Praise for Dore Gold's 2003 *New York Times* bestseller

# HATRED'S KINGDOM

"If you read one book to understand the roots of al-Qaeda's fury, it should be this one."
—R. JAMES WOOLSEY, former director of the CIA

"You won't find the newly published *Hatred's Kingdom* in any Saudi bookshop, but it is so much in demand among high officials that the government has brought out a reprint of its own."
—DAVID HIRST, *The Guardian*

"Devastatingly documented…"
—WILLIAM SAFIRE, *New York Times*

"Gold argues persuasively that contributions from some of Saudi Arabia's wealthiest families, and from charitable arms of the Saudi government, were important for al-Qaeda's evolution."
—HUME HORAN, *Wall Street Journal*,
former U.S. ambassador to Saudi Arabia

"[a] thoroughly researched study"
—JOSEPH A. KECHICHIAN, *Middle East Journal*

"Indispensable reading"
—JEFFREY GEDMIN, *Die Welt*

"Ambassador Gold blows the lid off the dangerous stream of support to terrorist and extremist groups. If the Saudis do not move to extinguish the fire they have been fueling, they will themselves be consumed by it."
—RICHARD PERLE, former assistant secretary of defense

"…certain for many years to remain the standard work on the political and terrorist effects of Wahhabism in Saudi Arabia, the Islamic world, and the West."
—DR. JOSHUA TEITELBAUM, Moshe Dayan Center for Middle Eastern
and African Studies, Tel Aviv University, in the *Jerusalem Report*

"*Hatred's Kingdom* author Dore Gold, former Israeli ambassador to the UN, explores in great detail the connection of Saudi Arabia and Wahhabi preachers to 9/11 and global terrorism. Gold pulls together shocking evidence of how Saudi Arabia, our ally, have used their billions in oil revenues to finance world-wide terrorism."
—JAMES TARANTO, *Wall Street Journal*

# The Fight for Jerusalem

# The Fight for Jerusalem

## RADICAL ISLAM, THE WEST, AND THE FUTURE OF THE HOLY CITY

# Dore Gold

Since 1947
**REGNERY**
**PUBLISHING, INC.**
*An Eagle Publishing Company • Washington, DC*

N. J. Dawood, *The Koran* (London: Penguin Books, 2000).

Cataloging-in-Publication data on file with the Library of Congress
ISBN 978-1-59698-029-7

Published in the United States by
Regnery Publishing, Inc.
One Massachusetts Avenue, NW
Washington, DC 20001
www.regnery.com

Distributed to the trade by
National Book Network
Lanham, MD 20706

Manufactured in the United States of America

10   9   8   7   6   5   4   3   2   1

*To my sisters, Paula and Debbie, whom I miss every day*

# Contents

# A Note on Terms

In order to assist the English-speaking reader, the spelling of Arabic terms throughout this book has been based on common usage in the United States and the United Kingdom (i.e., spellings commonly used by major newspapers and government agencies), and not on formal transliteration of literary Arabic. Additionally, Arabic terms that have been incorporated into standard American dictionaries have not been italicized. Common usage has also guided the rendering of Hebrew terms throughout the text rather than the formal rule of transliteration.

In keeping with the current usage by scholars and historians, this book will identify dates with the terms BCE (Before the Common Era) and CE (Common Era), rather than the more familiar BC and AD. These expressions correspond to the same period.

# The Battle for Historical Truth

Jerusalem was almost lost in July 2000, when the future of its ancient Old City was first put on the negotiating table. President Bill Clinton convened what would become a fifteen-day marathon summit at Camp David to fully resolve, once and for all, the Israeli-Palestinian conflict. Israelis and Palestinians were sealed off in the presidential retreat in Maryland and pressured to hammer out a final agreement. The whole event was a political long shot. Relations between the leaders, Israeli prime minister Ehud Barak and PLO chairman Yasser Arafat, were close to hostile and the pre-summit preparation was poor.[1] Nevertheless, Barak agreed to a stunning proposal: Israel would cede to the Palestinians sovereignty over most of East Jerusalem's suburbs, sovereignty over the Old City's Muslim and Christian quarters, and "custodianship" over Judaism's holiest site, the Temple Mount.[2] Since the Israel Defense Forces had captured Jerusalem's Old City in the Six-Day War in June 1967, no Israeli prime minister had proposed redividing the city. Now it was happening.

Barak's willingness to partition the Old City was especially astounding, as this was the spiritual heart of Israel's capital. A walled enclave located just inside the former border designating the eastern half of the city, the Old City occupies just over half a square mile and is divided into Jewish, Muslim, Christian, and Armenian quarters. It is home to some of the holiest sites of the world's three major Abrahamic religions. The Temple Mount is the most sensitive location. A hilltop platform complex, the thirty-five-acre Temple Mount is the former location of the biblical First Temple (the Temple of Solomon), which stood from the tenth century BCE until its destruction by the Babylonians in 586 BCE. The Second Temple was constructed on the same site and stood from 515 BCE until the Romans demolished it in 70 CE. The Temple Mount is now largely off-limits for organized Jewish prayer, which instead is conducted at the Western Wall, a retaining wall from the Second Temple located adjacent to and just below the Temple Mount.

The Temple Mount is also the third holiest site to Muslims, who refer to it as *Haram al-Sharif* (the Noble Sanctuary). It is now home to two major Islamic shrines. The first of these, the Dome of the Rock, built in the late seventh century, houses the rock from which Muhammad is said to have ascended to heaven to receive the commandment for Muslim prayers. The second site is the al-Aqsa Mosque, the largest mosque in Jerusalem, completed in the early eighth century. Not far from the Temple Mount, in the Christian quarter, stands the Church of the Holy Sepulchre. It was originally built by the Roman emperor Constantine in the fourth century at Golgotha, the site where Jesus was crucified. The church is venerated by Christians as the location of Jesus's tomb and is a major site for Christian pilgrimage.

When Barak was proposing the city's redivision at Camp David, most Israelis still remembered that after seizing East Jerusalem in 1948, Jordan's Arab Legion completely evicted the Jewish population from the Old City. The Jewish Quarter was set aflame, its homes were looted, and dozens of synagogues were destroyed or vandalized. Tombstones from the ancient Jewish cemetery on the Mount of Olives were converted into latrines. For the following nineteen years, Jews were prevented from praying at their holy sites, including the Western Wall. The Jordanians also barred Christian institutions from buying land and otherwise restricted the rights of Jerusalem's Christian population, which dropped by over 50 percent during the period of Jordanian rule. Upon capturing the Old City in 1967, Israel decided on a new approach to governing the city—it adopted a law protecting the holy sites of all religions and guaranteeing their free access to all worshipers.[3]

Barak's mentor, the late Israeli prime minister Yitzhak Rabin, had declared in October 1995 that Jerusalem must always remain the united capital of Israel. He proclaimed this during his very last parliamentary speech, one month before his assassination. Rabin was born in Jerusalem and had commanded the victorious Israeli forces that unified the city in 1967. He understood that only Israel could safeguard Jerusalem's freedom. Enjoying bipartisan support in Washington for years, Rabin's position on a united Jerusalem was endorsed by the U.S. Senate in 1995 in the Jerusalem Embassy Act, which passed by an overwhelming 93–5 vote. Its co-sponsors included both parties' senatorial leaders, Republican Bob Dole and Democrat Tom Daschle—two politicians who agreed on little else. Jerusalem looked like a closed issue. Yet now with the Camp David proposals, Arafat suddenly had over half of Jerusalem's Old City within his grasp.

Barak was playing a dangerous diplomatic chess game with Rabin's legacy and with the history of his own people. His offer to Arafat is inexplicable in light of his advance knowledge, gleaned from his military intelligence chiefs, that Arafat had no intention whatsoever of making peace. Additionally, the threat of violence hung in the air. Sandy Berger, Clinton's national security advisor, had warned in a Tel Aviv speech two months before Camp David that failure to advance the peace process would probably lead to an armed confrontation; indeed, while Berger was speaking, skirmishes between armed Palestinians and Israeli soldiers had already broken out. Furthermore, Arafat's agents for psychological warfare were running summer camps where, according to the *New York Times*, tens of thousands of Palestinian teenagers were "learning the arts of kidnapping, ambushing and using assault weapons."[4] The environment was hardly conducive to making peace.

Barak, moreover, had lost his parliamentary majority back home. Given the unprecedented concessions he planned for Camp David, Natan

Sharansky—who had spent nine years in a Soviet prison camp, fortifying his hopes by reciting the ancient Jewish incantation "Next Year in Jerusalem"—led a revolt as three parties abandoned Barak's coalition. Even Barak's own foreign minister, David Levy, refused to accompany him to Camp David and resigned shortly after the summit. In fact, Barak's flight to Washington was delayed due to a no-confidence vote in his government held just before takeoff. Thus, Clinton was convening a high-stakes summit at which his Israeli partner had no mandate to surrender parts of the Israeli capital.

What, then, were Barak's real intentions? If Arafat agreed to his proposals, Barak would bring the Israeli people a historic peace treaty formally ending the Arab-Israeli conflict. He would then be in a strong position to call new elections. If Arafat refused, Barak calculated that the Palestinian leader would be exposed before the entire world as the main obstacle to a comprehensive Middle Eastern peace. Barak tried to control the risks by making his proposals indirectly to Arafat through Clinton, so that his offers could not be pocketed as a binding commitment by Israel to surrender Jerusalem. And he took solace that the negotiations were based on the principle that "nothing is agreed until everything is agreed." If refused at Camp David, the unprecedented Israeli offer would be off the table—at least in theory.

Ultimately, the Camp David summit ended in total failure after Arafat rejected Barak's overture. But Jerusalem's fate still hung in the balance for the remainder of Clinton's presidency. In his final weeks in office, Clinton acted on Palestinian requests to develop "bridging proposals" on all the disputed subjects, including Jerusalem. In November 2000, two days after the election of George W. Bush, a lame-duck Clinton declared, "I've got ten weeks left in office and want to use that time to produce a comprehensive agreement, a historical agreement."[5] The clock was ticking for Clinton, and his negotiators worked furiously to secure a momentous peace agreement for his legacy. This urgency would affect the fate of Jerusalem, for Israel's negotiating position was further shaved down with each new negotiating round.

Clinton's peacemaking efforts were completely removed from events on the ground. On September 29, 2000, barely a month after the Camp David summit ended, Arafat used a visit to the Temple Mount by Ariel Sharon, then head of Barak's parliamentary opposition, as a pretext for launching a long, violent insurrection. Palestinians rioted in response to Sharon's visit, leaving over two dozen Israeli police injured. The next day, 22,000 Palestinian worshipers gathered for Friday prayers on the Temple Mount. Subsequent investigations revealed that Palestinian agents incited some of the worshipers to attack Jews praying at the Western Wall below with stones that had been secured in advance.[6] It was the eve of Rosh Hashana—the Jewish New Year—and Israel was forced to evacuate the packed Western Wall plaza, which was quickly carpeted with rocks.

Arafat called his new war "the al-Aqsa intifada." The name was intentionally misleading, implying the Temple Mount's al-Aqsa Mosque was in danger. It also reflected an effort to mobilize the Palestinians and to signal to the wider Arab world the start of a campaign to capture Jerusalem. The PLO's Radio Palestine called on Palestinians to rush to defend the Temple Mount, while Hamas, the terror organization that began as the Palestinian branch of the fundamentalist Muslim Brotherhood, distributed leaflets to the same effect. Since that time, Israelis have suffered a never-ending wave of Palestinian sniper, rocket, and suicide bombing attacks, mostly directed at civilians.

The Palestinians claimed the violence began as a spontaneous reaction to Sharon's visit to the Temple Mount. But Arafat's minister of communications, Imad Faluji, freely admitted the planned, organized nature of the campaign to a Lebanese Arabic newspaper: "Whoever thinks the Intifada broke out because of the despised Sharon's visit to the Al-Aqsa Mosque is wrong," he declared. "This Intifada was planned in advance, ever since President Arafat's return from the Camp David negotiations."[7] And Jewish holy sites were clearly a priority target. Following gun battles around Joseph's Tomb—the burial site of the biblical figure—Israeli troops withdrew from the area on October 7 after Palestinian police officials promised to protect the tomb. The policemen then stood aside and watched as a

Palestinian mob looted and demolished the shrine.[8] Many Palestinian police joined in. If Arafat was waging this sort of war—stoning Jewish worshipers at the Western Wall and destroying other holy sites—could he be depended upon to safeguard the holy sites of the world's three great faiths in Jerusalem?

## Why the Clinton Team Sought to Divide Jerusalem

What drove the Clinton administration to continue advocating new, even more dramatic proposals for dividing Jerusalem under such conditions? Some argue it was purely out of concern for Clinton's legacy. Clinton had earlier tied the prestige of his presidency to the Middle Eastern peace process. On September 13, 1993, he had stood with then Israeli prime minister Rabin and PLO chairman Arafat on the White House lawn, stretching his arms around them in an approving embrace as the two shook hands. The famous ceremony had marked both sides' agreement to the Declaration of Principles. The signing of this document, hammered out secretly by Israeli and Palestinian negotiators over the previous nine months in Norway, had launched the Oslo Peace Process. Clinton had made a huge political investment in this process over the following seven years. Certainly, he wanted to forestall its total collapse.

To be fair, Clinton did not initiate the Camp David meeting; it was Barak who repeatedly insisted on convening the high-risk summit. In fact, Clinton was at first a reluctant host, fearing American prestige would be damaged if the summit failed. According to diplomatic practice, the U.S. president only joins peacemaking negotiations once the parties have already bridged most of their differences. But despite the huge gaps that remained on the eve of Camp David, Clinton and Barak became locked in a diplomatic embrace that kept them engaged, even when each had serious doubts about the wisdom of continuing. For most of the Clinton peace team, achieving a peace settlement—any peace settlement—became a goal in and of itself.

Aside from presidential prestige, there were clearly policy considerations driving U.S. engagement as well. One American school of thought had always maintained that an Arab-Israeli peace settlement would be a panacea for the problems of the entire region from Morocco to Iran. Secretary of State Madeleine Albright, for example, described Barak's initial Camp David concessions on Jerusalem as nothing less than "a breakthrough that could change the whole future of the Middle East."[9] And occasionally, specific U.S. interests were raised. During the Oslo period, some policymakers argued that Arab-Israeli peacemaking would help the U.S. create Arab coalitions for the dual containment of Iraq and Iran. They adhered to this view despite the highly questionable premise that Arab states would risk vital interests by agreeing to a U.S. military presence simply because an ideological grievance of theirs had been addressed.

Then there was the issue of terrorism. Outside of the peace team, some high-ranking U.S. government officials hoped that in his last months in office Clinton would attack Osama bin Laden and al-Qaeda. Richard Clarke of the National Security Council later recalled, "Time was running out on the Clinton administration. There was going to be *one* last major national security initiative and it was going to be a final try to achieve an Israeli-Palestinian agreement [emphasis added]."[10] Thus Clinton apparently chose to court Arafat instead of making the elimination of bin Laden his first priority. In theory there was no reason why he couldn't do both. But as Clarke implies, every administration needs a primary focus. So Clinton put all his chips on brokering a deal between Arafat and Barak.

Clarke consoled himself with the logic behind the administration's choice: "If we could achieve a Middle East peace much of the popular support for al-Qaeda and much of the hatred for America would evaporate overnight."[11] But the evidence for his analysis was thin. Heavy U.S. engagement in Arab-Israeli peacemaking since 1993 had not reduced al-Qaeda's rage one iota; indeed, its attacks on U.S. interests continually escalated during the very same period. Notably, just two months after Camp David, al-Qaeda attacked the USS *Cole* in Yemen, killing seventeen U.S. sailors.

As the Clinton team pressed ahead with new peace proposals after Camp David and elicited further Israeli concessions, al-Qaeda continued to plan and train for its ultimate operation—the September 11 attacks on New York and Washington. There simply was no correlation between

America's Middle Eastern peacekeeping efforts and the motivation of al-Qaeda. Nonetheless, some administration officials continued to link the two issues, insisting that ever more Israeli concessions would help put out the flames of anti-Western hostility or at least lower their intensity.

Jerusalem and the struggle against Israel were not irrelevant to al-Qaeda and other jihadist networks; they were simply not their highest priority, as Professor Bernard Lewis noted in 1998.[12] For the leading architects of al-Qaeda's strategy, other stages in the battle against the West would precede the jihad against the Jewish state. For example, Abdullah Azzam, Osama bin Laden's Palestinian mentor, argued in his book *From Kabul to Jerusalem* that the liberation of Afghanistan was a precursor to the war for Jerusalem.[13]

After Azzam was assassinated in 1989, bin Laden's most influential ideological associate became Ayman al-Zawahiri, the leader of an Egyptian jihadist group who would become bin Laden's deputy in 1998. Like Azzam, al-Zawahiri put off the struggle for Jerusalem to the distant future. Echoing Azzam's strategy in a 1995 article titled "The Way to Jerusalem Passes through Cairo," al-Zawahiri argued that the worldwide jihad had to begin by vanquishing the anti-Islamist regimes across the Arab world—what he called the "Near Enemy." Jerusalem, he wrote, "will not be opened until the battles in Egypt and Algeria have been won and until Cairo has been opened."[14]

Despite mounting concerns about terrorism, Clinton remained focused on the Oslo Process through the end of his presidency. By late December 2000, he had privately laid out to both sides a comprehensive plan to solve the conflict's "core issues." This was not, ostensibly, a formal U.S. proposal, but rather an outline of the feasible "parameters" of a peace settlement. Clinton again insisted on dividing the Old City between Israel and the Palestinians, but this time he offered the Palestinians sovereignty over the Temple Mount, as opposed to the more limited Camp David offer of custodianship. The Western Wall would remain under Israeli jurisdiction, while control of the Christian Quarter, with its holy sites like the Church of the Holy Sepulchre, would go to Arafat.

Regarding the rest of East Jerusalem, Clinton moved past the Camp David proposal of Palestinian sovereignty over most of the suburbs.

Instead, he recommended Palestinian sovereignty over all neighborhoods populated by Palestinians and Israeli sovereignty over areas inhabited by Jews;[15] given the city's demographics, the plan would have turned Jerusalem into a checkerboard of sovereignties, with different governments controlling the equivalent of the red and black squares. Clinton gave both sides four days to accept or reject his ideas. He added that if either side turned down the "Clinton Parameters," they would be pulled off the table—it was a take-it-or-leave-it deal.[16] Arafat rejected the plan in a letter written to Clinton on December 25, 2000, refusing to concede even Israeli sovereignty over the Western Wall.[17] Ignoring his own vow to discontinue the initiative, Clinton invited Arafat to Washington for further consultations.

At the White House on January 2, 2001, Arafat once again rejected Clinton's plan. Yet Clinton still kept the proposal on the table, even publicizing its contents for the first time in a speech at New York's Waldorf Astoria hotel on January 7, 2001—just under two weeks before the end of his presidency. The details, however, had already reached the public by then. In late December, Israel's chief of staff (and later defense minister), Lt. General Shaul Mofaz, had told the Israeli cabinet that the Clinton Parameters, if implemented, would endanger Israel's security. This harsh assessment was splashed across the headlines of Israel's largest newspaper, *Yediot Ahronot*, on December 29.

Despite Barak's conditional acceptance of the Clinton plan, Israelis rallied against it. On January 8, over 400,000 Israelis gathered outside the walls of the Old City to protest the proposed division of Jerusalem in the largest demonstration in Israeli history. Israeli officials seemed oblivious to the furious public backlash against their diplomacy. The negotiations had taken on a momentum of their own, as Israel crossed one diplomatic redline after another. Some Israeli officials even explored the idea of crafting a UN Security Council resolution incorporating parts of Clinton's plan for Jerusalem, thus having Barak's concessions locked in by the international community's leading authority.

Within weeks, however, the threat to Jerusalem's unity was lifted—at least for the time being. Clinton was replaced on January 20, 2001, by George W. Bush, who had no inclination to continue Clinton's fruitless diplomacy. Around three weeks later, on February 7, Barak was forced to call new elections due to the loss of his parliamentary majority just before Camp David. He was replaced as prime minister by Ariel Sharon in the biggest electoral landslide in Israeli history. The Bush administration formally notified Sharon's representatives that Clinton's ideas were history. Barak's concessions were not binding, since no agreements were signed. Bush brought a new approach to the issue. He would not invite Arafat to the White House for pointless meetings. (Indeed, given Arafat's role in directing Palestinian violence, Bush wouldn't even shake his hand.) Although Bush did not explicitly commit himself to keeping Jerusalem united, he clearly was abandoning the Camp David legacy.

Sharon first met President Bush in the Oval Office on June 26, 2001. The two agreed that the Clinton Parameters would not be the starting point for future negotiations. Accepting Sharon's premise that Israel should not negotiate under fire, Bush informed his Israeli partner that he was not going to impose on Israel any more onerous peace plans. With the intifada raging, the U.S. would no longer obsessively court Yasser Arafat. As for Jerusalem, in public and in private Sharon presented a new, unequivocal Israeli position: "Jerusalem will remain united under the sovereignty of Israel."[18]

## Temple Denial—the Birth of a Political Creed

Although negotiations to divide Jerusalem were frozen, a new front in the fight for the city opened up. In the history of global struggles, parties often have acquiesced to borders or territorial claims without formal agreement—they accept the status quo because they are incapable of changing it. They understand that some historical doors are simply closed. Japan, for example, is not going to recapture the Kurile Islands, which it lost to Russia in 1945. Islamic empires, moreover, halted their frontal assault on Europe in 1683 with the Ottomans' defeat at the gates of Vienna. This door remained closed for centuries, until the arrival of millions of North African and Turkish immigrants in Europe encouraged radical Islamic leaders to believe the assault on the continent could be resumed. When historical doors of this sort are shut, a long truce sets in. But when they are opened, enormous historical forces are unleashed, often resulting in a furious wave of violence lasting until a new balance of power is attained. The Camp David proposals reopened precisely such a historical door.

From 1967 until 2000, the door for Israeli withdrawal from Jerusalem was largely closed. The first hint of a crack began when the 1993 Oslo Agreements declared the subject of Jerusalem to be an issue for future negotiations. While Rabin prevented this procedural agreement from becoming a substantive concession, the Camp David summit and its imme-diate aftermath swung the door wide open. Barak and Clinton expected that unprecedented Israeli concessions would convince the Palestinians of the Israelis' genuine commitment to peace. But instead, the breaking of Israeli diplomatic taboos opened up a Pandora's box. In return for his peace offer, Barak received a new war against Israel.

But the Palestinians' battle for Jerusalem incorporates more than just the frontal, military assault of the intifada. Its first stages entailed a campaign by Arafat to completely delegitimize the Israeli claim to the city. This began on the ninth day of the Camp David summit, when Arafat subjected Clinton to a lecture of staggering historical revisionism. His central argument was that the biblical temples never existed on the Temple Mount or even in Jerusalem. Arafat baldly asserted that "There is nothing there [i.e., no trace of a temple on the Temple Mount]," further insisting that "Solomon's Temple was not in Jerusalem, but Nablus."[19] As a Christian, a shocked Clinton responded that "not only the Jews but I, too, believe that under the surface there are remains of Solomon's temple."[20] Arafat changed his story two years later to further distance the Temple from Jerusalem, telling the London-based Arabic daily *al-Hayat*, "They found not a single stone proving that the Temple of Solomon was there, because historically the Temple was not in Palestine [at all]."[21]

Arafat undermined his credibility among many Westerners, for his ahistorical claims not only rejected fundamental elements of the Hebrew Bible, but also directly contradicted core Christian beliefs about the life of Jesus derived from the New Testament. Nonetheless, his doctrine of "Temple Denial" quickly became a new Palestinian dogma that was even repeated, with the firmest conviction, by Western-educated Palestinian officials who are assiduously courted by the international media.

For example, Nabil Sha'ath, a high-ranking Palestinian minister trained at the University of Pennsylvania's Wharton School of Business, told *Al-Ayyam* newspaper, "Israel demands control of the Temple Mount based on its claim that its *fictitious* temple stood there [emphasis added]."[22] Sa'eb Erakat, a frequent Palestinian spokesman on CNN, tried to Islamicize the biblical Temple a month after Camp David when he told a French reporter, "For Islam there never was a Jewish temple at Al-Qods [Jerusalem] but a 'distant mosque.'"[23] And Yasser Abd Rabbo, a Palestinian negotiator and former Palestinian minister of cabinet affairs, told *Le Monde* there was no archaeological evidence that the Temple ever existed on the Temple Mount.[24]

Arafat's eventual successor, Mahmoud Abbas (Abu Mazen), also embraced Temple Denial. The Jews "claim that 2,000 years ago they had a temple," he declared. "I challenge the claim that this is so."[25] Unlike Arafat, Abbas cultivated a moderate image in the West, which even elicited an invitation to the Bush White House. But on the issues of Jerusalem and Temple Denial, he was as hardline as Arafat and the rest of the PLO leadership. Arafat's espousal of Temple Denial had established a precedent for Palestinian diplomacy and propaganda. Once Arafat had realized at Camp David that a historical door had been opened for Jerusalem, he set about systematically dismantling the core Jewish claim to the city that had been accepted as axiomatic by Western civilization for centuries.

Temple Denial spread across the Middle East like wildfire from the editorial pages of *al-Jazirah* in Saudi Arabia to well-funded international seminars in the United Arab Emirates. It even subtly slipped into the writing of Middle East–based Western reporters. Thus *Time* magazine's Romesh Ratnesar in October 2003 described the Temple Mount as a place "where Jews *believe* Solomon and Herod built the First and Second Temples [emphasis added]."[26] In three years, Arafat's campaign had convinced a leading U.S. weekly to relate the existence of Jerusalem's biblical temples as a debatable matter of religious belief rather than historical fact. Arafat had moved the goalposts of historical truth.

Temple Denial found fertile ground in the Arab world's universities, particularly those with a more radical Islamist perspective, where it would affect an entirely new generation. A lecturer in modern history at Saudi Arabia's Muhammad bin Saud Islamic University repeated a popular variation of Temple Denial in 2000, when he published research arguing that King Solomon's Temple was in fact a mosque.[27] In mid-November 2005, a Jordanian lecturer in Islamic law at Jordan University claimed on Saudi television, "The Jews dug forty meters into the ground, and found nothing. There is no indication that a temple existed there. Brothers, they are making fun of you. Unfortunately, we are unwittingly legitimizing this nonsense of theirs. This is nonsense."[28]

Lecturers in Jordan also tried another tactic; they recruited European historians to their cause. Organizers of a project on the history of Jerusalem at Yarmuk University in northern Jordan, for example, found two German contributors to contend that the kingdoms of David and Solomon never existed.[29] This thesis reflected the arguments of an older school of European thought known as the "Copenhagen School," named after two Danish history professors and their supporters who claimed the biblical stories of David and Solomon were fictions invented hundreds of years later.[30] The school's adherents dismissed the entire biblical narrative of the Book of Kings, covering around 450 years of Jewish history from the end of King David's reign to the Babylonian captivity, as a "myth."[31] They further argued that there is no archaeological evidence that David and Solomon ruled ancient Israel, or that their dynasty constructed the "fabled" First Temple.

This group, however, suffered a huge setback in 1993, when an inscription was found in Aramaic, the language of the kingdoms of ancient Syria, on a basalt stele tablet at Tel Dan in northern Israel. The engraving detailed the invasion of ancient Israel by an Aramean king from Damascus: "[I] killed Jehoram son of [Ahab] king of Israel and [I] killed [Ahaz]iahu son of [Jehoram kin]g of the House of David." While archaeologists had to reconstruct some of the inscription's letters, the reference to the "House of David" was completely intact. The stone was dated to 835 BCE, less than a century after the reign of King Solomon.

The debate over King David and King Solomon continued in academia nonetheless. Nadia Abu El Haj, an assistant professor of anthropology at Columbia University's Barnard College, published a book in 2001 with the prestigious University of Chicago Press dismissing the biblical account of the First and Second Temples as "a national-historical tale"[32] and denouncing much of the existing research on the period as "pure political fabrication."[33] Moreover, a new theory soon emerged in academia charging that even if the House of David existed, the early biblical monarchs were no more than village leaders. Capturing the spirit of these new academic trends, *Harper's* magazine ran a March 2002 cover story provocatively titled "False Testament" that showcased the new theory that "the Davidic Empire" was "an invention of Jerusalem-based priests." The author described the Kingdom of Judah—the southern Israelite kingdom with its capital in Jerusalem that lasted for approximately 350 years—as merely a "Jewish outpost."

The *Harper's* article concluded, "Indeed, the chief disagreement among scholars nowadays is between those who hold that David was a petty hilltop chieftain whose writ extended no more than a few miles in any direction and a small but vociferous band of 'Biblical minimalists' who maintain that he never existed at all."[34] In either case, according to the logic underpinning these theories, no Israeli kingdom existed that could have constructed monumental buildings as described in the Bible like the palaces of David and Solomon—or, by implication, the Temple of Solomon.

But in the summer of 2005, Israeli archaeologist Eilat Mazar excavated an immense stone structure just south of the Temple Mount, where biblical accounts place King David's palace. The excavation, still in its initial phase at the time of this writing, has already shown that the structure, dating to the tenth century BCE, and with walls between six and eight feet thick, sat on top of a previously discovered stepped-stone fortification as tall as a twelve-story building.[35] A seal of a scribe to the last King of Judah was found on the site.

The "minimalists" had suffered yet another blow. Jerusalem, under the United Monarchy of David and Solomon, could no longer be credibly characterized as a minor village. But the academic debate over the veracity of the biblical narrative had political consequences—important Western academics had become potential allies for Middle Easterners seeking to deny the historical legitimacy of Israel's claim to Jerusalem. Such academics failed to see the irony that their mostly secular perspectives were being drafted into the services of radical Islam.

## A Secret Archaeological War

The Palestinian leadership advanced the creed of Temple Denial on two contradictory tracks; while they adamantly maintained that the Temple of Solomon was fictitious, they simultaneously attempted to destroy any archaeological evidence proving otherwise. Their control of key archaeological sites was rooted in the special arrangements Israel itself had implemented for the Temple Mount. Following the liberation of Jerusalem's Old City in the Six-Day War, the Israeli government extended Israeli law, jurisdiction, and administration to the eastern part of Jerusalem on June 27, 1967. According to Israel's Supreme Court, this made East Jerusalem an integral part of the State of Israel. Nevertheless, Israel refrained from interfering with the administration of the Muslim holy sites on the Temple Mount by the East Jerusalem Waqf, whose officials continued to be appointed in Amman by Jordan's Ministry of *Awqaf* (Religious Endowments) Affairs.

These arrangements eroded during the early Oslo period, when the Israeli government adopted two conflicting policies on the administration of the Temple Mount. Rabin sought to enshrine Jordan's special status on the Temple Mount by writing it into the 1994 Treaty of Peace between Israel and Jordan. His foreign minister, Shimon Peres, however, had sent a secret letter on October 11, 1993, to the PLO through the Norwegian foreign minister, Johan Jorgan Holst, assuring the continued operation of Palestinian institutions in East Jerusalem—some of which were clearly intent on displacing Jordan's role on the Temple Mount.

The PLO sought to exploit the Holst letter to weaken Jordan's position on the Temple Mount. On September 19, 1994, the PLO-controlled Palestinian Authority created its own Ministry for Waqf Affairs in East Jerusalem. The Jordanian-PLO rivalry intensified in October following the death of Jerusalem mufti (Islamic religious leader) Sulayman al-Jabari. Jordan named a new mufti, Sheikh Abd al-Qadir Abadin, while the PLO appointed its own candidate, Sheikh Ikrima Sabri. The PLO was launching an all-out campaign to displace Jordan's authority throughout the city.

The Palestinian-controlled Waqf sought to erode Israel's prerogatives on the Temple Mount as well. This effort began in September 1996, when the Waqf first expelled archaeological supervisors with the Israel Antiquities Authority from the Temple Mount. Although periodically allowed to return, the Waqf in September 2000 permanently barred the Israeli supervisors from the Temple Mount, where the Waqf was constructing two huge underground mosques inside the Temple Mount itself. The Waqf employed hundreds of trucks to move some 13,000 tons of unsifted rubble from the First and Second Temple periods, including archeological artifacts, which was dumped in various waste sites throughout Jerusalem. In March 2001, it was reported that the Waqf had brought a heavy stonecutter onto the Temple Mount and was slicing columns and cutting other stones from ancient structures.

What was in the piles of debris that the Waqf dug out? Subsequent sifting of these piles by an Israeli archeological team under Dr. Gabi Barkai showed precisely what the Waqf was seeking to destroy. Barkai, for example, found a clay seal from the Temple Mount with Hebrew writing. On the third line of the ancient seal was the name *Immer*, which is the last name of a man, Pashur Ben Immer, whom the Book of Jeremiah describes as an important priest in the First Temple. Looking at a set of broken lines above the name *Immer*, Barkai concluded that the seal belonged to a relative of Pashur named Galihu Ben Immer.[36] The clay seal proved that a noted priestly family member at the time of ancient Israel was involved in administering the Temple Mount. The seal added to a previous discovery by Barkai also indicating biblically-based Jewish religious practices in Jerusalem during the time of the First Temple. Years earlier, he had discovered in burial chambers from the First Temple period two tiny silver scrolls used as amulets that contained the oldest Hebrew-language biblical inscription ever found. The engraving reproduced verses from the Book of Numbers (Chapter 6: 24–26) known as the Priestly Benediction: "The Lord, Bless You and Protect You, The Lord Make His Face Shine Upon Thee and Be Gracious to Thee, May the Lord Lift Up His Countenance Upon You and Grant You Peace."

Barkai's discoveries were hardly the only archaeological or written evidence beyond Jewish religious writings to corroborate the Temples' existence. Ancient historians from the Roman era such as Josephus have provided detailed descriptions of the Second Temple as well as the planning and execution of its destruction by Titus, the son of Roman emperor Vespasian, and his successor. Indeed, any tourist visiting the famous Arch of Titus in Rome can see how the Roman conquest of Jerusalem was commemorated over nineteen centuries ago with engraved images of Roman soldiers triumphantly carrying the Temple vessels, including trumpets and the seven-branched Menorah (Jewish candelabra), as spoils of war.

Throughout Jerusalem's Old City, a variety of everyday items have been found that bear the mark of the Tenth Roman Legion—the unit that destroyed the Second Temple. Stone plaques with Greek inscriptions from the time of King Herod warning non-Jews not to enter certain areas of the Temple have also been uncovered. The excavation of the street level just below the Temple Mount revealed huge blocks of stone that toppled down during the Temple's destruction, including a site with a Hebrew inscription reading "To the Trumpeting Place." This corresponds with Josephus' account of a corner of the Temple Mount where the Temple trumpet was blown to mark the beginning of the Sabbath.

Aside from the archaeological evidence, Temple Denial is refuted even by the most sacred Islamic texts. Although the Koran contains no explicit references to Jerusalem, a famous verse that opens Sura 17, known as "The Night Journey," reads: "Glory to Him who made His Servant go by night from the Sacred Mosque to the Farther Mosque [*al-masjid al-aqsa*]." To understand this verse, we must consult the classical exegesis from the commentaries on the Koran that are cited by Islamic scholars to this day.

In the *al-Jalalayn*, named after the "two Jalals" who lived in the ninth and tenth centuries, the authors explain that the "Sacred Mosque" was in Mecca and the "Farther Mosque" was *bayt al-maqdis*, the plain meaning of which is the Temple. (The Arabic term is strikingly close to the Hebrew term for the Temple, *bayt ha-miqdash*.) Abdullah ibn Umar al-Baydawi, the most authoritative Koranic commentator, also explains the term "Farther Mosque" as the *bayt al-maqdis*; he adds that when Muhammad made the Night Journey, there was no mosque yet built in Jerusalem.[37]

Therefore, according to Islamic tradition, during the Night Journey Muhammad traveled on a winged, horse-like beast called *al-Buraq* from Mecca to Jerusalem, which was known as the city that once housed the Temple. Abu Jafar Muhammad al-Tabari, a leading Koranic commentator known as one of the greatest historians of the Islamic world, confirmed this interpretation. Writing in the ninth century during the zenith of the great Abbasid caliphate, al-Tabari penned an account of the conquest of Jerusalem by the second caliph of Islam, Umar bin al-Khattab. At one point, al-Tabari relates that Umar finished praying and then went to the area where "the Romans buried the Temple [*bayt al-maqdis*] at the time of the sons of Israel."[38]

It was noteworthy that the Koran itself had no doubts about the existence of David and Solomon, who appear as kings in Sura 27. It also describes Solomon's palace, which it says impressed the queen of Sheba with its splendor. Early Islam did not seek to eradicate ancient Israel. It confirmed many of its traditions through Islamic religious narrative.

Throughout the twentieth century, even extremist Muslim leaders and organizations still acknowledged the Temple's existence. For example, a guide to the Temple Mount was published in 1935 by the Supreme Muslim Council, which at the time was headed by Hajj Amin al-Husseini, the notorious pro-Nazi mufti of Jerusalem. Concerning the Temple Mount ("Haram al-Sharif"), the guide stated without equivocation that "Its identity with the site of Solomon's Temple is beyond dispute." This mimicked the language of an earlier guidebook the council had written in 1924. Thus the claims of Arafat and his acolytes throughout the Arab world that the Temples never existed in Jerusalem are refuted not only by the archaeological record, but also by Islam's greatest authorities and even by Arafat's radical predecessors.

## The War against the Holy Sites

During the intifada, Palestinians launched a concerted, armed campaign against non-Muslim holy sites, with attacks quickly spreading outside Jerusalem. The destruction of Joseph's Tomb discussed earlier was a telling example. The acquiescence of the Palestinian police in the tomb's demolition indicated that the attacks were orchestrated with official sanction. After the furious Palestinian mob ripped the shrine apart with sledgehammers, the ruined dome was painted green to symbolize that this was now an exclusively Islamic site.[39] Palestinian officials promptly put forward their own religious claim to the site. "This shrine in Nablus is basically and has always been a sort of holy man's shrine, a Palestinian place," declared Palestinian cabinet minister Hanan Ashrawi.[40] Five days later a Jewish holy site in Jericho, the ancient Shalom al Yisrael synagogue which dated back to the sixth century, was also sacked. The mob burned its holy books and relics in public.[41]

As Arafat's intifada raged over the next two years, the attacks on holy sites reached Bethlehem's Church of the Nativity, held sacred by Christians as the birthplace of Jesus. The Oslo Accords had given the Palestinian Authority jurisdiction over Bethlehem, and like other PA-controlled cities, terrorist groups converted it into a major base of operations for attacks inside Israel, especially in Jerusalem. After a Palestinian suicide bomber killed thirty Israeli civilians celebrating Passover at the Park Hotel in March 2002, Israeli forces entered PA-controlled cities in order to dismantle the terrorist infrastructure. On April 2, 2002, thirteen armed Palestinians from Arafat's own Tanzim militia, as well as from the Hamas and Islamic Jihad terror groups, seized the Church of the Nativity to evade capture by Israeli troops. They held the clergy hostage, while more than a hundred Palestinian bystanders were trapped inside as well.

A thirty-nine-day standoff ensued between the Israeli army, which refused to storm the church compound, and the terrorists inside. At one point, in an effort to force an end to the stalemate, the gunmen set fire to the Orthodox Christian and Franciscan sections of the compound, according to Israeli commanders on the ground.[42] Ultimately, the terrorists surrendered as part of an arrangement brokered by the European Union that allowed them to go into exile in Europe. The clergy then requested that Israeli forces enter the church to find and dismantle some forty explosive devises that the gunmen had left behind. A Franciscan cleric noted that the attackers stole icons, candelabra, and other religious objects that looked to be made of gold. Catholic priests described how their captors tore up

Bibles and used their pages as toilet paper.[43] In short, one of Christianity's holiest sites was thoroughly desecrated by adherents of the very same political movement that seeks control over Jerusalem's holy sites.

The attacks on the antiquities of non-Islamic faiths were part of a broader onslaught against holy sites across the Middle East and South Asia by radical offshoots of Islamist groups. The campaign initially gained notoriety when the Taliban, upon conquering Afghanistan's Bamiyan Valley in 1998, first attacked giant Buddhist statues there that were nearly 2,000 years old. Despite an international outcry, it finished off the statues in 2001 using truckloads of dynamite.

In the last decade, sectarian violence has mushroomed in many other countries, not even sparing Islamic holy sites. Strife between Sunnis and Shiites erupted in Afghanistan, Pakistan, Iraq, and other nations where the two groups had heretofore coexisted in relative peace. In 2003, Sunni Muslim extremists connected with al-Qaeda repeatedly sent suicide bombers to attack Shiite mosques in Pakistan and especially in Iraq, where the overthrow of Saddam Hussein was followed by an orgy of violence between Muslim sects. Christian churches also came under repeated bombing attacks in Pakistan and Iraq, while Muslim extremists inflicted a wave of violence on Egypt's Coptic Christians beginning in 1998. In 2004, radical Islamic insurgents connected to Abu Musab al-Zarqawi's al-Qaeda network bombed six Iraqi churches in one day.

This Islamist radicalization and the accompanying attacks on religious sites stemmed from two elements—a religious-ideological impetus and money—that originated in a single source: Saudi Arabia. In Afghanistan, local Islamic traditions deriving from India like the Deobandi school were infused with militant *salafi* doctrines imported from the Arabian peninsula and financed by petro-dollars supplied by Saudi Arabia and other Arab Gulf states. The salafi creed was based on both the Saudis' *Wahhabi* movement and the doctrines of Egypt's Muslim Brotherhood, which itself was inspired by Wahhabism. The Saudi *ulama*, or religious leadership, forged links with a variety of radical Islamic movements, including the Muslim Brotherhood, through the global network of Wahhabi charities under their control. Through these charities, the Saudis funded many radical religious schools in Afghanistan and Pakistan, which in turn propagated Wahhabi and salafi teachings of militant jihad.[44] This ideological input was instrumental in the emergence of the jihadist movements that fought the Soviets in the 1980s and evolved into al-Qaeda in the 1990s.

One key trademark of Wahhabism is the tendency of its adherents to vandalize religious sites—even Islamic ones. Insisting on extreme monotheism, Wahhabis view religious ceremonies at tombs and shrines as a form of polytheistic saint-worship. As Saudi-financed Wahhabism spread globally over the last ten years, attacks on such sites became more common in locations as diverse as Indonesia, Chechnya, and Iraqi Kurdistan. Wahhabis view Shiites, who elevate Muhammad's son-in-law, Ali, to near-divine position, as heretics deserving inferior status. Certainly Wahhabis would not grant Shiite holy sites unconditional protection. It is of historical interest to note that in 1805 when a Wahhabi army conquered Medina, the second holiest city in Islam, it even assaulted the tomb of Muhammad.

These harsh doctrines also deny protection to Jews and Christians, who are condemned as infidels. George Cattan, a Palestinian Christian intellectual, links the recent overall decline of Middle Eastern Christianity to the rise of salafism, citing the fate of Egypt's Christian Copts as one example: "The spreading of the Islamic movement and extremist Salafi views throughout Egyptian society led to the removal of Copts from the Parliament, municipalities, labor unions and [other] prominent positions, and limitations began to be imposed on the building and renovation of churches. Some [churches] were [even] attacked and burned down, and Christians were accused of heresy."[45]

The rise of Sunni Muslim militancy did not provoke the clashes over Jerusalem between Israel and the Palestinians, but it certainly affected how holy sites were treated by Islamist militants. As Cattan notes, "In the West Bank and Gaza, armed Islamic movements regard Palestine as a Muslim waqf [religious endowment], and call to defend the places holy to the Muslims while disregarding places holy to the Christians."[46]

Concrete links exist between these outer rings of Islamic militancy and the Palestinian world. For example, the militant Hamas movement, whose power among the Palestinians has been steadily growing in the last decade, was funded by the same Wahhabi charities that backed the Taliban and other jihadist groups in the 1990s.[47] Likewise, the writings of Saudi Wahhabi clerics like Sheikh Sulayman al-Ulwan and Sheikh Hamud bin Uqla al-Shu'aibi, who supported the ideology of al-Qaeda and Osama bin Laden, appeared on the Hamas website and were taught in Hamas schools.[48]

## Jerusalem as a Trigger for an Apocalyptic Global Jihad

One aspect of the growth of jihadist militancy in the Middle East is, in fact, directly tied to the Jerusalem issue—the spread of Islamic apocalyptic thought. According to Islamic doctrine of recent centuries, the concept of jihad has evolved into an eschatological concept reserved for the future. Accordingly, pious Muslims are expected to proselytize their religion and gain converts worldwide, an activity known as *da'wa*. Then, at the apocalyptic end of days, mainstream Muslims envision that a great, armed jihad will result in the subjugation of the entire world to Islam. Militant Wahhabism, however, reverses the order of da'wa and jihad, advancing jihad to the present day as a precursor for spreading Islam.

Hence, almost by definition, militant Islam is an apocalyptic movement preparing in the present for a final confrontation with the West and with others opposed to its agenda. It brings scenarios from the end of days to the here and now. It is therefore not surprising to find apocalyptic references in the speeches of jihadist leaders like Abu Musab al-Zarqawi, the former head of al-Qaeda in Iraq. Before his death at the hands of coalition forces, al-Zarqawi declared in 2004, "Behold, the spark has been lit in Iraq and its flames will blaze, Allah willing, until they consume the Armies of the Cross in Dabiq." The statement refers to a battle heralding the last Days of Judgment that is expected to occur in northern Syria.[49]

Jihadist apocalyptic references appear in various guises, though most relate to prophecies about a major confrontation with the West. This theme does not originate in the Koran, but rather in Islamic oral traditions known as *hadith*. One does not have to look hard to find allusions to this apocalyptic battle in jihadist proclamations. For example, Sheikh Yusuf al-Qaradhawi, the spiritual head of the Muslim Brotherhood, refers to "the signs of the victory of Islam," including its impending conquest of Europe. He relates prophecies that both Istanbul and Rome will be conquered, postulates that the fall of Rome is near, and follows this with a discussion of the global dissemination of Islam.[50]

Abu Qatada, a jihadist cleric who served as bin Laden's representative in Britain, took this scenario one step further, explaining the symbolic importance of conquering Rome for Islam's ultimate, apocalyptic battle: "Rome is a cross. The West is a cross and Romans are the owners of the cross." The Muslims must target the West, Abu Qatada explains, adding: "We will split Rome open. The destruction must be carried out by sword. Those who will destroy Rome are already preparing the swords. Rome will not be conquered with the word but with the force of arms."[51] A Saudi cleric appearing on the *al-Jazeera* television network in April 2006 took up the theme, reminding his viewers that "whoever is familiar with the Sunna and Hadith knows that a battle against the enemies of Allah awaits on the horizon."[52] In much of the apocalyptic literature, a great war between the Muslim forces and Rome represents one of the signs that the end of days is about to commence. And rhetoric about this upcoming clash is clearly on the rise.

Significantly, Jerusalem plays a key role in these apocalyptic traditions. According to the Islamic version of the end of history, a messianic figure known as the *Mahdi* (the rightly guided one) will appear and establish his headquarters in Jerusalem.[53] He is preceded by the arrival of the Antichrist, known in Islam as the *dajjal*. According to this eschatological scenario, Jesus will also return, proclaim the supremacy of Islam, and smash all the world's crosses. Then Jesus and the Mahdi together will wage war against the dajjal.[54]

Over the centuries, several important mainstream Muslim thinkers from Ibn Khaldun to Rashid Rida have raised serious questions regarding all this speculation about the dajjal and the Mahdi. Nonetheless, this religious belief has spread rapidly across the Middle East in recent years, gaining particular momentum in Egypt and among Palestinians after the

September 11 attacks.[55] It has also found considerable backing in jihadist circles close to the Wahhabis and Hamas. Yet few Western policymakers had even an inkling of these doctrines when they discussed the future of Jerusalem.

The Mahdist scenario unquestionably has influenced some Islamic militant groups that envision Jerusalem as the seat of a future caliphate. Their ideology is driven by the importance they attach to replacing the Ottoman caliphate, which served as the central authority of the Sunni Muslim world until it was dissolved after World War I. One such radical movement, Hizb ut-Tahrir, which originally emerged from the Muslim Brotherhood in Jordan in 1953, views the reestablishment of the caliphate as an essential precursor to the creation of a worldwide Islamic government.

Hizb ut-Tahrir is active in dozens of countries, including Great Britain. It claims to be peaceful but has engaged in violence, including the attempted assassination of Jordan's King Hussein in 1993. Regarded by terrorism experts as an al-Qaeda predecessor, the group also frequently organizes demonstrations on the Temple Mount. For organizations like Hizb ut-Tahrir, the achievement of Islamic control over Jerusalem would confirm their apocalyptic beliefs and significantly empower similar radical movements. It would spark the fevered imaginations of these movements' members, leading them to fight for a renewed caliphate with even greater conviction and force.

This threat is difficult to comprehend for many Western policymakers who adamantly believe the risk of violence and terrorism can be diminished by satisfying the essential grievances of militant movements. But is this assumption accurate? In order to analyze this supposition, we must first distinguish between defensive political movements (those that genuinely seek to fulfill the needs of the oppressed and downtrodden) and offensive political movements (those with completely aggressive intentions). This distinction helps explain how various withdrawals in the face of militant Islam in the Middle East have unexpectedly escalated hostilities.

The first, most famous case is the Soviet withdrawal from Afghanistan. The overwhelming majority of Afghan *mujahidin* fighters waged a defensive war to liberate their country. But for a small minority comprised mostly of foreign Arab volunteers, the Soviet withdrawal fed a larger, millennial image of an Islamic victory over a superpower. As adherents of salafi movements like the Muslim Brotherhood and Wahhabism, the Arab mujahidin concluded that their victory in Afghanistan would pave the way for them to replicate the Islamic conquests of the seventh century. Just as the armies of the early caliphs defeated the great powers of the day—Byzantium at the Battle of Yarmuk and Persia at the Battle of Qadisiyya—they too would crush the Soviet Union and eventually the United States.

Rather than returning home after their victory, these radicalized combat veterans created a new organization, al-Qaeda, to implement their offensive strategy against the West. The Soviet withdrawal had unexpectedly ignited a militant response. A new wave of Islamic militancy was being fueled not by political grievances, although these were frequently trotted out as a pretext for violence, but rather by a sense of triumph in the face of the perceived collapse of the movement's opponents.

This pattern was replicated on the Arab-Israeli front as well. In May 2000, the Barak government unilaterally withdrew all of Israel's forces from its self-declared security zone in southern Lebanon. Israel's static military positions in this area, which required continual reinforcement, had left its military convoys vulnerable to ground attacks by the Shiite guerillas of Hizballah. Most Israelis, reluctant to sustain further casualties in Lebanon, supported the withdrawal. But the move had the unintended consequence of radicalizing Palestinians, who were stunned that a small militia of approximately 2,000 Hizballah fighters could force Israel out of Lebanon. It was the first time the Israelis withdrew under fire. Arafat even complained to Shlomo Ben Ami, who would become Barak's foreign minister, that Hizballah's perceived victory had created pressure on him to emulate the organization's violent tactics.[56] And this is precisely what Arafat did, launching the intifada just four months after Israel's withdrawal from Lebanon.

Hizballah took away the same lesson. Hizballah's leader, Hasan Nasrallah, declared that Israel's national will was as thin as a spiderweb. Hizballah promptly began preparing for another round of war, undertaking a massive military buildup, including the construction of a network of underground bunkers along the Israeli border and the procurement of thousands of short-range missiles. And war did indeed erupt again on July 12, 2006, following a Hizballah cross-border attack in which several Israeli soldiers were killed and two were kidnapped. Israel's withdrawal from Lebanon had not diminished Middle Eastern violence, but rather provoked a new explosion of terrorism.

The final example of a withdrawal galvanizing the jihadist movement is Ariel Sharon's unilateral "disengagement" from the Gaza Strip in August 2005. Sharon had hoped that by pulling Israeli troops and settlers out of Gaza, he could secure U.S. and international approval of Israel's retention of strategic areas in the West Bank. But once again the Palestinians had a different perspective, viewing the withdrawal as a victory for their armed resistance. By then, it should have come as no surprise when the satisfaction of a major Palestinian grievance in Gaza actually provoked an upsurge in violence and extremism among Palestinians. After the pullout, militants used Gaza as a base to continuously launch Qassam rockets against southern Israel and to attack Israeli troops along Gaza's northern border, while weapons smuggling greatly intensified across the Gaza-Egyptian border in the south. The forces for moderation among Palestinians were pushed aside, leading to the victory of Hamas in elections to the Palestinian Legislative Council in early 2006.

The Gaza withdrawal also allowed for the formation of al-Qaeda cells in Gaza for the first time. Western diplomats had believed that Israeli disengagement from Gaza would undercut one of al-Qaeda's rallying cries, yet what emerged on the ground was a new al-Qaeda sanctuary. The strategy of neutralizing militant Islam through concessions had backfired once again. In Afghanistan, Lebanon, and Gaza, withdrawals in the face of a radical Islamic threat only strengthened the will of terrorist organizations and emboldened them, almost guaranteeing much larger conflagrations in the future.

In light of this history, let us ask the questions that concern us in this book: How would militant Muslims, in the Palestinian territories and worldwide, react to an Israeli withdrawal from eastern Jerusalem and a redivision of the Holy City? If the holy sites were turned over to a Palestinian government, would this defuse the rage of militant Islamist groups toward the West, or would it be upheld as a vindication of militant ideologies and a sign of the prophesized apocalypse? As previously noted, al-Qaeda ideologues envision that Jerusalem will only be captured after the toppling of secular Arab regimes. But if this sequence were reversed by events, would al-Qaeda be likely to establish itself in a Jerusalem bereft of Israel's security presence in hopes of making the Holy City the seat of a new caliphate?

Following Israel's withdrawal from Gaza, Hamas leaders like Mahmoud al-Zahar expressed confidence that the pullout would invigorate the mujahidin fighting against the United States in Iraq and Afghanistan. An Israeli withdrawal from Jerusalem would be even more explosive. It would inspire jihadist forces from South Asia to the Middle East as well as their offshoots living in the heart of Europe, thus creating enormous new energy for their global campaign. A new, Clinton-style agreement to divide Jerusalem would surely reignite the global jihad, even if the deal were conceived for the express purpose of containing it. In short, mishandling the Jerusalem issue could have disastrous worldwide consequences.

Most of the diplomacy over Jerusalem in the last decade has been premised on the need for a solution that is acceptable to both sides. Clinton was driven by this assumption, spending countless days refining endless proposals in hopes of coaxing the parties toward an agreement. The failure of these methods necessitates a new approach. Instead of prioritizing a mutually acceptable agreement, the West must first identify its primary interests in the Jerusalem question, and then seek out solutions that will safeguard those interests. The difference in approaches is reminiscent of the distinction columnist Charles Krauthammer once drew between the Carter administration's overall foreign policy goal (producing international agreements) and that of the Reagan administration (defending U.S. national interests). The point here is not to take sides in U.S. partisan politics, but rather to demonstrate that fundamentally different approaches exist to solving vexing diplomatic issues, some of which are more successful than others.

The above narrative has identified two significant interests that the international community shares regarding Jerusalem. First, adherents of all faiths must be guaranteed freedom of worship, with free access to their respective holy sites. Almost every major international actor affirms this necessity, yet it is inevitably lost during actual negotiations. In the continuing negotiations after Camp David, the fact that militant Palestinian groups, some tied directly to Arafat, were attacking Jewish worshipers at the Western Wall and torching holy sites just outside Jerusalem did not cause anyone involved in the talks to question the wisdom of transferring Jerusalem's holy sites to Arafat's control.

Today, the rising power of Hamas adds an even stronger Islamist component to any analysis of the possible fate of Jerusalem's holy sites under Palestinian rule. The Palestinians themselves compared local Hamas rule in the West Bank town of Qalqiliya to that of the Taliban; it is not hard to imagine how fundamentalist Islamic governance would affect the great churches of the Old City. Would any Westerner today seriously propose putting the Church of the Holy Sepulchre under a Taliban-like regime? Diplomats must refocus their efforts to prioritize the following question: who will best protect the freedom of all faiths in Jerusalem and their access to the holy sites?

Secondly, the international community has a vested interest in assuring that Jerusalem does not turn into a spark igniting the entire region in flames. Yet the Camp David record indicates enormous ignorance as to why Jerusalem is likely to become a much more volatile issue in the event of an Israeli withdrawal. International diplomats should conduct a thorough investigation of the religious connections of each of the great faiths to Jerusalem and their political implications. They should question their own assumptions: Is it really true that mainstream Islam cannot accept, under any circumstances, leaving Jerusalem under non-Islamic sovereignty? Is the continuation of the current situation truly bound to provoke an armed conflict, or is the division of the city more likely to ignite such a scenario?

The Christian world acquiesced to Islamic rule over Jerusalem for centuries without demanding the city's return. This status quo was only upset by the assault on the Church of the Holy Sepulchre by the Shiite-led Fatimid caliphate, which ultimately sparked the First Crusade in 1096 along with a strong dose of millennialism. Might mainstream elements in the Islamic world today also eventually adopt a similar acceptance of the status quo as long as Islam's holy sites are safeguarded? Will mainstream Muslims necessarily insist on exerting political sovereignty in Jerusalem as well?

History shows that Jerusalem was not always the highest priority for the centers of power in the Islamic world at large. For example, right after the launch of the First Crusade, the dominant Islamic force at the time, the great Abbasid caliphate in Baghdad, whose rule is regarded by many Muslims as a kind of golden age of Islam, did not initiate any military campaigns against the Crusader presence in Jerusalem. It was only when Crusader forces, based in what is today Jordan, began directly threatening the Arabian peninsula, home to the holy cities of Mecca and Medina, that Saladin began his campaign in 1187 to vanquish the Crusader Kingdom and capture Jerusalem. In short, it was Saladin's desire to defend the first and second most holy sites in Islam that provoked him to wage war over the third. And Saladin's grandson actually negotiated away Islamic control over Jerusalem to the Holy Roman Emperor in 1229—with a provision for the protection of Islamic holy sites.

A related question is: which of the great faiths has a pluralistic vision for the Holy City rooted in inter-religious tolerance, and which is committed to an exclusivist agenda? Unarguably, a Jerusalem authority that restricts religious freedoms is more likely to turn the city into a volatile source of constant crisis than an authority that recognizes a modus vivendi among the different faiths. And Judaism has already proven its tolerant outlook on Jerusalem and its holy sites. Ancient Judaism believed in freedom of worship in Jerusalem, even permitting non-Jews to offer sacrifices at the Temple. Of course, neither Christianity nor Islam yet existed for most of the Temple periods, but history nevertheless shows that while Jews did not typically proselytize, they still believed in a universalist mission emanating from their control of Jerusalem.

The soldiers of the First Crusade murdered Jerusalem's entire Jewish and Muslim populations when they first captured the city in 1099. It was Saladin, like a previous Muslim conqueror of Jerusalem, the caliph Umar bin al-Khattab, who allowed the Jews to return. Today, radical trends in the Islamic world have superseded the relative tolerance it has displayed at certain times in the past. And for the militant jihadists who assign Jerusalem an apocalyptic role, even a limited form of inter-religious coexistence has been replaced by visions of historical confrontations marking the end of days. It is impossible to analyze intelligently Jerusalem's future without delving into its past, where we find intermittent periods of coexistence that provide a glimmer of hope against the wave of militancy currently roiling much of the Arab world. An accurate understanding of the Holy City's past has become a matter of urgency, given the continuing campaign by Palestinian leaders to distort Jerusalem's history completely.

This book will first establish the historical record of Jerusalem as a point of departure for thinking about its future. It will take the position that only a free and democratic Israel can truly safeguard the city for all the world's faiths. After we look at the religious approaches of the three great faiths to Jerusalem, and analyze the past diplomatic struggle over the Holy City, the main alternatives raised for Jerusalem's future must be considered: Islamic control through the Palestinians, UN internationalization, and continuing Israeli rule. It will be demonstrated that the first two options would be far more destabilizing for Jerusalem, and indeed for the entire Middle East, than the maintenance of the status quo, given some of its unique features.

One of these features is Israel's continuation of the practice of allowing the Jordanian Ministry of Religious Endowments to administer the Muslim holy sites on the Temple Mount. While Christian churches can administer Jerusalem's Christian holy sites, the lack of a separation between church and state in the Islamic world necessitates that a moderate Arab government represent Muslim interests. As discussed earlier, a struggle was under way between Jordan and the Palestinian Authority over this religious role. In any case, continuing Israeli rule in a united Jerusalem can be accompanied by Jordan's administrative role in the Islamic shrines on the Temple Mount, Israel's full sovereignty notwithstanding.

The struggle for Jerusalem today is being waged against a background of the larger clash between radical Islam and the West. We have already discussed how, contrary to conventional wisdom, an Israeli pullback from Jerusalem would be likely to exacerbate that struggle by galvanizing the Islamic world's most militant elements. There is another side to this argument as well: Jerusalem can serve as a litmus test for the progress of a more moderate, tolerant trend in Islam. Today, most of the Christian world has no objection to the principle of Israeli sovereignty in Jerusalem. At the time of the Crusades, such acquiescence would have been unthinkable. Even as late as 1948, some Christian advocates of Jerusalem's internationalization could not countenance Jewish sovereignty in any part of the Holy City. But this attitude has since passed and is unlikely to resurface, so long as Christian holy sites are protected.

Were such a shift to occur in the Islamic world, it would have significance beyond the narrow confines of the Israeli-Palestinian conflict, for it would signal that the renewed jihadism that was born in Afghanistan in the 1980s and spread by al-Qaeda and its affiliates thereafter had truly subsided. Jerusalem has always sat on an inter-civilizational fault line between the East and West. It is where civilizations can collide or learn to coexist. In this sense, Jerusalem is more than the center of spirituality for millions of believers; it is also one of the keys to world peace.

# PART I

## The Religious Dimension of Jerusalem

# Chapter 1

# Jerusalem: The Legacy of Ancient Israel

Jerusalem emerges as both the political and religious capital of ancient Israel in the Hebrew Bible, which refers to the Holy City nearly 700 times. Jerusalem was also "the goodly mountain" that Moses saw from afar across the Jordan River when he beseeched God to allow him to enter the Promised Land.[1] Consequently, the memory of Jerusalem and its key historical elements—the House of David (the Israelite dynasty established by King David, the first ruler of the united Kingdom of Israel) and the Temple (first built by David's son, Solomon)—remained at the heart of the collective identity of the Jewish people for centuries, even after ancient Israel lost its independence. But the city's unique importance in the development of Judaism is not limited to the early biblical period alone, for Jerusalem became permanently fixed in the hopes and prayers articulated by the prophets of Israel for the future of their nation.

It is essential to look back at the city's biblical history to understand why, for three millennia, Jerusalem has remained central to the Jews' spiritual aspirations and national unity. Before the reign of King David, Jerusalem was situated along the boundary separating the lands of the Israelite tribes of Benjamin and Judah. Although it was technically within

the tribe of Benjamin's territory, the city had not been formally incorporated by any tribe and was still largely inhabited by the Jebusites, along
with other Hittite and local peoples.[2]

As a result, as the twelve tribes of Israel settled throughout Canaan,
Jerusalem was one of the last areas left outside all of their jurisdictions.
Thus the city provided a convenient neutral ground to serve as the
Israelites' united capital once King David captured it from the Jebusites in
1000 BCE. David believed the new capital could bind the tribes together
as a single people under the authority of his newly created United Monarchy. So he situated himself there rather than in Hebron, where he had previously ruled over the Tribe of Judah.

Undoubtedly, Jerusalem's status as the Jewish people's eternal national
and spiritual focal point was not sealed until after David's reign, when his
son and successor, Solomon, constructed the Temple. He built this on Mt.
Moriah, where Jewish tradition taught that Abraham had been tested generations earlier with the binding and near sacrifice of his son, Isaac. It was
also where Jacob slept and dreamt of a ladder serving as the link between
heaven and earth (Genesis 28:11).[3] The site seems to fulfill prophecy from
Deuteronomy, which foreshadows the Temple as Israel's sole religious center: "But look only to the site that the Lord your God will choose amidst
all your tribes as His habitation, to establish His name there" (12:5). For
the ancient Israelites, the Temple linked the religious practices of the
Davidic monarchy with the monotheistic legacy established centuries earlier by their ancestors, Abraham, Isaac, and Jacob, and conveyed in revelation to Moses.[4]

What was the Temple's significance to the Israelites? In 1961, an
ancient Judean tomb dating from roughly 700 BCE was discovered with a
Hebrew inscription that is one of the earliest testaments to the existence
of the First Temple. It read: "The (Mount of) Moriah Thou hast favored,
the dwelling of Yah, YHWH."[5] In short, the Israelites viewed the Temple
as the House of God. They never believed that God physically dwelled
inside the Temple, as was the belief concerning the gods of pagan temples,
but rather that the Temple represented the earthly place where man could
come closest to God. Indeed, the word in biblical Hebrew for the burnt

offering made in Temple ceremonies was *korban*, which did not mean "sacrifice" but rather was derived from the word *kirvah*, or "closeness." In later centuries, rabbinic literature would assert that the Temple was situated opposite the "Gate of Heaven."[6]

The idea that Jerusalem was home to the divine presence, or even brought the individual closer to that presence, was a powerful stimulant to both the development of the city and the unity of the Israelite nation. Worshipers flocked to the capital, where the Temple service bonded the people together in acts of religious piety. Pilgrims streamed to Jerusalem both for Yom Kippur (the Day of Atonement), when the nation's sins were forgiven, and for three yearly festivals: Pesach (Passover), Shavuot (Pentecost), and Succot (Tabernacles).[7] Indeed, to this day these holidays are known as the three pilgrimage festivals.

The Temple of Solomon had two main functions. First, it served as the permanent home to the altar where the sacrificial service was conducted (according to biblical law this service was led by priests descended from Moses' brother, Aaron). Additionally, a sanctuary within the Temple called the Holy of Holies housed the Ark of the Covenant containing the original Ten Commandments. In Hebrew, this area was called the *debir* (pronounced *dvir*) which, according to rabbinic literature, came from the same root as *dibur* (speech) and referred to the place from where God's word went forth to the world.[8] The Holy of Holies could only be entered once a year, and only by one person—the High Priest. Moreover, according to the Oral Law of Judaism, it was built over the *even shetiyya* (foundation stone)—the point at which the creation of the world began. This assertion would be incorporated into the *Zohar* (Book of Splendor), which serves as the foundation of *Kabbalah*, or Jewish mysticism.[9]

Thanks to the vital role played by its Temple in Jewish ritual, Jerusalem eclipsed all other Jewish religious sites and became the faith's spiritual center. Even Mt. Sinai, where Moses received divine revelation, could not compete with Jerusalem, for it was the Ark of the Covenant and its sacred contents that retained the sanctity of the Sinai revelation. By housing the foundation stone and the Ark of the Covenant, the Temple linked together two moments of divine intervention on earth: the creation of the world and the revelation of the Ten Commandments at Sinai. It would tie the particularistic faith of the ancient Israelites to a universalistic mission. And because the Sanhedrin, the supreme legal body of ancient Israel, was housed on the Temple Mount as well, the whole area linked the evolution of Judaic common law, especially in the Second Temple period, with principles derived from divine revelation.

The Temple replaced the Tabernacle, or Tent of Meeting, as the focal point of Jewish ritual. The Tabernacle was a large tent in which the same Temple services were conducted while the Israelites were in the Sinai desert during the exodus from Egypt. Afterward, as the Israelites moved through Canaan, they established a number of temporary locations for the Tabernacle—Gilgal, Shiloh, Nov, and Giveon—before it finally came to rest in Jerusalem. If the Tabernacle's portability symbolized the period of the Israelites' wanderings, then the Temple represented the permanent home they planned for Jerusalem. The Prophet Isaiah stressed this point in his description of the Temple as "a tent that shall not be transported. Whose pegs shall never be pulled up and none of whose ropes shall break" (Isaiah, 33:20).

## Recent Debate about the House of David

Even before King Solomon erected the Temple, King David built up Jerusalem as a national capital with international influence. According to 2 Samuel (5:9–11), David fortified the "surrounding area" around Jerusalem. He purchased the threshing floor of the Jebusite Araunah on the adjacent Mt. Moriah, where King Soloman would later build the Temple. King Hiram, the Phoenician ruler of Tyre, sent cedar logs to Jerusalem along with a mission of carpenters and stonemasons who assisted in building a new royal palace.

Outside of Jerusalem, David waged military campaigns from Aram to Moab and down to Edom in the east, as well as against the Philistines in the west. King Solomon consolidated David's empire, forging alliances and engaging in international trade through a fleet of ships in the Red Sea. We learn in 1 Kings that the fame of Solomon, who became known for his great wisdom, "spread among all the surrounding nations" (5:11). In short,

Jerusalem under the United Monarchy was the capital of an internationally renowned kingdom.

As previously noted, historians have recently begun questioning the veracity of the biblical account of David and Solomon's United Monarchy. A small but growing school of "minimalists" cite purportedly scientific evidence challenging much of the biblical narrative. Niels Peter Lemenche of the University of Copenhagen has gone so far as to accuse the author of the Book of Kings of "making it up."[10]

Indeed, the discussion among the minimalists grouped around the "Copenhagen School" has been tersely summarized as a disagreement over whether King David was just a "petty hilltop chieftain" or a complete historical fabrication.[11] This would make the Jerusalem of the tenth century BCE more of a village outpost rather than a national capital unifying the twelve Israelite tribes. And a hilltop chieftain would obviously have been incapable of financing the construction of the royal palaces described in the Bible or assembling the manpower with the engineering skills needed to erect them, much less the Temple of Solomon.

Yet several important sources corroborate the biblical narrative. In the summer of 2005, Israeli archaeologist Eilat Mazar excavated an immense stone structure south of the Temple Mount—just where the Bible relates that King David's palace stood. This has not yet been either proved or disproved as David's palace, but construction of a structure of such enormous dimensions was clearly beyond the means of a petty village chieftain. With walls between six and eight feet thick, it sat atop what archeologists called a "stepped-stone fortification" that Mazar judged to be the height of a twelve-story building.[12] The unique style of hewn stones discovered nearby was rare for central Israel at the time, but consistent with Phoenician construction work of the sort that would have been brought in by King Hiram of Tyre.

Pottery found underneath the structure dated to the twelfth and eleventh centuries BCE, indicating a likelihood that the structure itself was built in the tenth century BCE, when King David ruled. Additional pottery fragments show that the building was utilized for several hundred years through the sixth century BCE, toward the end of the Kingdom of

Judah, one of the successor kingdoms to the United Monarchy. Mazar also found an ancient bulla used as a seal for official documents, implying that the structure was some kind of governmental facility. The seal read "Belonging to Yechual ben Shelemiah ben Shovi," a name mentioned in the Book of Jeremiah (37:3) as a minister of King Zedekiah, the last King of Judah from the House of David.

Archeological evidence from later periods also attests to the House of David as a powerful historical dynasty. Ironically, much of this evidence is provided by Israel's ancient enemies, whose records show that David's name was still popularly associated with the entirety of the Israelites' territory even after his death. After the reign of Solomon, the United Monarchy split into the kingdoms of Israel and Judah, which were both invaded by the Egyptians under Shishak I in 925 BCE. Engravings found in Karnak in Egypt refer to Shishak's military campaign in "the highlands of *Dwt*." Given the tendency of ancient Egyptians to transcribe "d" in Semitic languages as "t," the phrase likely means the "highlands of David," or the Judean hills in the Kingdom of Judah.[13]

Later, Mesha, the king of Moab, celebrated in what is called the "Moabite Stone" his campaign against the son of King Omri of Israel and his seizure of territories previously controlled by the "House of [D]avid."[14]

Finally, stone fragments found in Israel's Tel Dan archaeological site in 1993 attest to the victory against both Israel and Judah by Aram-Damascus, a kingdom to the north of ancient Israel in what is today Syria. The fragments' inscription contains a boast that its author killed the kings of both Israel and Judah. The latter king, it says, was of the "House of David."[15] The habit in these foreign inscriptions of referring to the "House of David" rather than using simple geographic terms is indicative of the fame and prestige that David's United Monarchy long enjoyed throughout much of the ancient Near East and the status derived by ancient Egyptian, Moabite, and Aramean rulers from defeating his successors.

The evidence even impressed the skeptics, who were forced to acknowledge the significance of the Tel Dan discovery in particular. Notably, Israel Finkelstein and Neil Asher Silberstein, who have been prolific in challenging the veracity of the biblical narrative, concluded: "Thus, the house of David was known throughout the region; this clearly validates the biblical description of a figure named David becoming the founder of the dynasty of Judahite kings in Jerusalem."[16]

Archaeologists have also discovered "Solomonic gates" around the remains of fortified cities, as described in 1 Kings (9:15).[17] This verse details how Solomon erected a wall at Gezer after previously building walls around Hazor, Megiddo, and Jerusalem. The fact that walls and gates excavated in Hazor, Megiddo, and Gezer are remarkably similar means that the Bible did not simply compile a list of separate building projects, but rather detailed a unified plan to erect royal fortifications across Solomon's kingdom.[18]

The massive size of these fortifications undercuts the argument that Solomon was a minor village chieftain. Moreover, as noted archaeologists like Yigael Yadin have demonstrated, the six-chamber gates uncovered at each of these sites closely resemble the description of the gate in the court of the Temple of Solomon described by the Prophet Ezekiel.[19] True, Ezekiel offered a prophetic vision, but he had been a priest in Jerusalem prior to his exile in Babylon and his detailed account of the Temple gates seems to reflect an eyewitness account.[20] In any case, Charles Warren's initial excavation of parts of what are believed to be Solomonic gates in Jerusalem back in the 1860s greatly complicate the argument that Solomon was but a village chief; one of the gates' towers was estimated to be seventy-nine feet long, sixty-two feet wide, and nearly forty feet high.[21]

## Political Freedom and Religious Spirituality

Beyond the issue of whether Jerusalem was really the capital of a great kingdom in ancient Israel, there is the further question of what exactly Jerusalem signified for its people and their faith. The biblical narrative is striking in that the Temple's construction is the only event dated in relation to the exodus from Egypt (it was built 480 years afterward), which implies that the exodus only truly ended upon the conquest of Jerusalem and the completion of the Temple (1 Kings, 6:1).

This characteristic demonstrates that securing political freedom in Jerusalem and across Israel was a prerequisite for building the Temple. The

Israelites' spiritual achievements were limited as long as they were nomadic or under foreign tutelage. Political sovereignty was therefore a prerequisite for fully realizing their spirituality; the fulfillment of their faith required that they be a free people in their own homeland.

In fact, Judaism itself was always inextricably tied to a commitment to political freedom. For example, the Israelites had to free themselves from slavery and escape from Egypt before they could receive the revelation of the Torah at Mount Sinai. They institutionalized the commitment to freedom in the holiday of Passover, which commemorated their liberation from slavery and their emergence as a free people. Even beyond the Jewish world, the Bible's narrative of the exodus from Egypt became a paradigm for national liberation movements throughout history.[22]

This link between the spirituality of the ancient Israelites and their determination to preserve the liberties gained through political independence is evident throughout the history of ancient Israel. Sometimes it was a converse relationship as well—the spiritual decay led to political decline. During the period after the reign of King Solomon, as the religious commitment of the ancient Israelites weakened, the durability of their national self-rule came into question. As already noted, the United Monarchy split in 930 BCE into the kingdoms of Israel and Judah. Under Solomon's son, Rehoboam, the Kingdom of Judah went through a period of spiritual decay, even permitting idolatry.

The biblical prophets perceived a direct link between the adoption of idolatrous rituals and a decline in national morality.[23] Idolatry rituals included practices such as child sacrifice to the god Molech. Engaging in such foreign practices eroded the Israelites' national values relating to the fight against social injustice, as well as the nation's moral fortitude, thus leaving it vulnerable to foreign enemies. This process of decline ultimately ended in the exile of the inhabitants of both Israelite kingdoms.

As the Israelites came under increasing threats of external invasion, Judah's kings at times tried to restore the ritual purity—and ultimately the moral fiber—of their ancestors and thereby reestablish the nation's security. King Joash (837 BCE–800 BCE), or Jehoash, under the influence of the high priest Jehoida, purified the Temple of foreign religious practices, but later allowed paganism to return. He resisted external aggression, but the Kingdom of Judah remained weak and vulnerable.

His grandson, King Uziah (785 BCE–734 BCE), with the help of his son and regent, Yotam, revived Judah's strength and reestablished Judean control in the Negev down to the Red Sea. The biblical narrative notes the son's religious commitment as well: "Yotam did what was right in the sight of the Lord" (2 Kings 16:2). The Hebrew Bible repeatedly testifies to this intimate connection between the spiritual commitment of ancient Israel and its national strength in resisting the hegemonic ambitions of Egypt to the south and the kingdoms of Mesopotamia to the north.

In 720 BCE the Assyrian Empire conquered the Kingdom of Israel and deported much of its population. Many of the refugees streamed into Jerusalem, which significantly expanded during this period. Assyria then waged war against the Kingdom of Judah as well. An Assyrian inscription found on a prism-shaped black stone detailing King Sennacharib's campaign against Judah says of the Judean king, Hezekiah, "himself I made a prisoner in Jerusalem, his royal residence, like a bird in a cage."[24] In any case, the Assyrians did not subject Judah to the same fate as the Kingdom of Israel, but they reduced it to a vassal state of the Assyrian Empire and limited the political and religious freedom of its inhabitants. With its political autonomy highly circumscribed, the Kingdom of Judah was more prone to adopt alien religious practices from the now dominant Assyrians.[25]

Under Judean king Josiah (640 BCE–609 BCE), as Assyrian power began to wane, the Kingdom of Judah began reasserting its political independence.[26] Josiah took back from Assyria many territories of the former Kingdom of Israel, extending Judah's rule to the northern Galilee and the Mediterranean coast. With its freedom restored, the kingdom began reestablishing its original religious practices as well. Josiah, according to 2 Kings (23:24), purged foreign cult worship from Assyria: "the mediums, the idols, and the fetishes—all the detestable things that were to be seen in the land of Judah and in Jerusalem, did Josiah put away." He sought to eliminate any traces of the Assyrian religion in the Holy City,[27] dismantling alternative altars and centralizing all Jewish religious practice in Jerusalem alone.

Consequently, the Bible's next verse assigns Josiah a unique and remarkable status: "There was no king like him before who turned back to the Lord with all his heart and soul, and might, in full accord with the Teaching of Moses, nor did any like him arise after him." Josiah ritually cleaned the Temple and renewed the Passover sacrifice, which had not been offered in centuries.[28] Josiah's religious revival undoubtedly reinvigorated the citizenry of the Kingdom of Judah both morally and spiritually, thus assisting him in reestablishing the national strength that Israel once enjoyed under his Davidic predecessors.[29]

In 586 BCE, Nebuchadnezzar, king of Babylonia, attacked Jerusalem, destroyed the Temple of Solomon, and took the Judeans into exile in Babylon along with their king, Zedekiah. The Psalms (137) recorded the sentiment of the exiles who sat "by the waters of Babylon." Asked to perform their ritual music, the exiles asked themselves: "how can we sing the Lord's song on alien soil?" The psalm then declares, "If I forget thee Oh Jerusalem, let my right hand wither." The exiles' spiritual malaise was tied to their national status as stateless refugees.

The Jews reconsecrated Jerusalem with the completion of the Second Temple in 515 BCE, a few decades after King Cyrus of Persia crushed Babylonia and allowed the Judean exiles to return to Jerusalem and reestablish their self-government. Coins have been found from the Persian period engraved with the word "Yehud," which was the name of the new Jewish commonwealth in which Jerualem served as the restored capital.

However, the descendants of King Zedekiah, himself a direct descendant of King David, remained in Babylon under Persian rule; there they continued the House of David through the institution of the Exilarch (*Resh Galuta*), the leader of the Jewish community in exile. The line of the Exilarchs, who eventually moved to Baghdad, continued into the Islamic period until the Mongol invasion of the mid-thirteenth century. Yet this continuous Davidic institution in the Diaspora did not detract from the centrality of Jerusalem and its rebuilt Temple for the Jewish people worldwide. For example, the biblical Ezra brought several thousand Judean exiles back to Jerusalem in 459 BCE. Nehemiah records a total of 42,360 exiles who ultimately left Babylon for Jerusalem (7:66).

# Particularism versus Universalism in Judaism's Treatment of Jerusalem

Judaism can be interpreted as a highly particularistic religion because of its focus on the biblical history of the Jewish people. Unlike Christianity and Islam, Judaism did not generally proselytize among other nations, though it was open to converting Gentiles who expressed interest in monotheism. This particularism within Judaism could lead to the expectation that Jews would rule Jerusalem in an exclusivist way, without regard to the sensitivities of the other great faiths. The Bible offers glimpses of this intolerance—from the time the tribes of Israel first crossed into Canaan until the era of King David, Israel's early leaders waged repeated wars against the idolatry of the surrounding polytheistic nations.

Yet Judaism always contained an underlying universal ideal that is evident even in the meaning of the various biblical names for Jerusalem. In the Book of Genesis (22:2) Abraham is told by God to take his son Isaac to the "Land of Moriah." The *Midrash*—part of the early rabbinic literature compiled after the destruction of the Second Temple—breaks down various possible Hebraic roots of the word "Moriah," which is understood to mean the place where instruction (*hora'ah*), religious awe (*yir'ah*), or light (*orah*) "went forth to the world."[30] In short, the religious acts associated with Mt. Moriah have universal meaning for all mankind.

The Midrash offers further examples of this tendency toward universalism in its analysis of the word "Jerusalem" itself. In Genesis, Abraham calls Jerusalem "the place which the Lord will show" (*yir'eh*). But Jerusalem, according to the Midrash, already had the name Shalem, which it was given by Shem, the son of Noah. Thus Jerusalem is not only relevant to the tradition of Abraham, the Midrash concludes, but rather to all the sons of Noah—in other words, to the rest of mankind. Therefore, it suggests that God chose the name Jerusalem (*Yerushalayim*) as a combination of *Yir'eh* and *Shalem*.[31]

The Temple service reflected the universalistic role envisioned for Jerusalem. In dedicating the Temple, King Solomon said that prayers would be offered there by "a foreigner who is not of your people Israel, but rather comes from a distant land" (1 Kings 8:41). In Isaiah, God described the Temple as "a house of prayer for all people" (56:7). Furthermore, foreigners were involved in the construction of both Temples; foreigners sent by King Hiram of Tyre helped to build the First Temple, while Ezra (6:3) cites a royal decree stipulating that expenses for the Second Temple's construction will be borne by the royal treasury of Cyrus, King of Persia.

Temple services were intended not only to benefit the Israelites; sacrifices were regularly offered to promote peace for the entire world. The Temple sacrifices on the festival of Sukkot, according to Numbers (29:12–31), required an offering of seventy bulls over a seven-day period. The Talmud (Sukkah 55:B) explains that these rituals were offered for the atonement of the seventy nations of the world which, according to Genesis (10:2–29), constituted the sum total of all humanity.

According to biblical law, non-Jews were in fact permitted to offer sacrifices at the Temple, a practice that became particularly widespread during the Second Temple period. The historian Josephus names numerous kings across the entire Near East known to have brought sacrifices to the Temple, including Ptolemy III and Antiochus VII. He also claims that Alexander the Great brought an offering to the Temple during his campaigns in 331 BCE.[32]

Whether Alexander actually reached Jerusalem is the source of some dispute. The Talmud records a meeting between Alexander and Simon the Just, the Temple high priest, though the latter lived much later than the former.[33] Leaving Jerusalem to meet the Macedonian army, Simon persuades Alexander not to destroy the Temple by arguing, "Is it possible that (with regard to) the (very) house in which we pray for you and for your empire that it should not be destroyed?"[34] Alexander was convinced and spared the Temple. The entire story illustrated that prayers were offered at the Temple for other nations. It was also common for non-Jewish leaders to send gifts to the Temple throughout the Second Temple period. Darius, King of Persia, and even Augustus Caesar both did this. Undoubtedly because of the Temple, Pliny the Elder wrote that Jerusalem was the most famous city in the East. In short, the Temple had significance for large parts of the ancient world.

But Judaism's ancient universalism had its limits. The Bible denounces the adoption by certain kings of Israel and Judah of Canaanite and Babylonian pagan cults as a corruption of monotheism. Furthermore, while foreign leaders were initially welcomed to partake in the Second Temple's ceremonies (as long as they did not impose their religious practices on Jerusalem), the introduction by Seleucid ruler Antiochus Epiphanes of foreign deities inside the Temple in the second century CE helped spark the Maccabean revolt, which was also fueled by his decision to make Sabbath observance and circumcision punishable by death. The Maccabees rededicated the Temple, which was commemorated with the holiday of Hanukkah. They had little patience for their own co-religionists who supported the Selucids' Helenizing policies.

After the destruction of the Northern Kingdom of Israel, the Assyrian Empire settled colonists from different nationalities in the Samarian hills. These groups eventually merged into a people known as the Samaritans, who practiced a mixed religion reflecting their various countries of origin. When the Samaritans sought to join Jews returning from exile in Babylon in rebuilding the Temple, they were rebuffed. Although Judaism may have demonstrated considerable openness toward other nations, its adherents showed little tolerance for their own sectarians. According to Josephus, Alexander the Great eventually allowed the Samaritans to build their own altar on Mount Gerizim, near what is today Nablus.

## The War for the Freedom of Jerusalem

During the Second Temple Period, Jews in the Holy Land lived in a commonwealth whose independence was constantly threatened. Initially an autonomous area called *Yehud* within the Persian Empire, the commonwealth maintained a similar status under its succeeding rulers, the Hellenistic empires. Under the Hasmoneans, it regained the territorial size and the degree of independence enjoyed under the United Monarchy. But its autonomy gradually eroded as the Hasmonean kingdom came under the increasing influence and control of the Roman Empire.

This process began when the Roman general Pompey entered Jerusalem in 63 BCE, accelerating in 37 BCE when the Romans installed

Herod as king of Judea though he was neither a Hasmonean nor from a Davidic family.[35] By 6 CE, Judea was formally annexed to the Roman Empire, sparking the first Jewish resistance movements. Roman oppression worsened with the accession in 37 CE of Emperor Caligula, who viewed himself as a god and demanded that his statue be erected in the Temple. He ordered an army to march on Jerusalem, kill anyone who refused his demands, and enslave the entire population of Judea if they did not submit.

Caligula died before these orders could be executed, but Rome's local governors in Judea, known as procurators, became increasingly corrupt and abusive of the Jewish population. Beginning with Pontius Pilate (governing from 26–36 CE) this trend climaxed with the appointment of Gessius Florus (governing from 64–66 CE), whose oppressive policies provoked a Jewish rebellion.

The Great Revolt of the Jews against Roman rule began in 66 CE. The primary account of these events comes from Josephus, who was originally a commander of Jewish forces in the Galilee, in what is today northern Israel.[36] Josephus recorded the warning of Agrippa II, the pro-Roman king who ruled over the Galilee, to his Jewish subjects against their impending rebellion. Agrippa felt that they were too politically immature to handle freedom, and too confident "about the prospects of independence." Rome was the ancient world's greatest imperial power and these Jewish insurgents planned to wage all-out war against it without supplies, financial backing, or a fleet that could challenge the Roman navy. The risks, cautioned Agrippa, were just too great.[37]

After addressing the political situation in Jerusalem, Agrippa dismissed the Jews' demands for liberty: "As for your new passion for liberty, it comes too late." Perhaps the Jews could have successfully resisted when Pompey had invaded, he argued, but they didn't. He reminded the Jews that the Athenians and Macedonians all accepted Roman domination, adding, "other nations by the thousand, bursting with greater determination to assert their liberty no longer resist." He then asked: "Will you alone refuse to serve the masters of the whole world?" But the speech was in vain. The Jews refused to submit, for their religious freedom was fundamentally tied to their political liberty.

In their first act of defiance, the Temple priests ceased offering sacrifices for Rome and for Caesar.[38] The Jewish revolutionaries, as Josephus notes, "took advantage of the general disturbance" then convulsing the Roman Empire, which was afflicted by internal power struggles and civil strife.[39] And the Jewish revolt had implications for Rome beyond the Galilee, for it could undermine the entire social order in Roman-controlled Judea; indeed, in Judea, the revolt was accompanied by an internal social revolution. Simon bar Giora, one of the leaders of the Jewish Revolt, not only proclaimed "freedom for the slaves," but he actually implemented this policy in much of the Judean territory that came under his control. Peasants streamed into his army, which rapidly grew to a force of 20,000 to 40,000 men.[40] Furthermore, the revolt threatened the power of the Sadducees—Jewish families from whom Rome chose the Temple's high priests.

The revolt lasted from 66 CE to 73 CE. It broke out under the rule of the Roman emperor Nero, who dispatched to Judea his trusted general Vespasian, an experienced commander who had fought throughout the empire's western provinces. Having previously subdued a German revolt, Vespasian understood how to deal with rebellions.[41] He began his campaign with a scorched-earth policy in the north. Roman troops destroyed entire Jewish towns in the Galilee as well as the fortress of Gamla in the Golan Heights, where 5,000 Jews took their own lives rather than fall into captivity. Vespasian himself became emperor during the war and was forced to return to Rome. So his son, Titus, completed the campaign and led the final Roman offensive against Jerusalem. Jewish militias that had fought Vespasian in the Galilee poured into the Holy City prior to the final Roman assault. In May 70 CE, the Romans broke through Jerusalem's outer walls. On August 28, 70 CE—the ninth of the Hebrew month of Av—the Romans broke through to the inner courts on the Temple Mount and crushed some 6,000 Jewish insurgents who died defending their sanctuary.

The Roman forces then set the Temple on fire and destroyed it entirely. Titus had consulted with his war council over the Temple's fate. The Roman historian Tacitus reports that Titus had asked if it made sense to "overthrow a sanctuary of such workmanship, since it seemed to many that a sacred building, one more remarkable than any other human work, should not be destroyed." Titus thought that sparing the Temple "would testify to the moderation of the Romans." But he later decided "that the Temple should be destroyed without delay, in order that the religion of the Jews and Christians should be more completely exterminated."[42] The Romans were equally determined to eliminate the genealogical House of David; the Roman Tenth Legion had orders to hunt down and execute any Jew claiming to be a descendant of King David.[43] The Romans enslaved or crucified thousands of Jewish survivors around Jerusalem. The violence also threatened members of Jerusalem's incipient Christian community, many of whom had fled the Roman onslaught in Jerusalem by moving to cities like Pella in Transjordan.[44]

Returning to Rome, Titus was greeted with a triumphal parade that showcased the gold and silver booty from his campaign. The Romans forced hundreds of Jewish prisoners to march in the procession, including the leaders of the revolt, Simon bar Giora and John Gischala. Titus had previously displayed Jewish prisoners in similar processions held across Syria, but this time he added a new element to entertain the crowds—bar Giora was executed publicly in the Roman Forum. Titus built an arch of triumph near the Forum to eternalize his victory, while Rome issued coins commemorating the occasion with the inscription *Judaea Capta* (Judea Captured) and *Judaea Devicta* (Judea Vanquished).[45]

But Titus's effort to "exterminate" Judaism failed. His father, now Emperor Vespasian, gave permission to the great sage Rabbi Yohanan ben Zakai to establish a school of Jewish law at Yavneh. Moreover, after the Temple's destruction, the Jews were determined to recover their political freedom and rededicate the Temple as their national-religious center. Jewish resistance forces held out against Rome for several years after the fall of Jerusalem in remote fortresses like Masada in the Judean Desert. Additionally, Diaspora Jews revolted against Rome between 115 and 117 CE.

## The Second Jewish Revolt

The Bar Kochba revolt in Judea in 132–135 CE was the final expression of national resistance to Rome. Sources differ as to what triggered the rebellion. According to the Roman historian Dio Cassius, Emperor

Hadrian provoked his Jewish subjects by erecting a temple to Jupiter precisely where the Temple had stood in Jerusalem. Other accounts claim Jews were enraged by Hadrian's decision to rename Jerusalem after himself and rebuild it as an entirely pagan city.[46] Still others argue that Hadrian had banned circumcision. The Talmud, for its part, recounts that the Romans denied religious freedom throughout Judea.[47]

The revolt's leader was Shimon bar Kosiba. He acquired the nom de guerre of Bar Kochba, meaning the "son of the star," indicating that many regarded him as a messianic figure. The era's leading Jewish sage, Rabbi Akiva, connected to Bar Kochba the biblical verse, "There shall step forth a star out of Jacob" (Numbers 24:7). Maimonides would write nine hundred years later that this was a position adopted by most of the sages of that era.[48]

In the 1960s, Israeli archaeologists exploring inside caves in the Judean desert uncovered letters Bar Kochba had sent to his men. These were signed with the more modest appellation Bar Kosiba, rather than with his more famous messianic title. The caves yielded additional artifacts, including wool ritual fringes (*tzitzit*) used on the corners of prayer shawl (*talitot*) to this day,[49] and phylacteries (*tfilin*)—the black prayer boxes and straps worn by Jews during their weekday morning prayers.[50] The letters and surrounding findings demonstrate that Bar Kochba observed the detailed commandments of the Jewish religion. Bar Kochba clearly emerged from Jewish mainstream society, which was not factionalized during his rebellion as it was during the first anti-Roman revolt. Bar Kochba's efforts even seem to have secured the support of the Sanhedrin, the highest Jewish religious court.

Bar Kochba commanded a guerilla force that, in the first two years of the rebellion, scored repeated victories against Roman armies. This concerned the Roman authorities, who feared the revolt could destabilize other parts of the empire. According to the Roman historian Dio Cassius, both Jews and non-Jews throughout the Roman Empire supported the revolt. He reported that "many outside nations, too were joining" the rebels, adding "the whole earth, one might almost say, was being stirred up over the matter."[51] Thus Roman rulers for the second time perceived a threat to their empire emanating from Jewish rebels; during the earlier Great Revolt of 66–70 CE, Josephus writes, reports of initial Roman "reverses in Judea" had filled Emperor Nero with "consternation and alarm" as he sought to prevent "the spread of the infection to the surrounding nations."[52]

Given this historical background, Emperor Hadrian urgently needed to defeat the Bar Kochba revolt. He appointed Julius Severus, the commander of Roman forces in Britain, to lead the campaign. Units from eight legions from across the empire marched to Judea to put down the insurgency. (In comparison, the German revolt against Rome in 9 CE only earned three legions.)[53] The Romans felt they needed to defeat the Jews whatever the cost.

Early in their campaign, Bar Kochba's forces captured Jerusalem and completely drove the Roman military out of Judea.[54] Bar Kochba's confederates minted coins to celebrate these victories that were dated "Year One of the Redemption of Israel." This was a symbolic act asserting the Jews' political sovereignty. The guerilla insurgency had quickly metastasized into a full-blown war of national liberation covering all of Judea out to the Mediterranean coast.

Jerusalem was central to the revolt—a testament to its power as a symbol of Jewish spirituality and political freedom. The centrality of Jerusalem to the rebels was symbolized on some coins with an engraving of the Temple. Whereas Roman coins that depicted pagan temples typically displayed a pagan god between the temples' columns, the Bar Kochba coins showed the Ark of the Covenant in this position. The opposite side displayed the palm branch (*lulav*) used in prayer during the festival of Sukkot—one of the main holidays for pilgrimage to Jerusalem. Many Bar Kochba coins additionally contained the inscription "For the Freedom of Jerusalem"— a clear reference to the insurgents' ultimate war goal.

Did this inscription refer to other people's freedom as well? To answer this, we must analyze the general attitude of the rebellion's leaders toward non-Jews. Dio Cassius claims that non-Jews fought alongside the Jews, and it is known that Samaritans joined forces with the Jews as well, despite their past religious enmity.[55] In fact, one of the Bar Kochba letters is a

Greek-language missive by a non-Jewish insurgent named Ailonos, who refers to his fellow Jewish soldiers as "brothers."[56]

Yet the early church historian Eusebius, who was a pro-Roman bishop of Caesaria, cited an earlier second-century writer named Hegesippus in arguing that Bar Kochba in fact persecuted Christians. Much of the criticism focuses on Bar Kochba's compulsory military conscription of Christians, but he instituted this measure across Judea for Jews and Christians alike.[57] His letters make clear that he recommended strict measures be taken against those who evaded wartime military service regardless of religious affiliation. He thus viewed Christians as part of a potential coalition of free peoples who must fight Roman oppression. He saw Christians more as possible allies than as religious adversaries. After all, during the years of the two anti-Roman revolts, the Jewish and early Christian communities were still closely linked, with their definitive break yet to come.[58]

The Romans defeated Bar Kochba south of Jerusalem at the fortress of Beitar in 135 CE. Dio Cassius estimated that more than a half million Jews died during the rebellion. He reports that 985 villages were "razed to the ground" so that "nearly the whole of Judea was made desolate," and the Romans again enslaved many Jews. Roman losses were apparently considerable as well. This was attested to by Emperor Hadrian's written report to the Senate in which he left out the traditional imperial opening: "I and the legions are in health."[59]

Hadrian died three years later, but not before instituting a series of laws designed to crush any lingering national spirit among the Jews. He banned the celebration of Hanukkah, which reminded Jews of the rededication of the Temple; he prohibited the eating of *Matza* (unleavened bread) on Passover, which reminded Jews of their freedom from Egyptian bondage; and he banned public study of the Torah.[60] The Romans, moreover, tortured and killed Rabbi Akiva and many other leading religious sages.

Judea was renamed *Syria-Palestina*, or *Palestina* for short, in order to eradicate permanently the memory of Jewish independence. The new name was taken from the Greek translation of *Pleshet*, the Land of the Philistines. Judea was depopulated of its Jewish population; many sought refuge up north in the Galilee, which became a new center of Jewish learning.

In Jerusalem, the Romans sought to eliminate any sign of Jewish civilization. For the religious quest of the Jews to reestablish their spiritual capital was tied to their determination to win their political freedom. And that freedom undermined Rome's imperial rule. In short, the Romans, too, understood that Jerusalem was not only the beacon of Jewish heritage but also a symbol of freedom and liberation that they feared could spark unrest across the empire.

The Romans banned the Jews from Jerusalem and scrupulously imposed this law for centuries thereafter. They applied the injunction to Jewish Christians as well, which affected the early development of the Church. Over the years, a special exception to the ban was only permitted on the ninth day of the Hebrew month of Ab, when Jews fasted and mourned the destruction of the Temple. They would approach the western retaining wall of the Temple Mount, which was the closest they could approach to the Holy of Holies, and chant the Book of Lamentations. Thus the Western Wall became known also as the Wailing Wall. Despite this state of affairs, the Jewish people retained hope for salvation from their early rabbinic tradition that the divine presence (*Shekhinah*) would never abandon the Western Wall.[61]

## Jerusalem and Judaism after the Fall of Judea

Despite the flowering of Jewish life in the Galilee, Jews never forgot Jerusalem. The same was true of Jewish communities in the Diaspora. Although the failure of the two Jewish revolts led the rabbinic leadership to abandon its active opposition to Roman hegemony,[62] this did not affect Jewish views of Jerusalem. Jewish communities began building synagogues so that congregations would face Jerusalem during prayer. In the early twentieth century, a synagogue dating back to the second or third century was discovered near the Euphrates River in Syria. Called the *Dura Europos*, the structure contained a niche for holding Torah scrolls that was decorated with paintings of the Temple in Jerusalem. The painted area included a depiction of the binding of Isaac, which according to tradition also occurred on the Temple Mount.[63]

Engravings over the entranceways of synagogues built in the third and fourth centuries across the Galilee and Golan Heights display some common themes. Three symbols linked with the Temple almost always appear. The first two are the palm branch from the pilgrimage festival of Sukkot and the ram's horn (*shofar*) that is sounded on various religious holidays. Both of these had special significance since the great sage Yohanan Ben Zakai had instructed that they be used exactly as they had been when the Temple existed, as a memorial to its destruction.[64] The third engraving was a candelabrum (*menorah*), which was one of the most noted Temple fixtures as well as a symbol of the struggle for freedom and religious renewal against the Seleucids. All three items tied the early synagogues directly to the collective memories that Jewish communities retained of their destroyed Temple.

Following the Second Temple's destruction and the Jews' banishment from Jerusalem, the city's memory was preserved in the main Jewish prayers used to this day. The "Eighteen Benedictions" recited three times a day include a prayer for Jerusalem: "O return in mercy to Jerusalem thy city, and dwell therein as thou hast spoken; O rebuild it soon, in our days (as) an everlasting building, and speedily establish therein the throne of David. Blessed art thou, O Lord, the (Re) builder of Jerusalem."

These references to Jerusalem are twofold: first, a call to reestablish the city as the dwelling place of the divine, which plainly means rebuilding the Temple and restoring Jewish sovereignty through "the throne of David." In the grace after meals a shorter supplication was also instituted: "Rebuild Jerusalem, the Holy City, soon in our days. Blessed art Thou O Lord, who in his mercy rebuilds Jerusalem." These prayers placed Jerusalem at the core of Jewish belief and consciousness.

The Jews did not yearn passively. They still demonstrated their readiness to act on their aspirations. Their return to Jerusalem, however, depended largely on the willingness of foreign rulers to overturn Hadrian's edicts. The promotion of Christianity by Roman emperor Constantine in 324 CE greatly complicated these efforts, for early Roman Christianity attached a religious significance to the Temple's destruction and the Jews' exclusion from Jerusalem: they proved that God had rejected the Jews and that Judaism was a defeated religion.

Forty years later, Roman emperor Julian sought to restore paganism. Among various edicts designed to weaken Christianity's role in the empire, he repealed Hadrian's law and allowed the Jews to return to Jerusalem. Jews streamed back to resettle in their Holy City. Archaeologists excavating along the Western Wall in the 1970s found a Hebrew inscription quoting from the Book of Isaiah: "You shall see (this) and your heart shall rejoice, Your limbs shall flourish like grass" (66:14).[65] This message, likely carved during Julian's reign, captured the enthusiasm felt among Jews upon their return to Jerusalem.

Jerusalem's Jews quickly began planning for the Temple's reconstruction. This seemed a real possibility, for Julian, whose hostility to Christianity later earned him the moniker "Julian the Apostate," committed to help rebuild the Temple and even appointed officials to oversee its construction. The plan, however, was disrupted by a major fire at the Temple site caused by either arson or an earthquake. Julian was killed shortly thereafter in battle against the Persians and his successor, Jovian, restored Christianity as the empire's official religion. Most important, Jovian reactivated Hadrian's ban on Jewish settlement in Jerusalem.

Despite this setback, the Jews refused to reduce Jerusalem to a mere ritual symbol. Rather, they vowed to return and waited—for centuries— for the opportunity to do so. A substantial Jewish presence survived in Byzantine Palestine outside of Jerusalem. Estimates vary as to the size of this community. Writing in the fifth century, the Christian monk Bar Sawma claimed that the Jews and pagans combined constituted a majority in Byzantine Palestine,[66] and that Jews and Samaritans were still governing the land. In his monumental *History of Palestine*, Professor Moshe Gil suggests that much of this population was comprised of direct descendants of the first Jews to move into the Holy Land during the days of Joshua bin Nun.[67] The sages writing in the Jerusalem Talmud at this time debated whether most of Byzantine Palestine was already "in the hands of the Gentiles" or still "in the hands of the Jews."[68]

Following Jovian's restoration of Hadrian's laws, Jews once again began beseeching Roman rulers to overturn the ban on Jewish settlement in Jerusalem. In 425 CE, the Jews of the Galilee wrote to Byzantine empress Eudocia seeking permission to pray on the ruins of the Temple. Receiving a favorable response, they wrote to the Jewish communities of Persia and Rome, "You shall know that the time of the dispersion of our people is at an end, and from now onwards the day of our congregation and salvation has come, for the Roman kings have written a decree to hand over our city Jerusalem to us."[69] But the Church establishment ultimately ended Eudocia's gestures toward the Jews, who were left again to pray for their deliverance.

The Jews saw another opportunity to take back Jerusalem in the early seventh century, just before the rise of Islam. The Persians conquered what had been Judea from the Byzantine Empire, capturing Jerusalem in 614 CE. The Armenian historian Sebeos described the Jews' reaction to the Persian campaign: "As the Persians approached Palestine, the remnants of the Jewish nation rose against the Christians, joined the Persians and made common cause with them." The Persians even installed a Jew, Nehemiah ben Hushiel ben Ephraim ben Joseph, to rule the city.[70]

But this regime was short-lived. Hoping to accommodate their Roman Christian subjects, the Persians apparently withdrew their support for any Jewish self-government. Moreover, in 629 CE the Byzantine emperor Heraclius reconquered Jerusalem, where the former anti-Jewish edicts were again renewed. The city's new rulers banned public recital of Judaism's core prayer, the *Shema*, and executed many Jews or evicted them to neighboring countries. Five years later, the Byzantines required all the empire's Jews to become baptized. This harsh regime did not last long, however, for in 638 CE Muslim armies from Arabia conquered Jerusalem, thus opening a whole new chapter in the Holy City's history.

Thirteen hundred years would pass between the last Jewish self-government in Jerusalem in 614 and the establishment of a Jewish national home under the British that would later become the State of Israel. During that time, Jerusalem would remain the center of Jewish national aspirations as well as religious ritual. But the quest to return to Jerusalem was not left as an eschatological task for the distant future. Jews returned to Jerusalem whenever the bans on Jewish settlement were lifted; thus many Jews came back to the Holy City after the second caliph of Islam defeated the Byzantines, establishing a new Jewish Quarter that was populated until the First Crusade. Jerusalem's main Jewish synagogue in the first decades of Islamic rule, known as "the Cave," was located under the Temple Mount, at the point along the Western Wall closest to the Holy of Holies.[71]

According to Muslim sources, in these early years of Islamic rule, Muslim authorities put between ten and twenty of the new Jewish residents in charge of sanitation on the Temple Mount until 717, when the Ummayad caliph Umar ibn Abd a-Aziz replaced them with slaves.[72] The Jewish population apparently grew in Jerusalem in these years. The Muslim historian al-Muqaddasi, writing at the end of the tenth century, complained that there were not enough learned Islamic religious leaders in Jerusalem and that most of the city's inhabitants were Christians and Jews.[73] It is significant that during this period of early Islam, the presence of non-Muslims on the Temple Mount was not an issue.

During the following centuries, the greatest rabbis of the Diaspora made the pilgrimage to Jerusalem, including Maimonides (Rambam) in 1166 and Nachmandides (Ramban), who established a synagogue there in 1267. The great Hebrew poet and philosopher Judah Halevi left Muslim Spain in 1140 for Egypt in order to emigrate to his ancestral homeland. Some accounts have him dying in Jerusalem. There was also immigration to Jerusalem from the West. Three hundred rabbis from France and southern England came to reside in Jerusalem between 1209 and 1211, once the twin threats emanating from the Crusades and the Mongol invasions had passed.[74]

The reestablishment of Crusader rule interrupted this preliminary return to Jerusalem, and the new authorities resettled the recently returned Jews in Acre. But a new wave of Jewish immigrants arrived in the fifteenth century from Spain. The Israeli historian Binyamin Kedar discovered an account of the voyage of Jewish immigrants from Spain to the port of Jaffa: "Old and young, women and youths and infants, they went up to Jerusalem and there built [houses]."[75] Leading Jewish religious scholars at the time supported this exodus, although it caused some Spanish Jewish leaders to complain about the depopulation of Spain's Jews.[76]

Large numbers of Italian Jews also arrived in Jerusalem at this time. As Jerusalem's Jewish population grew more self-confident, it became involved in a dispute with Christians over control of the Tomb of David on Mt. Zion. In response, to cut off the influx of Jews to Jerusalem, the Catholic Church issued a papal order in 1428 prohibiting sea captains from carrying Jews to the Holy Land. The Venetians and Sicilians followed suit, barring their ports to Jews sailing to Jerusalem. But many European Jews nonetheless found their way to the city, including Rabbi Ovadiah Bartinurah, the commentator of the Mishnah, who moved to Jerusalem in 1488, where he was later buried.

Upon arriving in Jerusalem, these immigrants found a city with poor security. The Mamluk sultans of Egypt, who controlled Jerusalem from the thirteenth to the early sixteenth centuries, left Jerusalem without any walls, making it vulnerable to repeated Bedouin attacks. The Ottomans' conquest of the city in 1517 temporarily improved the security situation, especially after Sultan Sulayman the Magnificent rebuilt Jerusalem's walls, but later rulers neglected the city, and its security again deteriorated.

Yet Jewish scholars continued to encourage the reestablishment of a strong Jewish presence in Jerusalem. Rabbi Yitzhak Luria, the great sixteenth-century authority of Kabbalah, was born in Jerusalem and maintained an academy there as well as in Safed. Students of the leaders of the two main tendencies of European Judaism—the Baal Shem Tov, who founded the Hasidic movement, and the Vilna Gaon, who was the leading rabbinic authority for the more scholastic Talmudic academies of Europe—moved to Jerusalem in 1780 and 1808 respectively. The quest to return to Jerusalem bound Jews throughout the Diaspora together despite the evolution of differing strains of Judaism. For Jerusalem was crucial to the hope for redemption and the end of exile; in that sense, it was the aspiration to return to Jerusalem that safeguarded Jews' very identity over this long and difficult period.

Indeed, for centuries the two most widely practiced holiday prayers in Judaism, the Passover Seder and the final service for Yom Kippur, have ended with the declaration: "Next Year in Jerusalem." The liturgy of the Jewish faith thus connected Jerusalem with the festival of freedom and the day of atonement of man's sins. It also connected Jerusalem to the continuity of the Jews as a people. For at the end of a wedding ceremony, the groom crushes a glass with his foot to symbolically recall the destruction of the Temple, while he recites the verse: "If I forget you, O Jerusalem, let my right hand wither" (Psalms 137:5).

The Jews were not supposed to proselytize or spread their faith through military campaigns or by subjugating smaller nations. Their religion envisioned the ultimate redemption of all mankind through the observance by Jews of their commandments in a free Jerusalem that would serve both as their temple of prayer and as a welcoming site for members of other faiths seeking to direct their own prayers to the Almighty.

This vision was articulated by Philo, the great Greek-speaking Jewish philosopher toward the end of the Second Temple period. He made two insightful points about Judaism's relationship to other peoples. First, he noted that "throughout the world of Greeks and barbarians, there is practically no State which honours the institutions of any other." He continued, "We may fairly say that mankind from East to West, every country and nation and State, show aversion to foreign institutions, and they think they will enhance the respect for their own by showing disrespect for those of other nations. It is not so with ours."[77]

Secondly, Philo observed that Jewish practices at the time had a broader universalistic purpose. In fact, Philo expressed bewilderment at the widespread accusations he heard of Jewish exclusiveness: "And therefore it astonishes me to see that some people venture to accuse of inhumanity the nation which has shown so profound a sense of fellowship and goodwill to all men everywhere, by using its prayers and festivals and first-fruit offerings as a means of supplication for the human race in general."[78] Philo was explaining that the Temple service in Jerusalem was not just for the benefit of the Jewish people, but also for the salvation of mankind as a whole.

This idea was captured in Jewish eschatology by the prophet Micah (4:1–5). He envisioned that "in the days to come," Jerusalem will no longer be destroyed but rather "the Mount of the Lord's House shall stand firm among the mountains." There is no foreign subjugation of Jerusalem so that "instruction [Torah] shall come forth from Zion and the word of the Lord from Jerusalem." Divine peace will be extended to all the nations of the earth: "Nation shall not take up sword against nation."

Finally, Micah added that "all the peoples walk each in the names of its gods." Regarding the Jewish people, he prophesized "we will walk in the name of the Lord our God forever and ever." The prophecy means that all the nations will continue with their particular religious traditions, while recognizing God's role in the world.[79] Jerusalem, according to this vision, is where the particularism of the Jews supports a universalistic meeting point for all the world's religions.

# Chapter 2

# Christianity and Jerusalem

C hristianity was born in Jerusalem. According to all Christian traditions, the Holy City is the site of the most crucial events of the final days of Jesus of Nazareth: his teaching at the Temple, the Last Supper, his trial, and his crucifixion. It is the place of the celebrated Resurrection and the Ascension. It is where the New Testament tells that he performed miracles at the Pool of Bethesda and the Pool of Siloam.[1] The Gospels view Jesus as a descendant of King David, which provides yet another connection between the Christian faith and the capital from which the Davidic dynasty ruled. In the first few years after Jesus's death, most of his followers left their villages in the Galilee and settled in Jerusalem.[2] Finally, Jerusalem is the site of the establishment of the first Christian community, led by James.

In the New Testament, Jesus comes to Jerusalem for all the Jewish pilgrimage festivals—Passover, Pentecost, and Tabernacles—and visits the Temple for the "festival of dedication," or Hanukkah. Clearly, Jesus was intimately connected with Jerusalem, yet the New Testament demonstrates that early Christians held differing attitudes toward the city.[3] In the Gospel according to Luke, Jesus appears to his disciples after his crucifixion and tells them that the message of forgiveness of sins to all nations will begin in Jerusalem (24:47). After his ascension to heaven in Bethany, they return to Jerusalem "with great joy" and are "continually in the Temple blessing God" (24:53). The Gospel according to Matthew still calls Jerusalem "the Holy City" (27:53).

The Gospel according to John, however, displays a different attitude. After his encounter with the money changers in the Temple, Jesus implies that his mission essentially replaces the Temple: "Destroy this temple and in three days I will raise it up" (2:19). Although John explains that he was "speaking of the temple of his body" (2:21), the text could be interpreted as Jesus indicating that the connection between mankind and the divine presence will no longer be retained through the services of the Temple, but rather through his resurrection.[4] Later in John, a Samaritan woman asks Jesus whether she should worship on a Samarian mountain like her ancestors or in Jerusalem, to which Jesus responds, "the hour is coming when you will worship the Father neither on this mountain nor in Jerusalem" (4:20–21). This verse shows that Jerusalem's traditional spiritual role had been superseded by something else.

One explanation for the discrepancy in the Gospels' treatment of Jerusalem could be the chronological order in which the different versions were written; Luke was redacted relatively early, before the schism between Christianity and Judaism had fully set in, while John was written in a later period, when Christianity was already seeking to distinguish itself from the traditions of Judaism. Regardless, the different tones toward Jerusalem found in the various versions of the Gospels allowed for the evolution of divergent Christian attitudes toward the city.

In the first century, the theological diversity of the early Christian community reflected the diversity of the Gospels. In the first decades after Jesus's death, worshipers formed various religious groups to memorialize him, resulting in some fundamental theological fissures in early Christianity. Some looked back on Jesus as a righteous teacher in the tradition of the Old Testament prophets, while others, particularly in northern Syria, Asia Minor, and Greece, proclaimed Jesus's divinity and focused on the power of his martyrdom to redeem the world.[5]

The first Christian community was centered in Jerusalem.[6] The New Testament tells that Jewish Christians even brought sacrifices to the Temple. In Acts, the apostles Peter and John go up to the Temple at the hour of prayer (3:1). James was also a regular worshiper at the Temple. These early Christians observed Judaic law and were regarded by the rabbis as Jews, albeit ones who held some unacceptable views, like other Jewish sectarians at the time.[7]

Clearly, if Jerusalem's early Christian community was Jewish, then it would still regard the city as a national-spiritual capital, as all Jews did. According to Christian tradition, the Romans crucify Jesus around Passover and he ascends to heaven forty days later. In Luke, the apostles then return to Jerusalem and go to the Temple; that would correspond to the time of the festival of the Pentecost (*Shavuot*), which was one of the three pilgrimage festivals centered on the Temple. The apostles, like many Jews in Judea at the time, went to Jerusalem for prayer, demonstrating that Jerusalem was still central to the spiritual lives of the early Christians.

Yet this connection to the Holy City is noticeably absent in later writings. The downgrading of Jerusalem in later Christian writings may be attributable to historical events: the Temple's destruction in 70 CE, the defeat of the Bar Kochba revolt of 135 CE, and Hadrian's expulsion of the Jews from Jerusalem all contributed to the perception that Jerusalem was a fallen city whose ruin had been prophesized by Jesus.

Thus, after the passing of the original apostles who lived in Jerusalem, the evolving Christian faith minimized the city's spiritual importance until about the fourth century. The theological downgrading of Jerusalem in its earliest phase is largely attributable to Paul, who proselytized Christianity especially to Gentiles. It was Paul who drew a distinction between the present earthly Jerusalem, which he said was in a state of slavery, and Jerusalem above, which was free (Galatians 4:25–26).

In the letter to the Hebrews, often attributed to Paul, the author writes of a "new covenant" through Jesus that renders the previous Jewish one "obsolete," further noting that that which grows old "will soon disappear" (8:13). He then dismisses the "earthly sanctuary" of the first covenant, explaining that there is now a heavenly sanctuary that Jesus has entered (9:1–28). This spiritual focus on "heavenly Jerusalem" to the detriment of the earthly city quickly spread among Christians during the early Roman period.[8]

Paul, however, did not completely reject the old covenant or suggest that it was abrogated. In his letter to the Romans, he emphasizes its continuing validity: "I ask, then had God rejected his people? By no means! I myself am an Israelite, a descendant of Abraham, a member of the tribe of Benjamin. God has not rejected his people whom he foreknew"(11:1–2). The Jews had "stumbled," Paul says, but not fallen (11:11). Still, he does not lay out any special role for Jerusalem when he discusses the "remnant" of Israel (11:5). Paul focuses solely on the heavenly Jerusalem of the spirit, not on rebuilding the city of Jerusalem that was in ruins.

## Jerusalem's Declining Sanctity in the Early Church and Its Revival

Early Christian thinkers took these Pauline distinctions much further than Paul had envisioned. Marcion (85–160), for example, called for rejecting the Hebrew scriptures completely with their rich traditions about Jerusalem.[9] He wrote that the creator deity of the flesh from the Hebrew Bible had been replaced by a superior deity of the spirit revealed through Jesus. Jerusalem had nothing to do with the new concept of God that he was proposing. Roman church leaders ultimately condemned his ideas as heresy, but they continued to be debated for hundreds of years, indicating a lingering influence.

In contrast, Justin (100–65) sought to appropriate the Hebrew Bible for Christianity, which he called the "New Israel." The "Old Israel," in his view, was facing divine punishment, as evidenced by the desolation of its land and the destruction of its cities. The scriptures and rituals of the Christian Church had replaced the Israelites' homeland as the means to experience wisdom and religious worship, he argued.[10] Similarly, Irenaeus, the bishop of Lyon in the 170s, concluded that Jerusalem had once had a special status, but had become like vine branches that are cut away after bearing their fruit.[11]

The early Church's organizational structure in the Holy Land also reflected the downgrading of Jerusalem. The Church's chief representative there at this time sat in the old Roman imperial city of Caesarea instead of in Jerusalem, meaning the bishop of Caesarea had authority over the bishop of Jerusalem. Likewise in 234, the great Church father Origen chose Caesarea over Jerusalem as the site of his academy.[12]

In these early years there were multiple opinions on the significance of Jerusalem for the Christian faith. St. Gregory of Nyssa maintained in the fourth century, "When the Lord invites the blest to their inheritance in the Kingdom of Heaven, he does not include a pilgrimage to Jerusalem among their good deeds."[13] Later in the same era, St. Jerome, who lived in Bethlehem, would write that it was part of Christianity "to adore where His feet have stood and to see the vestiges of the nativity, of the cross, and of the passion."[14]

The emergence of Constantine as the Roman Empire's first Christian emperor greatly affected Christians' perception of Jerusalem, although in contradictory ways. After experiencing in 312 a vision of the Cross in battle over the Milvian Bridge in Rome and rallying his troops to victory, Constantine legalized Christianity and actively spread the faith throughout his realm. One of his predecessors, Diocletian, had decreed as late as 303 that all churches in his empire be destroyed. Constantine ordered that they be rebuilt at the expense of the Roman Empire.

Constantine became a major figure in the development of Christian theology, convening the Church's bishops together at the Council of Nicaea in 325 to develop a unified Christian doctrine.[15] His thinking was highly influenced by a key Church intellectual, Eusebius, who was the bishop of Caesaria. Sitting at Constantine's right hand at the Council of Nicaea,[16] Eusebius became Constantine's chief religious advisor as well as a leading theological writer in his own right. And Eusebius had strong ideas about the proper status of Jerusalem in Christian theology.

Asked whether Jerusalem still had some "theological significance," Eusebius succinctly summarized his view of the Holy City: "the Church of God has been raised up in place of Jerusalem that is fallen never to rise again."[17] He repeated this contention in various writings, such as his commentary on the Psalms in which he wrote that to think that Jerusalem is the city of God is the "mark of exceedingly base and petty thinking."[18] Eusebius even insisted on calling Jerusalem by its Roman name, *Aelia*, rather than the better-known Hebrew name that had been used for centuries. Eusebius was guided above all by a determination to preserve the distinctiveness of Christianity from Judaism. To him, the earthly Jerusalem was a purely Jewish interest. At Nicaea, similar considerations led the bishops to formally separate Easter from Passover and the Hebrew calendar.

In *Proof of the Gospel*, Eusebius further argues that Jerusalem's state of devastation and decline bore out the prophecies of the New Testament:

> When, then we see what was of old foretold for the nations fulfilled in our own day, and when lamentation and wailing that was predicted for the Jews, and the burning of the Temple and its utter desolation, can also be seen even now to have occurred according to the prediction, surely we must also agree that the king who was prophesied, the Christ of God, has come, since the signs of His coming have been shown in each instance I have treated to have been clearly fulfilled.[19]

Such arguments were amplified, to Jerusalem's detriment, by a growing emphasis during Constantine's time on the culpability of the city's Jews, as opposed to Rome's imperial policies, for Jesus's death.[20]

Despite Eusebius's influence, however, other forces influenced Christian thinking on Jerusalem, as well as that of Constantine, in a more positive direction. Constantine himself took an active interest in the city's biblical importance. At Nicaea, Constantine granted a request from Makarios, the bishop of Jerusalem, for permission to demolish the Temple of Venus that the Romans had built around the general location believed to be the site of Jesus's crucifixion and burial.[21] Constantine not only granted the request, but also decided to build a new church on the site consisting of the *Anastasis* (literally, resurrection) which was a rotunda over the tomb itself and a basilica (called the *Martyrium*). There was also a court containing the rock of Golgotha. The entire complex would become known in the West as the Church of the Holy Sepulchre. Understanding the depth of Constantine's convictions, Eusebius encouraged him to build a basilica that would be "the finest in the world."[22]

The Roman construction teams excavated the site, unearthing a rock tomb that was identified as the burial place of Jesus. They also located what they believed to be the precise hill on which he was crucified, Golgotha. Taken aback by the religious significance of the findings, Eusebius declared that the discovery was "contrary to all expectation."[23]

Constantine sent his mother, Helena, to observe and assist in the operation.[24] According to tradition, she was associated with another spectacular discovery at the site, that of the "True Cross" on which Jesus was crucified. Eusebius, who probably accompanied Helena in Jerusalem, wrote nothing of the discovery of the cross. Nonetheless, the date of its discovery became a religious holiday that was celebrated as far as Spain. Helena also ordered the construction of two key churches: the Church of the Nativity in Bethlehem at the birthplace of Jesus, and a church on the Mount of Olives where, according to the Book of Acts (1:6–12), Jesus ascended to heaven.

News of the discoveries and of the new Christian sanctuaries had an enormous impact on the status of Jerusalem in fourth-century Christianity. They quickly transformed the popular conception of Jerusalem from Eusebius's sinful city of ruins into a sanctified place that became a magnet of pilgrimage for Christians worldwide.[25] Christians found holiness in the paths on which Jesus walked, even if the holiness of the Temple no longer held theological significance for them.

Jerusalem's new appeal was welcomed by some Christian theologians who had always opposed Eusebius's view of the city. Cyril of Jerusalem, for example, maintained that any divine judgment against Jerusalem was not final, and in fact belonged to the past. For divine judgment, according to Cyril, had been directed specifically against the Temple, not against the city as a whole. God's punishment, in other words, had already been meted out. Now, with Rome becoming a Christian empire, Jerusalem could again be considered a holy city because it was now a Christian city.[26]

Moreover, the situation on the ground had changed. The Jerusalem that had been condemned had been under Jewish sovereignty; but over the years its population had changed. After Hadrian's defeat of Bar Kochba, most of the city's residents were pagan, as Jews were forbidden to live in the city and its environs. Even Eusebius admitted this: "Thus when the city came to be bereft of the nation of the Jews, and its ancient inhabitants had completely perished, it was colonized by foreigners."[27]

Years later, the fifth-century Christian scholar Jerome, who translated the Bible into Latin, would reiterate this point, arguing that the Roman capture of Jerusalem entailed the "slaying of its population" so that the city's slate, so to speak, was wiped clean. He explained that "new inhabitants" from Gaul, Britain, Armenia, Arabia, and Egypt had colonized Jerusalem so that the city could now be completely rehabilitated by its Byzantine, or Eastern Roman, rulers.[28]

The renewed Christian interest in Byzantine Jerusalem led to a new appreciation of the Jerusalem of the Hebrew Bible. For example, a late fourth-century pilgrim to Jerusalem named Egeria noted that the Church of the Holy Sepulchre displayed relics belonging to key figures from the Hebrew Bible like the ring of King Solomon and the horn with which the kings of Judah were anointed.[29]

The Temple Mount, however, did not benefit from the reversal in Jerusalem's fortunes; it remained largely in ruins as a testament to Rome's defeat and punishment of Judea. The Byzantine historian Eutychius noted, "The Byzantines, however, neglected it [the Temple Mount] and did not hold it in veneration, nor did they build a church over it because Christ our Lord said in the Holy Gospel 'Not a stone will be left upon a stone which will not be ruined and devastated.'"[30] It was as though the Byzantines rebuilt Jerusalem according to Cyril's distinction between the Temple area and the rest of the city.

The Temple Mount's lack of theological significance to Christianity in this period is evident in other ways as well. The Byzantines dismissed the Temple Mount's status as the "center of the world," assigning this designation to Golgotha instead.[31] Moreover, in 1897 a mosaic map of Byzantine Jerusalem was discovered. The artifact had been designed as the floor plan for a church in

Madaba, located in what is today Jordan. The map refers to many Christian holy sites in the city, but the Temple Mount does not appear.[32]

After Constantine, Byzantine emperors took an ongoing interest in Jerusalem. When Emperor Julian sought to revive paganism at the expense of Christianity, he still concentrated particularly on Jerusalem, even allowing Jews to return there, as previously noted. Jerusalem was a small city without much economic or military significance to the empire. It would seem an odd focal point for Julian's religious struggle, if not for its growing symbolic importance to the Christian world.

With Jerusalem's image thus rehabilitated, Constantine and his successors initiated massive construction projects in the city. Emperor Theodosius I constructed a church at Gethsemane, below Helena's church on the Mount of Olives. Eudocia, the wife of Theodosius II, restored the walls of Jerusalem and built additional shrines and churches. Finally, Justinian (527–565) sought to outdo his predecessors by building the massive Nea (New) Church in Jerusalem dedicated to Mary.[33] It is entirely possible that he conceived of this cathedral as a Christian substitute for the Temple, since it was located on a hill just opposite the Temple Mount and was constructed from stones taken from the destroyed Temple itself.[34] Justinian also built one of the great monuments of Byzantine architecture, the Hagia Sophia basilica in Constantinople. He reportedly exclaimed upon its completion, "I have outdone you, Solomon."

In the early seventh century, the Byzantines lost Jerusalem to the Persians, who in 614 confiscated Helena's True Cross and exiled the local Christian clergy. However, the Byzantine emperor, Heraclius, continued fighting for much of the ensuing fifteen years, finally defeating the Persians in 629 and regaining Jerusalem. (In less than ten years, he would lose the city again to the Muslims.) Heraclius triumphantly returned to Jerusalem bearing the True Cross, entering the city through the Golden Gate in emulation of Jesus's route in his final days.[35] For the Byzantines, Jerusalem was no longer a neglected backwater, but rather a holy city on the front lines of their most vital military struggles.

The Christian interest in Jerusalem was not confined to the Byzantines. With the unification of the Holy Roman Empire in the West under the Frankish king Charlemagne, Jerusalem became a subject of diplomacy between the Carologinians and the Muslims, who by then had conquered the city. Some accounts from the time report that in 800 Charlemagne received the key and standard of Jerusalem from the Abbasid caliph, Harun al-Rashid, who ruled over Syria and Palestine from Baghdad, although historians doubt whether this story has any factual basis.[36] But Charlemagne and his successors did become involved in Jerusalem, erecting a hospice, library, and new hostels to serve the needs of the Western pilgrims who were visiting the Holy City in ever greater numbers. Louis, Charlemagne's son, ordered each estate of his empire to make contributions for the Christians of Jerusalem.

Despite the city's renewed religious importance, Jerusalem's status remained inferior to that of some other Christian cities. Primary among these was Rome, as Catholic doctrine identified the bishop of Rome, the successor to the apostle Peter, as holding supreme authority over all other bishops. As for the Eastern Orthodox Church, after its formal schism with the Roman Catholic Church in 1054, Constantinople became the seat of the highest Patriarch of Orthodoxy. Aside from Peter, who had lived for a time in Jerusalem before becoming the first bishop of Rome, no subsequent pope visited the city until two millennia later with the visit of Pope Paul VI in 1964. The rule of Emperor Constantine had restored Jerusalem's status as a holy city, but not on the order of Rome or Constantinople.

## Toward the Crusades:
## Jerusalem as an Apocalyptic City

Jerusalem acquired sufficient Christian significance to inspire Pope Urban II to launch what became known as the First Crusade in 1095. Naturally there were factors beyond Jerusalem that mobilized Christian civilization for this campaign. Namely, the conflict between the Christian and Islamic worlds was no longer static; it had escalated dramatically in the second half of the eleventh century, especially in Spain and Italy, where the Muslims were in retreat in Toledo (1085) and Sicily (1091).

The situation was different in the East, where Islam was on the offensive. The Turkish Seljuks had seized much of Asia Minor, including Nicaea (1081), where Constantine had once established the Catholic creed. The Seljuks also captured Antioch (1084), the seat of one of Christianity's original patriarchates. Seeking a means to reunify Christendom after its great schism of 1054, Pope Urban II seized the opportunity when the Byzantine emperor, who was increasingly besieged by the Seljuks, sought out his help. Sixty thousand soldiers departed for the Holy Land within a year of the pope's call for the Crusade. They were followed by 100,000 more shortly thereafter. Hordes of peasants set out after the knights and soldiers as well.[37]

The Crusaders' precise motivation is difficult to pin down. Certainly Islam's military advance was nothing new, having begun in the seventh century. Meanwhile, Jerusalem had been under Islamic rule for more than four hundred years. There had been a brief Byzantine crusade of sorts to the Holy Land led by Emperor John Tzimisces in 975, during which the Byzantines briefly recovered Tiberias, Nazareth, and Caesaria—but not Jerusalem. In any case, Western powers had made no previous effort to take back the Holy Land for Christendom.

Perhaps the Christians were galvanized when the Fatimid caliph, al-Hakim, who controlled the Holy Land from Egypt, razed the Church of the Holy Sepulchre to the ground in 1009. Work teams sent by the Fatimid governor for this task were extremely thorough; they used pick-axes and hammers to demolish the tomb inside the church as well as the rock of Golgotha.[38] This desecration left an indelible mark on the whole Christian world. Nevertheless, it had occurred nearly ninety years before Pope Urban II's call to arms. Moreover, the Seljuk Turks had evicted the Fatimids from the Holy Land later in the century, after which the Church of the Holy Sepulchre had been rebuilt. Other factors must have been at play.

The destruction of the Church of the Holy Sepulchre in itself may not have been enough to provoke war, but that attack was not an isolated event. Europeans heard reports of atrocities throughout the following decades. After the Seljuk Turks consolidated their rule in Jerusalem, they massacred and looted many of its inhabitants. When Jerusalemites briefly rebelled, aided by the Seljuks' Fatimid rivals, the Seljuk rulers retaliated harshly, slaughtering 3,000 people in 1077.[39] Christian pilgrims to the Holy City were increasingly imperiled by the rivalry between the Seljuk Turks, who were loyal to the Sunni Abbasid caliphate, and the Fatimids, who were Shiites. Roughly thirty years before the First Crusade, Muslim marauders attacked 7,000 Christian pilgrims, led by the archbishop of Mainz, who were heading for the Jordan River.[40] Thus Pope Urban II was responding to cumulative grievances built up over time.

The address of Pope Urban II to the Frankish knights, clergy, and commoners who met at the Council of Clermont in France, where he first advocated what he called "the Jerusalem expedition,"[41] allows for some insight into the motivations behind the First Crusade. There is no official record of his remarks, but it is possible to reconstruct the speech from the various accounts of it that have been preserved. One of these, written twenty-five years later by Robert the Monk, summarized the pope's remarks as a "horrible tale" originating in Jerusalem and Constantinople about "a race from the kingdom of the Persians" that had invaded Christian lands and had "de-populated them by the sword, pillage and fire."[42]

The pope's call to action concentrated on Jerusalem: "Enter upon the road to the Holy Sepulchre: wrest that land from the wicked race, and subject it to yourselves." He added that "Jerusalem is the navel of the world," a "royal city" that was "in subjection to those who do not know God." Other versions relate that the pope lamented the fate of the great churches of Jerusalem, comparing it to the Old Testament account of the defiling of the Temple of Solomon.[43]

The pope's words made clear that Christendom, as represented by the Catholic Church, would no longer acquiesce to its enemies' control of the earthly Jerusalem. Islamic rule had not been challenged in the past, but over the last century it had proven to be an unreliable guardian of Christian holy sites and pilgrims. The overall Christian conception of Jerusalem had changed critically; the Holy City now had to be ruled by Christian powers.

Having personally witnessed the pope's address, Guilbert de Nogent, the abbot of Nogent, introduced apocalyptic themes into his account of Urban II's remarks: "With the end of the world already near...it is first necessary, according to prophecy, that the Christian sway be renewed in those regions either through you, or others, whom it shall please God to send before the coming of the Antichrist."

In other words, before any apocalyptic scenario could transpire leading to the second coming of Jesus, Jerusalem had to return to Christian hands. He added, "Consider, therefore, that the Almighty has provided you, perhaps, for this purpose, that through you He may restore Jerusalem from such debasement." Even if Pope Urban II did not use these exact words, the quotation is significant in that it indicates how people at the time understood and remembered the pope's message.[44]

Indeed, the idea that Christian control of Jerusalem was a prerequisite to the coming of the Last Days—a time when all of humanity would be judged and those who were saved would enter paradise—was widespread in Europe at the time.[45] Millennial speculation had been rife within Christiandom for the previous century as the year 1000 approached. In the Book of Revelation, Satan is bound for a thousand years in a sealed pit (20:1–3), but when the millennium passes, he is released from his prison for a final battle (20:7–10) after which a "new Jerusalem" descends from heaven. People understood from these verses that a war between a newly crowned emperor from the West and the Antichrist would take place in Jerusalem 1,000 years after Jesus had first defeated Satan and locked him away.[46] With the arrival of the year 1000, many Europeans anticipated the beginning of the battle of the Last Days and the second coming of Jesus.

People sought out explanations after the year 1000 when this scenario failed to unfold. Some proposed new dates for the apocalypse. But the argument must have found fertile ground that salvation was impossible so long as Christianity did not control Jerusalem. It appears that the apocalyptic vision of a New Jerusalem was particularly popular with the poorer segments of the population that followed the knights to the Holy Land. The knights themselves, in contrast, often joined the Crusade out of a sense of duty or even with the hope that they would be granted estates in the Holy Land.[47]

Although there is nothing inherently violent about millennial belief, this particular millennial expectation among the European masses unleashed tremendous violence in Europe itself, particularly against some of its oldest Jewish communities. Many of the peasants who comprised the "People's Crusade" believed that it was necessary to baptize all the Jews in order to usher in the Last Days; non-Christian belief had to be eliminated, and any Jews refusing to convert would have to be exterminated.[48] So long as any unconverted Jews remained, the Last Days could not arrive.

This was not just a theoretical matter. As the People's Crusade headed across Europe to the Holy Land, it passed by Jewish settlements along the Rhine. In some cases, the Crusaders gave these communities the choice of conversion to Christianity or death—and brutally fulfilled this threat against recalcitrant Jewish villagers. One of the leaders of these attacks was a feudal baron named Enrico, who fashioned himself as the Emperor of the Last Days. During the months of May and June 1096, he inspired Crusader mobs to massacre between 5,000 and 10,000 Jews in Worms, Mainz, Metz, and Cologne—three years before the main body of the Crusaders would reach Jerusalem.[49] Forcible conversion of non-Christians, in fact, was a violation of canon law. Some bishops opposed these mob attacks, but were largely unsuccessful at stopping them.[50]

Millennialism was also a factor in the dramatic increase in the volume of Western pilgrimage to Jerusalem in the eleventh century. What had been a steady flow, according to one observer, was becoming a flood.[51] Both nobles and commoners from Italy, France, Hungary, and Germany set out for the Holy City; one historian at the time described an "immeasurable multitude" trekking to Jerusalem.[52] This trend not only strengthened the general awareness of Jerusalem in the West, but also provided the groundwork for the success of Pope Urban II's appeals.

The ideas that Pope Urban II presented at Clermont spread quickly, though he undoubtedly lost control over how they were portrayed. He encouraged the bishops attending his address to propagate his call for action when they returned home.[53] His message motivated the cream of the European aristocracy to lead the military campaign, including Duke Bohemond of Taranto, a Norman from southern Italy; from the Low Countries, Duke Godfrey of Bouillon and his brother Baldwin; Raymond, count of Toulouse; and Robert Curthose, duke of Normandy and son of William the Conqueror.[54] The call from Clermont reached most centers of Western Christendom.

Pope Urban II undertook an extensive speaking tour across France to spread his message and recruit Crusaders. His appeals had an enormous impact on the view of Jerusalem within Christendom, popularizing apocalyptic traditions and tying earthly Jerusalem to religious speculation about the Last Days. Jerusalem thus became the most important objective of the First Crusade.

This became apparent as the Crusader armies approached the Holy City in the summer of 1099 after waging a successful campaign in Asia Minor, where they had recovered Nicaea and Antioch. The Fatimids, who had recaptured Jerusalem in 1098 from the Seljuk Turks, sent delegates to the Crusader commanders at this point to work out a joint alliance against the Seljuks. The Fatimids offered the Crusaders all of Syria in exchange for the Fatimids' retention of control over the Holy Land.

Several years earlier this might have been a tempting offer. Pope Urban II had already accomplished one of his most important war goals— the relief of the Byzantine Empire from encirclement by the Seljuks. But with the Crusaders rapidly advancing without any real opposition, the Fatimid offer was now insufficient. So the Crusader armies pressed on to Jerusalem. A month before their arrival, the Fatimids offered a new deal: a guaranteed right of Christian pilgrimage to Jerusalem in exchange for the Crusaders' acquiescence to Fatimid control of the Holy City. After the Crusaders rejected the offer, the Fatimids evicted from Jerusalem much of the Christian population. Many sought refuge in Bethlehem, just to the south.[55]

Jerusalem's population at this time numbered about 20,000, but the population tripled with the influx of rural Muslim refugees fleeing the invading armies. Despite being Shiites, the Fatimids were able nonetheless to recruit militias from the local Sunni Muslim population to defend the city's walls. They faced 1,300 knights and 12,000 additional "able-bodied men."[56]

Whether Jerusalem's Jews knew of the attacks against the Jewish communities along the Rhine is not known. Nonetheless the Holy City's Jews joined the Muslims in defending the city. Most likely, both the Sunni Muslims and Jews had some idea of their likely fate if the Crusaders sacked the city.

The Crusaders breached Jerusalem's walls at the Jewish quarter, putting the Jews' houses and synagogues in the main line of attack.[57] The bloodbath that followed as the Crusader armies poured into the Holy City was graphically recorded in eyewitness accounts by the Crusaders themselves:

> Now that our men had possession of the walls and the towers, wonderful sights were to be seen. Some of our men—and this was the more merciful course—cut off the heads of their enemies; others shot them with arrows so that they fell from towers; others tortured them longer by casting them into the flames. Piles of heads, hands and feet were to be seen in the streets of the city. It was necessary to pick one's way over the bodies of men and horses. But these were small matters compared to what happened in the Temple of Solomon [that is, the al-Aqsa Mosque], a place where religious services were ordinarily chanted. What happened there, if I tell the truth, it will exceed your powers of belief. So let it suffice to say this much at least, that in the Temple and porch of Solomon men rode in blood up to their knees and bridle reins.[58]

Some historians believe the Crusaders embellished such accounts since they varied greatly from Muslim recollections.[59] But the Crusaders unquestioningly conducted horrible massacres. According to one Arabic account, Jews who gathered together in their synagogues were burned alive "by the Franks."[60] A Jewish account from a letter written around 1100 simply recorded, "The Franks arrived and killed everybody in the city, whether of Ishmael or of Israel; and the few who survived the slaughter were made prisoners."[61]

When the Fatimid commander, Iftikhar al-Dawla, surrendered the citadel of Jerusalem on July 17, 1099, the Crusaders allowed survivors to leave the city and head for Ashkelon, which remained under Fatimid jurisdiction. The Crusaders then forced Muslim and Jewish prisoners to clear out the dead bodies that littered the Holy City's grounds. They also enslaved some Jews, transporting them to places like southern Italy, which was under Norman control. Other Jewish prisoners were ransomed to the Jewish community of Ashkelon.[62]

The motivation of the Crusaders in Jerusalem appeared to differ from that of the peasant hordes who had conducted the massacres along the Rhine several years earlier, as there were no reports in Jerusalem of forced conversions to Christianity. This evinces that millennialism was not a primary motivating force for the Crusader knights. Back in Europe, however, the return of Jerusalem to Christendom aroused the religious imagination of important clergy.

Writing ten years later, a number of French Benedictines, including Robert the Monk, Abbot Guilbert of Nogent, and Baldric of Bourgueil, described the Crusader conquest of Jerusalem as a sign of divine intervention.[63] For Robert the Monk, it was the greatest event in world history since the Crucifixion; in the near future, he declared, the Antichrist would appear in Jerusalem and the battle of the Last Days would begin.[64]

Unlike the Byzantines, who left the Temple Mount in ruins, the Crusaders treated the area as a sacred site. They took over the Islamic shrines, calling the Dome of the Rock the *Templum Domini* (Temple of the Lord) and the al-Aqsa Mosque the *Templum Salomonis*. King Baldwin II of Jerusalem made the *Templum Salomonis* his palace; it would also become the residence of the Knights Templar, a strict religious order dedicated to protecting Christian pilgrimage in the Holy Land.

Within a few months of their conquest of Jerusalem, the new Crusader authorities banned non-Christians from living inside the Holy City—a law that was strictly enforced.[65] Since the Crusader regime felt that the population of Jerusalem was too small to sustain the new Christian city they planned to establish, they brought in European as well as Middle Eastern ("Syrian") Christians as colonizers.

The Crusades made Jerusalem a bigger focal point for Christianity than ever before. But the intensity of that interest diminished in later centuries. Christianity lost Jerusalem to the Islamic world after Saladin captured the city in 1187. Christian religious interests were not protected by the new Muslim overlords, who razed the church at Gethsemane in 1219. The Crusaders briefly regained control once more in the thirteenth century, but following the final loss in 1292 of what was known as the Latin Kingdom of Jerusalem, the city became an increasingly peripheral concern for the Christian world.[66] The Latin patriarchate of Jerusalem was essentially abolished in 1291 and was represented in Rome by churchmen who held the title but had no influence on the ground. The Christians sensed that their historical door for control of Jerusalem had closed, so they turned their attention to other matters.

In the ensuing centuries, Christianity largely lacked a unified theological position on Jerusalem, especially after the Reformation and the emergence of numerous Protestant sects. Martin Luther, for his part, was not a proponent of pilgrimage to Jerusalem.[67] Yet in seventeenth-century Calvinist Holland, Christian political theorists like Hugo Grotius and Petrus Cunaeus looked to the Jerusalem of the Hebrew Bible as a model for fashioning a new central government for the Dutch republic.[68] For several centuries after the Reformation, Protestants played a relatively small role in Jerusalem itself, where responsibility for the holy sites was chiefly in the hands of the Catholic, Greek Orthodox, and Armenian churches.

But Protestant churches began building up a presence throughout the entire Near East in the early nineteenth century, focusing mostly on missionary activity and the spread of Western education reform. The Anglican Church established its first bishopric in Jerusalem in 1841. This was shortly followed by the return to Jerusalem of the Latin patriarch from Rome in 1847 and the transfer of the Greek patriarch from Istanbul to Jerusalem at roughly the same time.

In Jerusalem, a Protestant community established the "American Colony" outside the walls of the Old City. This provided social and educational services to members of all religious groups while scrupulously avoiding missionary activity in order to win their subjects' trust. Such activities represented a new approach to Christianity's involvement in the city. Yet certain legacies from the past continue to affect Christian theological approaches to Jerusalem to this day.

## Diverging Christian Views of Jerusalem in the Modern Era

Christianity currently has three main schools of thought with respect to Jerusalem.[69] These theological approaches do not neatly correspond to one Christian church or another, but rather may be found in various forms within all the main religious movements, sometimes provoking deep disputes among a single church's congregants.

Firstly, there is a supersessionist view of Jerusalem that questions whether Jerusalem retained any special theological significance after the coming of Jesus. This group adheres to "replacement theology," which posits that a new Christian covenant has superseded the covenant of the Hebrew Bible. The German Protestant theologian Karl Ludwig Schmidt summarized the supersessionist view of Jerusalem: "Jesus, the Messiah rejected by his people, prophesied the destruction of Jerusalem. Jerusalem has been destroyed, so that it will never again come under Jewish rule."[70] In his view, having replaced Israel as the focus of God's concern, the Christian Church had become "Israel after the spirit."

Although Schmidt rejected the base anti-Semitism that permeated Nazi Germany, in which he lived, adherents of this philosophy tend to harbor a generally negative, or at least dismissive, view of the Jewish people. Some supersessionists fold these views into liberation theology. With the original covenant of the Jewish people no longer applicable, they say, God's biblical promises to the ancient Israelites must be universalized and especially applied to the world's poorest communities. Politically, supersessionists reject any Jewish claims to Jerusalem based on the Hebrew Bible. Currently, they are at best ambivalent about Jerusalem's future political status, and in some cases they strongly support Islamic and Arab claims to the city.

Second, there is an incarnational approach that views Jerusalem, the site of the great events of the New Testament, as a unique holy city. Just as

Jews cherish Jerusalem because they associate God's presence with the city's Temple Mount, incarnationalists view the city as sacred because it was once home to the divine presence through the body of Jesus. This is often borne out by Christian pilgrims in Jerusalem, who find a special sanctity in those areas where Jesus walked and conducted his mission.

A third approach is the restorationist view, which is inspired by the restoration of the Jewish people to the Holy City in modern times. Frequently called Christian Zionists, adherents of this view denounce replacement theology and the supersessionist approach to Jerusalem.

William Blackstone was a well-known Christian Zionist. As an early Christian advocate of the return of the Jews to Israel, Blackstone petitioned U.S. president Benjamin Harrison in the early 1890s to hold an international conference to "consider the condition of Israelites and their claims to Palestine as their ancient home." He helped make Christian Zionism a mainstream position in the United States by enlisting more than four hundred prominent Americans in support of the idea, including clergy from the Methodist, Congregational, Baptist, and Presbyterian churches. Leading members of the judicial and legislative branches of the U.S. government also signed on.[71]

As Christian Zionism evolved, it diverged significantly from many other Christian trends in one other important respect. As previously noted, during the Crusades many Christians believed that the military campaign to recapture Jerusalem for Christianity would accelerate the coming of the "Last Days." The overall view that man's actions could hasten the Second Coming later became part of Protestant traditions as well. But historically, many Christian Zionists tended to be dispensationalists who believed they were powerless to alter the timing of the Apocalypse.[72] The return of the Jews to Jerusalem, according to their interpretation, is a divine sign that confirms their dispensational understanding of the Bible.

In the late nineteenth and twentieth centuries, Christian Zionism spread to many Protestant communities in America and in England. It also appeared to carry great weight in the Anglican Church, contributing to the eventual emergence of the Balfour Declaration in 1917, which called for the establishment of a Jewish homeland in Palestine. Chaim Weizmann, speaking as Israel's first president, noted the strongly supportive position of the Archbishop of Canterbury in 1938 when he argued in the British House of Lords against removing Jerusalem from a future Jewish national home:

> It seems to me extremely difficult to justify the ideals of Zionism by excluding them from any place in Zion. How is it possible for us not to sympathize in this matter with the Jews? We all remember their age-long resolve, lament, and longing: "If I forget thee, O Jerusalem, let my right hand forget her cunning."[73]

During this period, replacement theology and supersessionism declined across Christianity, especially after the Holocaust, as critics of these views charged that they fueled Christian anti-Semitism.

By the 1940s, the Catholic Church showed signs of becoming reconciled with the notion of Jewish control of Jerusalem. As the British prepared to withdraw from Palestine in 1947, the Vatican still formally supported the internationalization of Jerusalem under UN supervision. But it also showed a willingness to acquiesce to either Jewish or Muslim rule there so long as Christian holy sites were protected. In its formal correspondence with the UN secretary-general in 1947, the Church declared, "We are completely indifferent to the form of the regime which your esteemed committee may recommend, provided the interests of Christendom, Catholic, Protestant, and Orthodox, will be weighed and safeguarded in your final recommendations."[74]

The Church's local representatives in the Holy Land made the same point: "Should there be a non-Christian State we recommend that measures—international guarantees—be embodied in any arrangement with the new State that may be possibly set up."[75] Still, the transformation of the Church's attitude had not been complete. Even in 1950, Vatican diplomacy at the UN still lent its support to the idea of Jerusalem being internationalized, but its position on this issue was evolving.

In early 1999, Archbishop Jean-Loius Tauran, the Vatican's foreign minister, summarized the emerging position of the Catholic Church on the Jerusalem issue:

In the beginng, the Holy See supported the proposal for internation-alizing the territory, the "corpus separatum" called for by the United Nations General Assembly Resolution 181 of November 29, 1947. In the years that followed, although the objective of internationalization was shown to be unattainable, the Holy See continued to call for the protection of the Holy City's identity. It consistently drew attention to the need for an international commitment in this regard. To this end, the Holy See has consistently called for an international juridical instrument, which is what is meant by the phrase "an internationally guaranteed special status."[76]

Tauran clearly stated that the Holy See did not claim "any competence to enter into territorial disputes between nations."

This shift that occurred in the Catholic Church was even more dra-matically exemplified by the pilgrimage of John Paul II to Jerusalem in March 2000 and his visit to the Western Wall—which, along with the Temple Mount, was largely viewed in some early Christian circles as the symbol of an obsolete covenant between God and the Jews.[77] It was not the first papal visit to Jerusalem in modern times. Pope Paul VI had vis-ited Jerusalem in 1964, when it was divided between Israel and Jordan. But this was the first visit of a pope to a united Jerusalem, whose Old City was under Israeli control.

During that visit, the pope went right up to the ancient stones of the Western Wall and inserted a note in the cracks between them reading, "God of our forefathers, you chose Abraham and his descendants to bring your Name to the Nations: we are deeply saddened by the behavior of those who in the course of history have caused these children of yours to suffer, and asking your forgiveness we wish to commit ourselves to gen-uine brotherhood with the people of the Covenant."[78]

The pope's language, a clear rejection of replacement theology, was as significant as the symbolism of his pilgrimage to the holiest site in Judaism—the site of the Temple Mount in Jerusalem. For what Pope John Paul II had written was that the Jewish people were still the people of the covenant and were not associated with a "former," now irrelevant covenant. And if the older covenant still stands, according to the Vatican's latest pronouncements, then by implication the Hebrew Bible is still valid and its holy sites, especially Jerusalem, are still sacred.

Given the predominance of both the incarnational and restorational approaches to Jerusalem in the contemporary Christian world, the fate of the Holy City is tied to Christian spirituality today more than it has been in many years. Over the past fifty years, the theological connection between Christianity and physical Jerusalem—as opposed to heavenly Jerusalem alone—has grown significantly and the Church is unlikely to revert any time soon to its former ambivalent attitude.

# Chapter 3

# Jerusalem as the Third Holiest Place in Classical Islam

The religion of Islam was born in the Arabian city of Mecca, not far from where Muhammad bin Abdullah, of the Hashemite clan of the Quraish, received his first revelation of the Koran in the year 610 in a cave on a mountain known as *Jabal Nur* (the Mountain of Light). Mecca was also the vicinity of the hill Mina where Abraham had been tested, according to Islamic tradition, and brought his son Isma'il—and not Isaac, as in the Hebrew Bible—for sacrifice, only to be halted by the last-minute intervention of Gabriel. According to the Koran (2:127), Mecca was where Abraham and Ismail rebuilt the Holy House of worship, the Ka'bah, in accordance with a divine commandment, that had been originally founded by Adam. This was the "first house of worship to be built for mankind" (3:96). The Koran states that "Pilgrimage to the House is a duty to God for all that can make the journey" (3:97). Indeed, this pilgrimage to Mecca, called the *hajj*, is one of the five pillars of Islam.

The secondary center of sanctity for Islam was the Arabian city of Medina, where Muhammad and his early followers migrated and obtained refuge from persecution in Mecca in an event that became known as the *hijra*. Years later this 250-mile flight from Mecca northward to Medina would be used to mark the beginning of the Muslim calendar. It was also in Medina where Muhammad established the foundations of the first Islamic state before conquering Mecca itself some years later. Medina was additionally a place of further revelations of the Koran, which are distinguished as being either Meccan or Medinan verses.

Mecca may have been the most important spiritual center of Islam, but Medina would become its first political capital where Muhammad would spend the rest of his life and his immediate successors, the caliphs, would establish their seat of government. Medina was originally called Yathrib in pre-Islamic times; its Islamic name was derived from the city being called *Madinat al-Nabi*—literally, the "City of the Prophet." Medina also became Muhammad's place of burial. Those making pilgrimage to Mecca would often come to Medina as well to visit the tomb of the Prophet.

These very traditions of the location of Abraham's near-sacrifice of his son and the establishment of the holiest house of worship, and a center of religious pilgrimage were all special attributes of Jerusalem according to the Jewish faith. In Islam, they were applied exclusively to the holy city of Mecca, making the Arabian city the unquestionably primary center of sanctity for Muslims worldwide. Moreover, while Jerusalem served additionally as the political capital of ancient Israel as well, this role in early Islam was assumed by the holy city of Medina. Both Mecca and Medina were, additionally, locations where divine revelation was given and the Koran was communicated to Muhammad.

By comparison, according to Islamic tradition the divine message received by Muhammad in Jerusalem, as described below, was of a much more limited nature. Given this background it is not surprising that a clear prioritization emerged for ranking the importance of these holy cities; there is a *hadith*, or oral tradition, according to which Muhammad stated, "One prayer in my Mosque [in Medina] is worth ten thousand prayers, and one prayer in the Aqsa Mosque is worth a thousand prayers, and one prayer in the Sacred Mosque [of Mecca] is worth one hundred thousand prayers."[1]

If Jerusalem was to emerge in effect as the third holiest city in Islam, what unique events in the new Arabian faith would transpire there so that it would acquire this special status? For Jerusalem appears in the Koran only implicitly, in the first verse of Sura 17, which has been the subject of considerable interpretation and analysis: "Glory to Him who made His Servant go by night from the Sacred Mosque (*al-Masjid al-Haram*) to the Farther Mosque (*al-Masjid al-Aqsa*) whose surroundings We have blessed, that We might show him some of Our signs." The "servant" in the verse is the Prophet Muhammad, and the "Sacred Mosque" is located in Mecca.

But what exactly is the "Farther Mosque"? The farther mosque could not have been in Medina, since Muhammad's "night journey" occurred in 620 prior to the migration of his Muslim community from Mecca to Medina in 622. According to an early Muslim interpretation, the "Farther Mosque" was in heaven and the verse essentially described the ascent of the Prophet Muhammad, from which he later returns. However, what emerged as the more accepted interpretation was that Muhammad's Night Journey, described in the Koranic verse, was to Jerusalem.

Islamic traditions outside of the Koran provided the details of this interpretation of the verse. Muhammad was asleep one night near the Ka'bah in Mecca when the angel Gabriel woke him up and brought him over to a winged, horse-like beast called *al-Buraq* that he mounted and flew to the Temple Mount in Jerusalem, in what became known as *al-Isra'*, or "Night Journey." Al-Buraq had the body of a horse with wings, a woman's face, and a peacock's tale.[2] There are traditions that Muhammad flew from Mecca to Sinai, then to Bethlehem and some say Hebron before arriving in Jerusalem.[3]

Upon arrival, al-Buraq was tied to an iron ring alongside the gate to the "Farther Mosque" (in the last hundred years, a tradition developed that the ring was along the Western Wall). According to his own account, Muhammad prayed there, kneeling twice. Then, led by Gabriel, Muhammad was received respectively at each of the Seven Heavens by Adam, John and Jesus, Idris (Enoch), Aaron, Moses, and finally Abraham. At the height of his ascent, Muhammad rose up to the Divine Presence, in an event called *al-Mi'raj*, where he received the commandment for prayer, initially fifty times a day and reduced later to five.

Muslim theologians debated whether the Night Journey and the Ascent were part of a vision—that is, some kind of spiritual experience—or an actual event that physically occurred. The idea that it was only a vision was supported by the famous Sufi scholar Hasan al-Basri (642–728) and even more importantly by Aisha (613–678), the daughter of Abu Bakr and favorite wife of Muhammad, who in her later years was frequently consulted on Muhammad's sayings and practices.[4] The idea that the Night Journey was only a vision was also the position adopted by Caliph Mu'awiya, who would establish the Ummayad caliphate in Damascus in 660.[5] However, these interpretations would not prevail in the Islamic world. The majority orthodox view that emerged was that Muhammad bodily went on the Night Journey to Jerusalem while he was awake.

There remains the question of what was the "Farther Mosque" (*al-Masjid al-Aqsa*) cited in the verse. The greatest Islamic commentators of the Koran recognized that this required some explanation. For example, Abdullah ibn Umar al-Baydawi, the most authoritative interpreter of the Koran, notes that the famous al-Aqsa Mosque in Jerusalem didn't even exist when Muhammad's Night Journey occurred. Indeed, if Muslims believe that the Night Journey took place in 620, and it is known that the Islamic conquest of Jerusalem only took place seventeen years later in 637, then no mosque could have possibly been standing at the time.

Jerusalem was in fact under Persian rule during these years; non-Muslim rule in Jerusalem did not prevent Muhammad from making his Night Journey or experiencing the religious experience of ascent, according to the Koranic narrative. But factually there was no mosque yet built. For this reason, al-Baydawi and other Koranic commentators, such as al-Jalalayn, conclude that the "Farther Mosque" in the Koran was *bayt al-maqdis*—which best translates to "the Holy Temple;" indeed *bayt al-maqdis* is very close to the Hebrew term for the Temple, *bayt ha-mikdash*.[6] (This undoubtedly led the translator of the Koran for Penguin Books, N. J. Dawood, to translate *al-Masjid al-Aqsa*, which is normally rendered as the "Farther Mosque," as the "Farther Temple"; Dawood's translation is supported in a subsequent Koranic verse (17:7) that describes the destruction of the Temple of the Israelites and uses the term *al-masjid* as well, and which is translated as "Temple" in the "official" Saudi Arabian English version of the Koran by Abdullah Yusuf Ali).[7] *Bayt al-maqdis* became a name for Jerusalem which was shortened to al-Quds over time.

There were still those among the earliest Islamic scholars who challenged this sort of interpretation of the Night Journey by insisting that the "Farther Mosque" was not located in Jerusalem but rather in heaven. This rendition of the Night Journey somewhat diluted the Islamic connection to Jerusalem for those who adopted it. For example there was the case of Ja'far al-Sadiq (699–765), who was a descendant of Muhammad and a renowned religious scholar in the early Islamic period. His students in Medina included the founders of two of the four main schools of law in Sunni Islam, the Hanafi and Malaki schools. He himself was regarded as the founder of the main school of Islamic law for Shiites, and one of the pivotal figures in the development of Shiism in general.

On the issue of Jerusalem, there was a tradition attributed to Ja'far al-Sadiq that he was asked which mosques are to be praised. He answered by referring only to the mosque of Mecca and the Prophet's mosque in Medina. Then he was asked, "What about the al-Aqsa Mosque?" He answered that the al-Aqsa Mosque was in Heaven, and that was where the Prophet Muhammad was carried. Ja'far al-Sadiq then heard the remark, "People say that al-Aqsa is in Jerusalem." Rather than debate the point, he just answered that the mosque of Kufa was superior to that of Jerusalem.[8] This interpretation may have affected the importance of Jerusalem for Shiism, which had many other holy shrines for pilgrimage.

The Night Journey may be the main source of Islam's religious connection to Jerusalem, but it is not the only connection. For within the traditions outlined above is also a short description of the acknowledgment that Muhammad gives to the previous monotheistic religions with attachments to Jerusalem; he prays with Moses and Jesus, but he also leads them in prayer, taking precedence over the previous prophets.[9] There is a clear dualism conveyed here. On the one hand, a requirement can be inferred to respect the monotheistic predecessors to Islam. But on the other hand, there is also a reminder that it is Muhammad who leads them in prayer. For in the Islamic view, Judaism and Christianity may have been legitimately true religions for the time when they were revealed through their prophets, but they were corrupted by their followers and superseded by the more complete revelation of the Koran.[10]

Indeed, Islam inherited the founders of the earlier religions; not only do Abraham, Moses, and Jesus appear in the Koran, but so do David and Solomon, who are also regarded as earlier prophets that are appropriated by Islam. In this way, Jerusalem became important to Islam not only due to the Night Journey, but also because it had been important for key events in the growth of both Christianity and Judaism, which Islam saw itself ultimately correcting and even replacing.

This dualism is also reflected in the direction of prayer in Islam, the *qibla*. There is no explicit reference in the Koran to what was precisely "the first qibla"; nonetheless it became commonly understood in Islamic tradition that Muslim prayer was directed originally toward Jerusalem. But two years after the flight of Muhammad from Mecca to Medina in 622, Muhammad is instructed to change the direction of Muslim prayer from Jerusalem to Mecca. The original choice of Jerusalem has been explained by the fact that the Ka'bah in Mecca was still a polytheistic shrine and was hence an unfitting direction of prayer for Muhammad's new monotheistic faith.

There is also the view that Muhammad might have expected the Jews of Medina to convert to Islam, attracted partly to its adoption of Jerusalem as the direction of prayer just as in Judaism. Disappointed by their refusal to abandon their old faith, Muhammad may have preferred Mecca as a direction of prayer, since this would have additionally reinforced the morale of the Meccan exile community, known as *al-Muhajirun*, which accompanied him in Medina and was loyal to the new faith. The new direction of prayer did not mean that the old one was theologically discarded. True, Jerusalem was no longer the direction of Muslim prayer, but by virtue of it once having served this role, it acquired sanctity for Islam that was not abandoned.

## Jerusalem under Early Islamic Rule

The dualism inherent in the Islamic approach to the previous monotheistic faiths would provide a basis for enormous fluctuation in how Islam dealt with Christians and Jews in general, and with Jerusalem in particular, during the period of Islam's initial military expansion. The Koran certainly preaches tolerance toward the adherents of the earlier faiths: "Be courteous when you argue with the People of the Book, except with those among them who do evil. Say: 'We believe in that which has been revealed to us and was revealed to you. Our God and your God is one. To Him we submit'" (29:46). But there are contrary precepts as well, for it is also written in the Koran, "Fight against such of those to whom the Scriptures were given...who do not embrace the true Faith, until they pay tribute out of hand and are utterly subdued" (9:29).

Thus it becomes possible to conclude that periods of relative Islamic tolerance existed based on the more liberal verses in the Koran. But there was also an oppressive tradition that could be invoked by later generations that would seek to place humiliating restrictions upon both Christians and Jews.[11]

These very different early Islamic traditions from the time of the Koran led to periods of harsh treatment of other monotheistic faiths that were punctuated by intervals of relative tolerance. For example, the Jewish population of Medina, whose ancestors were survivors of the Jewish revolts against the Romans five hundred years earlier, was eliminated and its properties were distributed to the Meccans who followed Muhammad to Medina.[12] In 628, Muhammad led a military expedition against the northern Arabian oasis of Khaybar; he allowed the Jews living there to stay and practice their religion, but they had to forfeit their lands that they could still work if they paid half their harvest to their new Muslim owners.[13] In later years, the defeat of the Jews of Khaybar came to be viewed as a turning point in the history of the first Islamic military campaigns. For radical Islamic theorists, Khaybar set the stage for the most important victory of Muhammad that followed—the conquest of the holy city of Mecca for Islam.

This mixed pattern of militancy and tolerance was also replicated after the death of Muhammad in 632. The first caliph, Abu Bakr (632–634), who was chosen by the consensus of the leadership of the Islamic community, only ruled for two years. It was under his brief rule that the expansion of Islam beyond the Arabian peninsula was formally launched. There is a tradition that when Abu Bakr gave instructions to his armies as the campaign northward began, he stated, "You will meet people who have set themselves apart in hermitages; leave them to accomplish the purpose to which they have done." Essentially Abu Bakr was telling his troops to spare Christian monasteries, though he gave harsh orders about how to deal with those who shave their heads and leave a band of hair.[14]

Abu Bakr was followed by Umar bin al-Khattab (634–644), who decreed that Jews and Christians should be removed from Arabia in order to fulfill a statement made by Muhammad on his deathbed: "Let there not be two religions in Arabia."[15] Umar indeed evicted the rest of the remaining Jews from the area of the Hijaz, including from Khaybar, and sought to complete the expulsion of Christians from Najran. But in the border regions between Arabia and Byzantine Palestine, Umar allowed the Jews to remain unharmed.[16] The Khaybar Jews settled in Jericho, in Byzantine Palestine, while Najran's Christians sought refuge in Syria and Iraq.[17] It seemed that there was a harsh doctrine applied against the other monotheistic faiths inside Arabia, while outside Arabia, the early Islamic rulers would develop a modus vivendi with the other monotheistic faiths that was also subject to considerable fluctuations depending on the policies adopted by individual rulers.

Already during the brief rule of Abu Bakr, Islamic armies reached the southern parts of Byzantine Palestine. Some elements of their policies toward the adherents of the previous monotheistic religions could already be discerned. The earliest of these invasions more closely resembled tribal raids rather than wars of conquest. These raiding expeditions succeeded in moving deeper into Byzantine Syria as the military and economic power of the Byzantine Empire declined; for example, Arab tribes positioned just north of Arabia who were paid for centuries to militarily contain these raids actually lost their Byzantine stipends. And since the tribes in Arabia who had entered the early Muslim community were prohibited from raiding each other, they needed an external outlet for their raiding practices. The aim of this warfare was not only booty, but also to offer protection to captured peoples, who were required to make payments to the expanding

Islamic state. It is doubtful at this stage that there had been a well-developed doctrine of extending the religion of Islam by conquest.[18]

Nonetheless, the patriarch of Jerusalem at time, Sophronius, warned in his sermon on Christmas Eve 634 that the Christian world was facing an outright invasion and not just limited Bedouin attacks. He reported that Christian religious institutions were threatened. The invading "Saracens" had made it impossible to travel the short distance from Jerusalem to Bethlehem. A few days later, he expanded in another sermon on the consequences of the military moves made by the new invaders, stressing the destruction of Christian monasteries, the plundering of cities, and the burning of villages.[19] Sophronius did not see the Arab invasions as local raids alone. In his sermon he declared that the Saracens "boast that they would conquer the entire world."

There was already evidence that the armies had plans to colonize the Holy Land. For example, in the surrender of Tiberias and Beit Shean, half the inhabitants' homes had to be handed over to the Muslim armies. Agricultural taxes and poll taxes were also instituted for non-Muslims.[20] With the accession of Umar as caliph, the character of these military operations changed; they were reinforced and escalated. Umar indeed bore the title "Commander of the Faithful."[21]

Jerusalem had not yet fallen to the Arab armies. In 636, Khalid bin al-Walid, Abu Bakr's leading general who had overseen the great victories of Arab armies against the Persians in Iraq, defeated the Byzantines at the Battle of Yarmuk, forcing Byzantine emperor Heraclius to abandon Syria-Palestine in its entirety. However, Umar sacked Khalid bin al-Walid, who was given the appellation "the sword of Islam" and despite this reputation would not command the armies that would take Jerusalem. It would take another two years for the conquest of Palestine to be completed and the surrender of Jerusalem by the Byzantines to be secured.

What emerges from this timetable is the likelihood that Jerusalem itself was not a primary strategic objective of the advancing Arab armies.[22] In contrast to the Crusades, the Arab invasions did not set the capture of Jerusalem as their main goal. Indeed, many of these early conquests were much more a product of local forces exploiting opportunities created by immediate circumstances rather a result of some carefully crafted political design.[23] According to one of the oldest reports from the Arab conquests, a local tribal commander named Khalid bin Thabit al-Fahmi first set the terms of the Muslim armies for the surrender of Jerusalem: the open country of Palestine would belong to the Muslims, while Jerusalem itself would be untouched by the invading armies as long as its residents paid the tribute that was to be imposed on them.[24]

The great Muslim historian Abu Ja'far bin Jarir al-Tabari has recorded what is the traditional view of the actual fall of Jerusalem to Umar bin al-Khattab. Umar, who according to several accounts entered Jerusalem in intentionally modest camel-hair clothing, was anxious to see the area of the Temple Mount and looked for David's place of prayer. According to the Byzantine chronicler Theophanes, Umar "demanded to be taken to what in former times had been the Temple built by Solomon."[25] Historians may argue among themselves whether Umar actually went to Jerusalem at the time, as they question the historicity of other religious traditions, but what is more important is that the record of his visit has become part of the heritage of Islam, and hence its details served as a source of religious direction for subsequent generations.

Christian sources wrote that Umar visited Jerusalem's churches, including the Church of the Holy Sepulchre, but would not pray in one of them in order to preclude future Muslim claims on a Christian holy site. It may have been that Sophronius encouraged Umar to go to the Temple Mount, since the Christian community at the time had no religious interest in the area. Upon entering the Temple Mount compound, according to al-Tabari, Umar asked Ka'b al-Ahbar, a Yemenite Jew who had converted to Islam and accompanied the caliph, about what the proper direction of prayer should be. Ka'b answered that they should pray "toward the rock." In another version, Ka'b suggested that they should place a mosque behind the "foundation stone" so that "the two directions of prayer—that of Moses and that of Muhammad—merge with one another."

What Ka'b was suggesting, in essence, was that Umar pray in the direction of both the Holy of Holies and Mecca at the same time. Umar apparently rejected Ka'b's proposal of directing Muslim prayer toward the foundation stone: "O Ka'b, you are imitating the Jewish religion!" He further explained, "we were not commanded to venerate the Rock, but were commanded to venerate the Ka'bah."[26] Umar's warning to Ka'b reflected a theme that would resurface in Islamic religious thought every few centuries: Islam must avoid absorbing innovations, known as *bid'a*, in its original practices that are borrowed from other faiths.

Umar may not have been willing to sanctify the area of the foundation stone as the Jews were, but he nonetheless showed his respect for this holy site. He built a modest wooden mosque on the southern end of the Temple Mount; a Christian pilgrim named Arculf who visited Jerusalem in 680 described it as "an oblong house they [the Muslims] pieced together with upright planks and large beams over some ruined remains."[27] He had heard that it could hold 3,000 people. The golden Dome of the Rock over the foundation stone, which is frequently misnamed "the Mosque of Omar," would only be constructed decades later. But Umar clearly restored the Temple Mount after centuries as a holy site, even though Islam had not yet fully established for itself whether the old area of the Jewish Holy of Holies possessed any special sanctity and should be venerated.

It should be recalled that under the Byzantines, the Temple Mount became a garbage dump, and as noted earlier, their construction projects in Jerusalem were undertaken in other parts of the city. A Christian historian named Eutychius, writing in the ninth century, noted that "the Byzantines (Rum)" had neglected "the place of the rock and the area around it." He reported that the Romans had poured dirt over the rock "so that great was the filth above it." Eutychius wrote that Umar took his cloak and filled it with dirt that he dug out with his own hands. When the Muslims saw this they followed suit, clearing the rubble that had accumulated on the Temple Mount. Later Muslim accounts claimed that Umar forced the Christians to clear the rubbish that they had allowed to accumulate on the Temple Mount.

One of the points of controversy between the patriarch Sophronius and Umar was the future status of the Jews in Jerusalem. Umar apparently initially agreed to Sophronius's request that Jews continue to be banned from Jerusalem and its environs, in accordance with the Roman policy established by Hadrian and sustained by Constantine and his successors. If this was a key Byzantine demand to get Jerusalem to surrender peacefully, then it made sense for Umar to initially agree.

Umar incorporated this policy into the final terms of surrender that were presented to Jerusalem and incorporated into a document that would be called the "Covenant of Umar." He granted the residents of Jerusalem their security, adding "their churches will not be expropriated for residences nor destroyed; they and their annexes will suffer no harm and the same will be true of their crosses and their goods." There was an additional clause stating, "No constraint will be imposed upon them in the matter of religion." The big caveat in this early Islamic liberalism was the imposition of a discriminatory poll tax for non-Muslims called *al-jizya*. Reflecting the concerns of Sophronius with the return of the Jews, the "Covenant of Umar" also stated, "No Jew will be authorized to live in Jerusalem, with them."[28]

Within a few years, there were good reasons for Umar to change his mind about the question of Jewish settlement in Jerusalem. The Jews still represented a large portion of the population of Palestine, and economically they may have been its most important component.[29] Moreover, Umar did not go back on his word to Sophronius; he apparently renegotiated the ban on Jews. The Jews had requested that two hundred Jewish families be allowed to resettle in Jerusalem. The patriarch was only willing to agree to fifty. Umar took a compromise position, allowing seventy Jewish families from Tiberias to settle in Jerusalem.[30] A Jewish text known as the "Mysteries of Shimon Bar Yochai," reflecting the sentiments that were possibly felt in that era, would claim, "The second king [second caliph] who will rise from Ishmael will be a lover of Israel and will repair their cracks and the cracks of the temple."[31]

Jewish chronicles from the period in fact report that a group of Jews joined the Muslims in removing the rubbish from the Temple Mount under Umar's supervision. The Jews who returned to Jerusalem "took a pledge upon themselves to maintain the cleanliness of the Temple Mount area."[32] This was recorded from a Jewish source, but Muslim accounts also verified these arrangements. They added that there were twenty Jewish servants responsible for sanitation on the Temple Mount for several decades, until the reign of Caliph Umar ibn Abd al-Aziz (717–720), who were also made exempt from the poll tax (jizya) that was exclusively applied to non-Muslims.

There is a historical debate over whether Umar permitted the Jews to build their own synagogue and academy on the Temple Mount platform in an area away from the site where the Temple had stood.[33] There is no historical debate, however, over the fact that with the Islamic conquests, the Jews who returned to Jerusalem established their main synagogue, which was called "the Cave," (*al-Maghar* in Arabic) underneath the Temple Mount; its entranceway was a gate in the Western Wall that was located at the closest point possible to the Holy of Holies above.[34] All these accounts attest to a striking degree of tolerance for the adherents of the pre-Islamic monotheistic religions in seventh-century Jerusalem. Clearly the exclusivist restrictions with respect to non-Muslims in Mecca and Medina did not apply in the holy sites of Jerusalem.

Years later, other documents emerged called "The Covenant of Umar" that outlined the regulations that non-Muslims took upon themselves under Islamic rule in exchange for protection. Though attributed to Umar himself, the texts of these documents have not been dated any earlier than the tenth or eleventh centuries—about five hundred years after the death of Umar. These later versions of the "Covenant of Umar" contained severe limitations on religious freedom, such as a ruling that non-Muslims must not build new houses of prayer. It even stated that non-Muslims must not make repairs in houses of worship that have fallen into ruin.[35]

There were also restrictions on the public display of religious objects like the cross, and the holding of public processions on Palm Sunday. Ironically, Umar and his immediate successors did not impose these restrictions in seventh-century Jerusalem. The Jews clearly needed to build new synagogues, since they had not resided in Jerusalem for five hundred years because of Roman restrictions. Not only did the Jews build a synagogue under the Temple Mount, but another synagogue has been excavated next to the southwestern corner of the Temple Mount that has been dated to the reign of Umar.[36]

What was significant was that these positions were taken during the period of the first four caliphs of Islam, who would be later known as "the rightly guided caliphs" (*al-Rashidun*). Since they were actual companions of the Prophet Muhammad, these ancestors (*al-Salaf*) served throughout Islamic history as the most authoritative source for Islamic law and practice. Retrospectively, Muslims came to look upon this period as a "Golden Age" of the caliphate. Indeed, many modern Islamic fundamentalist movements are known as *salafi* movements because they seek to restore the pure Islam practiced at the time of the early caliphs, before it was corrupted by outside influence when the Islamic empires of the Middle Ages expanded and incorporated the traditions of many of their subject populations.

## The Ummayad Caliphate's Political Interest in Jerusalem

It was unquestionably the Ummayad caliphate, following the first four "rightly guided caliphs," who initially molded many aspects of the Islamic connection to Jerusalem that elevated the status of Jerusalem in early Islam. However, the traditions and sayings extolling Jerusalem that the Ummayads would propagate were mostly based on political considerations and dynastic rivalries.[37] It was during the Ummayad caliphate that the Koranic verse about the "Farther Mosque" in Muhammad's Night Journey came to be specifically identified with Jerusalem.[38] The shift from the "rightly guided caliphs" to the Ummayads was rapid. Umar was assassinated in 644 as was his successor, Uthman, some twelve years later. That brought to power Ali ibn Abi Talib, the son-in-law of Muhammad and his closest living relative. Mu'awiya, who came from the Ummayad clan in Mecca and had been appointed commander of the army in Syria and Palestine, decided to challenge the leadership of Ali and establish a new dynasty of his own.

This history had an indirect impact on Jerusalem, for during the course of these struggles for succession, new regional political and spiritual centers of Islam were created. For example, Ali moved his seat of government from Medina to Kufa in Iraq. Ali was murdered in Kufa in 661, like his predecessors. His tomb was erected in Najaf, another Iraqi town four miles from Kufa, and it would become an important center of pilgrimage for Ali's supporters, who became known as the Partisans of Ali, or simply the Shiites.

Ali had two sons who, from a Shiite perspective, should have become his successors. First there was Hasan, who abdicated in favor of Mu'awiya and the Ummayads. His younger brother, Hussein, however, refused to acknowledge Mu'awiya's son, Yazid, as the successor to the caliphate. This led to a clash between the forces of Hussein and an Ummayad army on October 10, 680, at the Iraqi town of Karbala, where Hussein was killed and where his tomb would become yet another site of pilgrimage for Shiite Islam.

Mu'awiya and his Ummayad successors sought to create their own spiritual and political centers of power. It was Mu'awiya who would shift the seat of the caliphate from Medina, which had been the first capital of the first Islamic state, to Damascus. Mu'awiya also had himself proclaimed caliph in Jerusalem in 660. He served as caliph for twenty years, until 680. Islamic historians report that Ummayad rulers also sought to transfer the pulpit of the Prophet Muhammad from Medina to Syria, where they ruled.[39] Oral traditions associated with Mu'awiya religiously extolled the territories under Ummayad control. Regarding the region of Syria, known as *al-Sham* in Arabic, he is said to have stated, "Go to al-Sham, for it is God's choice of His countries." He would stress the sanctity of all of Syria, calling it "the Land of Resurrection."[40]

Generally, the dynastic struggles in the Islamic world would affect the relative importance of its holy cities, creating new centers of pilgrimage while downgrading other spiritual centers or even making them inaccessible. For example, at the end of the reign of Yazid, as the second Ummayad caliph, Abdullah ibn al-Zubair seized Mecca and proclaimed himself the new caliph. He would control Mecca from 683 through 692.

It was the fourth Ummayad caliph, Abd al-Malik (685–705), who in this period of the rival caliphate of ibn al-Zubair decided to erect the Dome of the Rock on the Temple Mount. It was not designed as a mosque; it was a golden-domed octagonal sanctuary over what had been the foundation stone in the Jewish faith. During this very period, the Ummayad rulers were concerned that upon making the hajj, their subjects in Syria would be forced to declare their loyalty to the rival caliphate of Ibn al-Zubair in Mecca.

Shiite historians, who had little sympathy for the Ummayads, have related that Abd al-Malik, or his son al-Walid, decreed that the Dome of the Rock in Jerusalem should temporarily be the place of Muslim pilgrimage instead of the Ka'bah in Mecca, which was controlled by the Ummayads' rival.[41] One of these historians attributed to Abd al-Malik the statement that pilgrimage to Jerusalem should be equated to pilgrimage to Mecca.

But this thesis does not appear in the works of most of the classic Muslim historians of the ninth century, who describe in detail the conflict between Abd al-Malik and Ibn al-Zubair.[42] Moreover, it would be highly unlikely that an Ummayad caliph would suspend the pilgrimage to Mecca, which had been one of the five pillars of the Islamic faith. Nonetheless, the Ummayads still had a direct political interest in elevating the importance of Jerusalem in order to compete with the rival caliphate in Mecca.

Was this the source of Abd al-Malik's decision to build the Dome of the Rock? Did he wish to provide a monument that would enshrine Muhammad's Night Journey to Jerusalem and his ascent to Heaven? In 688, when the work on the Dome of the Rock began, the Night Journey alluded to in the Koran had not yet been definitively linked to Jerusalem.[43] The spectacular Arabic calligraphy along the walls of the Dome of the Rock does not even mention the Night Journey.

Instead, the main interior inscriptions appear to be directed against the still-substantial Christian population of Jerusalem: "Praise be to God, who begets no son, and has no partner." There is also a similar sentence: "He is God, one eternal. He does not beget, nor is he begotten, and He has no peer."[44] Some of the inscriptions are whole verses lifted from the Koran, while others are just newly written texts.[45] The strongest inscriptions on the Dome of the Rock were placed on copper plates right over its eastern and southern gates: "The Unity of God and the Prophecy of Muhammad are true" and "the Sonship of Jesus and the Trinity are false."[46] Inside, the inscriptions concluded with a call to the People of the Book to adopt Islam.[47]

None of the inscriptions seek to challenge the centrality of Mecca in Islam, which further undermines the argument that the Ummayads hoped to make Jerusalem an alternative site of pilgrimage. This also perhaps explains Abd al-Malik's motivation to build the Dome of the Rock—he wanted an Islamic structure that would rival Constantine's Church of the Holy Sepulchre.

In general, the Ummayads used architecture to symbolize the challenge they sought to pose to the previous supremacy of the Byzantine Christians. Mu'awiya's armies even reached the walls of Constantinople in 668 and again in 674. Clearly, the Ummayads were on the front line of Islam's war against the Byzantine Empire. Undoubtedly, this affected the behavior over time of the Ummayads toward their Christian subjects.

Abd al-Malik's son, al-Walid (705–715), who would build the great al-Aqsa Mosque at the southern end of the Temple Mount, also altered some of the great Christian houses of worship in his realm. He converted the Cathedral of St. John the Baptist in Damascus into the famous Ummayad Mosque.[48] He removed the dome of a church in Baalbek, in what is today Lebanon, for the al-Aqsa Mosque in Jerusalem.[49] Restrictions on building new houses of worship began to appear during the Ummayad caliphate, particularly under Umar II (717–720).[50] All of this was very different from the behavior of the first Umar, who wouldn't even pray at the Church of the Holy Sepulchre because he didn't want later generations of Muslims to convert it into an Islamic holy site.

One theory for the greater degree of tolerance exhibited during the first hundred years of Islamic rule was that the Arab conquerors who subdued these lands were still a minority needing the cooperation of the subject peoples that they ruled. As the demography of Syria and Palestine changed over the decades, there would be less political necessity for taking into account the religious needs of non-Muslims. Over time the special taxes imposed by Islamic rulers on non-Muslims like the *jizya* (poll tax) and the *kharaj* (land tax) took their toll on these demographic balances, increasing the number of adherents to Islam. But in Jerusalem, the demography of its residents did not change so quickly.

The great Muslim traveler and geographer al-Muqadassi (948–990), who was a native of Jerusalem, would note as late as the tenth century that the Holy City's "Christians and Jews have the upper hand." He complained that "the mosque is void of either congregation or assembly of learned men."[51] From his descriptions, three hundred years after the Arabs took Jerusalem from the Byzantines, it was still not a fully Islamic city.

During the Ummayad period, the caliph Sulayman considered for a time making Jerusalem his capital but he never carried through with the plan. Nor did the Ummayads or their predecessors adopt the Byzantine capital of Palestine, Caesaria. Instead, they preferred to make the new city of Ramle their administrative center. Over time, the Islamic world would adopt many different imperial capitals: Medina, Damascus, Baghdad, Cairo, and Istanbul. But Jerusalem would never become the capital of any Islamic empire.

## Rising Islamic Ambivalence about Jerusalem

The defeat of the Damascus-based Ummayad caliphate and its replacement by the Abbasid caliphate based in Baghdad would have enormous implications for the status of Jerusalem. The Ummayad caliphs were frequent visitors to Jerusalem and built palaces for themselves in the Holy City. The more distant Abbasids gradually lost interest in Jerusalem; the greatest of the Abbasid caliphs, Harun al-Rashid (786–809), would make hajj to Mecca every other year and was frequently in Syria because of his war against the Byzantines. Nevertheless, he never bothered to come to Jerusalem. His son, al-Ma'mun (813–833), also refrained from ever visiting the Holy City.

This increasing ambivalence about Jerusalem also appeared in religious writings at the time. Thus, if during the Ummayad period many traditions were spread about the merits of praying in Jerusalem, during the Abbasid caliphate an alternative religious view developed that explicitly demoted the value of prayer in Jerusalem and even advised against visiting the Holy City altogether.[52] Al-Mansur (754–775), the second Abbasid caliph, did visit Jerusalem on his way home from the hajj to Mecca. The al-Aqsa Mosque had been in ruins because of an earthquake ten years earlier. When he was asked by local Muslims to rebuild the great mosque, he replied that he had no money. He suggested they melt down the gold plating used in the Dome of the Rock in order to pay for the needed repairs. His successor ordered that the al-Aqsa Mosque be rebuilt, but insisted that provincial governors subsidize the project themselves.[53]

Al-Ma'mun ordered some building initiatives at the Islamic shrines on the Temple Mount. The most famous of his repairs, however, was his removal of the tiles on the Dome of the Rock that credited the Ummayad caliph Abd al-Malik with its construction. In their stead, he installed new tiles bearing his own name. The date of construction, however, was not altered. During the reign of al-Ma'mun, Jerusalem suffered from famine and became depleted of much of its Muslim population.[54] Subsequent peasant revolts that the Abbasid authorities failed to put down also contributed to demographic decline in the city. In the ninth century, the absence of any strong Abbasid presence led to a deterioration in the security situation in Jerusalem as well as increasing local outbursts against its non-Muslim communities. In 964, half of the outer court of the Church of the Holy Sepulchre was seized and a mosque was erected on it.

Shortly thereafter, Jerusalem came under the domination of the Fatimid caliphate, which made Cairo its capital. The dynastic name "Fatimid" alluded to the dynasty's claim to be descendants of Muhammad through his daughter Fatima and Ali. It was a dynasty that was religiously based on an offshoot of Shiism and would become a major competitor with the Sunni Abbasid caliphate. The Fatimids initially treated their Christians and Jews well, even using them in the state bureaucracy. However, the Fatimid caliph al-Hakim (996–1021) severely persecuted Christians and Jews, culminating in his order to destroy the Church of the Holy Sepulchre in September 1009. Until the arrival of the Crusades in 1099, Jerusalem would change hands several times between the Fatimids and the Seljuk Turks, who were loyal to the Abbasid caliph in Baghdad.

The relative neglect that the Abbasids demonstrated toward Jerusalem provides an important backdrop to their reaction to the fall of the Holy City to the Crusaders in 1099. Muslim refugees reached Baghdad for an audience with the caliph, al-Mustazhir. He expressed his deep sympathy and compassion to them. But he only ordered an inquiry into what exactly had happened in Jerusalem and nothing came out of this investigation.[55] Certainly there was no immediate military response to the Crusader assault.

It seemed as though the Abbasids were almost apathetic about the loss of Jerusalem. As in the past, this had theological underpinnings: leading scholars in Islamic law strongly opposed the special religious status that had been granted to Jerusalem in some Islamic circles, especially by Muslim mystics, known as Sufis. They condemned aspects of this veneration of Jerusalem as an innovation—*bid'a*—that was being added to Islam.[56]

It was not a baseless concern. Jerusalem had changed over the previous century. During the years of Fatimid-Shiite rule, classical Sunni scholars did not feel as comfortable in Jerusalem as they had in the past. In the early eleventh century a Jerusalem Muslim resident named Abu Bakr al-Wasiti described the rituals that were performed at the Dome of the Rock. These involved anointing the foundation stone with some prepared mixture and burning incense inside the sanctuary. All these practices were completely alien to Islam.[57] The religious calendar followed by local Muslims at the Dome of the Rock in al-Wasiti's descriptions appeared to be borrowed more from Judaism than from Islam; the main activities observed in the sanctuary were reserved for Monday and Thursday, the weekdays that Jews traditionally read from the Torah during the morning service.[58]

Nasir-i Khusra was a Persian traveler who visited Jerusalem in 1047 and recorded his impressions of religious life in the Holy City on the eve of the Crusades. He described a practice that was followed by local Muslims who were unable to make the hajj to Mecca of performing religious rites in Jerusalem that were normally followed around the pilgrimage to Mecca. Apparently, local Muslims would circle the Dome of the Rock, offer animal sacrifices, and engage in chanting that was typically reserved for Jabal Arafat in Mecca.[59] It was as though Jerusalem could serve as an alternative religious center, which would have entailed a significant modification of Islamic law.[60] Nasir-i Khusra also wrote about the presence of Sufi Muslims who had their own places of prayer on the Temple Mount;

there were no notable Sunni *ulama*. The practices that he witnessed and recorded in Jerusalem indicated the intensity of local Muslim involvement in the Holy City but such reports could have also alienated the main Islamic authorities at the time who ruled the Abbasid caliphate from Baghdad.

## Jerusalem as a Trigger for Jihad: Saladin Recovers the Holy City While His Successors Give It Away

The mobilization of the Islamic world for a counter-crusade to take back Jerusalem would take decades to accomplish. A new appreciation for Jerusalem arose with new dynastic struggles that began in the Arab world with the rise of Imad al-Din Zangi, the son of a Turkish slave, and his son Nur al-Din, who carved out a new empire for themselves in the area of Mosul and Allepo. Nur al-Din sought support for his military campaigns across the Fertile Crescent from the Abbasid caliph in Baghdad. He explained in a letter that his ultimate goal was "the expulsion of the cross-worshipers from the al-Aqsa mosque."[61]

Nur al-Din would use the cause of Jerusalem to serve his territorial aspirations.[62] Indeed, in this period of the mid-eleventh century a new type of literature called *Fadail al-Quds*, or praises of Jerusalem, became widespread. Nur al-Din's great general, a Kurdish warrior named Salah al-Din, or Saladin, was born in Tikrit and would become Nur al-Din's successor. Saladin repeated his predecessor's declarations about liberating Jerusalem. He had two burning passions that he hoped to realize: replacing the Shiite caliphate of the Fatimids with a Sunni regime and waging jihad against the Crusaders.[63]

Awareness of the issue of Jerusalem had undoubtedly grown in the core of the Islamic world in this period. In the early twelfth century the Syrian Muslim scholar Ali ibn Tahir al-Sulami sought to revive the idea of jihad, which in his view had been in abeyance for too long.[64] He focused on the need to take back Jerusalem, emphasizing that the Muslim recovery of the Holy City would set the stage for much greater military victories against the West, including the conquest of Constantinople: "We have heard in what we have heard of a sufficiently documented *hadith*, mentioning in it that the *Rum* (Rome, or more accurately the Byzantines) will conquer Jerusalem for a set period of time, and the Muslims will gather against them, drive them out of it, kill them all except a few of them, (and) then pursue their scattered remnants to Constantinople, descend on it and conquer it."[65]

In this way, the conquest of Jerusalem was a critical prerequisite for defeating the main global opponent to the Islamic world at the time and conquering its capital.

But what actually triggered Saladin's final offensive against the Crusaders were other considerations that had nothing to do with Jerusalem directly. Reynald of Chatillon controlled the fortress of Kerak in what is today southern Jordan, which was close to the border with Arabia. Kerak was like a forward defense line of the Crusader kingdom.

Reynald of Chatillon used this position to raid Muslim caravans with pilgrims bound for Mecca. In so doing, he was prepared to violate agreements between Saladin and the Crusader king of Jerusalem. He made incursions into the Hijaz, the Islamic holy land where the holy cities of Mecca and Medina were located. His ships attacked and pillaged Muslim shipping in the Red Sea and posed a threat to the ports of the Hijaz. At one point in 1182 he landed an invasion force in the Hijaz that was stopped only a day's march from Mecca.[66]

In 1186, Reynald took one more step that would finally ignite Saladin against the Crusader kingdom. He raided once again a rich caravan, only this time it included one of Saladin's sisters. In the aftermath of the attack, Saladin was quoted as saying, "the taking of that caravan was the ruin of Jerusalem."[67] Reynald of Chatillon's direct military threat to the heart of Arabia, combined with his attacks on all caravan traffic, would push Saladin to put an end to the Crusader kingdom in Jerusalem once and for all.[68]

Saladin put together the largest army he had ever commanded, with close to 30,000 soldiers in the Hauran, located in southern Syria. On June 30, 1187, he crossed the Jordan and in July engaged and overwhelmingly defeated a smaller Crusader force of 20,000 in the Battle of Hittin, near Tiberias. By October 2, 1187, Jerusalem surrendered to Saladin after a two-week siege.

In the aftermath of Saladin's victory, there was a determined effort to re-Islamize Jerusalem. Previous Islamic buildings that had been converted to churches became Muslim shrines again. The golden cross on the al-Aqsa Mosque, which had been made into a church by the Templars, was pulled down by Saladin's soldiers. Bells were also removed from church towers.[69] St. Anne's Church, which marked in Christian tradition the birthplace of the Virgin Mary and the place of burial of her parents, was turned into a mosque and its adjoining convent became a school for the study of Islamic law.[70] A monastery for Sufis was created in the former residence of the patriarch of Jerusalem adjacent to the Church of the Holy Sepulchre.[71] Western Christians—members of the Latin Church—were expelled by Jerusalem's new rulers, although adherents of the Eastern churches were allowed to stay. The Greek Orthodox Church was given custody over the Church of the Holy Sepulchre.[72]

Like Umar bin al-Khattab, Saladin allowed the Jews to return to Jerusalem; the initial members of the newly revived Jewish community came from Ashkelon in 1190. They were followed by new Jewish immigrants from North Africa and as far away as France and England. Eventually, right after the Third Crusade, Latin Christians would be permitted to make pilgrimage to Jerusalem.[73] Saladin concluded an agreement in 1192 with the leader of the Third Crusade, Richard the Lion Hearted, king of England, which allowed the return of Western pilgrims to Jerusalem. But the agreement also acknowledged the Crusaders' political position along the coast of Palestine; if Saladin sought to destroy the Crusader state, he ended up recognizing a part of it.

Nonetheless, Saladin's victory over the Crusaders enhanced the religious status of Jerusalem in the Islamic world. But would this new status be preserved by his successors? Saladin died in 1193; the Ayyubid dynasty that he established had rulers in Syria and Egypt who would become rivals. Saladin's nephew, al-Mu'azzam, would become the sultan of Damascus and also ruled over Jerusalem. In 1219, as the Fifth Crusade achieved military successes in Egypt, al-Mu'azzam ordered the destruction of all of Jerusalem's fortifications; he assumed that the Crusaders would have no problem recapturing the city and would then turn it into a forward base of operations against other Islamic territories. Indeed, he wrote: "If the Franks conquer it [Jerusalem] they will kill all whom they find there and will have the fate of Damascus and the lands of Islam in their hands."[74] Jerusalem was again viewed as a pivotal point in the struggle between the Christian West and the Islamic world.

After al-Mu'azzam razed the walls of Jerusalem it was again depopulated, with women, children, and the elderly fleeing the Holy City and taking up residence in Cairo, Damascus, and Kerak in Transjordan.[75] A Muslim historian, al-Maqrizi, wrote in the fifteenth century that al-Mu'azzam "caused all the inhabitants [of Jerusalem] to leave, [with] only a few remaining."[76] Jerusalem was defenseless and its situation only worsened in the years that followed. Al-Mu'azzam, the Ayyubid ruler of Syria, had also to contend with his brother and dynastic rival, al-Kamil, the ruler of Ayyubid Egypt. In order to build up his power against al-Mu'azzam, al-Kamil concluded a ten-year treaty in 1229 with Holy Roman Emperor Frederick II according to which Jerusalem would be returned to Christian rule, provided that the Muslims could still manage their religious affairs on the Temple Mount.

The text of the agreement read:

> The Sultan cedes Jerusalem to the Emperor or to his representatives. The Emperor may do as he desires regarding the fortification of the city and other matters. Al-Aqsa Mosque, known to the Christians as the Temple of Solomon and the Dome of the Rock or the Mosque of Omar, known as the Temple of the Lord, and all the area of *Haram al-Sharif*, that is, the Temple Mount area, will remain in the hands of Muslim authorities, who will worship there in accordance with their laws, including the muezzin's call to prayer. The keys of the gates of the *Haram al-Sharif* will also remain in Muslim hands. A Christian desiring to go to the *Haram* to pray will be permitted to do so.[77]

The agreement of Ayyubid Egypt with the Holy Roman Emperor led to a further deterioration of the situation in Jerusalem. Frederick instituted the old regulations of the Crusaders that prohibited Muslims and Jews from living in Jerusalem, although he honored his commitment to allow Muslim prayer on the Temple Mount. Still, the supreme Muslim authority in Jerusalem had to maintain its seat outside the Holy City in the town of al-Birah. Moreover, after further hostilities between Ayyubid Egypt and Ayyubid Syria, the Syrian successors of Saladin decided to revise Frederick's previous agreement over Jerusalem with new concessions in order to win Christian political support against the Egyptians: as a result, Ayyubid Syria agreed to remove the Muslim presence from the Temple Mount altogether.[78]

Despite these setbacks for Muslim interests in Jerusalem, the Holy City had become a religious site that many Muslims around the Middle East would seek to visit. Still, even Saladin's great victory in 1187 never altered the religious status of Jerusalem as the third holiest city in Islam, after Mecca and Medina, according to Islamic thinkers at the time. Pilgrimage to Mecca was clearly defined as hajj, and was one of the five pillars of Islam, while a "pious journey" or visit to Jerusalem was technically called *ziyara*.[79]

## Islamic Reservations about Excessive Veneration of Jerusalem

The Mongol invasions of the thirteenth century affected both the physical and spiritual status of Jerusalem. Turkish tribes fleeing from the Mongols moved into the Middle East, including the Khwarizmians, who were recruited as allies by the Egyptian Ayyubids. The Khwarizmians overran Jerusalem in 1244 and devastated what remained of the Holy City. Jerusalem was further depopulated; mostly local Christians remained, who had been tolerated by the Crusaders as well.

There was virtually no Muslim population left.[80] With the invasion of the Mongol armies of Genghis Khan's grandson, Hulagu, into Palestine, Jerusalem was virtually deserted; most of its residents fled from the advancing Mongol armies. After the defeat of the Mongols by the Mamluk armies from Egypt, whose sultan had intermarried with the Ayyubids, Jerusalem came under the new Mamluk Empire, based in Cairo.

The Mongols in the Middle East had become Muslims, but a growing concern was evident among Islamic thinkers about the authenticity of their conversion as well as the influx of foreign ideas that they brought into Islam. In this period there was an understandable desire of religious authorities to return to the original Islam that was spread by Muhammad and his successors, without the influence of other faiths.

The leading force for this movement was the fourteenth-century reformer Taqiyy al-Din ibn Taymiyya. He was not only concerned with the Mongols, for Ibn Taymiyya argued against what he judged was an inappropriate level of devotion to Jerusalem that was still evident in some Islamic circles. His legal opinions were extremely significant, as centuries later his views on jihad and other religious matters would inspire the most militant elements in the Islamic world, from the founders of the Wahhabi movement in Arabia to the jihadists around al-Qaeda.

Ibn Taymiyya was blunt: "And in Jerusalem, there is not a place one calls sacred and the same holds true for the tombs of Hebron."[81] In his view, the term sacred only applied to sites in the Arabian peninsula. The glorification of the foundation stone was a practice of the Jews and some Christians. During the period of the first four "rightly guided caliphs," he pointed out that there was no Dome of the Rock: "they did not glorify the rock." He explained that it was built by the Ummayad caliph Abd al-Malik in order "to deter" Muslims from going to Mecca, which was ruled by the rival caliphate of ibn al-Zubayr. He completely rejected the notion that there was an imprint of the foot of Muhammad in the foundation stone dating back to the Night Journey and his ascent to Heaven. Ibn Taymiyya reserved his harshest criticism for Muslims who performed unique religious rites in Jerusalem that were prescribed for Mecca alone; he specifically referred to the circumambulation of the Ka'ba, which was not to be performed in Jerusalem.

Jerusalem, he explained, had once been the *qibla*—that is, the direction of Muslim prayer. But that had been changed. The Ka'bah was the only direction of prayer. He added: "One who, today, regards the rock (in Jerusalem) as the qibla and prays towards it is a renegade apostate who must repent." He then warns, "Either he seeks repentance or he is killed."[82] Ibn Taymiyya was controversial; local authorities in Cairo and Damascus imprisoned him for his ideas. Yet when he died 20,000 Syrians attended his funeral and his tomb became a place of pilgrimage (something he would probably have condemned). His critique of the excessive vener-ation of Jerusalem was a minority opinion, although he left students like Ibn Kathir who adhered to his views.

What Ibn Taymiyya's writings nonetheless demonstrated were the reli-gious dilemmas for Islam that were created with the initial glorification of Jerusalem in the aftermath of Saladin's victory in 1187 over the Crusaders. The dilemma was not new, for the resistance to adopting Judaizing ten-dencies into Islamic practice dates back to the first visit of the caliph Umar to the Temple Mount with his recently converted Jewish guide, Ka'b. And this problem reappeared during the Abbasid caliphate, as explained above.

However this struggle worked itself out, on the ground the Mamluks, who were the new Islamic power governing Jerusalem from Cairo in the years 1260 through 1517, essentially left it in its ruined state. True, they dedicated many new religious establishments for Sunni Islam. Yet during this entire period of roughly 250 years, they would not rebuild the city's walls, leaving Jerusalem wide open for repeated Bedouin raids. Indeed, in 1348, a Bedouin attack on Jerusalem drove out all its inhabitants.[83] The resulting insecurity affected its ability to attract new immigrants to fully repopulate the city as well as assure its economic growth. The Mamluks would only appoint low-level officials to govern the Holy City. Moreover, Jerusalem became for the Mamluks a place to exile officials who had fallen out of favor with the Mamluk establishment.[84]

In the period of Saladin, Jerusalem was directly tied to the ideal of jihad. His recovery of Jerusalem was seen as a turning point in the war between the Christian empires and the Islamic world. But with the Mam-luks there were other battles that had become more important. The great Mamluk military leader Baybars crushed the Mongols in 1260 at Ain Jalut, and afterwards set his sights on destroying the remaining Crusader cities along the Mediterranean coast. Mamluk prestige was derived from these victories and not from Saladin's conquest of Jerusalem a century earlier. This somewhat separated the idea of jihad from the issue of Jerusalem and may have contributed to a reduced sense of involvement on the part of the Mamluks in the affairs of the Holy City over time.[85]

In fact, under the Mamluks, the situation for Christians and Muslims in Jerusalem worsened. There was an increase in the appropriation of

Christian buildings.[86] The most famous case at the time was that of the complex of Christian buildings on Mt. Zion that included the Tomb of David, which was revered by Jews, and the Coenaculum, where Jesus and his disciples took part in the Last Supper. The Mamluk sultan ordered the destruction of the church on Mt. Zion.[87] Restrictions on the visit of non-Muslims to the Temple Mount were also instituted, although these may have dated back to the Ayyubid period as well. Arnold von Hartff, a European visitor to Jerusalem in 1496, wrote, "no Christian or Jew is suffered to enter there or draw near, since they say and maintain that we are base dogs and not worthy to go to the holy places on pain of death, at which I was frightened."[88]

There was also a tendency to strictly enforce the prohibition preventing non-Muslims from building new places of worship. Repairs were also restricted. When part of the thirteenth-century synagogue of Nachmanides (Ramban) collapsed in 1473, a Muslim mob sought to prevent it being repaired and demolished it. To his credit, the Mamluk sultan Qaytbay ordered it rebuilt. But that was also indicative of the problem that Jerusalem faced. With no strong central government to protect minority religious rights, non-Muslims were vulnerable to local initiatives against them, even beyond the measures that the central government in Cairo sometimes also took against these communities.

Jerusalem's fortunes began to change when the Ottoman Empire replaced the Mamluks in 1517.

Under Sultan Sulayman the Magnificent (1520–1566) the walls of Jerusalem were rebuilt. New tile work was commissioned for the Dome of the Rock and it was in this period that the Temple Mount area came to be commonly known as *al-Haram al-Sharif* (the Noble Sanctuary).[89] Jerusalem was clearly a priority for Sulaiman; he invested in its water system by constructing canals and fountains. His Russian-born wife, Roxelana, created Jerusalem's most important charitable institution at the time, which subsidized a mosque, a madrassa (religious school) and hospice for students and the poor.[90]

Sulayman also sought to repopulate the Holy City; indeed, its population nearly tripled in size by the mid-sixteenth century. In 1525,

Jerusalem had a total population of 4,700 but by 1553 the population had risen to 13,384.[91] Under Sulayman, repairs of minority houses of worship were permitted, the most famous case being the restoration of the Church of the Holy Sepulchre in 1555. With the Ottoman Empire serving as refuge for Jews expelled from Spain as a result of the Spanish Inquisition in 1492, Suleyman was not averse to seeing the Jewish population of Jerusalem grow as well during this period. Indeed, in Tiberias he gave over large tracts of land to his Jewish advisor, Don Joseph Nasi, for new Jewish settlements. Finally, he issued an official edict permitting the Jews to have a place of prayer at the Western Wall.[92]

Sulayman was sultan at the zenith of the Ottoman Empire. In the West, his armies overran Belgrade and Hungary and reached the gates of Vienna, while in the East he secured Baghdad from the Persians. His treatment of his Jewish subjects indicated that it was possible for a great leader of one of the most powerful Islamic empires in history to demonstrate respect toward both pre-Islamic faiths. But this period of relative tolerance for some minorities under Ottoman rule would not remain permanent. Moreover, as in the case of the Mamluks, whenever the interest of the Ottoman central authorities in Jerusalem declined, the security of the Holy City became threatened by local developments. There was a renewal of Bedouin raids in the late sixteenth and in the seventeenth centuries. A local Ottoman governor named Muhammad ibn Faruk imposed heavy taxes on non-Muslims, especially Jews, some of whom he imprisoned and tortured.[93] Many Jews left Jerusalem to seek security in Safed.

And as Ottoman relations with the Western powers deteriorated, local authorities in Jerusalem suspected that Christian monasteries were being used as weapons depots, so that orders were issued to have them searched.[94] As late as the 1820s the Ottoman governor of Damascus, Mustafa Pasha, sent forces to Jerusalem to put down a local rebellion. Around Jerusalem, they plundered churches and monasteries. These vicissitudes in the security and access to religious sites in Jerusalem would make guarantees of religious rights in the Holy City a growing concern of global powers, as well as an issue that would increasingly dominate international diplomacy over Jerusalem's political future.

# PART II

# The Diplomatic Struggle
# over Jerusalem

# Chapter 4

# Jerusalem and the Birth of Modern Israel

Jerusalem was the magnet that pulled the Jewish people back to their ancestral homeland well before the creation of the State of Israel in 1948. The turning point in Jewish immigration to Jerusalem had already come about during the early part of the nineteenth century because of important political shifts inside the Middle East itself. Specifically, the conquest in 1831 of Ottoman Palestine by the forces of the Egyptian leader Muhammad Ali led to a liberalization of local policies toward non-Muslims in Jerusalem, thereby setting the stage for a significant and steady growth of its Jewish population, which had already begun to expand in the previous centuries. It was in this period that permanent foreign consulates began to spring up in Jerusalem—the British consulate was the first to open up in 1838.

The Egyptians' better treatment of non-Muslims emanated from their desire to win the approval and backing of the European powers against the crumbling Ottoman Empire. In this new environment, the Jews of Jerusalem were permitted to repair and rebuild their synagogues.[1] Access to the Western Wall improved. Moreover, natural disasters played a part in the demographic changes in Jerusalem; an earthquake in 1837 in Safed and Tiberias caused many in these Jewish communities to seek refuge in Jerusalem. When the Ottoman Empire took back Jerusalem from the Egyptians in 1840 with European backing, it was not in a position to roll back many of the reforms instituted by the regime of Muhammad Ali.

Thus the demographic growth of the Jewish community of Jerusalem continued. Foreign consulates sometimes gave a more accurate picture of the breakdown of Jerusalem's changing population, since the census taken by the Ottoman Empire had been notoriously inaccurate. Often it did not take into account many of the new immigrants to Jerusalem; non-Muslims who appeared in these Ottoman records would be expected to pay special taxes like the jizya (poll tax), and therefore did not have an interest in being immediately registered.[2] The Jewish immigrants to Jerusalem in this period came from all parts of the world: Yemen, North Africa, Persia, Russia, and the Austro-Hungarian Empire.

New data became available in time. In 1842, a Prussian consulate was established in Jerusalem. It estimated that Jerusalem had a total population of 15,150 in 1845, of which 7,120 were Jews. In 1864, the British consulate reported to London that while the total population of Jerusalem during the previous year had still been about 15,000, there were 8,000 Jews (the British also estimated that there were 4,500 Muslims and 2,500 Christians).[3] This constituted a clear-cut Jewish majority in Jerusalem for the first time since Roman armies under the command of Hadrian had defeated Bar Kochba in the second century. By the beginning of the First World War in 1914, there were 45,000 Jews in Jerusalem out of a total population of 65,000.[4]

These demographic changes served as the backdrop to how the Western powers began to think about the future of Jerusalem as the decay of the Ottoman Empire accelerated during the nineteenth century. European statesmen from Lord Palmerston to Lloyd George became fascinated with the idea of a Jewish national rebirth.[5] After his invasion of Egypt in 1798, it was Napoleon Bonaparte who first issued a call for the Jews of Asia and Africa to join him in reestablishing ancient Jerusalem.[6] The French army moved northward along the coast of Palestine and never reached Jerusalem. But for decades thereafter, as the Ottoman Empire opened up to foreign visitors and the general awareness of the Jewish return to Jerusalem grew, so did the sense that the Jews possessed historical claims to the Holy City.

For example, as noted earlier, the American Methodist minister William Blackstone wrote a petition in 1891 to President Benjamin Harrison and Secretary of State James Blaine calling for restoring Palestine to the Jewish people. He observed that in 1878, under the Treaty of Berlin, the European powers had given Bulgaria to the Bulgarians and Serbia to the Serbs. He argued that the Jews had never given up their title to the land of their ancestors, but were instead "expelled by force." Significantly, Blackstone's petition was backed by the chief justice of the U.S. Supreme Court, Melville Fuller, the Speaker of the House of Representatives, T. B. Reed, members of Congress like William McKinley, who would become president (1897–1901), and many industrial giants, including J. P. Morgan and John D. Rockefeller. The perception of Jewish rights to Palestine had become widespread among the legal and political elites of the United States.[7]

Blackstone's focus on Western diplomacy over Jewish rights in Palestine was consistent with another general trend in that era. European powers were pressing the Ottoman Empire to safeguard religious liberties in Jerusalem and were using their consulates to monitor whether the situation on the ground was changing. In 1852, the Ottoman Empire published an edict, or *firman*, determining the rights and powers of the various churches in five Christian holy places. This arrangement became known as the status quo. It received international recognition in 1856 through the Treaty of Paris and again in 1878 through the Treaty of Berlin.[8] The status of the holy sites of Jerusalem was thus very much on the agenda of international diplomacy in the latter part of the nineteenth century.

# Recognition of Jewish Historical Rights at the League of Nations

During World War I, the Ottomans' alliance with Germany provoked Britain to abandon its decades-long policy of protecting the Ottomans from European encroachments. Instead, British officials struck alliances against the Ottomans with local Arab rulers in the Arabian peninsula as part of a plan for dismembering the Ottoman Empire.[9] The Western allies, after defeating the Ottomans, hoped to redraw the map of the Middle East with new states and national leaders, many of which owed their very existence to the intervention of the British. A key part of this effort was the British promulgation in November 1917 of the Balfour Declaration, which called for creating "a national home for the Jewish people" in Palestine.

The British Army captured Jerusalem in December 1917. Around three years later, the Ottoman Empire officially relinquished its sovereignty in the Treaty of Sèvres over all the former Asiatic provinces it had controlled for four hundred years since 1517. It was significant that this decision was taken before the Ottoman caliphate had been disbanded and the sultan replaced by a secular Turkish government. Though the Treaty of Sèvres was not ratified by the Ottoman Empire, it set into motion the legal basis for the Allied powers to consider who might constitute its successor in Jerusalem and in the former districts of Ottoman Palestine as a whole.

What began in Sèvres in 1920 was completed in 1923 with the Lausanne Treaty, when the newly created Republic of Turkey, which had replaced the Ottoman Empire, affirmed that it "renounces all rights and title whatsoever over or respecting the territories situated outside the frontiers [of Turkey] laid out in the present Treaty."[10] Sensing that a vacuum of sovereignty had been created by the Turkish renunciation, representatives of the Zionist Organization worked intensely to secure international recognition of Jewish claims in Palestine. Specifically, they first and foremost asked the victorious Allied powers to "recognize the historic title of the Jewish people to Palestine and the right of the Jews to reconstitute in Palestine their National Home." They explained that the Jewish people had not left their ancestral homeland by choice, but rather had been driven out through violence. Moreover, they had never ceded their rights over the centuries.

The recognition they sought was indeed achieved with the British Mandate for Palestine; the Mandate document opened with a clause in its preamble that provided the first international recognition of the claims of the Jewish people to their ancestral homeland: "Whereas recognition has thereby been given to the historical connection of the Jewish people with Palestine and to the grounds for reconstituting their national home in that country..."[11] It specifically referred to the Balfour Declaration of the British government from November 1917, which first called for creating "a national home for the Jewish people" in what had been Ottoman Palestine. How the term "national home" was understood at the time was illustrated by the U.S. intelligence recommendations to President Woodrow Wilson at the 1919 Paris Peace Conference: "It will be the policy of the League of Nations to recognize Palestine as a Jewish state as soon as it is a Jewish state in fact. It is right that Palestine should become a Jewish state, if the Jews being given the full opportunity, make it such."[12]

Significantly, the League of Nations Mandate did not create new rights, but rather acknowledged a pre-existing right which, in the view of the international community at the time, had clearly not been forfeited by the Jewish people or suspended by international law after successive empires occupied and ruled Jerusalem and the rest of the area of Palestine in the intervening centuries. Indeed, while the mandate documents for Syria and Iraq called on the French and the British to "to facilitate the progressive development" of these mandates "as independent states," the Palestine mandate related to the need to "secure the establishment of the Jewish national home, as laid out in the preamble."

This had legal significance, for the declarative language about the historic rights of the Jewish people that appeared in the preamble was linked to the binding operative language of the Palestine Mandate. When the Council of the League of Nations confirmed the Mandate in July 1922, it acquired the force of law. Indeed, a member of the Permanent Court of International Justice, the predecessor to the International Court of Justice in the Hague, would comment that the adoption of the Mandate for Palestine by the League of Nations, and in particular its call for creating a Jewish national home, was "an International Legislative Act."[13]

Did the League of Nations Mandate award Jerusalem to the Jewish national home as well? What is clear is that there is nothing in the League of Nations Mandate that could be interpreted as excluding Jerusalem from the Jewish national home. There was no call for internationalizing Jerusalem.[14] Special provisions were written for the holy places. The League of Nations undertook in the Palestine Mandate "the securing of the Holy Places." It committed itself to "the free exercise of worship" in those areas. At the same time, the Palestine Mandate sought to specifically protect Islamic rights by stating, "Nothing in this mandate shall be construed as conferring upon the Mandatory authority to interfere with the fabric or the management of purely Moslem sacred shrines, the immunities of which are guaranteed."

After the adoption of the Mandate for Palestine, Arab critics like the famous Lebanese-born Greek Orthodox publicist George Antonius challenged its legality throughout the interwar period. For example, they argued that the support Britain gave for the creation of a Jewish national home contradicted the wartime commitments that Sir Henry McMahon, the British high commissioner in Egypt, gave to the Sherif Hussein of Mecca in 1915 for the independence of the Arab areas that had been under Ottoman control. These commitments served as the basis of the Great Arab Revolt against the Ottomans that was facilitated by T. E. Lawrence (Lawrence of Arabia).

The British response to this charge was summarized by Winston Churchill in 1922, who as colonial secretary argued that during the negotiations with Hussein, the British had specifically excluded certain territories from the area of Arab independence: what had been the Ottoman district (*vilayet*) of Beirut, covering much of what is today Lebanon and Israel, as well as the main Ottoman district in the area of Palestine—"the Sanjak of Jerusalem."[15]

In the McMahon-Hussein correspondence, the British had sought to remove from the future Arab state those parts of greater Syria that had substantial minority populations: "the portions of Syria lying to the west of the districts of Damascus, Homs, Hama, and Aleppo cannot be said to be purely Arab, and should be excluded from the limits demanded." Hussein tried to change British policy nonetheless. But he confined his response to seeking only the incorporation of the viyalets of Aleppo and

Beirut in the area under his control. He argued that Muslims knew how to treat Christians well based on the precedents set by the second caliph, Umar bin al-Khattab. However, in this effort to get a revision of Britain's commitments, he wrote nothing about the issue of Jerusalem.[16]

It is possible that Hussein's omission of Jerusalem reflected his understanding of the limits of what he could possibly achieve from his British allies. Alternatively, since he had been discussing with British authorities since 1914 the possibility that he would establish a new Arab caliphate to replace the older caliphate of the Ottoman sultan, it might have been expected that he would at least take a public stand for the record on the issue of Jerusalem. Yet it is equally possible that Hussein's failure to emphasize the importance of Arab control of Jerusalem emanated from traditional Islamic priorities.

As the king of the Hijaz region, as he came to be known, he was already in possession of the two most important holy cities of Mecca and Medina. He needed to consolidate his power in Arabia, especially in light of the growing strength of those who might threaten him most directly like the Wahhabi forces of the Saudis who ruled in the neighboring Nejd plateau. For this he needed strong British backing. Whatever was Hussein's ultimate motivation in his dealings with the British, there was a widespread sense among Arab nationalists that he had been doublecrossed.

The question over the precise contents of the McMahon-Hussein correspondence was largely put to rest when McMahon himself broke his silence on this dispute in a letter to the *Times* on July 23, 1937, in which he wrote, "I feel it my duty to state, and I do so emphatically, that it was not intended by me in giving this pledge to King Hussein to include Palestine in the area in which Arab independence was promised. I also had every reason to believe at the time that the fact that Palestine was not included in my pledge was well understood by King Hussein."[17]

This became particularly evident in the diplomatic agenda presented by Hussein's representatives at the 1919 Paris Peace Conference.

Indeed, the Arab delegation to the Paris Peace Conference seemed willing to acquiesce, albeit conditionally, to the Jewish national home. Its leader, Emir Faisal, Hussein's son, who would years later become king of

Iraq, came to Paris also serving as the main spokesman of the Arab national movement. Formally, he led the delegation of the Kingdom of Hijaz, but since it was emerging as the only fully independent Arab state at the time, Faisal hoped to add other Arab regions that had previously been under Ottoman rule to his father's kingdom.[18]

Faisal had just successfully led the Arab Revolt against the Ottoman Empire. His words still carried great weight with Arab nationalist elites. His portrait was displayed at nationalist rallies in Damascus or in Jerusalem. He had a pan-Arab delegation in Paris that included Palestinian Arabs who would later play a leading role in the Palestinian national movement. It also included Nuri al-Said, the future prime minister of Iraq in the 1950s. While later pro-Soviet propaganda would portray the entire Hashemite clan as British lackeys, in 1919 he was fighting for Arab rights against the machinations of the British and the French. When it came to the question of Palestine, Faisal envisioned that as a result of his postwar diplomacy, his father would control a large Arab state over much of the Middle East, and under such conditions, he was supportive of Jewish proposals in Paris: "Our Deputation here in Paris is fully acquainted with the proposals submitted yesterday by the Zionist Organization to the Peace Conference, and we regard them as moderate and proper. We will do our best, so far as we are concerned, to help them through; we will wish the Jews a hearty welcome home."[19]

Faisal concluded a written agreement on January 3, 1919, with the Zionist leader Chaim Weizmann, the future first president of Israel, envisioning two states emerging in the former Ottoman territories: "the Arab state and Palestine." The agreement stated that "all necessary measures shall be taken to encourage and stimulate immigration of Jews into Palestine on a large scale." Britain's secret understandings with France for dividing the Middle East into spheres of influence had in the meantime been disclosed, so that Faisal was seeking Arab-Jewish coordination to forestall any possible betrayal by the European powers of their commitments to both national movements. For this reason, Faisal added a handwritten reservation to this first Arab-Israeli agreement specifying that he would only carry it out if his political agenda for an Arab state was addressed by the Allied powers.

At about the same time, in his formal memorandum to the Paris Peace Conference seeking Arab independence, Faisal purposely left out Palestine, explaining that "the Arabs cannot risk assuming the responsibility of holding level the scales in the clash of races and religions that have in this one province, so often involved the world in difficulties."[20] He voiced no special concerns about Jerusalem. A British Royal Commission observed at the time that "if King Hussein and the Emir Faisal secured their big Arab state, they would concede little Palestine to the Jews."[21]

There was something to this British analysis in one important respect. During this period, the common terms of reference for Arab nationalism and self-determination were very broad and were not based on a local identity in one small region alone. For example, in the aftermath of the Paris Peace Conference, Arab nationalists in Damascus organized a General Syrian Congress in July 1919 that described Palestine as "the southern part of Syria." The resolution of the Congress stated, "we ask that there should be no separation of the southern part of Syria, known as Palestine, nor of the littoral western zone, which includes Lebanon, from the Syrian country."

While critics of the Palestine Mandate charged that it compromised the principle of self-determination, its supporters retorted that it only sought to create a Jewish national home in a very small portion of the territories slated to eventually become independent. The main problem for Emir Faisal and the Syrian Congress was that because of secret British wartime commitments to France, the Arabs were not even going to obtain their "big Arab state." Syria was not going to become independent, but rather it would instead fall under the jurisdiction of another League of Nations Mandate that would be run by the French, who did not want the Hashemites in Damascus. This clearly undermined the basis for any possible Arab-Jewish understanding at a very embryonic stage of the Middle East conflict.

But a more profound debate over the relative merits of the various claimants to sovereignty was also revealed in the immediate postwar years in the arguments employed by international jurists on both sides. If the Arab claim to Palestine, including Jerusalem, was based on a region-wide Arab ethnic nationalism, those defending the Jewish legal claim asked how long had the Arabs as a political body actually been in control of this territory. The various Arab caliphates ruled for a little over four hundred years; from that time onward, Palestine had been ruled by the Seljuq Turks, Crusaders, Kurds (Saladin), and various other Turkish dynasties. Thus Ernst Frankenstein, a German-Jewish jurist who lectured at the Academy of International Law in the Hague, concluded that the Arabs did not have "continuous and undisturbed possession" of Palestine, thereby undercutting their legal claim.

Moreover, he insisted that most of the inhabitants of Palestine were not the descendants of its original indigenous population, but rather many were immigrants themselves. It was true that between the Crusades and the Mongol invasions, large parts of Palestine, and especially Jerusalem, had been depopulated. The total population of Jerusalem in the mid-nineteenth century was about the same as in the mid-sixteenth century—14,000 to 15,000 residents—and that was after it had been reduced even further during the period of the Mamluks. The Arabic-speaking populations had been somewhat replenished in the rest of Palestine by the constant stream of Bedouin and neighboring immigrants from Egypt and Syria in recent centuries, and especially with the rise of the Jewish national home.[22] The issue of Arab immigration into Palestine, which was raised by those advancing the cause for Jewish national rights, may have been controversial with many British authorities but it nonetheless made an impact in 1939 on President Franklin Delano Roosevelt, who concluded, "Arab immigration into Palestine since 1921 has vastly exceeded the total Jewish immigration during the whole period."[23]

Still, after the First World War, there was a local Palestinian Arab leadership in Jerusalem that had served in various religious and municipal capacities since at least the thirteenth century. The leading family in Palestinian Arab politics, the Husseinis, regarded themselves as *ashraf*, meaning they traced themselves back to the family of Muhammad in Arabia. According to one estimate, they came to Palestine in the eighteenth century.[24] According to another estimate, they first arrived in Palestine in the twelfth century, but they only moved to Jerusalem during the fourteenth century.[25] The al-Khatib family in Jerusalem that served the Muslim shrines on the Temple Mount could be traced to the city of Hama, in northern Syria.[26] In contrast, the al-Khalidis were an original Palestinian Arab family of notables.[27] These leading families also served in many of the governing institutions of the Ottoman state. But with the dissolution of the Ottoman Empire, this leadership still felt that it had to rely on the broader Arab world to stake its diplomatic claims.

Thus, with this legal background, the Jewish leadership came to the diplomatic table with two main arguments. While Arab nationalists could not assert their rights to keeping Palestine within a larger Arab Syrian state on the basis of recent history, the Jewish people had an ancestral right that was acknowledged by the supreme body in the international community at the time: they had a right of self-determination. They were the true indigenous population of the country that had been forcibly removed, but their bond with the land had never been severed. In addition, in Jerusalem, at least, the Jews had restored an overwhelming majority even without the help of the British, the Balfour Declaration, and the League of Nations Mandate.

Nevertheless, the issue of self-determination created enormous confusion in diplomatic circles throughout this period. Indeed, Robert Lansing, the U.S. secretary of state at the Paris Peace Conference, asked whether the right of self-determination applied to a territorial area, to a whole community, or to a race. Legal authorities on behalf of the Jewish cause asserted that the principle of self-determination applied to the Jewish people outside Palestine as well as those already residing in Palestine.

The argumentation on behalf of the restoration of the Jewish homeland appeared to have made a dent. Even though the British government was backing away from its initial enthusiastic backing of the return of the Jewish people to Palestine, the Palestine Royal Report that it issued in 1937 made many of the same claims that Jewish jurists had raised: "Palestine was different from other ex-Turkish provinces. It was, indeed, unique both as the Holy Land of the three world-religions and as the old historic homeland of the Jews. The Arabs had lived in it for centuries, but they had long ceased to rule it, and in view of its peculiar character they could not now claim to possess it in the same way as they could claim Syria or 'Iraq.'"[28]

Moreover, the Palestinian Arabs themselves still made their national claims in broader Arab nationalist language. Thus Awni Abdul Hadi, a

Palestinian pan-Arabist leader who was the secretary general of the Arab Higher Committee in British Mandatory Palestine (and Faisal's private secretary at the Paris Peace Conference), appeared before Britain's Peel Commission in 1937 and still stated, "There is no such country [as Palestine]! Palestine is a term the Zionists invented! Our country was for centuries, part of Syria."[29] In any case, President Woodrow Wilson, who was the greatest advocate of self-determination at the close of the First World War, saw no contradiction between the cause of Jewish nationalism and his quest to protect the freedom of the peoples liberated from the Ottoman Empire. Indeed, he would emerge as a strong supporter of Zionism and the reestablishment of the Jewish national home.

How did the debate over the legality of the British Mandate affect the issue of Jerusalem? Some observers have argued that since the mainstream Zionist movement was essentially secular, it only had a minimal interest in Jerusalem.[30] Instead, they insisted, the Zionist Organization preferred rural land development in the Galilee and the formation of agricultural communities like kibbutzim. But the assumption that the Jews had lost interest in Jerusalem during this period was simply false. The Jewish Agency, which from the 1920s onward served as the quasi-government of the Jewish community of Palestine, located its headquarters in Jerusalem; the decision to put the Jewish Agency in Jerusalem even had international recognition, since it was proposed by the League of Nations itself in September 1922. In fact, the name for the entire movement to restore the Jewish people to their land was "Zionism," which was extracted from the Jewish longing for "Zion"—the biblical name that was synonymous for Jerusalem.

And when the British first considered partitioning Palestine in 1937 with the Peel Commission Report, which proposed to remove Jerusalem from the Jewish state, the Jewish leadership rejected the idea out of hand, declaring that "Jewish Palestine without Jerusalem would be a body without a soul."[31] True, Chaim Weizmann, then serving as president of the Zionist Organization, and David Ben-Gurion, the chairman of its executive, accepted the idea of partition in principle, but they still sought to revise the proposed borders and to increase the total area slated for Jewish sovereignty.[32]

# The United Nations Tries to Internationalize Jerusalem and Fails

The Second World War revolutionized the international political constellation facing the leadership of the Jewish Agency in Palestine, but not the legal rights that had already been established for its rebuilding of the Jewish homeland. It also did not alter its legal rights in Jerusalem. True, the League of Nations was formally liquidated in April 1946. But the new United Nations that replaced it had been established during the previous year. Its charter was drafted with an awareness that the UN would serve as an improved successor organization to the League of Nations.

For example, Article 80 of the UN Charter protected any existing rights of states and of "any peoples or the terms of existing international instruments [i.e. the Mandate for Palestine] to which Members of the United Nations may respectively be parties." This article became known as "the Palestine clause" because it was drafted in response to Jewish legal representations at the UN's founding conference in San Francisco. It essentially preserved the rights of the Jewish people to their homeland that had been formally acknowledged for the first time by the League of Nations Mandate.[33]

The revelations of the murder of six million Jews by the Nazis unquestionably made the argument for Jewish statehood even more compelling. Simultaneously, the war had seriously weakened its original sponsor, Great Britain, which had already retreated from its commitments to support the creation of a new Jewish homeland when it seriously curtailed Jewish immigration to Palestine on the eve of the Second World War. In April 1947, the British government decided to refer the issue of Palestine to the UN General Assembly instead of the Security Council, acutely aware that it could only receive political recommendations from the former body, which would still leave it with considerable leeway in the future. The UN General Assembly then established a special commission called UNSCOP whose majority proposal recommended the partition of Palestine into Jewish and Arab states that were to be tied together by an economic union.

Significantly, the UN Partition Plan did not assign Jerusalem to either the Arabs or the Jews, but rather envisioned the creation of a special international entity that it called a *Corpus Separatum*. In short, the UN was proposing the internationalization of Jerusalem and its placement under UN administration. This part of the Partition Plan posed a tough dilemma for the Jewish Agency; after all, the League of Nations did not strip the Jewish homeland that it envisioned of Jerusalem. Moreover, Jerusalem had a strong Jewish majority: there were 99,320 Jews and 65,000 Arabs (40,000 Muslims and 25,000 Christian Arabs).[34]

The Jewish authorities concluded that it was better to have a Jewish state with UN approval, without Jerusalem for now, than not to have any Jewish state at all.[35] But in accepting the Partition Plan proposal, Dr. Abba Hillel Silver, speaking on behalf of the Jewish Agency, still urged the inclusion of the Jewish section of Jerusalem in the Jewish state. He added that the Jewish state would reserve the right to seek territorial modifications, apparently in reference to the area of Jerusalem.[36] This was not a far-fetched line of policy since there was an important caveat in the UN plan that made it bearable for the Jewish side: the internationalization of Jerusalem was essentially an interim measure that the UN was suggesting for ten years. At the end of the period, the residents of Jerusalem would be "free to express by means of a referendum their wishes as to possible modifications of the regime of the City." Thus, the Jewish Agency was not forced to surrender Jerusalem after 2,000 years of Jewish yearning. Given the Jewish majority that existed, it essentially only had to put off Jerusalem's incorporation into the Jewish state to a later period.

True, the *Corpus Separatum* covered an area that went beyond Jerusalem's municipal borders. It included Arab towns like Bethlehem and many other villages, giving the two populations approximate demographic parity. Nonetheless, even within this wider area, a future Jewish majority could be assured with immigration; a six-nation UN working group on internationalization left open the possibility of future Jewish immigrants coming into Jerusalem under the UN regime.[37] In any case, much of this was highly theoretical; the Jewish Agency formally notified the UN that it accepted the UN Partition Plan on October 2, 1947. The Palestinian Arabs, represented by the Arab Higher Committee, had already rejected the Partition Plan in a formal statement to the UN on September 29,

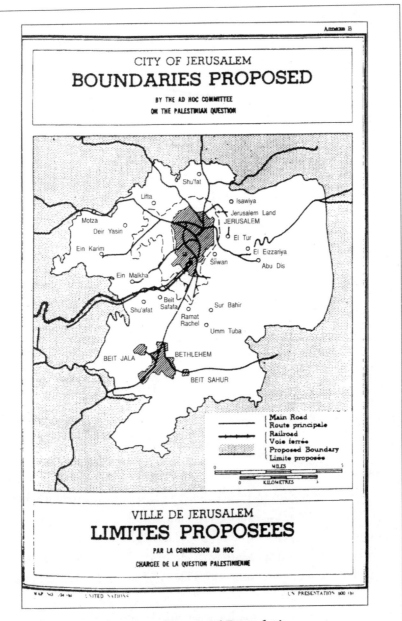

Jerusalem: Proposed Boundaries,
According to UN General Assembly Resolution 181,
Corpus Separatum

1947. Without Arab acceptance of the UN proposals, it was doubtful that the detailed territorial components of the Partition Plan would ultimately be implemented on the ground.

Nonetheless, on November 29, 1947, the UN General Assembly approved the Partition Plan by adopting Resolution 181 by a two-thirds majority. The U.S. and the Soviet Union backed partition, while Britain abstained. The Jewish Agency lent its support to the plan, but the representatives of the Palestinian Arabs and the Arab League firmly opposed the UN action and even rejected its authority to involve itself in the entire matter. The UN took upon itself certain commitments with respect to Jerusalem as a result of the passage of Resolution 181. It pledged "to ensure that peace and order reign in Jerusalem" and that it would "promote the security, well-being and any constructive measures of development for the residents." It empowered the newly created UN Trusteeship Council to draft and approve a detailed statute for UN administration of the Holy City. This was a necessary legal step for the UN to assume the responsibilities of the British Mandate after its termination.

But no Jerusalem statute was adopted. On May 14, 1948, the UN General Assembly convened in special session to determine whether to assume formal responsibility for Jerusalem as the Partition Plan had proposed. The UN determined that it would have to take action before the Mandate expired on May 15. But the UN failed to adopt any proposal giving it legal responsibility for Jerusalem that would enable it to become the effective successor to the British Mandate as the General Assembly had envisioned. Essentially, by its inaction, the UN created a vacuum that the Arab states could argue they were seeking to fill. Certainly there was no UN umbrella over Jerusalem that would have given the Arab states pause before sending their troops into what might be seen as UN territory. This made a full-scale invasion of British Palestine, and of Jerusalem in particular, almost inevitable.

Unsurprisingly then, the Egyptian government officially notified the UN Security Council on May 15, 1948, of the following declaration: "now that the British Mandate in Palestine has ended...Egyptian armed forces have started to enter Palestine." Their purported purpose was "to establish security and order in place of chaos and disorder." King Abdullah of Transjordan cabled the UN secretary-general with a similar announcement the next day.

By invading Palestine after the formal termination of the British Mandate and the declaration of independence of Israel on May 15, 1948, the Arab states were essentially seeking to overturn violently a resolution that had been overwhelmingly adopted by the UN, including its provisions for the internationalization of Jerusalem. There was little doubt at the time about who was to blame for the war. Trygve Lie, the UN secretary-general, flatly stated, "The invasion of Palestine by the Arab states was the first armed aggression which the world has seen since the world war."[38]

Jerusalem was immediately attacked from all sides. Arab irregulars overran its northern suburbs of Neve Yaakov and Atarot. Iraqi troops were positioned near the suburb of Talpiot. On May 19, King Abdullah's Arab Legion, commanded by British officers, reached Jerusalem; its tanks reached just north of the Old City's walls and unleashed an immense artillery barrage.[39] The Arab Legion was soon joined in the Old City by Egyptian volunteers from the Muslim Brotherhood, the militant Islamic fundamentalist organization that had been founded in 1928 and would give birth to many jihadist organizations several decades later.

In the meantime, regular Egyptian forces attacking from the south had occupied Kibbutz Ramat Rachel.[40] The Egyptians also took up positions at Mar Elias Monastery on the outskirts of Bethlehem, from where they pounded Jerusalem with artillery shells that reached the area of the Old City's Jaffa Gate.[41] The security situation in Jerusalem was rapidly deteriorating for its Jewish residents, who had already been under siege for months and lacked regular supplies of food and water.

Who would protect the nearly 100,000 Jewish residents in Jerusalem who found themselves completely surrounded? Would the UN send forces to protect the international zone it had pronounced in 1947 but failed to create during the following year? On April 1, 1948, the future foreign minister of Israel, Moshe Sharett, appeared before the UN Security Council and requested the provision of armed forces to halt the deterioration in Jerusalem. The British were preparing to leave and not providing any security. Chaim Herzog, who would later become president of Israel, served at the time as a liaison officer between the pre-state Haganah and the British; he warned Sharett in a March 1948 cable that the Jewish community in Jerusalem was facing "total annihilation unless [an] international force [was] dispatched."[42] Sharett gave an ominous description of what was happening in Jerusalem and to its holy sites that should have elicited some UN response:

> As the Mandate now draws to an end, instead of coming under an international regime which would maintain the civilized standards of its government, Jerusalem seems about to fall, as most of its holy places have already fallen, into the clutches of the most fanatical and impious elements in the country... Sheikh Yasin Bakri, has boasted in public of his prowess in sniping at Jewish funeral parties on the way to the hallowed cemetery on the Mount of Olives. He has been photographed by Cairo newspapers in the act of directing fire from the walls of the Haram enclosure [the Temple Mount], the so-called Mosque of Omar. When we see other photographs of this person, photographs which have been submitted to the Security Council, receiving courtesy visits from the British Area Commander of Jerusalem, we are forced to assume that he is considered in some quarters as a suitable custodian of the holy sites. He has proclaimed another success: for the first time since Roman days, Jewish worshipers are now forcibly prevented from having access to the Wailing Wall, the greatest sanctuary of the Jewish faith.[43]

Months later he protested to the UN that "the shelling of Jerusalem from outside by foreign armies is proceeding with unabated fury, and ancient Jewish synagogues in the Walled City are being destroyed one after the other as a result of Arab artillery fire."[44] And the UN's own subsequent report on Jerusalem verified many of these charges: "Many religious buildings, however, are located in areas where heavy fighting has occurred, and some of them have been destroyed." The report stated that "the Church of the Holy Sepulchre has been hit once, with no appreciable damage. The Church of Dormition in the Old City has been severely hit, but its walls are still standing." Even the Dome of the Rock on the Temple Mount had suffered shelling.[45] The UN did not assign blame for these attacks, but it was clear that most of the heavy firepower—including artillery and tanks—in the Jerusalem area was possessed by the invading Arab armies. The UN Security Council was not moved to offer protection to the holy sites. No international forces were dispatched. The growing risks to Jerusalem's population also did not alter UN behavior. David Ben-Gurion, who would become Israel's first prime minister, remarked in April 1948, "The Jews of the Old City of Jerusalem have been under siege for several months. Jewish Jerusalem as a whole is almost completely cut off from the rest of the country and under constant threat of starvation."

Since the end of 1947, Jerusalem's lifeline to the coast along the road to Tel Aviv had come under increasing attacks by Palestinian Arab irregulars. The road from the ports of British Palestine along the coastal plane to Jerusalem went through a narrow gorge and was hence extremely vulnerable to sniper fire from surrounding hills. Supply vehicles were moving only in convoys. By May 12, 1948, Arab forces had shut off the pumping stations that supplied water to Jerusalem's population.

The only military action undertaken to lift the siege of Jerusalem was by the Jewish underground forces, for no UN troops were ever sent to intervene. Already in April 1948, in the first major offensive action ordered by the Jewish Agency leadership, Operation Nachshon was launched to clear the Jerusalem corridor and open up access to the Holy City. The Palmach, the elite Jewish strike force, took the initiative and seized the Kastel, a strategic position held by Arab irregulars that overlooked the last stretch of the Jerusalem–Tel Aviv road. To open the rest of the Jerusalem corridor, the Harel brigade of the Palmach was established under the command of Yitzhak Rabin, the future prime minister of Israel. The UN was completely irrelevant.

Attacks and counter-attacks intensified with no UN intervention as civilian casualties mounted. There were Palestinian Arab losses like at Deir Yassin, where an armed assault by Jewish underground movements led to roughly two hundred dead. There were also attacks on Jewish convoys inside Jerusalem, like the ambush and murder of eighty Jewish doctors and medical staff on the way to Hadassah Hospital on Mt. Scopus. There was still a British military post fewer than two hundred yards away from the massacre of the doctors, but the soldiers did not intervene. And the UN was unmoved; it maintained a hands-off policy.

Ultimately, security would only be assured for Jerusalem after May 15, 1948, by the newly created Israel Defense Forces, which broke the siege and fought to protect its encircled Jewish-populated areas from external attack. There were limits, however, to what the new Israeli army could accomplish. On May 28, 1948, the Jewish Quarter of the Old City surrendered to the Arab Legion. Its remaining Jewish population was evicted. The Old City's synagogues like the Hurva, which was first built in 1705, were burnt down.[46] Nor was the thirteenth-century synagogue of Nachmadides spared. A total of fifty-eight synagogues and study halls were ultimately demolished or desecrated.

What did this succession of events mean for the international legal status of Jerusalem, especially in light of the UN's abdication of its responsibility to its residents? At the end of the First Arab-Israeli War, Prime Minister David Ben-Gurion addressed the newly formed Israeli parliament, the Knesset, on December 5, 1949. With the stabilization of Arab-Israeli frontiers through a series of armistice agreements, the UN was again considering internationalization based on its General Assembly resolution from 1947—Resolution 181. Ben-Gurion reminded the UN of its failure to protect Jerusalem:

> We are not setting ourselves up as judges of the United Nations, which did not lift a finger when other States, members of the United Nations, openly made war on the decision adopted by the General Assembly on 29 November 1947, and tried by armed force to prevent the establishment of the State of Israel, to blot out Jews living in the Holy Land and to destroy Jerusalem, the Holy City. But for our successful stand against the aggressors acting in defiance of the United Nations, Jewish Jerusalem would have been wiped off the face of the earth. The whole Jewish population would have been annihilated and the State of Israel would have never arisen.

Ben-Gurion did not want to reject Resolution 181. The Partition Plan's recognition of the Jewish right to statehood was an important achievement for Israel; it even appeared in Israel's Declaration of Independence. Nonetheless, he was prepared to renounce formally the idea of internationalization that had failed the residents of Jerusalem so miserably. Thus, Ben-Gurion announced, "We cannot today regard the decision of 29 November 1947 as being possessed of any further moral force since the United Nations did not succeed in implementing its own decisions. In our view, the decision of 29 November about Jerusalem is null and void."[47]

He declared instead that "Jerusalem is an organic and inseparable part of the State of Israel and is an inseparable part of the history and religion of Israel and of the soul of the people." He warned the UN that the new State of Israel was not going to give up whatever parts of Jerusalem it controlled: "The people which faithfully honored for 2,500 years the oath sworn by the Rivers of Babylon not to forget Jerusalem—this people will never reconcile itself with separation from Jerusalem."[48]

Within a week, however, the General Assembly voted to restate its commitment to the internationalization of Jerusalem. Supporting this measure was an odd coalition of Communist, Islamic, and Latin American countries. The U.S., Canada, and Britain voted against. Ben-Gurion responded on December 13, 1949. He understood that the world's concern with Jerusalem principally emanated from a concern over the fate of its holy sites. So in the early part of his address, he reiterated, "We respect and shall continue to respect the wishes of all those States which are concerned for freedom of worship and free access to the Holy Places, and which to safeguard existing rights in the Holy Places and religious edifices in Jerusalem." But he made clear that Israel would not agree to Jerusalem being separated from the Jewish state, declaring that he was moving the Knesset from Tel Aviv to Jerusalem: "for the State of Israel there has always been and always will be one capital only—Jerusalem the Eternal."[49]

On what basis could Israel assert its sovereignty in Jerusalem? Clearly the UN Partition Plan did not supersede or replace the rights of the Jewish people that were recognized by the League of Nations in the Mandate and preserved by the UN Charter through Article 80. Moreover, the Mandate for Palestine had been a binding legal document—an international treaty—

while the UN General Assembly proposals were only a non-binding recommendation that had been rejected outright by one side.[50] By definition, UN General Assembly resolutions were only recommendations, in any case. Of course, had the Partition Plan been accepted by both parties, it could have become an internationally binding agreement, but that had not occurred.

Moreover, the Partition Plan's division of Palestine was drawn under the assumption that the two states it envisioned, along with the international regime for Jerusalem, would be cooperating peacefully. But with the categorical rejection of the plan by the Arab side and its use of force to prevent its implementation, the borders and other detailed elements of partition that the UN was proposing could not have any legal standing.

For example, the proposed economic union between the Jewish and Arab states was a dead letter in light of the war and the hostile relations between the parties that ensued. Whatever positive value such economic cooperation might have offered, political realities on the ground rendered it unworkable. Similarly, the UN proposal for the internationalization of Jerusalem proved impracticable. Changed circumstances had arisen. This provided yet another reason why it never became a legally binding obligation for the new State of Israel or any UN member states. In short, according to legal scholars, the lines of the Partition Plan had been overtaken by events on the ground.[51]

Israel had suffered heavy losses in the war. Six thousand Israelis had been killed, which amounted to 1 percent of the new state's entire population.[52] A quarter of those losses, or close to 1,500 Israelis, died in the war over Jerusalem alone.[53] This was significant, for a thesis advanced among Israel's critics has long argued that Jerusalem was not particularly important for the Zionist movement.

The history of the First Arab-Israeli War proved the exact opposite. One of the more subtle illustrations of the importance of Jerusalem was the intense effort Israel made to take the fortress of Latrun that was held by the Arab Legion. Situated along the road connecting Tel Aviv to Jerusalem, Latrun was a key strategic position near the entrance to the hills leading up to the Holy City. Ben-Gurion ordered four separate attacks on Latrun, prioritizing it despite the critical situation along other fronts.

While the Israel Defense Forces failed to dislodge the Arab Legion, it nonetheless prevented those forces from reinforcing the Arab armies in Jerusalem itself, thus helping to avert the fall of the rest of the city.

In 1949, at the end of the First Arab-Israeli War, Israel reached a series of armistice agreements with all the Arab states along its borders (no such agreements were reached with Iraq, Saudi Arabia, and Yemen, each of which also had sent troops). After Israel signed an armistice agreement with Jordan (formerly Transjordan) on April 3, 1949, that left the Old City and its holy sites on the other side of the newly created boundary, had Israel agreed to give up the core of Jerusalem?

During the negotiations over the armistice agreement, it was the Jordanian side that insisted on putting into the document Article II/2, which stated that the agreed-upon boundaries were only military lines and not final political borders: "It is also recognized that no provision of this Agreement shall in any way prejudice the rights, claims and positions of either Party hereto in the ultimate peaceful settlement of the Palestine question, the provisions of this Agreement being dictated exclusively by military considerations." The Jordanians apparently wanted to preserve their territorial claims to lands that were inside of Israel. By doing so, they in effect also kept open Israeli claims to territories that were lost as a result of war and might be the subject of future negotiations.

The first test of these principles occurred in April 1950, when the Jordanian parliament declared that it approved "the complete unity between the two banks of the Jordan, the Eastern and Western, and their amalgamation in one single state." Jordan had annexed the territories that it militarily controlled after its 1948 invasion: the West Bank and eastern Jerusalem. The British government recognized the Jordanian annexation, though it did not extend that recognition to Jordanian-controlled Jerusalem. On May 3, 1950, Israeli foreign minister Sharett formally rejected the Jordanian move in an address to the Knesset, referring to his government's formal statement:

> The decision to annex the Arab areas west of the River Jordan to the Hashemite Kingdom of Jordan is a unilateral step to which Israel is

not a party in any way. We are connected with the Hashemite Kingdom of Jordan through the Armistice Agreement, which we will
uphold rigorously. This agreement does not include any final political settlement, however, and no such settlement is possible without
negotiations and a peace treaty between the sides. It must be evident,
therefore, that the question of the status of the Arab areas west of the
River Jordan remains open as far as we are concerned.[54]

During the parliamentary debate, he went into considerably more
detail on the issue of Jerusalem. Responding to the accusation that Ben-
Gurion's government had abandoned Israel's rights to Jerusalem's holy
places, he declared, "We have never abandoned them, and we have said as
much, and no side doubts that we adhere to our claim to our share and our
rights in the Old City of Jerusalem."[55]

Indeed, during Israeli-Jordanian negotiations a year earlier, the idea
of a Jewish return to the Jewish Quarter was seriously discussed.[56] No
agreement of this sort was reached, but it was clear from both public statements and private contacts that Israel sought to preserve its rights in
Jerusalem even though it had lost the Old City in 1948. In sum, Israel was
not going to initiate any wars of conquest to take these territories from
Jordan, but it was also registering that it had not acquiesced to the loss of
any part of these lands, particularly without completing peace negotiations
first.

Clearly, Israel sought to retain whatever it could in Jerusalem, but it
understood that it would have to take upon itself international commitments in so doing. In fact, upon rejecting the UN's internationalization
proposals, Ben-Gurion had stressed that Israel, as a newly born state, had
obligated itself to protect religious freedom and to safeguard the holy sites
of all religions. He explained that this commitment was contained in
Israel's Declaration of Independence.

The armistice agreements had an added significance in Israel's struggle against the internationalization of Jerusalem: the agreements did not
mention UN General Assembly Resolution 181 or its proposal for a *Corpus Separatum* in Jerusalem. And when the UN Security Council convened

on August 11, 1949, to endorse all the armistice agreements with the adoption of Resolution 73, it confirmed the prioritization that postwar diplomacy was giving to these bilateral arrangements, for the Security Council also made no reference to Resolution 181.

Against the non-binding proposal of the UN General Assembly there were now binding bilateral treaties between Israel and each of its neighbors; from the standpoint of international law, there was no question that these agreements had far greater legal weight than the UN's failed internationalization plan, which had clearly been overtaken by the events of 1948–49. Nonetheless, the UN General Assembly still sought ways to implement an international regime for Jerusalem until at least 1952, despite the UN's total failure in protecting Jerusalem during wartime.

Israel strongly opposed these efforts. The Jordanians also had little interest in seeing the UN establish any authority in those sectors of Jerusalem under its own control. By 1953, the U.S. was backing off from internationalization, but the idea would constantly return for discussion within some foreign policy circles. The struggle against internationalization had involved a challenging question for the international community: who would better protect the holy places—the UN or the new State of Israel? After the First Arab-Israeli War, the answer was no longer in doubt. Only a free and democratic state could uphold religious freedom and protect Jerusalem. But it would still take decades for this to be recognized.

# Chapter 5

# Jerusalem, the Palestinian Arabs, and the Hashemite Kingdom of Jordan

The Palestinian Arabs based their political struggle against Britain's Palestine Mandate on the supposition that they were unfairly denied the right of self-determination that they deserved as the "descendants of the indigenous inhabitants of the country."[1] Moreover, in their view, the Jewish claim to the land was "based upon a historical connection which ceased effectively centuries ago."[2] They also argued that Great Britain's wartime pledges to Sharif Hussein of Mecca to support Arab independence across the Middle East superseded the subsequent commitments the British gave in 1917 to the Jewish people for a Jewish homeland in Palestine. Their earliest priority after the First World War was to stop the surging Jewish immigration into Palestine.[3]

Jerusalem was not the initial focus of the Palestinian Arabs' political struggle against the British Mandate. But it quickly became a rallying point principally due to the efforts of the man who would become the mufti of Jerusalem, Hajj Amin al-Husseini, who one Palestinian historian would call "the undisputed leader of the country's Arabs."[4] However, Jerusalem, with its Jewish majority, was not an ideal center for the Arab struggle. Other cities in British Mandatory Palestine could have taken a leading position in an anti-British revolt, including Jaffa, which had a larger Arab population, Haifa, or even smaller towns like Nablus. But Jerusalem had features that none of the other towns possessed—the most important Islamic holy sites after Mecca and Medina.

## The Era of Hajj Amin al-Husseini: Using Jerusalem as a Political Weapon

Some of the earliest demonstrations in which Hajj Amin al-Husseini participated chiefly protested the way the victors of World War I had cut off Palestine from Syria. On March 8, 1920, Husseini was involved in a protest organized on the day that Faisal, the son of Sharif Hussein of Mecca, was briefly proclaimed king of Syria. A month later he spoke during the Nabi Musa celebrations and at a procession on Jerusalem's Jaffa Road. Husseini held up a portrait of Faisal, shouting to the crowd, "This is your king."[5]

What began as a demonstration for preserving a united Syria deteriorated into a full-scale riot that left nine dead and more than 200 wounded.[6] In the aftermath of the violence, the British authorities amnestied Husseini and even appointed him as grand mufti of Jerusalem, hoping to co-opt him to work with the Mandatory government. In the meantime, the French invaded Syria and expelled Faisal, whom the British made king of Iraq.

Nonetheless, the Palestinian Arabs still hoped for union with Syria. When Winston Churchill, as secretary of state for colonial affairs, visited Jerusalem in 1921, a delegation from the Haifa Congress of Palestinian Arabs warned him against any "unnatural partitioning" of their lands. They advocated that the British adopt a five-point plan that included the abolition of the commitment to a Jewish "national home," a halt to Jewish immigration, and an end to the separation of Palestine "from her sister states."[7]

The British decision to appoint Hajj Amin al-Husseini as grand mufti in 1921 helped politicize the issue of Jerusalem and make it into much more of a focal point in the early years of the conflict, especially as the idea of unifying Palestine with Syria became increasingly unrealistic. He was not a religious scholar, lacking sufficient religious training to earn the title of Sheikh.[8] Nonetheless, toward the end of the year he was appointed president of the newly created Supreme Muslim Council, which gave him control over religious properties, appointments to religious courts, and budgets. He would use both these positions to revive the importance of Jerusalem among the Palestinian Arabs and in the wider Muslim world.

For example, the front of the al-Aqsa Mosque in the early twentieth century had become dilapidated. The mosque's structural stability, along with that of the Dome of the Rock, was in question. In 1923 and 1924, Husseini dispatched missions to India, Iraq, and Arabia in order to raise money for the restoration of al-Aqsa and for gold plating for the Dome of the Rock, thus spreading awareness of the rising tensions in the city. But his main opportunity to exploit the Jerusalem issue came in September 1928, when religious Jews preparing for prayers at the Western Wall on Yom Kippur put up a screen to separate the men's prayer area from that of the women. They bought mats and what the Muslims claimed was a larger ark than usual for their Torah scrolls.

There were two ways to interpret these actions; either the Jewish worshipers were challenging the status quo at the Wall in order to seize control over the area, or these small ritual changes were simply ceremonial acts that had been conducted in the past without dispute in accordance with quiet oral understandings with the local residents. Husseini decided on the severest possible interpretation of the whole affair, stating before the Supreme Muslim Council, "The Jews' aim is to take possession of the Mosque of al-Aksa [sic] gradually."[9]

In order to inflame Muslim opinion, Arab nationalists circulated doctored photographs of a Jewish flag with the Star of David flying over the Dome of the Rock. To make matters worse, Husseini instigated a move to change the paved area in front of the Western Wall, which was transformed from a cul-de-sac into an open thoroughfare. As a result, local Arab residents began walking through a revered Jewish area of prayer, sometimes even accompanied by donkeys. The combustible situation ultimately exploded, with mass rioting that spread across British Mandatory Palestine leaving 113 Jews and 116 Arabs dead and hundreds more wounded. The 1929 riots had proven that Jerusalem was an ideal fuse for igniting a wider conflict in Palestine.

Indeed the Palestinian Arab leadership at the time popularized the charge that: "the Jews' aim is to take possession of the Mosque of Al-Aqsa gradually on the pretense that it is the Temple, by starting with the Western Wall of this place, which is an inseparable part of the Mosque of Al-Aqsa." In fact, the heart of the Palestinian Arab argument at the time was that the Western Wall was also a Muslim holy site. According to Muslim traditions, it was where Muhammad tied his winged horse-like beast, al-Buraq, on whom he had miraculously flown from Mecca to Jerusalem before ascending to the heavens from the Temple Mount. In fact, Muslims called the area of the Western Wall *al-Buraq al-Sharif* (the Noble Buraq).

Husseini took his campaign abroad. In many parts of the Muslim world, word spread that Jews were "desecrating the Mosque of Omar"—a reference to the Dome of the Rock—even though the unrest of 1929 clearly only related to the Western Wall. He made himself president of a new General Moslem Conference. It created a "Society for the Protection of the Moslem Holy Places" which, in addition to the recently created "Committee for the Defense of the *Buraq-el-Sharif*," could be used to mobilize Palestinian Arabs to action. The General Moslem Conference passed resolutions opposing any action that advanced "the establishment of any right to the Jews in the Holy Barak area."[10]

Jewish observers at the time wondered whether all this activity emanated from sincere religious concerns or was motivated by purely political considerations. They questioned the holiness of the Western Wall to Muslims, wondering why, if this was true, Muslim authorities would help create a new thoroughfare in front of the Wall that donkeys would regularly soil with their dung.[11]

Muslim scholars in the past had disputed the exact location where al-Buraq was tied. Some identified this location with the Eastern Wall near the Golden Gate, while other scholars cited the Southern Wall of the Temple Mount. This last thesis became the orthodox view in the late seventeenth century.[12] Apparently the notion that al-Buraq was tied to the Western Wall emerged in the nineteenth century, possibly in response to the growing Jewish interest in acquiring rights around the Wall.[13] In the meantime, Jerusalem's Muslim community viewed the Western Wall as *waqf* property—land given centuries earlier as a trust to the Islamic state. Most waqf donations were made in perpetuity, although legal devices were invented during the Abbasid caliphate and in modern times to void waqf control of properties.[14]

The British tried to use their own good offices to settle the controversy over the Western Wall. In 1930 Husseini held an illuminating discussion on this topic with the British high commissioner in Palestine, Sir John Chancellor, that exposed many of the Jerusalem mufti's political considerations and especially his diplomatic strategy. Chancellor told Husseini that he essentially had two choices with regard to Jewish-Arab disputes over the Western Wall: either the Arabs could help formulate a compromise, or an international commission could impose a solution that would certainly be more favorable to the Jews than to the Arabs.[15]

From a European diplomatic perspective, Husseini should have accepted the first option. Husseini, however, preferred the second option, explaining that he would take the imposed solution over the negotiated agreement, which no matter how favorable to the Arabs would still somehow offend his "convictions."[16] In other words, if a diplomatic solution provided a better result for the Palestinian Arabs but still entailed the slightest concession, it was better to forgo such an arrangement, even if that created a far worse outcome for the Arab side.

The International Commission for the Wailing Wall, also known as the Shaw Commission, was appointed by the British with League of Nations approval. It still indicated that it preferred a voluntary solution to the controversy, but it ultimately drafted a decision formally confirming Jewish rights of access to the Western Wall. But, backing the British, it also accepted a highly restrictive interpretation of what these rights entailed. For example, the commission ruled that Jews could not bring benches or chairs to the Wall area, and an ark containing Torah scrolls could only be brought on special holidays. This reflected the commission's understanding of the status quo under the Ottoman Empire. But it also exposed an inherent contradiction in the terms of the British Mandate; on the one hand, the British undertook the "securing of free access to the Holy Places" and the "free exercise of all forms of worship," but on the other hand, they felt bound to maintain the previous status quo, even if it was discriminatory and conflicted with their commitment to religious freedom.

The commission did not contest the Muslim claim to ownership over the Wall and the pavement in front of it, but it utterly rejected the notion that al-Buraq was tethered in the area where the Jews prayed, suggesting that this location was further south. Hence it concluded, "Under these circumstances the Commission does not consider that the Pavement in front of the Wall can be regarded as a sacred place from a Moslem point of view."[17] It traced the Jewish use of the site for prayer back to the fourth century CE, adding for further corroboration the accounts of the Jewish traveler Benjamin of Tudela from 1167, written before the area was declared waqf property.[18] These results were totally unacceptable to the mufti and the Supreme Muslim Council, who now rejected the legal competence of any international body except a Shariah court to settle questions about Muslim holy sites.[19]

The commission report clearly failed to advance the mufti's agenda. Husseini then sought to further internationalize his struggle. The Supreme Muslim Council authorized him to invite Arab and Muslim leaders to a World Islamic Conference in Jerusalem slated for December 1931. When the conference opened the attendance initially looked impressive—about 130 delegates from twenty-two countries.[20] Important states were absent, though. Turkey did not attend and even sought to subvert the conference, concerned that it would become a forum for restoring the caliphate and undermining the secular regime of Ataturk. The Saudi leader, King Abdul Aziz ibn Saud, diplomatically explained that the invitation to the Jerusalem conference had arrived too late. In all likelihood a Saudi decision had been taken to boycott the whole event.[21] Their approach was colored by their experience in organizing the Congress of the Islamic World in Mecca back in 1926. That conference had ended acrimoniously, with its resolution to meet annually in Mecca coming to naught. Five years later, Ibn Saud was not going to lend his weight to a Jerusalem conference that might succeed where the Mecca conference had failed.

Clearly, Husseini had not convinced international Muslim leaders that Jews were threatening Islamic holy sites. In fact, the purpose of the whole event was not entirely clear. Husseini had stressed to invitees that the conference would deal with the Buraq al-Sharif. In his public call to the conference, however, Shawkat Ali said nothing about the Buraq al-Sharif, but rather spoke more generally about how Muslims might defend their civilization.[22]

Husseini's conference was convened on December 6, 1931, which corresponded on the Islamic calendar to the day that Muhammad ascended to the heavens from the Temple Mount. At the opening of the conference, Husseini's supporters resorted to their tried and true tactic of disseminating doctored photos, this time showing Jews with machine guns attacking the Dome of the Rock.[23] The use of this transparent propaganda alienated many delegates, who held a protest meeting at the King David Hotel presided over by Husseini's Palestinian rival, Ragheb Bey al-Nashashibi, the Jerusalem mayor.

Husseini's congress sought to establish a permanent body that would convene every two years. The executive committee of the congress was headed by Husseini, thus giving him a pan-Islamic title and platform for the first time. The congress also announced the need to establish an Islamic university in Jerusalem, which apparently was not looked on favorably by the religious leadership at al-Azhar in Egypt. Adopting a resolution proclaiming the sanctity of the Buraq al-Sharif,[24] the congress rejected the report of the "Wailing Wall Commission." Finally, it formally decided to deny Jews access to the al-Aqsa Mosque, despite the fact that Jews had their own religious reasons for staying away from the Temple Mount.

Notably, during these disputes over the Western Wall Husseini did not adopt the tactic later embraced by Yasser Arafat of denying in total the religious history of the Jews. For example, the Supreme Muslim Council, which Husseini had headed since 1921, published an English-language book in 1924 for visitors to the Temple Mount area titled *A Brief Guide to al-Haram al-Sharif Jerusalem*. The book's historical sketch of the site related that "the site is one of the oldest in the world. Its sanctity dates from the earliest (perhaps from pre-historic) times. Its identity with the site of Solomon's Temple is beyond dispute." The 1930 edition remained unchanged despite the 1929 Western Wall riots. The Supreme Muslim

Council did not engage in Temple Denial, as Arafat's generation would decades later.

Beginning in 1936, Jerusalem's position in Palestinian politics was greatly affected by what became known as the Arab Revolt, although the revolt did not initially break out in Jerusalem. Husseini and the Arab Higher Committee—another new body under his leadership—declared a nationwide strike. In July 1937, the British finally cracked down on the mufti, who hid out on the Temple Mount for three months.[25] The area had become a hiding place for weapons and explosives by Palestinian Arabs. In October 1937, Husseini fled British Palestine, first heading for Lebanon, then Iraq and finally Europe, where he met in Berlin with Adolf Hitler during November 1941 and became a close ally of the Nazi cause. (He would seek asylum after the war, fearing he would be prosecuted as a war criminal.) In the meantime, back in 1937, the Palestinian strike metastasized into an armed revolt, with volunteers arriving from neighboring countries.

Other leaders arose to lead the Palestinian Arabs' military struggle. A major side effect of the 1936 Arab Revolt was that rural chieftains in British Mandatory Palestine provided much of the revolt's leadership. Jerusalem, in fact, lost its pre-eminent place in Palestinian politics. For example, of the 281 Arab officers involved, only ten (or 3.5 percent) came from Jerusalem.[26]

It was noteworthy that prior to the adoption of the UN General Assembly resolution in November 1947 calling for the partition of Palestine, the representatives of the Palestinian Arabs did not make the issue of Jerusalem their primary focus. Jamal al-Husseini, the mufti's cousin, who presented the Palestinian Arab position before the United Nations, still used pan-Arab motifs in making the case of the Arab Higher Committee that he represented: "one consideration of fundamental importance to the Arab world was that of racial homogeneity." He explained that "the Arabs lived in a vast territory stretching from the Mediterranean to the Indian Ocean, spoke one language, had the same history, tradition, and aspirations." He referred to the threat of an "alien body" entering the Middle East region. He also spoke about a future constitutional organization for Palestine that would seek to guarantee to all "freedom of worship and access to the Holy Places." But this was clearly not the central thrust of his remarks.[27]

## The Jordanian Era in Jerusalem

As a result of the First Arab-Israeli War, Jerusalem was divided, with its Old City coming under the occupation of the Arab Legion of the Hashemite Kingdom of Jordan. Relations between Israel and Jordan over Jerusalem were supposed to be governed by their April 3, 1949, Armistice Agreement. According to Article VIII of the armistice, both sides undertook to guarantee free access to Mt. Scopus as well as the resumption of the "normal functioning" of its "cultural and humanitarian institutions." For Israel, this meant reopening Hebrew University and the Hadassah Hospital.

The same article also assured "free access to the Holy Places and cultural institutions and the use of the cemetery on the Mount of Olives." If Article VIII had been implemented, Israelis would have been able to visit the Old City of Jerusalem and pray at the Western Wall. The Jordanians were to obtain road access to Bethlehem and the provision of Israeli electricity to the Old City. To work out the modalities of these principles, the same article called on both governments to appoint representatives to a "Special Committee" that was supposed to formulate detailed plans.

True, there was a regular Israeli convoy to Mt. Scopus, but the Special Committee was disbanded even before its meetings got under way, so that no arrangements could be put in place for reopening Hebrew University or the Hadassah Hospital. More significant, Israelis were denied access to both the Western Wall and the Mount of Olives during the entire period of Jordanian rule. Jordan further barred non-Israeli Jews from the Western Wall, demanding that tourists present a certificate of baptism before a visa would be granted.[28] Formally, the Jordanians maintained that the scope of the Special Committee needed to be broadened to include other holy sites inside Israel such as those in Nazareth.[29] This demand, however, did not appear in the armistice.

The true motivation behind Jordanian policy in these years was revealed in a frank exchange on February 23, 1951, between Jordanian

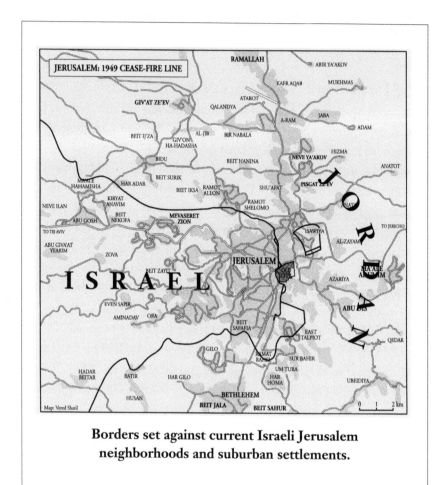

**Borders set against current Israeli Jerusalem
neighborhoods and suburban settlements.**

prime minister Samir al-Rifaʻi and an Israeli envoy, Reuven Shiloah. Al-Rifaʻi disclosed why his country had no intention of implementing its armistice obligations under Article VIII—Jordan simply had nothing to gain from the armistice any longer. Jordan no longer needed access to the Bethlehem road from Israel—the Jordanians had built another road instead—and the Old City would no longer need Israeli electricity after Jordan worked out a different source of electrical power.[30]

In the meantime, Israelis were also prevented from visiting all holy sites around Jerusalem that fell within Jordan's jurisdiction, including the tomb of the prophet Samuel northwest of Jerusalem, the tomb of the high priest Simon the Just inside Jerusalem, Rachel's tomb on the Jerusalem-Bethlehem border, and the Tomb of the Patriarchs in Hebron.[31] Israeli Muslims were blocked from visiting the Islamic holy shrines under Jordanian control. Israeli Christians did not fare much better; they were permitted to cross over and visit their holy sites once a year, on Christmas. The UN Security Council was notified on November 4, 1952, that "Jordan has declined thus far to meet in the Special Committee."[32] But in the years that followed, the UN did not intervene any further to safeguard religious freedom in Jerusalem even though the Jordanians were violating the 1949 Armistice Agreement, which the UN had been empowered to oversee.

Just after the 1948 war, Jordan's formal relations with Jerusalem changed very quickly. Previously, in December 1948, a congress of Palestinian Arabs had been convened in the West Bank town of Jericho that asked Jordanian King Abdullah to place the West Bank, including East Jerusalem, under the control of Jordan's Hashemite monarchy. Hashemite ties to Jerusalem had been steadily growing; when Abdullah's father, the former Sharif Hussein, died in 1931, he was buried in Jerusalem on the Temple Mount. Thus after the 1948 war, with its forces deployed in the West Bank and enjoying the support of many Palestinian Arabs, Jordan moved to solidify its control over its new Palestinian territories.

Jordan took decisive action in this regard in April 1950, when both houses of the Jordanian parliament formally annexed the West Bank and East Jerusalem, declaring the "complete unity between the two banks of the Jordan, the Eastern and Western, and their amalgamation into one single state, Hashemite Kingdom of Jordan, under the crown of His Hashemite Majesty King Abdullah ben al-Hussein the exalted."[33] Only two countries recognized these territorial changes; the first of these, the British, extended recognition with the qualification that it could not recognize Jordanian sovereignty over those parts of Jerusalem that the UN had proposed to internationalize. Only Pakistan gave unqualified recognition to the annexation. At least one leading Jordanian figure has contended that Amman was in effective control of its sector of Jerusalem from 1949 to 1967, but it had not acquired territorial sovereignty.[34]

The new, unified Hashemite Kingdom kept Amman, forty miles east of Jerusalem, as its capital. Government offices were transferred from Jerusalem to Amman, which also benefited from most of the Jordanian government's development funds. Amman grew dramatically from a small town of 22,000 people in 1948 to a city of a quarter million by 1961.[35] Some of this expansion undoubtedly stemmed from the arrival of Palestinian refugees from the 1948 war, but another contributing factor was the movement of West Bank Palestinians eastward in search of employment opportunities. By comparison, Jordanian Jerusalem only grew from 42,000 to 70,000 over an even longer period of time, from 1949 to 1967.[36]

During these years, prominent Jerusalem Arabs grumbled about the increasing primacy of Amman over Jerusalem. A typical complaint was uttered by a Jerusalem candidate to the Jordanian parliament. "See the palaces which are being built in Amman," he remarked, "those palaces should have been built in Jerusalem, but were removed from here."[37] Another reason for discontent was Jordanian radio's broadcasting of Friday prayers from a mosque in Amman instead of the al-Aqsa Mosque in Jerusalem.[38] Noticing that the British and U.S. ambassadors to Israel in 1954 were presenting their credentials to the Israeli president in Jerusalem, one Palestinian writer bemoaned that Israel had made Jerusalem into a capital while Jordan had reduced it "from a position of preeminence to its current place that does not rise above the rank of a village."[39]

This downgrading of Jerusalem unquestionably had a political background. During the Mandate period, the city was the center of power of the Jerusalem mufti, Hajj Amin al-Husseini. Seeking to displace Husseini's authority, King Abdullah had Husseini replaced as mufti in December 1948. Husseini was banned from Jerusalem, and in 1951 the Jordanians abolished the Supreme Muslim Council that he had headed.[40] The Jordanians also moved the Muslim religious appeals court from Jerusalem to Amman. The commemoration of the Nabi Musa festival, which had been effectively manipulated by Husseini for political purposes, lapsed in these years as well. In the meantime, the Jordanian government was providing public sector jobs and assistance to the regime's core supporters. These were the East Bank tribes, not the Palestinian Arabs on the West Bank and in Jerusalem.

The mufti turned out to be a persistent problem for the Jordanians. He remained active after the 1948 war from exile in Egypt. With the help of sympathizers in the Egyptian Army tied to the Islamic fundamentalist Muslim Brotherhood, he managed to escape on September 28, 1948, to Gaza, where an "all-Palestine government" was established a few days later on October 1. The mufti was declared president of a Palestine National Council that adopted a vote of confidence in the Gaza-based government. Not surprisingly, the mufti's council declared that Jerusalem would be its capital.[41]

The mufti's Gaza government was not recognized by a single state and it had no meaningful financial resources or armed forces. Yet it posed a political challenge to Jordan. Given this rivalry, it should have come as no surprise that King Abdullah would be vulnerable to assassination attempts. On July 20, 1951, Abdullah was shot dead by a Palestinian gunman at Friday prayers in the al-Aqsa Mosque. Just next to him was his grandson, Hussein, who would become king less than a year later. The mufti was widely believed to be the chief instigator of the assassination.[42]

Now that Jordan had unilaterally created a new political status for itself in Jerusalem, would it be more careful about observing its armistice responsibilities, particularly with respect to religious freedom? As previously noted, the wartime behavior of Jordan's Arab Legion in the Old City of Jerusalem had been contemptible. Colonel Abdullah al-Tal, the local legion commander, would later admit in his memoirs, "I knew the Jewish Quarter was densely populated with Jews... I embarked, therefore, on the shelling of the Quarter with mortars, creating harassment and destruction."[43]

Jordan thus played a role in reducing to rubble most of the Jewish Quarter, whose Jewish population was evicted or taken prisoner. Great study centers like the Porat Yosef Yeshivah were blasted with explosives. Religious sites that remained standing were often subject to a form of ritual desecration used throughout the Middle East—they were converted into stables. For example, outside the Old City's walls, this was the fate of the tomb of Simon the Just. Many desecrated synagogues, like the three prayer houses that made up the Yohanan Ben Zakai complex, were filled with donkey dung.

But responsibility for this religious vandalism did not fall on Jordan alone. The Arab Legion was British-trained and went into battle under the command of many British officers. There was concern expressed in the British parliament, particularly by Winston Churchill, about their participation in the assault on Jerusalem.[44] From May 19, 1948, when the Arab Legion's attack on the Old City began, until May 30, when the British officers were finally pulled out of Jerusalem, these officers shared responsibility for the destruction wrought by the Arab Legion in the Old City.

For example, the Hurva Synagogue, first built in 1705, was set on fire on May 27—that is, before the British withdrawal.[45] Palestinian Arab mobs were also involved in the acts of desecration that occurred in the Old City, and in fact may have been responsible for a far greater proportion of the destruction than the Arab Legion.[46] There were also reports that the Arab Legion actually protected those Jews of the Jewish Quarter whom it did not take prisoner from local mobs as they filed out in retreat from the Old City through the Zion Gate.[47]

Still, the Arab Legion had operational responsibility for the situation in the territories that it occupied. And Jordan's mistreatment of holy sites and the religious interests of other faiths unfortunately continued after the 1948 war. Thousands of tombstones in the ancient Jewish cemetery on the Mount of Olives were removed and used to pave roads, to build fences, and for latrines in Jordanian military camps; their engraved Hebrew letters were still visible on the stones after they were used for these purposes. Many graves were torn open and the bones inside them scattered.[48] The number of tombstones affected by these acts of desecration was not insignificant—at least 38,000 of the 50,000 tombstones on the Mount of Olives were torn up.[49]

And, as already noted, the Jordanians refused to implement their responsibilities, according to the 1949 armistice, to give Israelis access to their holy sites in Jerusalem. Even in the small Israeli-controlled Mt. Scopus enclave, religious restrictions appeared; on November 30, 1964, the UN Truce Supervision Organization demanded in writing that Israel stop the traditional display of lights on the festival of Hanukkah atop Mt. Scopus because of Jordanian sensitivities.[50] Rather than regularly protesting the Jordanian refusal to open up the Old City to members of all faiths, its local representative in Jerusalem were busy restricting the expression of Jewish religious practice even further.

Christianity in Jerusalem also suffered setbacks. Starting in 1953, the Jordanians decided that Christian institutions would face restrictions in buying land in and around Jerusalem. There were worldwide protests against the Jordanian actions, leading the Jordanians to suspend the application of some of these provisions.[51] Nonetheless, according to one historical account, two years later the British consul-general wrote a cable about an "anti-Christian tendency" evident in Jordanian behavior.[52] By the 1960s Christian schools were told that they would have to close on Fridays instead of Sundays, which had been their past practice. In this difficult environment, the Christian population of Jerusalem declined from 25,000 in 1948 to 10,800 in 1967.[53] The bulk of that change in fact occurred after the 1948 war. Jordan, however, was forced to begin paying more attention to its treatment of Christians in advance of the visit of Pope Paul VI to Jordan and Israel in January 1964.

Israel developed a paradoxical relationship with the Jordanians. On the one hand, it had strong grievances against the Jordanian abuses with respect to the holy sites; on the other, both states were engaging in secret negotiations to conclude a peace treaty. These contacts were in fact well-advanced; indeed, Britain's representative disclosed in a private meeting in London during July 1949 that "King Abdullah was personally anxious to come to an agreement with Israel, and in fact, it was our [British] restraining influence which had so far prevented him from doing so."[54] Additionally, both states had a joint interest in forestalling the lingering internationalization initiatives that were still being proposed in the early 1950s at the UN.

It would be erroneous to conclude that during the period of its rule, Jordan essentially cut itself off from Jerusalem and was completely anti-Palestinian as well; Jordan always sought to invest in the area of the Temple Mount. Between 1952 and 1959, the Jordanians undertook a new restoration project at the Dome of the Rock. The U.S. began to receive reports in 1960 that Jordan planned to treat Jerusalem as a second capital and construct new offices there that served the central government in Amman. Washington warned Jordan that it did not approve of such an action.[55] From the mid-1950s, King Hussein would refer to Jerusalem as Jordan's "spiritual capital," although this had no practical meaning.[56]

During these years the Jordanians also appointed a number of leading Palestinian Arabs to senior positions in the Jordanian government. There was Awni Abdul Hadi from Nablus, who was a pan-Arabist but ended up joining the mufti's All-Palestine Government in Gaza; between 1951 and 1955 he was appointed Jordan's foreign minister and its ambassador to Cairo. Jerusalem's Anwar Nusseibah became Jordan's minister of defense and its ambassador to London. Hussein Fakhri al-Khalidi, who also came from Jerusalem, briefly became Jordan's prime minister in 1957. Jordan's overall goal was to enhance the Jordanian identity of its Palestinian citizens; moving Jordan's capital to Jerusalem would have produced the exact opposite effect—it would have built up the Palestinian identity of the entire Hashemite Kingdom.

## The PLO and Jerusalem

During the period of Jordanian rule, another political body would come to influence the struggle for Jerusalem: the Palestine Liberation Organization (PLO). It was founded in May 1964 by a conference of four hundred delegates meeting at the Intercontinental Hotel in Jordanian-controlled Jerusalem. Its first head, Ahmad Shukeiry, was a Palestinian who served as a Saudi Arabian diplomat until he fell out with the Saudi leadership. The early PLO was completely controlled by Egypt, which sponsored the proposal for its creation at an Arab Summit meeting in order to reduce the relative responsibility of the Arab states to resolve the Palestinian issue. The PLO covenant rejected Jewish claims to Palestine and the validity of the League of Nations mandate. But it did not specifically single out Palestinian claims to Jerusalem, which are not even mentioned in the covenant—either in its original version promulgated in 1964 or in its 1968 rendition.[57]

The early PLO had good reasons to leave Jerusalem out of its founding charter. It did not want to antagonize its Jordanian hosts, who had no intention of turning over Jerusalem to the PLO. There had already been a number of points of tension between Jordan and the PLO leadership over Jerusalem prior to the Jerusalem conference. For example, the Jordanians wanted the conference held in Amman or by the Dead Sea, while the Palestinians preferred the Old City. The Intercontinental Hotel was a compromise.[58] Any action that appeared as a PLO claim to Jerusalem was firmly opposed by the Jordanian leadership. In order to relieve the Jordanians, the PLO adopted a number of "final resolutions" in 1964 that included the following principle: "The PLO will not assert any territorial sovereignty over the West Bank, nor over the Gaza Strip, nor over the al-Hamma area [controlled by Syria]."[59]

Moreover, the Jordanians had considerable political leverage against any group challenging their supremacy in Jerusalem. They could play off other Palestinian groups against the PLO if the latter caused them trouble. Jordanian-PLO relations did in fact deteriorate as the Hashemite monarchy increasingly suspected that the PLO sought its overthrow. Jordan closed down the PLO office in Jerusalem on January 3, 1967, and Amman played the card of turning to the PLO's competitors. A few months later on March 1, 1967, there was a rapprochement between King Hussein and Hajj Amin al-Husseini, who was invited to visit Jordan. It was also the first time the mufti had returned to Jerusalem since 1937, when he escaped the British from his hideout on the Temple Mount.[60] In the mid-1960s, when it came to the issue of Jerusalem, the PLO had to acquiesce to Jordanian wishes and thus emphasized other Palestinian interests.

Yasser Arafat's takeover of the PLO in 1968 would make Jerusalem more of a cause for the organization in the years that followed. For one thing, Arafat claimed to have been born in Jerusalem; it was a vitally important biographical detail that he flaunted in order to enhance his credentials as a Palestinian Arab leader. In truth, Arafat was born in Cairo in 1929 to a father who was half-Palestinian and half-Egyptian. (His mother came from an old Jerusalem family.) And in order to build himself up with the Palestinian public, he would additionally argue that he was related to Hajj Amin al-Husseini. But apparently, while his father came out of the al-Husseini clan in Gaza, the Gaza Husseinis were not related to the

Jerusalem Husseinis. Arafat, in short, was not born to a family of Palestinian notables and to make matters worse, he wasn't even born in British Mandatory Palestine.[61]

For a short period of four years in the mid-1930s, Arafat's widowed father sent him from Cairo to Jerusalem to live with his mother's family. He was a child volunteer to one of the assistants to the mufti, who became for Arafat a figure to be emulated. In order to sustain the legend that he promoted about his past, Arafat would argue that he fought in the First Arab-Israeli War under Abdul Qader al-Husseini, who was both the mufti's cousin and one of the main Palestinian commanders who died in the battle for Jerusalem. Arafat did fight in the 1948 war, but not with the Palestinians as he maintained. Instead, he was recruited into the Egyptian units that were organized by the Muslim Brotherhood in Cairo.[62]

Even after Arafat's takeover of the PLO, certain aspects of the organization's unique approach to the Jerusalem question only became evident many years later. Arafat's real political constituency that sustained him in power over the years was located in the Palestinian refugee camps, first on the East Bank in Jordan, and then in Lebanon. The Palestinian elites in East Jerusalem were not part of that constituency and even presented a potential alternative leadership, at times, to Arafat's organization, which was based far away in Lebanon and later in Tunisia. Due to the PLO's refusal for several decades formally to renounce terrorism or meet any of the minimal pre-conditions that the U.S. set for a diplomatic dialogue, the East Jerusalem leadership would be able to meet U.S. secretaries of state, while Arafat could not even see a U.S. ambassador.

Because Arafat had a different political constituency, he was willing to agree to tactical concessions in Jerusalem that were unacceptable to the local leadership. In fact, looking ahead a number of decades, one of the reason that Israeli prime minister Yitzhak Rabin was willing to pursue a secret negotiating track with the PLO in Oslo—which eventually led to the signing of the Declaration of Principles in 1993 on the White House lawn—was precisely because the PLO was willing to exclude Jerusalem from any interim self-governing arrangements for the Palestinians. In contrast, a local Palestinian delegation to peace talks in Washington under the leadership of Faisal al-Husseini, who in fact did come out of the prestigious Husseini clan of the mufti, insisted on including East Jerusalem in any future Palestinian government. In short, the PLO position on Jerusalem was softer, so Rabin went with the PLO option.

Indeed, while Jerusalem played a central role in Yasser Arafat's rhetoric, he was willing to set the Holy City aside, when pressed in negotiations, in the years that followed. In 1996, for example, he agreed to close a number of Palestinian Authority offices in Jerusalem that violated the clauses of the Oslo Agreement, which confined the jurisdiction of his government to West Bank and Gaza Strip territory and excluded Jerusalem. The PLO's readiness to adopt such policies put it into conflict with some of the older East Jerusalem Palestinian leadership. It may have misled Israeli officials who hoped that the PLO would show such flexibility in future final status talks when Jerusalem's ultimate fate would be decided.

**The Heart of Jerusalem:** The Temple Mount is a thirty-five-acre plaza that was erected over two thousand years ago. It is where both the Temple of Solomon and the Second Temple once stood. It is also where the late seventh-century Dome of the Rock was erected by the Ummayad caliphs; its tile work dates back to the Ottoman Turks. Below it is the 187-foot Western Wall, where a part of the original Herodian retaining wall of the Temple Mount is exposed. It became, over the centuries, the main place of Jewish prayer because of its proximity to the Holy of Holies. The full length of the Western Wall is nearly 1,600 feet and may be accessed through the large arches on the left of the prayer area. *Photo © Kevin Frayer/Associated Press*

**The Failed Summit:** In July 2000, President Bill Clinton convened the Camp David Summit with Israeli prime minister Ehud Barak (left) and Palestinian Authority chairman Yasser Arafat (right). Barak broke with his predecessors and was willing to conditionally agree to redivide Jerusalem. Arafat refused all U.S. peace offers and shocked U.S. negotiators with his assertion that the Temple never even existed in Jerusalem. *Photo © Ron Edmonds/Associated Press*

**Temple Denial Spreads:** Arafat's rendition of the history of the Temple was repeated by his top aides who survived him (pictured here left to right): Mahmoud Abbas (Abu Mazen), Nabil Sha'ath, Sa'eb Erekat, and Yasser Abd Rabbo. Temple Denial also spread across the Arab world. In parallel there was a growing trend in Western universities to doubt the veracity of the biblical narrative, including the existence of the House of David. Some synergies developed between the Middle Eastern and Western academic deniers of biblical history. *Photos (from left to right): © Lawrence Jackson/Associated Press; © Adel Hana/Associated Press; © Amir Nabil/Associated Press; and © Amir Nabil/Associated Press*

**The Temple Vessels:** Any tourist in Rome walking under the Arch of Titus can observe its depiction of a Roman victory procession, in which the looted vessels from the destroyed Temple in Jerusalem were displayed. The arch was completed in 81 CE, ten years after the Roman victory over Judea. *Photo © Z. Radovan/www.BibleLandPictures.com*

**The Tenth Legion:** The Tenth Legion was one of four Roman legions that put Jerusalem under siege and destroyed the Temple between 66 and 70 CE. The third row of inscription on this Roman column in Jerusalem's Old City, near the Jaffa Gate, refers to LEGX. *Photo © Lea Giorgy*

**The Temple in Greek:** During the Second Temple period non-Jews also participated in its sacrificial services. Because the inner courts of the Temple were reserved for priests and other Temple functionaries, plaques written in ancient Greek warned Gentiles of these areas. A complete rendition of the entire plaque containing the above fragment, from the Israel Museum, is on the opposite page. A whole Greek plaque from the Temple Mount is housed in the museum in Istanbul, Turkey. *Israel Antiquities Authority/Photos © The Israel Museum, Jerusalem*

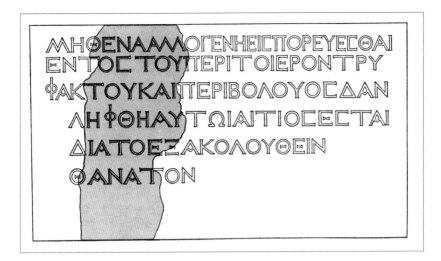

MHΘΕΝΑΛΛΟΓΕΝΗΕΙΣΠΟΡΕΥΕΣΘΑΙ
ΕΝΤΟΣΤΟΥΠΕΡΙΤΟΙΕΡΟΝΤΡΥ
ΦΑΚΤΟΥΚΑΙΠΕΡΙΒΟΛΟΥΟΣΔΑΝ
ΛΗΦΘΗΑΥΤΩΙΑΙΤΙΟΣΕΣΤΑΙ
ΔΙΑΤΟΕΞΑΚΟΛΟΥΘΕΙΝ
ΘΑΝΑΤΟΝ

**A Temple Warning:** The rules of the Temple area were regarded as divinely enforced religious law, as the stern warning in the top line above indicates: "Foreigner, do not enter within the grille and the partition surrounding the Temple." In the case of the Holy of Holies, only a ritually purified high priest could enter the area once a year on the Day of Atonement (Yom Kippur). *Israel Antiquities Authority/Photos © The Israel Museum, Jerusalem*

**The Trumpet of the Temple Priests:** The historian of the Jewish war against Rome, Josephus, describes the roof of the priests' chambers on the Temple Mount, where a priest would sound a trumpet to give notice that the Sabbath was approaching. Hebrew inscription on the above eight-foot-long stone says: "To the place of trumpeting." The stone was apparently hurled down by the Roman armies from the Temple area to the pavement surrounding the Temple Mount below over 1,900 years ago. *Israel Antiquities Authority/Photos © The Israel Museum, Jerusalem*

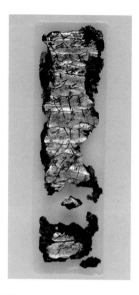

**First Temple Priestly Blessing:** This unrolled silver amulet from Jerusalem in the First Temple period (about 600 BCE) contains the biblical text of the priestly blessing in Numbers 6: 24–26.

*Israel Antiquities Authority/Photos © The Israel Museum, Jerusalem*

**The Golden Gate to the Temple Mount:** The Gate of Mercy or Golden Gate along the eastern wall of the Temple Mount is the oldest of Jerusalem's gates, dating back to the Herodian or Byzantine period. It leads from the area opposite the Mount of Olives to the Temple Mount. According to the Jewish tradition, it is where the messiah will enter Jerusalem. In Christian tradition, it is where Jesus entered the Temple Mount on Palm Sunday. During the Ottoman Empire, a Muslim cemetery was established in front of the gate, which had been completely blocked several centuries earlier. *Photo © Jean Marie Hosatte*

**House of David:** According to certain academic circles the whole biblical story of King David was made up hundreds of years later. Yet an Aramaic inscription discovered in 1993 at Tel Dan, in northern Israel, celebrates the victory of the Syrians against a "King of Israel" and the "House of David." The stone has been dated back to 835 BCE, less than a century after the reign of King Solomon.

*Israel Antiquities Authority/Photos © The Israel Museum, Jerusalem*

**Royal Seals of the Kings of Judah:** A whole school of European professors have argued that the Book of Kings was really "a myth." These are ancient royal seals from the period of the Kings of Judah who ruled in Jerusalem which prove the contrary. The top left seal says: "Belonging to King Ahaz (ben) Jotham, King of Judah" who ruled from 735 BCE to 715 BCE (2 Kings 16:1). The top right seal says: "Belonging to King Hezekiah (ben) Ahaz, King of Judah," who ruled from 715 BCE to 686 BCE (2 Kings 18:1). On the bottom is a seal (right) and its wax impression (left) that says: "Belonging to Jehoahaz, Kings' Son" (King of Judah, son of King Josiah) (2 Kings 23:31). Jehoahaz ruled as king briefly in 609 BCE.

*Photos (top) © Z.Radovan/www.BibleLandPictures.com; (bottom) Israel Antiquities Authority/Photos © The Israel Museum, Jerusalem*

**Monumental Structures in the City of David:** Skeptical accounts of the biblical narrative have included the assertion that David and Solomon were "village chieftains" incapable of building royal palaces and, by implication, the Temple. In recent excavations in Jerusalem's City of David, a monumental structure from the time of King David was found with walls between six and eight feet thick, raising the possibility that it might have served as the base of King David's palace. *Photo © Dr. Eilat Mazar*

**Bar Kochba Revolt against Rome:** In the above letter by Bar Kochba, written during his revolt against Rome in 132–135 CE, he seeks to recruit "Galileans," which some scholars interpreted as Christians. The Roman historian Dio Cassius only writes that "many outside nations" joined the revolt which caused "the whole earth" to be "stirred up." The emperor Hadrian feared the revolt could spark the hopes of enslaved peoples across the Roman Empire. *Israel Antiquities Authority/Photos © The Israel Museum, Jerusalem*

**For the Freedom of Jerusalem:** Bar Kochba coins indicated the purpose of the revolt: to liberate Jerusalem. One side of the Bar Kochba coin above (left) is a façade of the Temple with the Ark of the Covenant between the pillars. The other side, showing the "four species" used during prayer in the pilgrimage Festival of Tabernacles (Succot), reads: "For the Freedom of Jerusalem." *Photos © The Israel Museum, Jerusalem*

**The Evil Wind I: al-Qaeda Afghanistan:** Beginning in 1998, religious sites across the Middle East increasingly lost their traditional immunity when facing the forces of global jihad. When the Taliban came under the influence of al-Qaeda in Afghanistan and radical Wahhabi clerics who gave it support, the Afghan government decided in 2001 to destroy two-thousand-year-old Buddhist statues (see left) in the Bamiyan Valley, blasting them with explosives and reducing them to rubble (see right). *Photos © Associated Press and © Murad Sezer/Associated Press*

**The Evil Wind II: al-Qaeda Iraq:** In February 2006, al-Qaeda Iraq bombed one of the holiest sites in Shiite Islam: the gold-domed al-Askari Mosque in Samarra, sixty miles from Baghdad. The shrine is the burial place of the Tenth and Eleventh Imams and is next to the shrine of the Hidden Imam, where he went into concealment, according to Shiite tradition. *Photo © Hameed Rasheed/Associated Press*

**The Evil Wind III: Palestinian Radicals Attack Holy Sites:** Palestinian gunmen, police, and civilians stormed the biblical Tomb of Joseph on October 7, 2000, in the West Bank town of Nablus, trashing Hebrew texts while seeking to demolish the stone structure and cracking open its dome. *Photos © Lefteris Pitarakis/Associated Press*

**The Church of the Nativity in Bethlehem Becomes a Target:** Billowing black smoke came out of Bethlehem's Manger Square, next to the Church of the Nativity, where on April 2, 2002, a joint Hamas-Fatah Tanzim force of thirteen terrorists held the clergy as hostages for thirty-nine days.
*Photos © Peter DeJong/Associated Press*

**Hostages Seek Outside Help:** An unidentified Armenian cleric holds up a sign reading "Please Help" on April 23, 2002, from inside the Church of the Nativity compound. *Photos © Agence France Presse*

**The Church of the Holy Sepulchre:** The Church of the Holy Sepulchre was originally built by the Roman emperor Constantine. It was destroyed by the Fatimid caliph al-Hakim in the early eleventh century and then rebuilt. *Photos © Dallas and John Heaton/Stock Connection USA*

**The al-Aqsa Mosque:** The al-Aqsa Mosque is located on the Temple Mount, at its southern end. Pictured above are fully attended Muslim religious services that were held inside the al-Aqsa Mosque (at the time of Ramadan) in October 2006. *Photos © Mahfouz Abu Turk/Reuters Photo Archive*

**Jordan and the Muslim Holy Shrines:** Israeli prime minister Yitzhak Rabin shakes hands with Jordan's King Hussein at a ceremony for the Washington Declaration on July 25, 1994. One month before his assassination in November 1995, he insisted that Jerusalem remain a united city, keeping it under Israeli sovereignty. Rabin recognized at the ceremony above "the special role of the Hashemite Kingdom of Jordan in Muslim holy shrines in Jerusalem." He assured Hussein that Israel would "give high priority to the Jordanian historic role in these shrines" when the final status of Jerusalem is discussed.

*Photos © Richard Clement/Reuters Photo Archive*

**Jordan and the Dome of the Rock:** Jordan repeatedly undertook to renovate the Dome of the Rock under King Abdullah I and King Hussein. King Abdullah II, Hussein's son, maintained Jordan's traditional links to the upkeep of this shrine by recently replacing 2,000 square meters of carpeting covering its floors in October 2006. *Photos © Awad Awad/Agence France Presse*

**Israelis Stream to the Western Wall:** During the Feast of Tabernacles (Succot) on October 9, 2006, large numbers of Israelis participated in morning prayers at the Western Wall, which included the recitation of the priestly blessing. Below on the left is the continuation of the Western Wall northward near the point opposite the Holy of Holies and the Foundation Stone. *Photos © Oded Balilty/ Associated Press*

**For a United Jerusalem:** Prime Minister Benjamin Netanyahu (bottom right) addressed a joint session of the U.S. Congress on July 10, 1996, in which he reiterated the importance of a united Jerusalem under the sovereignty of Israel. Prime Minister Ariel Sharon made the same point in his first visit to Washington, D.C., in 2001, to meet with President Bush (above right). Here they are pictured in April 2004. *Photos (clockwise from left) © Lea Giorgy; © Mark Wilson/Photographer Showcase; and © Saar Yaacov/State of Israel, National Photo Collection*

# Chapter 6

# Jerusalem and the Arab-Israeli Peace Process

T he 1967 Six-Day War revolutionized the situation of Jerusalem by bringing about its reunification after nineteen years. More-over, the specific conditions out of which the conflict erupted created new legal rights and diplomatic terms of reference that would replace the armistice agreements of 1949; for the armistice agreements had patently failed, and something new was needed in their stead. But the immediate causes of the war were related to developments on other fronts. Military tensions along the Israeli-Syrian front rose steadily from April 1967, provoking the Soviet Union deliberately to mislead Egypt into believing that an Israeli strike on Syria was imminent.

As a result, the Egyptian regime under President Gamal Abd al-Nasser took three critical steps that led inevitably to war. First, Nasser massed 80,000 troops in Egyptian Sinai along Israel's southern Negev border. Next, to give credibility to his threat, the Egyptian president demanded that the UN Emergency Force that had been deployed for a decade along that sensitive border zone withdraw—and UN secretary-general U Thant complied.

Finally, Nasser announced a naval blockade of Israel's southern port of Eilat. All shipping between the port and the Red Sea and Indian Ocean was thus threatened by artillery positions Egypt had emplaced adjacent to the narrow Straits of Tiran, near the tip of the Sinai peninsula. The Egyptian president's military buildup had taken on a momentum of its own. He announced his intentions on May 26, 1967: "The battle will be a general one and our basic objective will be to destroy Israel."[1]

The Hashemite Kingdom of Jordan joined the emerging coalition of states backing Egypt. In late May, Jordan's King Hussein flew to Cairo and placed his armed forces under Egyptian military command. He then agreed to allow other neighboring states to deploy their troops on Jordanian territory, including in the West Bank near Jerusalem. Two Egyptian commando battalions joined nine Jordanian brigades in the West Bank, while one-third of the Iraqi Army traversed Jordanian territory and was poised to cross the Jordan River into the West Bank on June 5, 1967.

Meanwhile, as these hostile forces massed, the Jordanian representative to the UN in New York reminded the Security Council that the old 1949 armistice agreement "did not fix boundaries; it fixed the demarcation line."[2] For the Jordanians, the 1967 lines on the eve of the Six-Day War were not permanent international borders, but only military lines denoting where Middle Eastern armies had halted back in 1949. It was not clear that the representative understood the full implications of his statement, for it indicated that if Jordan sent troops over the armistice line, it was not crossing a recognized international border.

With a combined force of nearly 250,000 troops ringing Israel's borders and Egypt already announcing a blockade—which was legally an act of war—on the morning of June 5, two hundred Israeli fighter aircraft flew south to Egypt's airfields and destroyed the Egyptian air force on the ground. Israel's pre-emptive strike on Egypt took place at 7:45 in the morning. The timing was significant, as the exact sequence of events that morning would ultimately have enormous diplomatic and legal implications for the postwar claims of the warring parties, especially with respect to the future of Jerusalem.

The immediate question was whether King Hussein would now open up another front in the West Bank and Jerusalem or sit out the war. The question was resolved at 10:00 a.m. when Jordanian artillery opened fire on the Israeli side of Jerusalem, conducting massive indiscriminate shelling

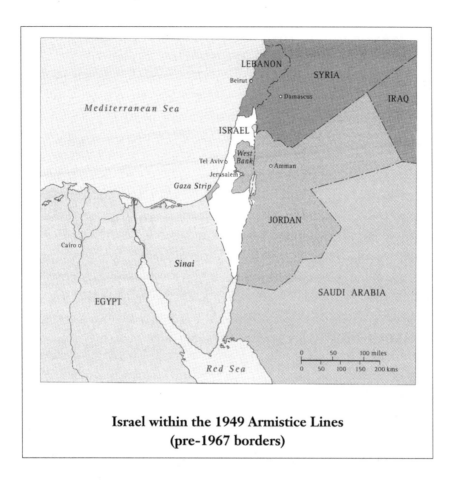

**Israel within the 1949 Armistice Lines**
**(pre-1967 borders)**

of civilian neighborhoods. Ultimately, some 6,000 artillery shells would fall on western Jerusalem, leaving 900 buildings damaged. Over 1,000 Israelis were wounded in Jerusalem alone, while the Jordanian barrage additionally set fire to the Church of the Dormition on Mount Zion.[3]

The Israeli government had sent King Hussein a simple message through the UN Truce Supervision Force commander in Jerusalem that reached him at about 10:30 a.m.: if the Jordanians "would not open hostilities," then Israel would not attack Jordan. Israeli foreign minister Abba Eban later recalled, "Jordan was given every chance to remain outside the struggle. Even after Jordan had bombarded and bombed Israel territory at several points, we still proposed to the Jordanian monarch that he abstain from any continuing hostilities."[4]

The message was ignored. A second Israeli message was sent later that morning, but Jordanian attacks only intensified. At 11:50 a.m. the small Jordanian Air Force began attacking targets in Israel, including infantry and armor.[5] Israel first responded against Jordan at 12:30 p.m. with air attacks against Jordanian airfields. In addition to the artillery barrage, Jordanian ground units crossed the 1949 armistice lines in Jerusalem. Israeli ground troops moved in response. In the ensuing war, the Israel Defense Forces captured the Old City of Jerusalem just three days later on June 8.

The rest of the West Bank was taken as well. Israeli defense minister Moshe Dayan, who had helped negotiate the cease-fire agreements with the Arab Legion during the 1948 war, announced, "The Israel Defense Forces have liberated Jerusalem. We have reunited the torn city, the capital of Israel. We have returned to this most sacred shrine, never to part from it again."[6]

## From Resolution 242 to Oslo

At the end of June 1967, Israel began extending its law and jurisdiction to eastern Jerusalem as well as to those strategic locations surrounding the Holy City that had been used by the Jordanians to bombard it. These were incorporated into the city's widened municipal boundaries. On June 27, 1967, the Knesset adopted the "Protection of Holy Places Law." The new law vowed that "the Holy Places shall be protected from desecration and any other violation." It also sought to protect "the freedom of access of the members of the different religions to the places sacred to them." The new law had teeth—anyone caught desecrating a holy place would be liable to seven years in prison.[7]

After the war, the Israeli government began repairing the churches damaged in the recent fighting or in the conflict of 1948. Israel signed an agreement on September 11, 1968, with fourteen churches and religious orders agreeing to pay them compensation for war damages regardless of whether Israeli or Jordanian forces had been the cause.[8] The Israeli government was determined to demonstrate its goodwill toward the religious institutions in the Holy City.

With respect to Muslim holy sites like the al-Aqsa Mosque and the Dome of the Rock, Israel continued their Islamic administration through

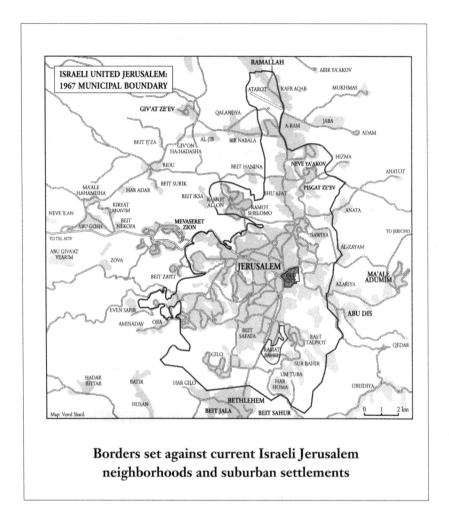

**Borders set against current Israeli Jerusalem
neighborhoods and suburban settlements**

the Jordanian Ministry of *Awqaf* (Religious Endowments), which retained
its responsibility for the Waqf employees on the Temple Mount. Since the
times of the British Mandate, Judaism's chief rabbis had ruled that the
Temple Mount had eternal sanctity and hence Jews should not enter any
part of the area. Observant Jews were aware that if they went on top of the
Temple Mount they might inadvertently step onto the Holy of Holies,
which was only to be entered one day a year by a high priest who had purified himself according to ancient traditions. Still, Israeli law now allowed
for Jews who did not observe these religious laws to enter the Temple
Mount area.[9]

Israel's policy to protect the holy places stood in stark contrast to the previous nineteen years of Jordanian rule during which numerous non-Muslim institutions were vandalized or otherwise mistreated. But in seeking to extend its laws to the parts of Jerusalem that its army had captured, Israel immediately transformed the fate of the Holy City into an intense subject of international diplomacy. The assertion of Israeli laws in a newly united Jerusalem created dilemmas for legal analysts seeking to judge the legality of the situation Israel had created.

For example, unless Israel extended its law to the Old City, it could not provide a legal basis for its new legislation protecting the holy places.[10] Moreover, on a more fundamental level, Israeli forces had not entered eastern Jerusalem or the rest of the West Bank as a result of a war of aggression or conquest, but rather because of a clear-cut war of self-defense. In short, it had captured territories from which it had been attacked.

These circumstances were clear to most observers at the time. In fact, the Soviet Union failed by an 11–4 vote in the UN Security Council in its attempt, taken in deference to its Arab clients, to have Israel branded as the war's "aggressor." Similar Soviet initiatives failed in the UN General Assembly, where it only got thirty-six states to support its stance against eighty who voted against it or abstained.[11] These were astounding numbers considering that the UN General Assembly was not particularly friendly to the U.S. or Israel following the emergence of the Non-Aligned bloc in the early 1960s.

Years later, the legal significance of this failure to designate Israel as the aggressor was elucidated by Stephen Schwebel, who would later serve as the State Department legal advisor, in a seminal article on the subject. Writing in the *American Journal of International Law* in 1970, he concluded, "... Israel has *better title* in the territory of what was Palestine, *including the whole of Jerusalem*, than do Jordan and Egypt [emphasis added]."[12] Later in his career, Schwebel would become president of the International Court of Justice in The Hague. His legal views, in short, carried great weight.

Schwebel's analysis was rooted in one other important distinction. Jordan's previous standing in Jerusalem had stemmed from an illegal invasion in 1948 that was branded by then UN secretary-general Trygve Lie as an act of "armed aggression."[13] Thus Schwebel was comparing the rights of states that entered a given territory illegally as a result of a war of aggression in 1948 to the prerogatives of one that entered the very same territory in a war of self-defense in 1967. He wrote, "when the prior holder of territory had seized that territory unlawfully, the state which subsequently takes that territory in the lawful exercise of self-defense has, against the prior holder, better title."

Schwebel's argument was strengthened by the fact that Pakistan was the only state to recognize Jordan's 1950 annexation of eastern Jerusalem; it would be difficult for other states to argue that Israel had illegally seized Jordanian territory if they did not recognize Jordan's sovereignty there in the first place. He added that in light of the circumstances of the 1967 Six-Day War "substantial alterations" of the old 1949 armistice lines, "such as recognition of Israeli sovereignty over the whole of Jerusalem" were completely "lawful."

When state boundaries are crossed during a war, international diplomats usually seek a restoration of the *status quo ante*—the territorial situation prior to the outbreak of hostilities. But in the case of Jerusalem, the status quo ante had been the product of an act of blatant aggression. Moreover, calling for a restoration of the status quo ante legally meant enshrining Jordan's discriminatory policies against the religious freedom of non-Muslim faiths, including their restricted access to Jerusalem's holy sites. A demand to return to this situation would have been untenable.

U.S. president Lyndon Johnson hinted at some of these dilemmas on June 19, 1967, when he outlined what he called the "five great principles of peace." He explained that the armistice system of 1949 had failed and a return to the pre-war situation "would not be a prescription for peace, but for a renewal of hostilities." On Jerusalem, he asserted, "There . . . must be adequate recognition of the special interest of the three great religions in the holy places of Jerusalem."[14] Subsequent U.S. statements in 1967 also stressed that "the safeguarding of the holy places, and freedom of access to them for all should be internationally guaranteed."

Thus, the initial American approach to the issue of Jerusalem after the Six-Day War focused on the protection of the holy places and not on restoring Jordanian control of the Old City. When the UN General Assembly voted on July 4, 1967, to support a Pakistani draft resolution condemning the extension of Israeli law to eastern Jerusalem, the U.S. notably abstained along with nineteen other countries. It did not condone Israel's moves in Jerusalem, but neither did it argue that the pre-war situation should be restored.

All these considerations were expressed in the most important UN Security Council resolution on Israel, one that would ultimately serve as the foundation of Arab-Israeli diplomacy for decades thereafter: UN Security Council Resolution 242, which called for the withdrawal of Israeli forces from territories it had occupied in the war and the creation of secure boundaries. The resolution was drafted by the British mission to the UN under its ambassador, Lord Caradon, with the active involvement of the U.S. mission headed by U.S. ambassador to the UN Arthur Goldberg, a former U.S. Supreme Court justice. It was adopted unanimously by all fifteen Security Council members on November 22, 1967, after intense diplomatic wrangling over its language.

The resolution's wording had several consequential features. First, Resolution 242 was not adopted under Chapter VII of the UN Charter, which was applied in cases of acts of aggression and threats to international peace (for example, the UN Security Council invoked Chapter VII when Iraq invaded Kuwait in August 1990). The Security Council was functioning at the time strictly within Chapter VI of the UN Charter, which deals with the peaceful settlement of disputes and the initiation of negotiations, arbitration, or mediation.[15] The fact that this was a Chapter VI resolution, instead of Chapter VII, meant that the resolution was not self-enforcing, which would have required a unilateral Israeli withdrawal from the territory in question. Instead, any withdrawal would first require negotiation and agreement between the parties.

Secondly, Resolution 242 did not call for a return to the status quo ante. Like all UN Security Council resolutions, Resolution 242 comprised a preamble, with general provisions, and operative paragraphs, which laid out the specific actions called for by the Security Council. The resolution's famous withdrawal clause appeared within the operative section. The clause stated that in order to reach "a just and lasting peace," one of the principles that needed to be applied included "withdrawal of Israeli armed forces from territories occupied in the recent conflict."

This language was the product of particularly painstaking diplomacy. For example, the Soviet Union initially demanded that the clause specifically call for a withdrawal of Israeli forces from *all* the territories that it captured. This was not just a specialized debate between the legal advisors of the U.S. and Soviet missions to the UN, but rather a fundamental political disagreement that reached up to the apex of power in both countries— that is, to President Johnson in Washington and Prime Minister Alexei Kosygin in Moscow.

Kosygin sent a direct message to the White House insisting that the resolution should at least call for an Israeli withdrawal from "the" territories.[16] Furthermore, in the next sub-paragraph, the resolution essentially called for the creation of new lines that would form "secure and recognized boundaries." Taking these two elements together, it was clear that the new resolution provided the basis for replacing the 1949 armistice lines with new borders that met these criteria.

Facing Johnson's strong opposition to any last-minute changes in the draft resolution, the Soviets backed off their demand to modify its language. The head of the Soviet delegation to the UN at the time, Deputy Foreign Minister Vasily Kuznetsov, nonetheless expressed his displeasure with the final language: "There is certainly much leeway for different interpretations that retain for Israel the right to establish new boundaries and to withdraw its troops only as far as the lines it judges convenient."[17] None of the opponents of the U.S. and Israel at the time were comforted by the UN's poor French translation of the phrase "from territories," with its clearly indefinite meaning, as *"retrait des forces armées Isreliennes **des** territories occupés"* [emphasis added], which included the definite article that the English version purposely kept out. The negotiations over 242 were conducted in English, hence by international diplomatic practice it was the relevant version to which all parties related.

Indeed, Professor Alan Dershowitz of Harvard Law School worked for Goldberg in 1967 as Resolution 242 was being drafted; he has written that the U.S. deliberately omitted the article *the* from the withdrawal clause "in order to permit the retention of territories necessary to assure secure boundaries."[18] Looking back on this debate three years later, George Brown, who was the British foreign secretary at the time, explained the significance of the final language adopted in Resolution 242: "The proposal said 'Israel will withdraw from territories that were occupied,' not from 'the territories,' which means that Israel will not withdraw from all the territories."

Having lost the battle over Resolution 242's operative language, the Arab states would focus subsequently on its preamble, which referred to "the inadmissibility of the acquisition of territory by war"—a principle taken out of the operative paragraphs of an earlier draft proposed by India (along with Mali and Nigeria) and put into the less significant preamble by British and U.S. legal teams in order to build support for the resolution as a whole. But operative paragraphs were what legally mattered at the UN, and this clause certainly could not be used to rule out territorial changes that stemmed from peaceful negotiations.

There was a third significant aspect of Resolution 242—it did not mention Jerusalem at all. On March 6, 1980, Goldberg wrote a letter to the *New York Times* explaining that this was intentional: "Resolution 242 in no way refers to Jerusalem, and this omission was deliberate."[19] He explained that he had never described Jerusalem as "occupied territory," adding that while he believed that the status of Jerusalem should be negotiable, from his viewpoint, the old armistice lines dividing the Holy City had lost their viability. The upshot of his message was that "Jerusalem was not to be divided again."

Goldberg's letter stemmed from his feeling that the policies he had defended in the UN were misrepresented by successive U.S. administrations, especially under President Jimmy Carter. But Johnson's policies on Jerusalem had actually begun to erode soon after he left office. For example, a *New York Times* editorial in July 1969 attacked the Johnson administration's past Middle East policies, asserting that while it had declared its refusal to recognize "any unilateral actions affecting the status of Jerusalem," its UN delegates abstained from a vote condemning Israel for its unification of the city. The editorial seemed to be pressuring the new Nixon administration to take a tougher line against Israel, implying that Washington should vote for UN condemnations of Israel for its actions in Jerusalem. Indeed, that very month, the U.S. voted for a resolution censuring "in the strongest terms all measures taken to change the status of Jerusalem."[20] Charles Yost, Goldberg's successor at the UN, called East Jerusalem for the first time "occupied territory."[21]

These distinctions would remain somewhat academic for the next few decades. Though the issue of Jerusalem was raised by Arab states in subsequent negotiations between Israel and its neighbors, all Israeli governments were adamant about retaining Jerusalem as a united city under Israeli sovereignty. The idea that the future status of the territories Israel captured in the 1967 Six-Day War required a negotiation between the concerned parties was made explicit with the adoption of UN Security Council Resolution 338 on October 22, 1973. Resolutions 242 and 338 provided the only agreed basis for all Arab-Israeli negotiations that followed.

At the end of the first Camp David summit in 1978 between Israel and Egypt, under the auspices of President Jimmy Carter, the two parties agreed to disagree on the issue of Jerusalem. Egyptian president Anwar Sadat and Israeli prime minister Menachem Begin signed an agreement leading to their 1979 peace treaty, while relating their different positions on Jerusalem in separate letters to Carter. Despite the omission of Jerusalem from the treaty itself, the Carter administration began arguing that the Palestinian Arabs in East Jerusalem could participate in any future elections for the Palestinian autonomous authority that was envisioned by the Camp David Accords.[22]

It was a position that would be taken up with greater force by President George H. W. Bush in the early 1990s. In the meantime, Begin may have been comforted that in 1980 the new U.S. presidential candidate, Ronald Reagan, was far more forceful on Israel's rights in Jerusalem than was President Carter. Reagan stated his position clearly: "An undivided city of Jerusalem means sovereignty for Israel over that city."[23] As president, Reagan continued to insist that Jerusalem remain undivided although in the 1982 Reagan Plan he added that "its final status should be decided through negotiations."[24] His basic position supporting changes of the old 1949 armistice lines more generally was forcefully echoed by his secretary of state, George Shultz, who declared on September 16, 1988: "Israel will never negotiate from or return to the lines of partition or to the 1967 borders."[25]

According to the 1993 Declaration of Principles between Israel and the PLO—also known as the Oslo Accords—Prime Minister Yitzhak Rabin approved a five-year interim agreement for Palestinian self-government, under what became known as the Palestinian Authority, in the West Bank and Gaza Strip. Jerusalem was clearly excluded from Palestinian jurisdiction, but the Israeli government did explicitly agree that the issue of Jerusalem would be discussed in the parties' final status negotiations alongside other issues like final borders, security arrangements, refugees, and Israeli settlements.

Palestinian negotiators detected that they had created a huge crack in the Israeli negotiating position. Up until that point, negotiator Nabil Sha'ath noted, Israelis had never accepted that the final status of Jerusalem would even appear on a written negotiating agenda—Jerusalem was simply off the negotiating table. Now, he felt that Oslo had called into question the "finality of their annexation."[26] He also tellingly noted that Oslo allowed Palestinians residing in East Jerusalem to vote in Palestinian Authority elections,[27] thus further opening the door to Arab claims on the city. Israel, however, ultimately only allowed such voting at Israeli post offices, so that Palestinian voting in Jerusalem resembled the casting of an absentee ballot for the French or U.S. elections and was not an expression of foreign sovereignty. Nevertheless, Oslo had created new possibilities in the Holy City for the Palestinian side. The local Palestinian leader Faisal al-Husseini happily noted, "in the Oslo Accords it was established that the status of Jerusalem is open to negotiations on the final arrangement, and the moment that you say yes to negotiations, you are ready for a compromise."[28]

But with Rabin as the Israeli leader, Husseini's assessment was wishful thinking. Rabin was born in Jerusalem. In 1948, he commanded the Harel

Brigade of the Palmach, which fought to keep the road to Jerusalem open to convoys with food and water for its encircled Jewish population. Less than twenty years later, he was the chief of staff of the Israel Defense Forces during the Six-Day War, when Jerusalem was reunited. His public statements on Jerusalem did not provide any hint that he was even considering redividing the Holy City.

For example, Rabin told a group of schoolchildren in Tel Aviv on June 27, 1995, "If they told us that peace is the price of giving up on a united Jerusalem under Israeli sovereignty, my reply would be, 'Let's do without peace.'"[29] And speaking in the Knesset on October 5, 1995, just one month before his assassination, Rabin laid out before Israeli lawmakers his vision of Israel's final map: "The borders of the State of Israel, during the permanent solution, will be beyond the lines which existed before the Six-Day War. We will not return to the 4 June 1967 lines." When it came to Israel's capital, Rabin left no doubt about his position—he insisted that Israel retain "a united Jerusalem."[30]

## The Barak Government's Shift on Jerusalem

The Camp David summit of July 11–24, 2000, was the first serious, official negotiation between Israel and the Palestinians over Jerusalem. It was also the first time since 1967 that an Israeli prime minister was willing to consider, albeit conditionally, specific proposals for redividing the city.

Prime Minister Ehud Barak was elected in May 1999, having committed himself to keeping Jerusalem united and carrying on the legacy of his mentor, Yitzhak Rabin. In May 2000 he declared on Jerusalem Day, "Only those who do not understand the depth of the total emotional bond of the Jewish people to Jerusalem, only those who are completely estranged from the vision of the nation, from the poetry of that nation's life, from its faith and from the hope it has cherished for generations—only persons in that category could possibly entertain the thought that the State of Israel would actually concede even a part of Jerusalem."

As late as July 10, 2000, the day before the Camp David summit began, Barak stood in the Knesset and pledged to Israeli lawmakers that retaining "a united Jerusalem under Israeli sovereignty" was a critical redline that could not be crossed in the upcoming negotiations. Barak was not the kind of Israeli leader one might expect would divide Jerusalem. One of Israel's most decorated soldiers, he had risen up the ranks of the Israeli military and commanded its elite commando unit, *Sayyeret Matkal*. He also served in many senior positions on the Israeli general staff, including head of military intelligence. When he was chief of general staff in 1993, he had warned the Rabin government of the dangerous security situation that the Oslo agreements would create for Israel.

Rabin groomed Barak after he left the army to be a future Israeli leader, if not his successor, making him a senior minister in the Rabin government. In 1995, when Rabin sought to extend formally the jurisdiction of the Palestinian Authority beyond its original foothold in the Gaza Strip and Jericho to the remaining Palestinian population centers in the West Bank, Barak refused to support this "Interim Agreement" from his post within the Rabin government. But at Camp David, Barak retreated from his previous positions and offered concessions to the PLO far beyond what Rabin had ever proposed.

President Bill Clinton had also previously supported a united Jerusalem. Just before the 1992 presidential elections, he told *Middle East Insight*, "I do recognize Jerusalem as Israel's capital, and Jerusalem ought to remain an undivided city." His ambassador to the UN, Madeleine Albright, also seemed to adhere to this position; when vetoing an anti-Israel resolution in 1994 in the UN Security Council, she declared, "We are today voting against a resolution . . . precisely because it implies that Jerusalem is occupied Palestinian territory. We simply do not support the description of the territories occupied by Israel in the 1967 war as occupied Palestinian territory."[31]

Moreover, as the Oslo process progressed, Clinton drew extremely close to Rabin, developing enormous trust and respect for the late Israeli leader and claiming to understand his thought process and political positions.[32] It is doubtful that Clinton would call for Jerusalem's redivision so long as Rabin was forcefully opposed. Indeed, there are indications that the U.S. was still not fully prepared for such a radical change in policy toward Jerusalem at the start of Camp David. According to Clinton's national security advisor, Sandy Berger, Clinton had no idea on the eve of Camp David that Barak was willing to consider redividing Jerusalem.[33] Thus, Clinton clearly did not convene the summit with the intention of dividing the Holy City.

Barak's diplomatic strategy on Jerusalem at Camp David was a complete mystery. Going into the summit, his military intelligence branch gave the Camp David negotiations a less than 50 percent chance of success.[34] There are two possible explanations for his negotiating positions; the first is that Barak, having lost his nerve after shedding his military uniform, was willing to sacrifice historic Israeli interests because, for reasons he never disclosed, he needed an agreement at all costs. Alternatively, Barak may have intended to exploit his unexpected flexibility on Jerusalem in order to expose Arafat's intransigence to the world, thereby ending the Oslo process that he, as chief of staff, had so strongly doubted from the beginning.

Perhaps Barak combined both these approaches; if his long-shot diplomacy worked, he would return to Israel with a monumental peace agreement. (Israeli public opinion polls had shown that firm opposition to some of his concessions could flip once the government presented them as a fait accompli.) And if Yasser Arafat did not reciprocate his flexibility, then "Plan B" would involve exposing the Palestinian leadership as the true obstacle to peace.

Still, there had to be some basis for the belief that the parties could reach an agreement if placed under the pressure cooker of summit diplomacy. Throughout the 1990s, a number of back channel efforts had probed the respective positions of Israelis and Palestinians on the most sensitive issues, including that of Jerusalem. The most famous of these efforts produced what came to be called the Beilin-Abu Mazen agreement. This was named after two men: the first, Yossi Beilin, as Israel's deputy foreign minister had conceived and promoted the 1993 secret Israel-PLO contacts that became the Oslo Agreement; and the second, Abu Mazen (also called Mahmoud Abbas), would eventually lead the Palestinian Authority after Arafat's death.

Most of the contacts between the Israeli and Palestinian teams that worked these back channels did not involve Beilin or Abu Mazen, but rather academics in their employ who met together between 1994 and 1995.[35] Reportedly, they secretly concluded a set of understandings on October 31, 1995—less than a week before Rabin's assassination. Whether they actually struck an agreement or not would become a source of tremendous controversy in the years that followed. The Israeli team had worked under what they thought were Rabin's redlines, especially his demand that there be no return to the 1967 borders and no redivision of Jerusalem.

One idea advanced was to expand the definition of Jerusalem to include Abu Dis. This was a Palestinian village just to the east of Jerusalem's municipal border but inside the County of Jerusalem, as defined by the Jordanians prior to 1967. This plan would give the Palestinians a capital in Jerusalem (though only in the village of Abu Dis) that they could call *al-Quds*, and Israel would retain control of a united Jerusalem. Both sides would put off talks about sovereignty in East Jerusalem to the future, so both camps could interpret the solution in different ways.

The Beilin-Abu Mazen final status document that contained these proposals was hailed by political commentators around the world as a great breakthrough that showed that an Israeli-Palestinian peace agreement was indeed obtainable if Israel made sufficient concessions. The document was leaked with great fanfare to *Newsweek* and to the Israeli newspaper *Haaretz*. From the outside, the whole effort looked as if it was supported by a well-oiled public relations team that seemed to be providing background briefings everywhere. It clearly affected the intellectual debate about the chances of finalizing an Israeli-Palestinian peace arrangement in Jerusalem and in Washington.

Writing in the *New York Times* in December 1997, Thomas Friedman firmly held that a credible plan "already exists" for resolving the Israeli-Palestinian conflict; he then explained that he was referring to the "final deal" reached by Beilin and Abu Mazen, with its special solution for Jerusalem.[36] Somewhat more understated, the chief Middle East negotiator for the U.S. Department of State, Dennis Ross, would later summarize the document's significance by asserting that "it showed that even the most existential issues could be resolved."[37] Indeed, reportedly, senior Clinton administration officials urged the parties in advance of Camp David that the summit be based on the Beilin-Abu Mazen paper in which, apparently, the Americans had great faith.[38]

The big problem with the Beilin-Abu Mazen Agreement was that there was no agreement. There was a detailed document, but Abu Mazen denied ever signing it. In a symposium some years later he maintained, "There were secret negotiations, but there is no secret agreement."[39] Abu Mazen would repeat this on Palestinian television in May 1999, saying "there is no document, no agreement, no nothing."[40] This was not just public posturing used to save face with Palestinian public opinion in response to reports of concessions he might have made, for Abu Mazen said the same exact things privately as well.

And when Arafat was shown the document, he didn't agree to it either, but rather commented that it served as a basis for further negotiations; in other words, he could pocket Israeli territorial concessions without having to guarantee that they were sufficient to cause him to sign a peace treaty in return. The document was also unacceptable to the Israeli side, for Rabin's successor, Shimon Peres, rejected the Beilin-Abu Mazen draft as well.

Negotiators familiar with the thinking of the Palestinian side admitted that they never agreed to accept Abu Dis as a substitute for Jerusalem, but rather saw it as a launching pad for acquiring influence in East Jerusalem prior to future negotiations over the fate of the Holy City. They believed they could use Abu Dis to obtain the Old City by osmosis. In other words, if the Beilin-Abu Mazen experience had influenced the Barak team to believe that the issue of Jerusalem could be successfully negotiated at Camp David, then they were operating on the basis of false pretenses.

This might have been further affected by reports from another secret channel in 2000 led by Shlomo Ben-Ami, Barak's minister of justice and later Israeli foreign minister, as well as by Gilead Sher, the head of Barak's office. The talks were held at Harpsund, the summer residence of Sweden's prime minister south of Stockholm. Though not specifically charged to probe the issue of Jerusalem at this stage, this channel also came back with optimistic reporting; Ben-Ami himself wrote afterward that "enormous progress" was made in the Stockholm talks.[41]

The diplomacy over Jerusalem at Camp David was designed so that the parties could consider ideas without binding themselves to the negotiating record of the talks. Several safeguards were put in place to this end. First, the Camp David summit was guided by certain ground rules. At the end of the summit, President Clinton reiterated that the talks had been based on the principle that "nothing is agreed until everything is agreed." Thus, even if the Israeli delegation found one point of a proposal to be acceptable, Israel did not make any firm commitment by expressing approval of the idea or by not rejecting it out of hand. The entire discussion at Camp David was hypothetical and contingent on Palestinian agreement on other matters.

Secondly, very little at Camp David was put in writing. Instead, the ideas raised in the summit were oral. Israeli position papers were not shared with other delegations but rather kept within the Israeli delegation.[42] This served as a further protection against any discussion of proposals becoming a binding commitment that could later be raised in future negotiations.

Finally, most of the ideas about Jerusalem were raised by a third party— the U.S. Barak tried to keep his direct contact with Arafat to a bare minimum and did not make proposals to him directly in one-on-one meetings. Because the proposals at Camp David were hypothetical, oral, and raised through a third party, in the event that the summit failed, the negotiating record was not supposed to serve as a new basis for future negotiations.

Jerusalem came onto the Camp David agenda in stages. On the fifth day of the summit, Barak asked Dennis Ross what he thought the Palestinians needed on Jerusalem to close a deal. Ross replied that in addition to "clear" Palestinian control of the Temple Mount, they would need sovereignty in part of East Jerusalem. Invoking the Beilin-Abu Mazen ideas, which he must have assumed partly guided Israeli thinking, Ross at this point understood that they did not provide a sufficient basis for reaching closure between the parties. He explained that a new Palestinian capital in Jerusalem called *al-Quds* could not simply comprise villages like Abu Dis outside of the city's municipal border. Barak was not very responsive to this initial assessment and he did not indicate a readiness to offer new concessions to meet what Ross perceived as the Palestinians' minimum demands.

Three days later, however, Barak appeared ready to budge. On the summit's eighth day, President Clinton slowly read to Arafat a proposal on Jerusalem that he claimed had already been endorsed by Barak. In fact, Barak had not accepted the U.S. proposals straight out, but was willing to consider them as a basis for negotiation if Yasser Arafat would do the same.[43] Barak's acceptance was conditional. This early U.S. proposal on Jerusalem was based on the following elements:

1. The establishment of the Palestinian capital in East Jerusalem itself, with Palestinian sovereignty in seven or eight of nine of its outer neighborhoods
2. Palestinian sovereignty over half of the Old City of Jerusalem—specifically the Muslim and Christian Quarters
3. What was called Palestinian "custodianship" over the Temple Mount—a term connoting control with less than full sovereignty[44]

From the U.S. perspective, Barak had gone as far as he could; it was now the Palestinians' turn to demonstrate flexibility. But Arafat rejected this scheme outright. Clinton got nowhere with Arafat, who held out for nothing less than full Palestinian sovereignty over all of East Jerusalem. According to one account, Ross had to admit, "This question of Jerusalem is very hard. We can't bridge the gap between the two positions."[45]

During the ensuing days at Camp David, Ross and his peace team spent an enormous amount of time working out new diplomatic language for the Jerusalem question that they hoped would be more acceptable to the Palestinians. The underlying assumption behind this effort must have been that the main diplomatic problem facing the parties at Camp David on Jerusalem was one of terminology. But much of this creative word processing was barely understandable in English, let alone when translated into Arabic for Arafat. Sometimes the proposed solutions were literally hard to imagine.

For example, Dennis Ross suggested to Palestinian negotiator Sa'eb Erekat that Israel retain sovereignty underneath the Temple Mount, while the Palestinians obtain sovereignty above—on top of the Temple Mount. Erekat didn't even bother to respond to these ideas. The Palestinians understood this proposal to mean that sovereignty would be divided "vertically and horizontally"—the Palestinians would control everything above ground, while Israel would have sovereignty over everything underneath.

The U.S. at one point entertained an Israeli request for a Jewish place of prayer on the Temple Mount itself. Arafat would obtain a headquarters, or a "sovereign presidential compound" (according to one version), inside the Waqf compound on the Temple Mount, access to which would be assured without any Israeli checkpoints through a tunnel, bridge, or special road from Abu Dis.[46] Abu Mazen recalled these kind of ideas as follows: "in Camp David...the Israelis and Americans were releasing test-balloons regarding solutions to the Jerusalem issues."[47] The Palestinians clearly felt their role was to shoot them down.

On the summit's twelfth day, Ross suggested that because the Temple Mount was so unique, "it should not be governed by traditional definitions of sovereignty." Thus a new idea was footed: the Palestinians would obtain "religious and administrative sovereignty" and Israel would retain "sovereignty in name only." Ross later commented dryly that "both sides were able to restrain their enthusiasm."[48]

Finally, President Clinton tried his hand at working new terminology to win Palestinian acceptance. He proposed that the Palestinians obtain sovereignty in the outer neighborhoods of East Jerusalem, limited sovereignty in the inner neighborhoods, sovereignty in the Muslim and Christian Quarters of the Old City, and what he called "custodial sovereignty" over the Temple Mount. Erekat came back with Arafat's answer: No.[49]

On July 23, 2000, one day before Camp David ended, Arafat summarized his position on Jerusalem in a way that left little room for flexibility: "I will not agree to any Israeli sovereign presence in Jerusalem, neither in the Armenian quarter, nor in the Al-Aqsa Mosque, neither in Via De La Rosa, nor in the Church of the Holy Sepulcher. They can occupy us by force, because we are weaker now, but in two years, ten years, or one hundred years, there will be someone who will liberate Jerusalem [from them]."[50]

Israel's proposed concessions, backed by the Clinton administration, did not soften the tone of the Palestinian leader; if anything, the peace conference appeared to have hardened his stance. Within two months, Arafat launched a new war against Israel that he would tie directly to the fight for Jerusalem, calling his struggle the "al-Aqsa Intifada."

## Jerusalem: A Case of Unbridgeable Gaps

Most commentators attributed the Camp David summit's failure to the differences between the parties over Jerusalem, although wide gaps remained over every one of the major issues that were discussed: borders, refugees, and security arrangements. Nevertheless, Sandy Berger, President Clinton's assistant for national security affairs, insisted that the parties refused to move forward on other Israeli-Palestinian issues before knowing whether their differences over Jerusalem could be resolved.[51] In this sense, Camp David was also a diplomatic litmus test of whether the positions of the parties to the Arab-Israel conflict over the issue of Jerusalem could, in fact, be bridged.

But once the Camp David experiment was over, what was the status of all the U.S. and Israeli "trial balloons"? The Israelis had put unprecedented concessions on the table. And the Clinton administration had also clarified U.S. ideas on Jerusalem that its predecessors had not articulated. Had U.S. and Israeli policy on Jeruslem been changed forever?

President Clinton still emphasized on July 25, "Under the operating rules that nothing is agreed until everything is agreed, they are, of course, not bound by any proposal discussed at the summit." Barak similarly sought to clarify the events of Camp David: "Ideas, views and even positions which were raised in the course of the summit are invalid as opening positions in the resumption of negotiations, when they resume. They are *null and void* [emphasis added]."

Realistically, despite the strong legal grounding of this position, both leaders would have to acknowledge the possibility that the Palestinians would not forget the extent of Israel's concessions while denying even a hint of their own. One of Barak's negotiators would lament years later that the Palestinians had a knack for forgetting their own concessions, particularly those from the pre-summit backchannel contacts: "The Palestinians retracted from understandings reached during the negotiations. The famous Beilin-Abu Mazen understandings of 1995 became, for the Palestinians, the 'Beilin-Abu-Beilin Understandings' [i.e., no Abu Mazen]. The document that was formulated in the 'Swedish Track' [Stockholm] . . . did not exist for the Palestinian Camp David negotiators."[52]

This dynamic explained how Israeli and American negotiators had misread the significance of the pre-summit contacts and assumed incorrectly that they signified the readiness of both parties to reach a final agreement. In fact, there was a huge chasm separating the Israeli and Palestinian positions on Jerusalem that seemed to have been papered over by some of the hyperbole prior to Camp David about a final agreement being within reach.

Israeli and U.S. officials had received excessively optimistic reports from a variety of back channel meetings between Israelis and Palestinians.[53] Back channels were normally used by governments because they provided so-called "plausible deniability" if their existence was revealed in the press (it could be said that these were just meetings of a few academics). But precisely because their results could be so easily denied, they were notoriously unreliable; their negotiators sat in posh European hotels, bereft of the sense of responsibility that an accredited diplomat would feel at an official summit like Camp David.

Peacemaking, like the conduct of war, can only succeed if it is based on accurate intelligence. The real lesson from Camp David was that Israel and the Palestinians have unbridgeable gaps over Jerusalem and that the summit's proposals were unworkable and should not be part of any future negotiating agenda. Indeed, additional talks over Jerusalem could further inflame the entire situation on the ground.

Yet members of Barak's government certainly did not act as though the Camp David proposals were off the table. As he sought to enlist Egyptian help in developing a new diplomatic formula for the Old City, acting foreign minister Shlomo Ben-Ami assured President Mubarak on August 24 that "We are not going back to square one." Ben-Ami explained that Israel was interested in setting down in writing a "paper to express what the parties understand is the product of Camp David on some core issues."[54]

Ben-Ami had his own vision for the Old City that differed greatly from the U.S. proposals:

A special regime in the Old City is what we should try to build. Since we have a two-kilometer square, this is the Old City and full of holy sites—Muslim, Christian, Jewish—populations that mingle in the Jewish Quarter, you have Jews in the Muslim Quarter. You have Jews and Muslims in the Armenian Quarter. Half of it is Jewish. So to divide sovereignty in such a limited space is ridiculous.[55]

The heads of the Catholic, Greek Orthodox, and Armenian Churches wrote to Clinton immediately after Camp David to protest that they had not been consulted about the proposals; they sought international guarantees for their protection in the event of any major change to their status in Jerusalem. President Clinton had just assumed that a compromise for the Old City must include Palestinian sovereignty over the holy places of Christianity in the Christian quarter—including the Church of the Holy Sepulcher—and that the Armenian quarter, which is also a Christian quarter, would stay under Israel.[56]

The Barak government also continued to seek new formulas after Camp David for resolving the Jerusalem issue. These efforts included nebulous proposals for "divine sovereignty" as a solution to the Temple Mount. Despite U.S. and Egyptian mediation efforts in these post–Camp David negotiations, nothing could close the gap between Israel and the PLO. The Palestinians were not interested in a "Holy Basin" with either shared or international control; they wanted Palestinian Arab sovereignty and would settle for nothing less.

## The Clinton Plan for Jerusalem

The Barak government pushed forward with its post–Camp David diplomacy, including consideration of new U.S. proposals for Jerusalem that were even more forthcoming for the Palestinians than the Camp David offers. On December 23, 2000, President Clinton met with Israeli and Palestinian negotiators in the White House and read aloud the new U.S. plan for Jerusalem. Just as at Camp David, Clinton did not present his proposals in writing.

U.S. officials referred to the plan as the "Clinton Parameters," indicating that the proposals only roughly set out the outlines of a possible settlement; a detailed agreement would require further negotiation between the parties. Significantly, according to notes taken by Giddi Grinstein, who worked for Israeli negotiator Gilead Sher, Clinton's oral presentation was to be regarded only as "the ideas of the president." And if the ideas were not accepted, Clinton stated, "they are not just off the table; they go with the president as he leaves office."[57] Clinton's proposals can be summarized as follows:

## Redivision of Jerusalem

The "general principle" put forward was that "Arab areas are Palestinian and Jewish areas are Israeli." This principle for assigning sovereignty was to be applied to the Old City as well. Clinton urged both sides "to create maximal contiguity." This new Clinton proposal was even more favorable to the PLO than the earlier Camp David ideas, since it transferred Palestinian residential areas in the inner neighborhoods around the Old City to full Palestinian sovereignty instead of just giving the Palestinians functional powers in the framework of Israeli sovereignty.

## The Temple Mount Taken from Israel

The Clinton proposals contained several alternative solutions for the Temple Mount:

1. Palestinian sovereignty over the Temple Mount and Israeli sovereignty over the Western Wall "and the space sacred to Judaism of which it is a part," or Israeli sovereignty over the Western Wall "and the Holy of Holies of which it is a part." This proposal would also contain a firm commitment by both sides not to excavate beneath the Temple Mount or behind the Western Wall.
2. Palestinian sovereignty over the Temple Mount and Israeli sovereignty over the Western Wall and "shared functional sovereignty over the issue of excavation," requiring the mutual consent of the parties before any excavation could take place. This second alternative eliminated the idea of Israeli subterranean sovereignty on the Temple Mount that was advanced at Camp David.

Clinton's final summary of his Jerusalem proposal was presented publicly in his parting address to the Israel Policy Forum at the Waldorf-Astoria Hotel in New York on January 7, 2001:

> First, Jerusalem shall be an open and undivided city, with assured freedom of access and worship for all. It should encompass the internationally recognized capitals of two states, Israel and Palestine. Second, what is Arab should be Palestinian, for why would Israel want to govern, in perpetuity, the lives of hundreds and thousands of Palestinians? Third, what is Jewish should be Israeli. That would give rise to a Jewish Jerusalem larger and more vibrant than any in history.

In these public remarks, he refrained from going into the same kind of detail about his proposals for the Temple Mount as he had in his private presentation in December.

The Palestinians had their own forceful argumentation against the Clinton Plan that they presented in the form of a letter from Arafat to Clinton:

> We seek, through this letter, to explain why *the latest American proposals, that were presented without any clarifications, do not meet the required conditions for a lasting peace.* In their present form, the American proposals may lead to the following . . . *partitioning Palestinian Jerusalem into several islands detached from one another as well as from the Palestinian state* [emphasis added].[58]

The Palestinian critique of the Clinton Plan, contained in the Arafat letter, included the formulas proposed for the Temple Mount: "it seems that the American proposal recognizes, in essence, the Israeli sovereignty underneath the Haram (al-Sharif), since it implies that Israel has the right to excavate behind the Wall (which is the same area underneath the Haram), but it voluntarily concede [sic] this right."[59]

Many negotiators blamed the failure of all these talks on Yasser Arafat personally and his rigid ideological positions. Shlomo Ben-Ami recalled how members of the Palestinian delegation at Camp David told their Israeli counterparts that Jerusalem and the Temple Mount were "Arafat's personal obsession," hinting that they themselves held a different opinion. But in reality even the more moderate Palestinian negotiators took a hard line on Jerusalem.

For example, Abu Mazen wrote a two-part article about Camp David in the London-based Arabic daily *al-Hayat* on November 23 and 24, 2000. His account shows that even he refused to recognize Israeli sovereignty over the Western Wall: "We agreed that they could pray near the Western Wall, but without our recognizing any sovereignty over it, based on the 1929 British Shaw Commission. The commission acknowledged that the Western Wall belongs to the Muslim Waqf, but the Jews were permitted to pray near it provided they did not blow the Shofar."[60]

Thus Abu Mazen invoked positions that had been crafted when the British Mandatory government was searching for a middle ground between Jewish demands for religious freedom in Jerusalem and the positions of Jerusalem mufti Hajj Amin al-Husseini, who was seeking to constrain and even roll back the Jewish presence. Was the PLO in 2000 seriously suggesting that Jews would be prohibited from placing benches and an ark for Torah scrolls in front of the Western Wall as in 1929? Were they going to try to ban the blowing of the shofar, or ram's horn, in Jewish ceremonies?

One further aspect of the Clinton Plan for Jerusalem should be noted, especially in its more detailed December 2000 version. Clinton proposed that regardless of which model Israelis and Palestinians decided upon for dividing sovereignty on the Temple Mount, they should put in place "an international monitoring mechanism." The use of international organizations was not an alien concept for either side. In fact, Arafat proposed through one of his aides that the Saudi-dominated Organization of the Islamic Conference (OIC) should become involved in the Temple Mount, even entrusting it with sovereignty. Recognizing that use of the OIC could give countries like Iran or Iraq a say in Jerusalem affairs, the Clinton administration told Arafat that it was a non-starter.[61]

For his part, Ben-Ami began to take an interest in a possible UN role on the Temple Mount. He certainly supported using the UN to help close an Israeli-Palestinian understanding over the Temple Mount in the future. For example, he explored the idea of taking the Clinton Plan and turning it into a new UN Security Council resolution that would have, in effect, served as a new authoritative interpretation of Resolution 242.[62]

This might have created some pressure on Arafat, but it would have also locked in Barak's concessions at Camp David and in the months that followed—even though they had not even led to an agreement—into a formal UN resolution that could bind a future Israeli government even if it opposed the Barak team's concessions. Given the fact that Barak's government had lost its parliamentary majority and was facing new elections, this would have been a cynical attempt to keep these controversial proposals alive no matter what happened at the ballot box.

And what would the U.S. do if asked to support such an idea? Ben-Ami admitted he had already sought the advice of the U.S. ambassador to the UN at the time, Richard Holbrooke, by October 2000 about inserting the UN into the Temple Mount issue. With this effort, Ben-Ami was looking for a way to use the UN Security Council to provide legitimacy to Arafat's custodianship over the Temple Mount. Holbrooke, to his credit, poured cold water over the idea of any UN engagement on the Temple Mount issue.[63] In its remaining months in office, even the Clinton administration declined to push for this new Security Council resolution that some on the Israeli side were considering.

The last chapter of Israeli-Palestinian negotiations during the Barak period took place in Taba, Egypt, during the latter part of January 2001. Unlike the Camp David summit and the Clinton Plan, the Taba negotiations were mostly bilateral, with only a low-level U.S. diplomatic presence. Foreign Minister Shlomo Ben-Ami heralded the Taba talks as producing a near breakthrough. "We have never been closer to an agreement," he exclaimed. Yet Ben-Ami's Palestinian counterpart, Abu Ala', offered the exact opposite assessment of the marathon talks: "there has never before been a clearer gap in the positions of the two sides."[64]

Abu Ala' appears to have presented the more accurate version. The Palestinian line seemed to have hardened on the issue of settlement blocs. The negotiating gaps between the parties actually widened at Taba.[65] Meanwhile, Israeli negotiators probed the idea of creating a special international regime for the "Holy Basin"—an area including the Old City and some nearby locations including the Mount of Olives cemetery. The Palestinians rejected the proposal, insisting on Palestinian sovereignty instead.[66]

Even on the question of the Western Wall, the Israeli and Palestinian positions were far apart. The EU Special Representative to the Peace Process (now Spanish foreign minister) Miguel Moratinos attended the Taba talks and his notes were published in the Israeli daily *Haaretz* on February 14, 2002; all he could write about the Western Wall was that the Palestinians acknowledged Israel's request for an "affiliation" with the Western Wall, but did not explicitly accept Israeli sovereignty over it. This sounded exactly like Abu Mazen's position as described in *al-Hayat* several months earlier.

The Israeli negotiating team appeared to be determined to press ahead for an agreement at all costs; they even probed ideas that had not been approved by Barak. For example, Ben-Ami reportedly told Erekat that he just wanted assurances that if the Palestinians obtain the Temple Mount, there would be no unilateral Palestinian archeological excavations in the area, since it was holy to the Jews. Erekat apparently refused, saying, "…we won't write anything about the area being holy to the Jews."[67]

## What Went Wrong

A careful analysis of the failure of the Camp David diplomacy over Jerusalem yields some lessons for future diplomatic initiatives, especially by Israel or the U.S. Despite the unprecedented concessions offered by Barak regarding Jerusalem, especially in comparison with every preceding Israeli prime minister since 1967, the PLO did not offer any corresponding readiness to compromise on territorial matters.

Arafat in essence insisted on receiving 100 percent of the West Bank, including East Jerusalem, and the Gaza Strip. He was only willing to concede land in these territories if he received equivalent compensation via a land swap from unpopulated territories inside of pre-1967 Israel like the arid Halutza area of the Negev. However, it should be stressed that Resolution 242 from November 1967, which had served until Camp David as the basis of Israeli-Palestinian agreements, did not articulate any need for a land swap;

it related only to the territories Israel captured in the 1967 Six-Day War. Unfortunately, due to Arafat's insistence, Israeli and U.S. negotiators became willing to explore the land swap idea, even though it exceeded the scope of the most central UN resolutions on the peace process.

The expression of Israeli interest in a possible land swap ended up as another de facto Israeli concession that failed to bring the parties any closer to an agreement, but it allowed the Palestinians to begin to erode even the 1949 Armistice lines. It certainly was not even clear whether the land swap concept, based on the Halutza area, could be applied to Jerusalem at all. Official Palestinian statements indicated little or no willingness to compromise on land inside the Old City of Jerusalem; residual Palestinian claims to sovereignty in the Jewish Quarter and even over the Western Wall were repeatedly voiced in the post–Camp David period.

Some Palestinians also sought special land swaps for Jerusalem, asking for land in the western side of the city in exchange for Israeli-populated areas in East Jerusalem. Finally, while Barak was willing to forgo exclusive Israeli sovereignty over the Temple Mount, albeit stipulating that he would not accept exclusive Palestinian sovereignty, the PLO would accept no alternatives to Palestinian sovereignty, period.

The Taba negotiations illustrated the problem Israeli negotiators had in reading Palestinian positions. Foreign Minister Ben-Ami asserted that the parties "had never been closer to an agreement." Yet the Palestinians presented a completely contradictory assessment; Sa'eb Erekat said that Taba "emphasized the size of the gap between the positions of the two sides."[68] It appeared that throughout the negotiating process from Camp David to Taba, Israeli and U.S. diplomats based their assessments of the Palestinians more on wishful thinking than on hard information.

The European Union also contributed to the failure of negotiation over Jerusalem. On March 1, 1999, the German ambassador to Israel, whose country was serving as the rotating president of the European Union, sent what is called a *Note Verbale* to Israel's Ministry of Foreign Affairs reviving the UN General Assembly's outdated 1947 proposal from Resolution 181 for internationalizing Jerusalem. This used the resolution's Latin term describing Jerusalem as an internationalized separate entity under UN control: "The European Union reaffirms its known position concerning the specific status of Jerusalem as a *corpus separatum*."

Internationalization had patently failed back in 1948; the UN hadn't lifted a finger to break the siege of Jerusalem, leading Prime Minister Ben-Gurion to declare in 1949 that the elements in Resolution 181 that related to Jerusalem were "null and void." Now the EU was resurrecting a super-annuated UN General Assembly resolution that had been utterly rejected by the Arab side in 1947 and had been abandoned afterwards by the Israelis after they had waged a bitter war, with no international help, in Jerusalem's defense. In any case, it had not been a legally binding international agreement, but only a failed recommendation of the UN.

The newly articulated EU position only radicalized the Palestinians. The official Palestinian Authority newspaper *al-Ayyam* quoted on March 14, 1999, the conclusion of the leading Palestinian negotiator, Abu Ala': "The [EU's] letter asserts that Jerusalem in both its parts—the Western and the Eastern—is a land under occupation." It should be stressed that Abu Ala' was thought by most Israelis to be pragmatic; he was the senior PLO official in the Oslo back channel that led to the Oslo Agreement. Yet even his position had hardened. The Arab states soon followed, with the six-state Gulf Cooperation Council, led by Saudi Arabia, issuing a press release on March 15, 1999, stating, "The Council again commended the European Union for its refusal to recognize Al-Quds, including the western section of the city...."

Just over a week later, Arafat emerged from a meeting with UN secretary-general Kofi Annan and spoke to reporters in Arabic about Resolution 181. On March 25, his representative to the UN, Nasser al-Kidwa, then wrote a letter to Annan that was released as a UN document in which he argued that the old partition boundaries from Resolution 181 were what the international community had accepted. This argument not only could be used to refute Israel's claims to East Jerusalem, but could equally be applied to West Jerusalem as well. In short, the EU had managed to make an intricate diplomatic issue even more impossible to handle, just over one year before Camp David.[69]

Part of the difficulty of bridging the gap between Israel and the PLO over the issue of Jerusalem, or over any final status issue for that matter, could stem from a more fundamental problem with the PLO's approach to peace negotiations that became evident during Arafat's Al-Aqsa Intifada: leading Palestinian spokesmen revealed that they ultimately had no intention of ever reaching a final peace with Israel.

Thus, Yasser Abd Rabbo, the Palestinian Authority minister of information, confessed on a television program broadcast on November 17, 2000 on the Qatar-based *al-Jazeera* network that "there is a consensus among Palestinians that the direct goal is to reach the establishment of an independent Palestinian state in the June 4, 1967, borders, with Jerusalem as its capital, [but] regarding to the future after that, it is best to leave the issue aside and not to discuss it."[70]

Less than a year later, Faisal al-Husseini was far more revealing about the PLO's ultimate intentions during the Oslo years. He compared Arafat's use of the Oslo peace process to a Trojan horse that allowed the PLO to get the Israelis to open "their fortified gates and let it inside their walls." The real strategic goal of the PLO, he explained, had been a Palestine "from the [Jordan] River to the [Mediterranean] Sea," and not a mini-state in the West Bank.[71]

These were not a few discordant voices, for other major Palestinian figures expressed the same views. There was Salim Za'anun, the chairman of the Palestine National Council, who stated in an official PA newspaper that the PLO covenant calling for Israel's destruction had never changed and hence remained in force. Sakher Habash was a hardline Fatah ideologue within the PLO, but nevertheless Arafat would request that he speak in various West Bank cities in his name; for example, he declared: "Experience proves that without the establishment of the democratic state *on all the land* peace will not be realized [emphasis added]." To give these words added authority, they were written up in the official Palestinian Authority newspaper *al-Hayat al-Jadida* on January 1, 2001.[72]

Nor were statements of this sort confined to the Arabic press. Marwan Barghouti was one of the heads of Arafat's Fatah movement in the West

Bank. He frequently mixed with Western reporters before he was convicted in an Israeli court for his involvement in orchestrating terrorist attacks against Israeli civilians during the intifada. In an interview appearing in the July 9, 2001, edition of *The New Yorker*, Barghouti admitted that even if Israel withdrew from 100 percent of the territories it had captured in the Six-Day War, the Israeli-Palestinian conflict would still not end. Like Sakher Habash he demanded the replacement of Israel with "one state for all the peoples."

Of course, these statements could be the product of the heated political environment created by the intifada. But throughout the post-1993 Oslo period, there was considerable evidence that the PLO leadership's ambitions extended beyond any arrangements within the 1967 lines, in accordance with UN Security Council Resolution 242, and extended into Israel itself. Arafat referred to the original Oslo Agreement as another Treaty of Hudaybiyyah—a temporary truce from the time of Muhammad.[73]

The repeated references of PLO spokesmen in 1998–99, including a reference at the United Nations, to the UN General Assembly Resolution 181 of 1947 as a *territorial* basis for a peace settlement further indicated that Palestinian ambitions stretched well beyond the West Bank and Gaza Strip. If these hardline positions were the true bottom line of PLO negotiators, then no diplomatic initiative could have closed the gap between the parties.

# PART III

## Radical Islam and Jerusalem

# Chapter 7

# The Evil Wind: Radical Islam, the Destruction of Holy Sites, and Jerusalem

The attacks on New York and Washington on September 11, 2001, and the militant ideology that spawned them had nothing to do with the issue of Jerusalem. The diplomatic struggle over the future of the Holy City had become dormant with the failure of the Camp David summit a year earlier and the sharp escalation of Palestinian suicide bombing attacks against Israelis, known as the Second Intifada, shortly thereafter. Al-Qaeda had already been at war with the United States since the early 1990s. Its list of grievances against the West had a clear order of priorities in the previous decade. First, it focused on removing the Western—and especially the U.S.—presence from Saudi Arabia. Second, it sought to free Iraq from UN sanctions. And then came Jerusalem, which al-Qaeda generally listed as only a tertiary priority.[1]

That Jerusalem was not the highest priority for al-Qaeda was not surprising. Al-Qaeda was not formed in response to one of the Arab-Israeli wars involving Jerusalem. It sprang up in the aftermath of the war against the Soviet Union in Afghanistan. Moreover, the worldview of its leader, Osama bin Laden, stemmed from a mixture of two militant Islamist movements in the Arab world: the Wahhabi movement in Saudi Arabia and the

Muslim Brotherhood of Egypt.[2] Wahhabism was an eighteenth-century Islamic movement originating in Central Arabia that was founded by a religious reformer named Muhammad ibn Abd al-Wahhab, who was largely inspired by the writings of the fourteenth-century Islamic scholar Ibn Taymiyah. Both of these religious leaders wrote polemics against Christianity, Shiism, and Sufi practices.[3]

In his youth, Ibn Abd al-Wahhab even copied by hand the works of Ibn Taymiyyah. In the 1990s Osama bin Laden would extensively quote both scholars, indicating the importance of their thinking in the formulation of his worldview.[4] Because of Ibn Taymiyyah's centrality to the world of Sunni militancy that gave birth to al-Qaeda, his religious positions on the issue of Jerusalem are important to recount. After all, it was Ibn Taymiyyah who warned Muslims at the time not to assign to Jerusalem any special sanctity, which was to be specifically reserved for Mecca alone. He was a critic of *bid'a*, or any innovation that might be added to Islam from other religions. He was also disturbed by Muslims performing special ceremonies while visiting the Temple Mount that were normally reserved for the Holy Mosque in Mecca.

This may have had some impact during the dawn of Wahhabism. It is noteworthy that in the late eighteenth and early nineteenth centuries, when the Wahhabis began their wars of expansion, they moved first and foremost to take Mecca and Medina. At a later stage they attacked the Shiite holy cities of Kerbala and Najaf. They also threatened Damascus, hundreds of miles from their base in Arabia. But they never directed their wars of conquest toward Jerusalem, which remained entirely out of their political orbit. Even today, in the modern Saudi state, Wahhabi clerics have inveighed against aspects of how Muslims celebrate Muhammad's Night Journey to Jerusalem.[5] According to Sheikh Muhammad bin Salah al-Munajid, improperly commemorating the Night Journey is nothing less than *bid'a*.[6]

The Muslim Brotherhood initially had a different position toward Jerusalem. The group was originally established in 1928 by Hasan al-Bannah in order to preserve Egypt as an Islamic society as it began drawing up a new national constitution after the fall of the Ottoman Empire and the disbanding of the caliphate in 1924. Many of the key figures who would help form al-Qaeda were influenced by the ideology of the Muslim Brotherhood leadership, which makes its history quite relevant to contemporary events. Despite its initial internal focus in its early years, the Muslim Brotherhood became intensely involved in the issue of Palestine, even sending military units to participate in the 1948 Arab-Israeli War. These were mostly active in the southern Negev theater and to a lesser extent in the Jerusalem area.[7]

However, the even more militant offshoots of the Muslim Brotherhood in Egypt during the 1990s advanced the principle that the road to the liberation of Jerusalem must begin in Cairo.[8] Their first priority was regime change in Egypt and the rest of the Arab world, so they directed their energies against the "near enemy" around them. Indeed, Ayman al-Zawahiri, who began his career in the Muslim Brotherhood and would become the deputy head of al-Qaeda under Osama bin Laden, wrote an article in April 1995 in *Al-Mujahidin* entitled "The Way to Jerusalem Passes Through Cairo."[9] He argued in the article that "Jerusalem will not be opened until the battles in Egypt and Algeria have been won."[10] His contemporary, Muhammad Abd al-Salam Faraj of the Egyptian Islamic Jihad, argued similarly that the liberation of Jerusalem must be waged under the banner of Islam and not by an "impious" leadership that he sought to overthrow.[11] In short, these organizations did not want to focus at this time on the war for Jerusalem; they preferred to try to assassinate Egyptian president Hosni Mubarak.

This logic was common in other parts of the Islamist world: it was adopted by Abdullah Azzam, the famous Palestinian mentor of Osama bin Laden, who emerged out of the Jordanian branch of the Muslim Brotherhood. Azzam wrote a book entitled *From Kabul to Jerusalem* establishing that victory in Afghanistan was a necessary prerequisite for taking Jerusalem.[12] This prioritization was also adopted by Abu Muhammad al-Maqdasi, the Palestinian mentor of Abu Musab al-Zarqawi in Jordan.[13] Khalid Sheikh Muhammad, who started out in the Kuwaiti branch of the Muslim Brotherhood, would encourage al-Qaeda to strike even further away from the Israeli-Palestinian conflict when he conceived of the idea of the September 11 strikes against the United States, which he would see through as their chief architect.

This idea's power was most evident in the case of Abdullah Azzam, mentioned above. In the late 1980s, Azzam could have just as easily returned to the West Bank and joined Hamas, the Palestinian branch of the Muslim Brotherhood that launched its first military campaign against Israel in 1987. He could have become one of its early leaders. Instead, Azzam, who had moved to Saudi Arabia in the late 1970s where he taught bin Laden at King Abd al-Aziz University in Jeddah, had other priorities. He relocated himself to distant Afghanistan to fight the Soviet Union, bringing his Saudi student bin Laden with him.

U.S. diplomacy on the Palestinian-Israeli issue had no effect on the ideology of Islamic militants like Azzam. As noted earlier, in September 1993, Clinton presided over the signing on the White House lawn of the Declaration of Principles, known also as the Oslo Accords, between Israel and the PLO. This generated the Gaza-Jericho Agreement in 1994 and the Interim Agreement in 1995 that dealt with the West Bank. More agreements followed: the Hebron Protocol in 1997, the Wye Agreement in 1998 and finally the effort to reach a final agreement at Camp David in July 2000, where the redivision of Jerusalem was proposed.

Yet during this period the al-Qaeda threat actually worsened, thus demonstrating that there was no correlation between U.S. activism on issues like Jerusalem and the scale of the terrorist threat to the United States. After the first World Trade Center attack in 1993, al-Qaeda struck Americans in Saudi Arabia in 1995, and then two U.S. embassies in East Africa in 1998. By 2000, al-Qaeda had attacked the USS *Cole* at the port of Aden in Yemen. And finally on September 11, 2001, the World Trade Center and Pentagon absorbed al-Qaeda's most lethal attack to date. The territorial disputes between Israel and the Palestinians were simply peripheral to al-Qaeda's agenda.

Al-Qaeda's war with the West was not a territorial conflict but rather was a far more fundamental one; along with challenging the "near enemy" represented by the current Arab regimes, bin Laden's organization hoped to defeat the West as a whole—"the far enemy"—and set the stage for a worldwide Islamic regime based on its militant interpretation of the religion. For many of its adherents, the goal was the reestablishment of a new global caliphate. Given the scale of these aspirations, the motivation of al-Qaeda did not emanate from a particular political grievance whose redress could weaken the organization's appeal. Its recruitment tapes utilized scenes of its battlefield victories from the Balkans to Chechnya as much as references to what it regarded as historical injustices. As a result, all the diplomatic energies invested in the 1990s in the resolution of the Israeli-Palestinian conflict did not affect the wider phenomenon of terrorism which the U.S. increasingly had to face.

## From Bamiyan to the Temple Mount

Jerusalem may not have been radical Islam's highest priority, but militant Islamic movements like the Taliban and al-Qaeda were nonetheless influencing the Middle East in ways that would have enormous implications for the future of the Holy City. Beginning in the late 1990s a wave of unprecedented acts of religious intolerance, chiefly expressed through violent attacks on holy sites, appeared to be sweeping over a large area from Morocco out to Pakistan. It was as though an evil wind was blowing across the Middle East, leaving a trail of desecrated and even decimated places of worship in its wake.

The most blatant example of this new wave, which captured headlines worldwide, occurred in early 1998 when the Taliban captured the Bamiyan Valley in Afghanistan, where two huge sandstone statues were located that depicted the Buddha. They were the largest Buddhist statues in the world, with one reaching a height of 165 feet and the other stretching 114 feet. They were also over 1,500 years old.[14] The Taliban made multiple efforts to destroy the statues. In July 1998, Taliban fighter aircraft bombed the sandstone mountain in which the statues were located. Later in September, Taliban forces blew off the head of one of the Buddhas with explosives and fired rockets at the groin area of the other. The statues were damaged but remained standing.

The Taliban became determined to completely eliminate the ancient statues, despite growing international efforts to protect them. On February

26, 2001, Taliban leader Mullah Mohammad Omar ordered the final destruction of the Bamiyan Buddhas "based on the verdict of Islamic scholars and the decision of the Supreme Court of the Islamic Emirate [of Afghanistan]." Secretary-General Kofi Annan interceded with the Taliban foreign minister to try to save the Buddhas. Neither the protests of the UN nor the international community, however, could stop them. A Taliban force came to Bamiyan from Kabul with a truckload of dynamite. Soldiers drilled holes in the torsos of the two statues, placed the dynamite charges inside, and detonated them, completely obliterating the Buddhas and reducing them to rubble. The entire operation was supervised by the Taliban defense minister.[15] And this was only the tip of the iceberg when it came to Taliban intolerance. Bamiyan was an area where the Hazaras resided; they were ethnically close to the Mongols and, more important for the Taliban, they were Shiite Muslims. The Taliban, who were militant Sunnis, tried to starve out 300,000 Hazara Shiites in Bamiyan; they managed to kill 5,000.

The assault on the Buddhist statues and the attempted mass murder of the Shiites was relatively new for Afghanistan, which did not have a long history of this kind of Islamic extremism.[16] Islamic armies from different dynasties had moved across Afghanistan since the seventh century. But no previous conqueror of Afghanistan had tried to eliminate the Buddhist statues. Was this a local phenomenon or part of a wider change in the Islamic world? As one writer noted, Islam had coexisted with pagan objects in the past, from the Sphinx in Egypt to the statues in Iranian Persepolis.[17] Why was this happening now?

The Taliban's religious traditions came out of the Deobandi Islamic schools of nineteenth-century India, which were not particularly extreme. What appeared to have radicalized the Taliban movement was an external source: the influence of Wahhabi Islam from Saudi Arabia on the ideological development of the Taliban leadership. After all, it was the Saudi religious leadership, the *ulama*, who advocated a Saudi relationship with the Taliban—this was especially true of Saudi Arabia's grand mufti in the 1990s, Sheikh Abd al-Aziz bin Baz, and the Saudi minister of justice Muhammad bin Jubair. Huge amounts of Saudi aid poured into the country, particularly from the large Islamic charities controlled by the ulama.[18] Jubair was known as "the exporter of the Wahhabi creed in the Muslim world." Finally, Osama bin Laden and al-Qaeda also served as important conduits of militant Wahhabism to the Taliban so that in time his worldview permeated senior levels of the Afghan leadership.[19]

The effects of Saudi influence became quickly apparent. There is little doubt that the financial dependence of the Taliban on Saudi Arabia and its clerics contributed to the formation of its religious and ideological outlook. The Taliban copied Wahhabi religious practices, even though when it came to the main four schools of Islamic law the Afghans traditionally had been followers of the Hanafi school, as opposed to the Hanbali school of law that was predominant among the Saudi Wahhabis. Despite these differences, the Taliban introduced religious police into Afghanistan that were modeled on the Saudi variety. Indeed, it is extremely likely that the new sectarianism that caused the Taliban Sunnis to attack Afghan Shiites also had Saudi origins.

For example, a *fatwa*, or religious opinion, signed by four members of the permanent committee of the Saudi ulama, including Sheikh bin Baz, asserted that the Shiites were not Muslims, but rather were to be defined as infidels.[20] Worse still was a fatwa issued in September 1991 by a member of the Saudi Council of Higher Ulama, Sheikh ibn Jibrin, arguing that Shiites were *rafida*—a term of opprobrium that can mean "disloyal" or even "apostate." According to ibn Jibrin, given that definition, killing them was not a sin.[21] Anti-Shiite doctrines had been part of Wahhabi Islam since the time of Muhammad ibn Abd al-Wahhab in the eighteenth century. But now those doctrines had the backing of the religious establishment of a modern Saudi state that was awash with petro-dollars, and were consequently being exported to the Saudis' Afghan client.

In order to attack religious sites that had existed undisturbed for hundreds of years like the Bamiyan Buddhist statues, the Taliban needed to internalize two messages from their Wahhabi mentors. First, they needed to see other religions—including Shiite Islam—in categories that no longer merited the protective status that Islam traditionally had granted to many groups during the various Islamic empires of the past.

This transformation was in fact occurring in Wahhabi Islam in Saudi Arabia. For the radical clerics there, Christians and Jews were no longer the "people of the book," deserving security within some second-class status, but were being called infidels. In fact, one Saudi cleric used this new demoted status for Christians and Jews to justify the use of weapons of mass destruction against them. Buddhists, or more precisely their ancient places of pilgrimage, did not have any basis for obtaining any better status than Christians and Jews.

Second, there needed to be a special religious sanction to destroy the religious sites that belonged to other faiths, especially after their status had been demoted. The Wahhabism exported by Saudi Arabia was rooted in an uncompromising campaign against *shirk*—any action that could be interpreted as polytheisitic, like saint or martyr worship that was frequently practiced by many religions around the tombs of holy figures. The Wahhabis particularly condemned those who petitioned these revered individuals to intervene on their behalf with God; in fact, a Muslim was not even supposed to mention the name of Muhammad in the opening of prayer, or to commemorate his birthday. In the eighteenth century, Muhammad ibn Abd al-Wahhab demolished the tombs of the companions of Muhammad, which had become objects of religious veneration.

The implementation of his doctrine reached the point that when Wahhabi armies entered Medina in 1806, they demolished many Islamic shrines and even planned to destroy the grave of Muhammad, which allegedly had led to polytheistic tendencies among Muslims. Stone idols, sacred trees, or rocks over which some Bedouin engaged in pre-Islamic religious acts of devotion were the original primary targets of destruction in Wahhabism's military campaigns. It was the Shiite adoration of Muhammad's son-in-law, Ali, and the almost divine attributes they assigned to him and his successors, from Hasan and Hussein, right out to the Twelfth Imam, that caused the Wahhabis to detest Shiism in particular, starting with the 1802 sacking of the Shiite holy city of Kerbala.

This Wahhabi insistence on destroying holy sites that might lead to polytheistic practices has in fact survived to the present day. No less that Sheikh bin Baz himself issued a fatwa in 1994 reading, "It is not permitted to glorify buildings and historical sites. Such action would lead to *shirk* because people might think the places have spiritual value."[22] This was not just a theoretical legal judgement; it was put into practice in 1998—within Saudi Arabia itself—when the grave of Amina bint Wahhab, the mother of Muhammad, was destroyed by bulldozers and gasoline was then poured over the site.[23] It doesn't take much imagination to consider how the same authorities would treat ancient statues that were revered by other faiths if that is how they treated Islamic tombs. In short, the Taliban's destruction of the Buddhist statues in Bamiyan was an act that fit the Wahhabi worldview like a glove.

In fact, while the destruction in Bamiyan itself was the work of the Saudis' Taliban protégés, important clerical figures in the Saudi religious establishment issued fatwas explaining their religious support for the Taliban's demolition of the statues. For example, there was Sheikh Hamud bin Uqla al-Shu'aibi, a hard-line establishment cleric, who later would back al-Qaeda's September 11 attacks on New York and Washington.[24] A similarly militant cleric, who had been admired by Osama bin Laden, was Sheikh Sulayman bin Nasir al-Ulwan, who also issued a fatwa backing the Taliban action against the Buddhist statues.[25]

These were not obscure individuals known only to the Saudi elites and their Taliban students. The writings of both these Wahhabi clerics had region-wide influence and were read by Islamic militants from Chechnya to Western Iraq to the Gaza Strip. The advent of the Internet simplified the worldwide proliferation of their ideas. For example, their religious rulings in support of suicide bombing attacks were featured on the website of Hamas, where a fatwa from a Saudi scholar was more common than the writings of Palestinian Islamists.[26]

This ideology was also disseminated through printed Wahhabi texts from Mecca. The writings of Sheikh al-Ulwan that appeared in such texts were studied in one of the top Hamas schools in the Gaza Strip, called the *Dar al-Arqam* Model School. Finally, with its oil wealth, Saudi Arabia was able to offer generous scholarships to students from around the Middle East to study in hothouses of extremism like the Islamic University of Medina. Many Palestinians took up these offers, so that the rulings of

Saudi Arabia's clerical establishment, including its most militant elements, became easily accessible to the whole Muslim world.

In addition to the Wahhabi support the Taliban received for destroying the Buddhist statues, it is important to stress the position of Sheikh Yusuf Qaradhawi, the most important spiritual authority for the worldwide Muslim Brotherhood, including its Palestinian branch, Hamas (see below). Qaradhawi's views were doubly important because of his regular appearances on the *al-Jazeera* news network, where he had his own television program. Despite his open support for abducting and killing Americans in Iraq, he was often received warmly in Europe, as he was during his 2004 visit to London, where he was hosted by Mayor Ken Livingstone. Initially, Qaradhawi opposed the assault on the Buddhist statues and made a high-profile trip to Afghanistan to urge the Taliban to halt their proposed destruction. He later explained on *al-Jazeera* that at first he opposed the attacks because he was concerned with their effect on the status of Muslim minorities in Buddhist countries. But after visiting Afghanistan, he changed his mind and actually praised the Taliban, explaining that they were concerned with outsiders coming to Afghanistan and worshiping the statues.[27]

Qaradhawi also associated himself with a 2006 Egyptian Islamic ruling against ancient Egyptian statues, declaring that "the statues of ancient Egypt are prohibited."[28] In fact, once the attacks on non-Muslim religious sites were legitimized in Afghanistan, it was not surprising to see the phenomenon spread across the entire Middle East and beyond. Wahhabi missionaries were seeking to cleanse Central Asia of the practice of venerating Muslim saints. In Iraqi Kurdistan, Islamic militants affiliated with pro-Wahhabi groups like *Ansar al-Islam* destroyed the graves of religious scholars, belonging to the Naqshabandi Sufi order, at which local Muslims recited prayers. In fact, in a July 2002 press release, the Patriotic Union of Kurdistan, led by Jalal Talabani, compared one such assault in a place called Bakhi Kon to the Taliban attacks on the Buddhist statues.[29] In April 2006, Talabani was elected the president of the new Iraq.

All these trends toward increasing religious intolerance converged in Iraq during the Sunni insurgency after the downfall of Saddam Hussein. The Sunni militant organizations that were heavily motivated by the

Wahhabi interpretation of Islam focused much of their internal campaign against the Iraqi Shiite population and its religious institutions. Shiite mosques were regularly targeted by Sunni suicide bombers. The most dramatic attack was carried out on February 22, 2006, by a team of two Iraqis and four Saudis who detonated bombs in the 1,200-year-old al-Askariya Mosque in Sammara, destroying the mosque's golden dome.[30]

The special sanctity of the al-Askariya Mosque was derived from its location as the burial place of the tenth and eleventh Imams, according to Shiite tradition. Additionally, it was regarded as the place where the Twelfth Imam vanished and went into hiding in 874. The attack represented an unprecedented escalation in the severity of the war on religious sites. There had been Sunni attacks on Shiite shrines in Iraq before; besides the 1802 Wahhabi assault on Kerbala, in 1843 an Ottoman Sunni governor stormed the shrines of Hussein and Abbas in Kerbala and desecrated them by turning them into stables.[31] But the internal war roiling Iraq since 2004 has been far more intense than anything that has occurred before. And modern war on holy sites quickly became contagious in Iraq's sectarian conflict; on the day after the attack on the al-Askariya Mosque, Shiite militas in turn attacked twenty-seven Sunni mosques in Baghdad, using small arms, rocket propelled grenades, and mortar rounds.

This intra-Islamic violence had direct implications for the dwindling Christian communities of the Middle East and South Asia, who also faced more attacks during this period. In October 2001, radical Islamists opened fire inside a Catholic church in Bahawalpur, Pakistan, killing fifteen men, women, and children. Sectarian bombings of Pakistani Shiite mosques were also on the rise at the same time. There were no Shiite mosques in Egypt to destroy, but nonetheless attacks against Coptic Christians increased, including the massacre of twenty-one Christians in southern Egypt in early 2000. Eventually, the intensifying persecution of Christians and other non-Muslims by radical Islamists could no longer be ignored.[32]

## The Winds of Intolerance Hit the Palestinians

How these trends affected the Palestinian Arabs during the same time period requires special consideration for the issue of Jerusalem. The dominant political force in Yasser Arafat's Palestinian Authority (PA) was al-Fatah. Its founders in the 1960s included a number of Muslim Brotherhood sympathizers, but it nonetheless sought to be perceived as a movement that would protect Christian and Muslim interests through its international arm, the PLO. Arafat spent a tremendous amount of energy cultivating a relationship with the Vatican, earning repeated audiences with the pope. The declared PLO goal for decades had been the replacement of Israel with a secular democratic state of Palestine.

Nonetheless, on the ground, the situation of Christians in areas controlled by the PA appeared to worsen in the 1990s. The PA itself was formed in 1994, a year after the signing of the Oslo Accords. The PA's draft constitution guaranteed that it would respect all monotheistic religions and guarantee freedom of worship, but also established Islam as the official religion and Islamic law as the primary source of legislation.[33]

And whatever were the principles of governance that Arafat announced, in parallel to his Palestinian Authority there was the Hamas movement. A militant Palestinian Islamist terrorist organization established in 1987–88, Hamas steadily gained strength throughout the 1990s. Fatah and Hamas were political rivals, and Arafat was even willing to have its members arrested in 1996 in reaction to U.S. pressure following a devastating series of Hamas suicide bombings that killed upwards of ninety Israelis.

But Arafat was also willing to closely collaborate with Hamas, signaling to its leadership that it should resume bombing attacks when it suited his interest, as was the case in March 1997. And since Fatah had no independent body of clerics, Hamas religious leaders were frequently employed by the Palestinian Authority. This collaborative relationship evolved to the point that Hamas eventually became a full military partner of Fatah in the confrontation with Israel in 2000. Fatah militias like the al-Aqsa Martyrs' Brigades began engaging in suicide bombings, following the lead of the Hamas religious leadership.

In this context, it is important to remember that Hamas declared itself in its founding charter as the Palestinian branch of the Muslim Brotherhood, whose own record with respect to Christian Copts and local Jews in

Egypt was extremely poor. Historically, the Muslim Brotherhood regarded them both as foreigners who had exploited Egypt's natural resources. It was the Muslim Brotherhood that first coined the language of "the Zionist-Crusading War" that would become one of the main idioms of al-Qaeda years later.[34] Its literature traced much of European imperialism to the political machinations of the Church: "The West surely seeks to humiliate us, to occupy our lands and begin destroying Islam by annulling its laws and abolishing its traditions. In doing this, the West acts under the guidance of the Church. The power of the Church is operative in orienting the internal and foreign policies of the Western bloc, led by England and America."[35]

Sayyid Qutb, the prolific ideologue of the Egyptian Muslim Brotherhood in the 1960s, would develop this theme further, blaming imperialism on "the Crusader spirit which runs in the blood of all Westerners." Subduing the Church was a constant theme of the organization's chief ideologues.

In short, the roots out of which Hamas grew were imbued with a strong anti-Christian predisposition above and beyond its more well-known anti-Israel positions. Hamas was a politically astute Islamist movement; it forged tactical alliances with local Palestinian Christians and even accepted them to its electoral slates. But its long-term ideological program for any territories that came under its control was molded by its affiliation with the Muslim Brotherhood and financial donations from Saudi Wahhabi charities which, by 2003, accounted for between 50 and 70 percent of its annual expenditures.

The effects of the arrival of Arafat's regime in the 1990s became most noticeable in the city of Bethlehem—the birthplace of Jesus and the location of the Church of the Nativity. Back in 1990, before the advent of the PA, when Bethlehem was under the Christian mayor Elias Freij and Israeli military control, Christians enjoyed a 60 percent majority in the city. This figure fell to 20 percent by 2001.[36] There were multiple causes of this dramatic demographic shift. Arafat gerrymandered Bethlehem's municipal boundaries to include large Muslim populations nearby, while his PA encouraged Muslims to immigrate to Bethlehem from Hebron and built large-scale housing projects for them there.

But there was also a massive emigration of Christians from Bethlehem. Contributing to this exodus was mounting social and economic discrimination as well as an environment of growing anti-Christian incitement. There were also many cases of land theft in which Christians were forced off their properties by an "Islamic fundamentalist mafia."[37] Holy sites were increasingly affected as well. Khaled Abu Toameh, the Arab affairs reporter of the *Jerusalem Post*, reported cases of Palestinian Muslims breaking into Christian monasteries to steal gold and other valuables. Christian cemeteries were also vandalized.

Priests and nuns were unable to stop these attacks and they received no help from the Palestinian security services. The Palestinian Anglican bishop, Riah Abu al-Assal, explained the growing anti-Christian environment in terms reminiscent of the views of the Muslim Brotherhood in Egypt: "Unfortunately, for Middle-Eastern Christians, we are perceived by some Muslims as stooges of the West. The extremists look on us as enemies."[38]

In this environment, religious sites generally lost the immunity that they had enjoyed in the past. This became particularly evident in the Palestinian war against Israel, known as the Second Intifada, at the beginning of which Joseph's Tomb in Nablus and the Shalom al-Yisrael Synagogue in Jericho were attacked by armed mobs and desecrated. Christian holy sites became targets as well. In October and November 2000, gunmen from Fatah's *Tanzim* militia took up positions near the churches of the mostly Christian town of Beit Jalla, next to Bethlehem, in order to open fire into the nearby Jewish neighborhood of Gilo. One Christian cleric noted the case of the Church of St. Nicholas where, he explained, Arafat's Tanzim militia hoped Israel's return fire would hit the church, sparking front-page headlines about Israeli attacks on churches.[39]

These attacks culminated in the dramatic invasion of the Church of the Nativity on April 2, 2002, when thirteen armed Palestinians from Hamas, Islamic Jihad, and Arafat's Tanzim militia blew open the church compound, forced their way inside, and seized clergymen as hostages. Wanted by the Israeli army, the gunmen seized the church knowing that the Israelis would be loath to raid a Christian holy site. While holed up inside, the terrorists looted church valuables, desecrated Bibles, and planted bombs (which Israeli soldiers ultimately defused). After nearly six weeks, the attackers emerged as part of a deal sending them off to exile in Europe.[40] This single event illustrated the strikingly divergent attitudes held by the Israeli soldiers and Palestinian armed groups, respectively, toward the sanctity of Jerusalem's holy sites.

As already noted, Hamas was a full military partner of the Palestinian Authority, the latter having been led by Arafat's Fatah movement during the early years of the intifada of 2000. At that time both movements worked together under a common umbrella or joint command called "The National and Islamic Forces." In the West Bank the National and Islamic Forces were commanded by Marwan Barghouti, the local head of Fatah.

Yet by 2006, Hamas was no longer a junior partner of Fatah, for in that year it won the Palestinian parliamentary elections. Just prior to the elections, a Hamas member of the Bethlehem city council suggested that the traditional Islamic tax on non-Muslims, the *jizya* or poll tax, be reinstated for Palestinian Christians as part of the imposition of Islamic law. In this new environment, George Cattan, a Palestinian intellectual, warned that the growing power of Palestinian Islamic movements was compromising the status of Christians and their holy sites: "In the West Bank and Gaza, armed Islamic movements regard Palestine as a Muslim *waqf* [religious endowment], and call to defend the places holy to Muslims while disregarding the places holy to Christians."[41]

## The Assertion of Palestinian Exclusivity in Jerusalem

To ascertain how all this affected Jerusalem during the period from 1993, when the Oslo Agreements were signed, until 2006, when Hamas won the Palestinian parliamentary elections, we must briefly review the Holy City's status during these years. Israeli prime minister Yitzhak Rabin may have launched the Oslo Accords in 1993, but he was determined to keep Jerusalem united under the sovereignty of Israel. Even the Israeli-Palestinian implementation agreements clarified that the jurisdiction of Arafat's Palestinian Authority would not apply to areas that were to be discussed in future final status talks—and Oslo defined Jerusalem only as a future subject of negotiations.[42] In short, the Palestinians had no legal standing in the Holy City according to the agreement that they themselves had signed.

Nonetheless, there were a number of ways through which Arafat's men sought to increase their power and influence in Jerusalem. While Rabin sought to enshrine Jordan's traditional status as the administrative care-taker of the Islamic shrines on the Temple Mount through the 1994 Washington Declaration and the subsequent Treaty of Peace between Israel and Jordan, his foreign minister, Shimon Peres, sent a secret letter of assurances to the PLO a year earlier on October 11, 1993, through the Norwegian foreign minister, Johan Jorgan Holst, assuring the continuation of Palestinian institutions in Jerusalem.

The PLO applied this Israeli assurance liberally. It created a Ministry for Jerusalem Affairs that was headed by Faisal al-Husseini, who was not a full voting member of the Palestinian cabinet, in order to preclude any Israeli protests about PA governmental activity in Jerusalem. This was a transparent ploy to begin penetrating Jerusalem contrary to the Oslo Accords, but it was backed by many European states whose foreign ministers visited Husseini's Jerusalem headquarters in Orient House.

Moreover, in the religious sphere, during September 1994 Arafat established the Palestinian Authority's Ministry for Waqf Affairs in East Jerusalem under Hasan Tahboub. This was an affront not only to Israel but also to Jordan, which had been recognized as the paramount authority in the Muslim shrines on the Temple Mount. Indeed, a month later, when the Jordanian-appointed mufti of Jerusalem died, the PLO rushed in and appointed its own mufti, Sheikh Ikrima Sabri, who managed to win out in a struggle for influence with his Jordanian competitor. Sabri was an extremist; born in 1939, he already belonged to the Muslim Brotherhood during the period of Jordanian rule in the West Bank.

The Israeli government took no action since it was torn between Rabin's pro-Jordanian approach to the holy sites in Jerusalem and Peres's commitments to the PLO. The Clinton administration, which had hosted and witnessed the signing ceremonies for the Israeli agreements with the Palestinians and Jordan, did not get involved. But this Palestinian Authority takeover, even if it was confined to issues of religious administration, was significant, for the Palestinian Waqf had been heavily penetrated by Hamas as well.

In the period that followed, numerous incidents demonstrated that the new Palestinian religious authorities were seeking to erode aspects of the previous status quo at Jerusalem's holy sites. The most dramatic of these occurred on April 9, 1997, when representatives of the Greek Orthodox Church alerted the Jerusalem municipality that Muslim workers associated with the al-Hanake Mosque, which was next to the Church of the Holy Sepulchre, had broken into rooms belonging to the Greek Patriarch and annexed them to the mosque. After these rooms were added to the mosque, they were sealed off to the area controlled by the Greek Patriarch.[43]

The entire initiative had been authorized by the Palestinian Authority Waqf. The main workers active on the site, however, were actually Israeli Arabs from Haifa and Jaffa who belonged to the Islamic Movement in Israel, which was a subsidiary of the Muslim Brotherhood and closely allied with Hamas.[44] The leader of its militant northern faction, Sheikh Ra'id Salah, was in contact with Sheikh Yusuf Qaradhawi on many issues.[45] Qaradhawi brought in the full ideological legacy of the Muslim Brotherhood. Although asked to head the organization, he instead emerged as its main spiritual guide. As noted before, Qaradhawi ultimately supported the actions of the Taliban against the Buddhist statues in Afghanistan's Bamiyan Valley. Now he was influencing Sheikh Salah.

Salah became a hard-liner; unlike the leadership of the southern faction of the Islamic Movement in Israel, he refused to let his members participate in national parliamentary elections.[46] Perhaps his family background contributed to the positions he adopted. He came from a Syrian Druze family that had converted to Islam before moving to Palestine.[47] He built up a close partnership with Dr. Mahmoud al-Zahar, the Hamas leader, who would become the Palestinian Authority foreign minister after Hamas won the 2006 Palestinian elections. He led delegations of his movement to meet with Sheikh Ahmad Yassin, the founder of Hamas. It was generally assumed that his faction benefited from the financial networks of the Muslim Brotherhood, based in Kuwait and Saudi Arabia.[48]

In the meantime, these workers began building a new two-story struc-ture in the mosque courtyard in a place that was adjacent to the northern wall of the Church of the Holy Sepulchre. The mosque had no building permit for the structure, which was intended to be a study hall for the Sufis. The al-Hanake Mosque dated back to the twelfth century and was dedicated by Saladin for the use of a Sufi order in Jerusalem, which still controlled the site. To make matters worse, all this construction eventu-ally collapsed an internal wall inside the Church of the Holy Sepulchre. In another era, a threat of this sort to one of the holiest sites in Christianity could have sparked a war.

What also made this added construction effort especially controver-sial was that it included a bathroom on the second floor that also shared a common wall with the Church of the Holy Sepulchre. The Fransciscans were enraged by this Muslim construction initiative. They noted that the roof of the new building was two feet higher than the Church of the Holy Sepulchre, which in their view constituted an added provocation, for they felt it was intended to demonstrate the superiority of Islam over Christian-ity.[49] The whole situation had become explosive.

Israel preferred that the Hashemite Kingdom of Jordan use its influ-ence with the al-Haneke Mosque to correct the situation. Turning to the Palestinian Authority would be completely self-defeating since it would only enhance the status of the PA in the heart of the Old City. Moreover it was the PA-controlled Waqf that was backing the assault on Church properties. But even the Jordanians were unable to dislodge the Islamic Movement and the al-Hanake Mosque from the Greek Orthodox rooms. Jordan simply offered the Greek Orthodox Church an ancient Byzantine church near Kerak that had been turned into a mosque. In exchange, the Greek Orthodox Church dropped its claim to the two rooms next to the Church of the Holy Sepulchre.[50]

The immediate crisis appeared to be defused. However, the Palestin-ian Waqf undoubtedly emerged from the incident emboldened, since it was able to overturn the status quo in Jerusalem and get away with it. Moreover, it had expanded the area where it could exercise control in the heart of one of the most sensitive holy sites in the Middle East. It was only a matter of time before a similar effort would be attempted in another potential tinderbox on the Old City of Jerusalem: the Temple Mount.

This upcoming clash would become evident in two stages. For years, Arab states had voiced their opposition to Israeli efforts to complete the development of the Western Wall area that formally began not long after the 1967 Six-Day War. The exposed area of the Western Wall used as a center of Jewish prayer was only 187 feet wide. There was another 1,050 feet of the Western Wall along the Temple Mount that was underground and which Israel completed excavating in the late 1980s. In 1991, the Western Wall Tunnel was officially opened, but it reached a dead end at the northwestern corner of the Temple Mount, requiring visitors to double back in order to exit to the outside world.

It would have made more sense for Israel to open up the northern end of the tunnel so that tourists could exit without having to do a U-turn and walk back the entire distance of the narrow underground tunnel. Tourists leaving the tunnel at the northern end would also pour into the tourist shops in the area of the Via Delarosa and increase the business of many Palestinian Arab shopkeepers.

The tunnels were full of rich archaeological discoveries including rooms from the times of King Herod, ballistae fired from Roman catapults against the Jewish defenders of Jerusalem during the Great Revolt when the Temple was destroyed, and many toppled stones from the Roman destruction from the Temple Mount above. Along the tunnels was the original masonry holding up the Temple Mount—including a 45-foot long stone weighing at least 550 tons. And at one area of the subterranean wall was a clearly marked point that designated where the Holy of Holies was located above. The potential for traffic of religious pilgrims from all over the world was enormous. Nonetheless, Israeli officials understood the sensitivity of the Islamic authorities to any changes in the area of the Temple Mount, so that even something as simple as the opening of an exit was usually proposed in consultation with the Waqf.

An opportunity to reach a quiet understanding over the opening of the Western Wall tunnel arose in early January 1996, when the Waqf authorities turned to the Israeli government, headed by Prime Minister Shimon

Peres, with a request to open up the heretofore sealed halls on the Temple Mount, known as Solomon's Stables, for Muslim prayers during Ramadan, when the numbers of Muslim visitors increases and there is a need for a covered area to give them shelter from the winter rains. Solomon's Stables, which included many subterranean halls, did not date back to the time of the United Monarchy of ancient Israel, but was actually a huge and largely abandoned structure that was used for stables by the Knights Templar after the First Crusade.

Neither side had an interest in giving the other a written agreement which stated that in exchange for opening up Solomon's Stables at the end of Ramadan, the northern end of the Western Wall Tunnel would be opened. In the past, agreements of this sort were usually concluded orally or in the form of a quiet mutual acquiescence to each side's requests. Representatives of the Minister of Police were absolutely certain that they had reached such a quiet quid pro quo from the Waqf authorities and reported this back to the Peres government. It was a strictly oral understanding. After Peres lost the 1996 elections to Benjamin Netanyahu, the new government apparently based its understanding of the Western Wall Tunnel/Solomon's stables tradeoff on a January 24, 1996, protocol from Peres's security cabinet.[51]

Following the election, however, the Palestinian Waqf stridently denied that it gave any acknowledgement of Israeli rights to open up the Western Wall Tunnel, while at the same time it significantly expanded upon the rights Israel granted the Waqf in Solomon's Stables, turning a one-time permit to use the area on Ramadan alone in the event of rain, into a license to construct an entirely new and permanent mosque inside the Temple Mount—for the first time in hundreds of years. The new mosque was to consist of Solomon's Stables and another underground structure known as the Ancient al-Aqsa Mosque.

From January 1996 through the rest of the year, the Waqf, assisted by Israeli Arab volunteers from the radical faction of the Islamic Movement, worked feverishly to complete the new mosque that covered an area of 1.5 acres. They claimed that the Ummayad caliph Marwan, the father of the caliph Abd al-Malik who built the Dome of the Rock, had used Solomon's

Stables as a mosque or prayer room in the past, although there was no historical proof of this. Most of the initial work involved installing huge amounts of marble flooring and lighting. On December 10, 1996, they opened the mosque with a mass prayer of 5,000 Muslims, although the area of the new mosque could have housed double that number.[52] The volunteers from the Islamic Movement were not seeking to take over control of the Temple Mount from the Palestinian Authority Waqf. To the contrary, they appeared to be fully coordinated.

As the work proceeded, the Israeli government could have sought to halt what the Waqf was doing without a building license. Instead, it preferred to assert Israel's sovereign rights in another area of the Temple Mount by opening up the northern end of the Western Wall Tunnel. Late at night on September 23, 1996, at the end of the Jewish fast of Yom Kippur, Prime Minister Netanyahu ordered the stones sealing the northern end of the Western Wall tunnel to be knocked out and an exit for the tunnel to be created. His cabinet based its decisions on the understandings that had been quietly worked out months earlier by the Peres government.

Arafat immediately launched an international campaign to force Israel to seal up the opening. He recruited the Arab League, which repeated his charge that the purpose of the tunnel was to collapse the al-Aqsa Mosque and to construct in its place a new Jewish Temple. In an official complaint to the UN Security Council, the Saudi representative to the UN sought action against Israel's "opening an entrance to the tunnel extending under the Al-Aqsa Mosque in occupied East Jerusalem."[53]

Of course, the Western Wall tunnel was not even near the al-Aqsa Mosque—it did not go under the Temple Mount, but rather followed a path that went parallel to the Temple Mount's western side. Nonetheless, despite the fact that the Saudi letter contained essential erroneous facts, it was not dismissed out of hand by the UN and would trigger full consideration of the Western Wall Tunnel by the Security Council.

The chronology alone should have led the Security Council to dismiss the Saudi letter. Most of the tunnel's excavation was completed back in 1987 and no damage was caused at the time to the area of the Muslim shrines; as already noted, that last stretch of the tunnel was dug out in

1991, and it involved uncovering a pre-existing tunnel that had been an aqueduct in Hasmonean times. In short, there was no new digging that had transpired in 1996 and certainly nothing remotely close to the al-Aqsa Mosque. All that had occurred was that a two-foot thick wall at the far end of the tunnel had been opened, so that it could be exited on both its ends.

The campaign against the Western Wall Tunnel had two aspects. First, after the UN Security Council considered the Saudi letter, it adopted Resolution 1073 that called for "the immediate cessation and reversal of all acts which have resulted in the aggravation of the situation, and which have negative implications for the Middle East peace process." This was an implicit call on Israel to seal the Western Wall Tunnel and it had the support of the Clinton administration, which could argue that the language of the resolution was softened and an explicit call on Israel to seal the tunnel was removed.

The second aspect of the campaign against the tunnel was more serious, for it involved outright violence. Initially there was no spontaneous reaction to the opening of the tunnel from the Palestinian street. As a result, the Palestinian Authority decided to incite mass rioting for three days; for the first time since the signing of the Oslo Accords, Palestinian security forces opened fire on Israeli soldiers, resulting in fifteen soldiers killed and about forty Palestinian fatalities.

The clear purpose of the international campaign and accompanying local bloodshed, which had been initiated by Arafat as well, was to force Israel to withdraw from exercising its sovereignty along the side of the Temple Mount, while the Palestinians would complete uninterrupted their effort to totally alter the status quo on top of the Temple Mount by finishing off their new mosque in Solomon's Stables.

Ironically, if any construction initiative threatened the stability of ancient structures on the Temple Mount or its outer walls, it was the completion of this new mosque and not the opening of the Western Wall Tunnel. Solomon's Stables were right next to the al-Aqsa Mosque, while the northern end of the Western Wall Tunnel was roughly 1,000 feet away. The goal here was Palestinian exclusive control of the Temple Mount and not some kind of modus vivendi between two monotheistic faiths. This was clearly a political battle for the future of Jerusalem and not a struggle based on any substance regarding the issues.

The efforts of the Waqf with radical elements of the Islamic movement in Israel to take over the Temple Mount continued. During 1997, the Waqf worked to take possession of another ancient structure that the Muslim authorities called the "Ancient Al-Aqsa" which was under the al-Aqsa Mosque and an adjacent school. It was opened for prayers during Ramadan 1999. The Waqf then argued that these underground mosques would need emergency exits. This led also in 1999 to it opening a huge gaping hole through which thousands of tons of ancient debris was removed and dumped in the neighboring Kidron Valley. Israeli archeologists sifting through this material found artifacts dating back to the First Temple period.[54]

What was clear was that the Waqf workers did not want anyone else to go through the material they had removed or identify it. Stones with decorations and markings were recut. Apparently, there were discoveries that the Waqf sought to hide. For example, one Waqf worker claimed to have seen writing on some stones in ancient Hebrew. He also observed five-pointed Hasmonean stars. Moreover, the trucks carrying the debris from the Temple Mount were followed to Jerusalem's municipal garbage dump, where it was unloaded and mixed with local garbage in order to make it difficult to separate out any historically significant artifacts. When the municipal manager of the city dump was informed that the trucks contained archaeologically significant debris, he redirected them to a clean zone; but after four trucks were told to move to this new area, the rest of the trucks simply stopped coming to the municipal dump.[55]

In July 2000, the director of the Waqf, Adnan Husseini, tried to clarify in the *Washington Post* what exactly the Palestinians were doing on the Temple Mount. He denied that any damage was caused to any archaeological remains. His argument had been proven patently false in light of what had been already found in the rubble the Waqf had removed from the Temple Mount and discarded in various dump sites around Jerusalem. He then explained why they were building new mosques like the "Al-Marwani Prayer Room" in Solomon's Stables: "The Waqf's work on the Haram al-Sharif is being done in anticipation of the thousands of Muslim pilgrims who will be able to visit the Haram after Palestinian-Israeli peace."[56]

It was a weak argument since the Waqf's work on Solomon's Stables began in 1996, well before any negotiations over the future status of Jerusalem were held. But Husseini had revealed an important intention of the Palestinian Authority, in the event that it secured the Temple Mount and most of the Old City in negotiations: to open up Jerusalem to much larger scale Muslim pilgrimage than the city had ever received before. Reliable sources close to the Palestinian Authority indicated that the PLO was considering new plans for eliminating many buildings in the Old City of Jerusalem to make way for new hotel construction on a massive scale in order to house the thousands of pilgrims that it hoped to attract.

By September 2000, Arafat launched a new round of violence against Israel, the pretext of which was the visit to the Temple Mount of Ariel Sharon, who headed at the time the Israeli parliamentary opposition. According to the Palestinian Authority minister of communications, Imad Faluji, the outburst of Palestinian violence that followed was pre-planned by Arafat months earlier; nonetheless, he would call his new war the "Al-Aqsa Intifada" in order to convey the idea that the al-Aqsa Mosque was somehow endangered and hence needed to be defended.[57] Exploiting this new political environment that Arafat had created, the Palestinain Author-ity Waqf took one more step to assert its claim to the area of the Temple Mount; it unilaterally closed off the area to regular inspections from the Israel Antiquities Authority. The Waqf also barred non-Muslim visitors from the Temple Mount.

With Israeli oversight removed, much of the heavier work on the underground mosques could move forward without any concern about its possible disclosure. In total, some 13,000 tons of unsifted archaeological rubble had been removed to city garbage dumps and other sites. A heavy saw was introduced inside the Temple Mount that was being used to cut and destroy ancient columns. Ironically, it was during this period that the Clinton administration and the Barak government were working feverishly to conclude an Israeli-Palestinian final status accord that would have divided the Old City of Jerusalem and granted formal recognition of Pales-tinian control of the Temple Mount.

In early 2001, both Clinton and Barak were replaced. Still, Prime Minister Ariel Sharon understood how a direct clash with the Waqf over the Temple Mount could ignite the whole Islamic world. As a result, his government undertook quiet measures intended to end the enormous damage caused by the Waqf activities. Primarily, he sought to limit the introduction of heavy equipment and machinery into the area of the Temple Mount. Bulldozers and heavy dump trucks would no longer be permitted to enter the Temple Mount to remove tons of ancient remains, although some heavy equipment was still spotted at times by groups of private citizens who reported these instances to the Israeli authorities.

The Waqf efforts, however, were not completely halted. Hundreds of Israeli Arab volunteers still streamed into Jerusalem to work on various new projects. The use of Israeli Arab manpower provided a regular supply of laborers, since the arrival of West Bank Palestinians might be halted in the event of a deteriorating security situation. As a result, by working together, the Waqf and the militant faction of the Islamic Movement in Israel continued their efforts to stake out an exclusive claim over the Temple Mount once their heavy construction projects were arrested.

For in the meantime, the Islamic Movement discovered thirty-seven underground chambers inside the Temple Mount, some of which have large halls. It has undertaken a fundraising drive throughout the Arab world to renovate these areas. Israeli authorities assumed that the work on these underground rooms was being undertaken to build additional mosques or to create a system of passageways connecting a network of prayer halls that the Waqf hoped to create. This would have converted the whole Temple Mount into one huge mosque, and could be used as yet another reason for keeping non-Muslims out of the area. The Sharon government ordered the clean-up of the underground areas halted in August 2001 after only a few of these large halls had been prepared.[58]

The following month, however, the Islamic Movement planned to import water from the Zamzam well in Mecca and pour it into ten cisterns that it had uncovered on the Temple Mount. According to Islamic tradition, the Zamzam was a spring that miraculously appeared before Hagar and Ishmael in the desert after they had exhausted the water they had in their possession upon leaving Abraham. The Zamzam well is located inside the Grand Mosque in Mecca and is only a short distance from the Ka'bah. Its waters come from the heart of the holiest site in Islam. During the first day of the hajj, pilgrims to Mecca drink Zamzam water as one of the religious rites that they perform.

While Zamzam water may be drunk outside of Mecca and is often given to the sick, since it is viewed as having a degree of holiness, it is associated with a religious ceremony that is performed only in Mecca. This raises the question of what the Israeli Islamic Movement planned to do with the Zamzam waters they hoped to store in great quantities on the Temple Mount. Some interpreted this act as an effort to elevate the holiness of Jerusalem for Islam to a status comparable to that of Mecca. True Muslim conservatives would have raised their eyebrows had the plan been implemented; going back to Ibn Taymiyyah, they had always objected to the adoption of Islamic religious rituals in Jerusalem that were normally reserved for Mecca. The sponsors of the project admitted that its purpose was to increase the number of Muslim visitors to the al-Aqsa Mosque.[59] In practical terms if Islamic authorities could argue that Jerusalem and Mecca shared the same sanctity, then they might also rule that non-Muslims must stay away from the Temple Mount, just as non-Muslims are forbidden to enter the area of Mecca. The Islamic Movement in Israel admitted that it had received the support and financial assistance of a number of international Islamic organizations, although it did not reveal their identities.

What seemed certain was that behind this plan was an effort to link directly the sanctity of Jerusalem to that of Mecca and thereby mobilize even greater support for the continuing efforts of the Waqf and the Islamic Movement to take over the entire Temple Mount. Despite all the difficulties, Israeli authorities succeeded in preventing the completion of the Zamzam waters project. The Islamic movement had hoped to ship the holy waters from Saudi Arabia to Jordan by tanker, and then to Jerusalem via the West Bank. Ultimately, the plan was successfully halted.

As with the earlier efforts of the Waqf to destroy Temple Mount antiquities, Israel needed to adopt a number of counter-measures to halt the anarchical situation developing under the religious administration of the Palestinian Authority. But it also needed to be certain that it would not provide an excuse for Arafat to incite a new religious war in response. This required a carefully calibrated strategy. Prime Minister Sharon had rolled back the Palestinian Authority presence in Jerusalem back in August 2001, when he closed down Orient House, the un-official PLO headquarters in East Jerusalem. This reassertion of Israeli control transpired without any incident.

The Temple Mount was a far more delicate matter. The Israeli government took its first move there in August 2003, when it reopened the Temple Mount to all international visitors after it had been closed off to non-Muslims for three years. The Israeli government insisted that the Temple Mount, which was one of the most important holy sites in Jerusalem, be made accessible to people of all faiths, in accordance with Israeli law. It was a principle that even the UN Security Council could not oppose.

The following year, Israel sought quietly to restore Jordanian influence on the Temple Mount and cut back the powers of the Palestinian Authority. Reportedly, Jerusalem's chief of police made a number of secret visits to Jordan for this purpose. Jordan raised approximately $4 million to repair the Dome of the Rock and the al-Aqsa Mosque, as it had done in the past, and thereby asserted its continuing role in the area in a very public way. Jordan had been paying Waqf salaries for years even in the period of Palestinian religious administration, but it now sought to be more assertive with these employees, who were apparently pleased with Jordan's rising interest. Moreover, the Waqf building projects over the last number of years on the Temple Mount had weakened its southern wall; Jordanian engineers arrived to suggest repairs.[60]

Nonetheless, the years of Palestinian Authority control had created the conditions that facilitated the infiltration of militant ideologies. These would be hard to counter, for throughout this period the Friday sermons given on the Temple Mount also became increasingly radical. The themes raised appeared to follow much of the jihadist agenda advanced by spokesmen of al-Qaeda. For example, an April 11, 2003, sermon attacked the current leaders in the Arab world describing their governments as "heretical Arab regimes." Since 2000 this had become a common theme in various

Temple Mount sermons. And, on November 12, 2004, Sheikh Yusuf Sneineh, one of the senior preachers in the al-Aqsa Mosque spoke before 32,000 worshipers at Friday prayers. He also called for the creation of a new caliphate, explaining that the only solution to the problems facing the Palestinians was the establishment of an Islamic state, whose flag will fly over the Temple Mount. The new state, he proposed, would be headed by an Islamic caliph.[61] While Jerusalem had never been the seat of any of the great caliphates of Islam in the past, there were calls among some clerics to convert the Holy City into the capital of the new Islamic caliphate they hoped to create.

The Palestinian Authority–appointed mufti, Sheikh Ikrima Sabri, added strongly anti-American themes to the Temple Mount sermons. Weeks before September 11, Sabri had gone so far to declare before worshipers, "Allah, bring destruction on the United States, on those who help it and on all its collaborators." He also called for the destruction of Great Britain.[62] His militant anti-Americanism continued years later. For example, on December 3, 2004, he charged the U.S. with waging a cultural war against Muslims, which was part of the "Crusader-Zionist attack on Islam." It was notable that these themes were still being voiced even after the death of Yasser Arafat and his replacement by Mahmoud Abbas (Abu Mazen), who had been courted by the Bush administration. It probably reflected the weak control of the Fatah leadership over the religious elements in the Palestinian Authority who were coming under the influence of other movements.

Multiple sources for this radicalization of the Temple Mount sermons can be identified. There were Hamas members who infiltrated the Temple Mount—like Sheikh Hasan Yousef, who spoke to a crowd in front of the al-Aqsa Mosque on April 10, 2005. Additionally, since September 2001, supporters of Hizb ut-Tahrir (the Islamic Liberation Party) often gave brief sermons on the Temple Mount after the main Friday prayers in the al-Aqsa Mosque.[63] One of the organization's strongest proponents among the Palestinians was a preacher named Sheikh Issam Amayra, who gave a monthly sermon in the al-Aqsa Mosque following the afternoon prayers. He would also give a weekly course during the month of Ramadan at the al-Aqsa Mosque itself.

The entry of Hizb ut-Tahrir to the Temple Mount was significant and had international implications. Members of Hizb ut-Tahrir assailed Egypt's foreign minster, Ahmad Maher, in December 2003, when he came to pray in the al-Aqsa Mosque. They also sought to surround the First Lady, Laura Bush, when she visited the Temple Mount in May 2005, but she was protected by the U.S. Secret Service and Israeli security guards. Hizb ut-Tahrir was extremely hostile to existing Arab regimes and those who supported them. According to its own platform, its paramount mission was the reestablishment of the Islamic caliphate, which will rule over the entire Muslim world instead of the present governments.[64]

Moreover, Hizb ut-Tahrir was regarded by Western analysts as an al-Qaeda precursor organization that provided ideological indoctrination to its members and thereby made them ideal recruits for more militant groups like al-Qaeda at a later stage; for this reason, one analyst called them "a conveyor belt for terrorists," meaning that once a Hizb ut-Tahrir member is adequately imbued with its radical Islamist agenda, he is ready to be passed along to groups that actually conduct military operations.[65] Hizb ut-Tahrir itself believed that the reestablishment of the caliphate was a prerequisite for declaring jihad. This distinguished the organization from the main jihadist networks like al-Qaeda. But like al-Qaeda it opposes all the existing regimes in the Islamic world and seeks their replacement.[66]

Hizb ut-Tahrir was founded in Jordanian-controlled East Jerusalem in 1953 by a Palestinian judge named Sheikh Taqi al-Din al-Nabhani. He came out of the Muslim Brotherhood but he felt that it had been too accepting of what he viewed as the Judeo-Christian–dominated Western state system.[67] Its religious outlook was based on Wahhabism. Despite its origins, it did not specifically state that Jerusalem had to be the seat of the new caliphate; it did not disclose its territorial ambitions.[68] Over the years, Hizb ut-Tahrir established secret cells in dozens of countries, perhaps in as many as forty, including many states in Europe and especially in the UK.

In much of the Arab world Hizb ut-Tahrir was illegal. The Germans belatedly outlawed the group in 2003; it had been revealed that September 11 mastermind Muhammad Atta had come under its influence. However, it was still active in Britain. Pakistani prime minister Pervez Musharaf warned the British government in the *London Sunday Times* on July 31, 2005, to shut down Hizb ut-Tahrir, right after the July 7, 2005, London subway bombings, thereby linking the presence of the organization with the new internal jihadist threats facing Britain. It seemed that Hizb ut-Tahrir was crossing over into terrorism or at least preparing the groundwork for the infiltration of al-Qaeda in key locations around the world.[69]

Now it appeared that Hizb ut-Tahrir had sympathizers among those Palestinians in Jerusalem who were giving sermons on the Temple Mount. Presumably, the Waqf was supposed to control who gave these sermons. The clerics who preached in the Temple Mount mosques were in many cases employees of the Palestinian Authority, for they also received funds from its Ministry of Waqf Affairs. Given that the Palestinian Authority was dependent on Saudi financial largesse and Egyptian political backing, it was surprising that it would permit such inflammatory rhetoric calling for the overthrow of the regimes that had been the bedrock of its support. The Waqf had clearly opened the door to the penetration of the Temple Mount by radical Islamist elements. Indeed, Hizb ut-Tahrir even held a mass rally on the Temple Mount on March 3, 2006.

Hizb ut-Tahrir was only a part of the problem that Jerusalem potentially faced. As already noted, several months earlier in January 2006, Hamas won the Palestinian Authority parliamentary elections and formed the new Palestinian government. In recent years Hamas had, in fact, shown signs of becoming even more radicalized. While to the international community it sought to distinguish itself from al-Qaeda, internally it appeared more ready to embrace aspects of its ideology and global agenda.

Thus a Hamas poster distributed in the West Bank in 2002 featured a portrait of its founder, Sheikh Ahmad Yassin, alongside portraits of the Chechen jihadist leader Khattab and of Osama bin Laden. The poster also listed the areas where global jihadist groups had been active: Afghanistan, Kashmir, the Balkans, and of course, Palestine. And when Israel completed its unilateral disengagement from the Gaza Strip in August 2005, Hamas leaders like Mahmoud al-Zahar, expressed their hope that the Israeli pullout would strengthen the morale of the *mujahidin* fighting the coalition in Iraq. Al-Zahar would become the Hamas foreign minister after the 2006 Palestinian elections.

Finally, on March 20, 2006, the head of the Hamas political bureau, Khaled Mashaal attended a Hamas fundraiser in Yemen that featured Sheikh Abd al-Majid al-Zindani, who had been designated by the U.S. Department of the Treasury as an al-Qaeda supporter and spiritual advisor to Osama bin Laden. Known to have actively recruited operatives for al-Qaeda training camps,[70] al-Zindani had fought with bin Laden in Afghanistan in the 1980s. Less than a week after the fundraiser in Yemen, the Hamas leadership visited Peshawar, Pakistan, where it was in contact with leaders of a Kashmiri jihadist group with close ties to al-Qaeda.[71] Thus, despite its denials, Hamas was increasingly reaching out to the forces of global jihad with whom it ideologically identified, while it was simultaneously seeking to be legitimized by Western powers who were anxious to see the Israeli-Palestinian peace process resumed.

What all this meant for the future of Jerusalem was becoming increasingly clear. Any expansion of Hamas influence in Jerusalem through the Palestinian Authority would open the door for even more radical Islamic elements to establish themselves in the Holy City. This had already been demonstrated in the Gaza Strip; after Israel withdrew completely from Gaza, where Hamas was already the predominant political power, it should not have come as a surprise that Israeli military intelligence determined that al-Qaeda cells had successfully infiltrated the area.

Indeed, Palestinian Authority president Mahmoud Abbas (Abu Mazen) verified the Israeli claim in the London Arabic daily *al-Hayat* on March 2, 2006, when he admitted that he too had received intelligence information indicating the presence of al-Qaeda operatives in both the Gaza Strip and the West Bank. Hamas made no effort to block al-Qaeda's infiltration efforts. It stood to conclude that if Hamas could harbor al-Qaeda cells in Gaza, then this might occur wherever Hamas could exercise its control. Potentially, Hamas was in a position in which it could easily repeat in 2006 what the Taliban had done a decade earlier by hosting terrorists associated with al-Qaeda.

What that could mean for the holy sites of Jerusalem had already become evident with the limited amount of authority that the Palestinians had taken from the Hashemite Kingdom of Jordan during the 1990s. In the surrounding areas under Palestinian control, the visible signs of religious intolerance were multiplying. Israel's withdrawal from the Gaza Strip in August 2005 was immediately followed by mob attacks on the synagogues it left behind, which were set on fire. More recently in September 2006, following the controversy in much of the Arab world over the remarks made by Pope Benedict XVI about how a Byzantine leader historically viewed Islam, two West Bank churches were hit by firebombs and a Greek Orthodox church in Gaza was attacked by two small explosive devices.

It seemed that in the Hamas-dominated Palestinian Authority there was a very short fuse that could be easily lit when unexpected events transpired with religious implications. Under such conditions, if Israel withdrew from most of the Old City of Jerusalem, as was proposed in the latter part of 2000, the future security of the holy sites of the three great faiths, as well as the freedom of Jerusalem more generally, would be clearly put at serious risk.

# Chapter 8

# Jerusalem as an Apocalyptic Trigger for Radical Islam

P resident Mahmoud Ahmadinejad of Iran established in the most dramatic fashion a direct connection between radical Islam's apocalyptic outlook and the future of Jerusalem. Facing a UN Security Council deadline for answering the demands of the international community that Iran freeze the production of enriched uranium, Ahmadinejad's government stated that it would give its answer on August 22, 2006. That date corresponded to the twenty-seventh of the month of Rajab, according to the Muslim calendar.[1] In Islamic tradition, that was the date when Muhammad flew on a winged horse-like beast, *al-Buraq*, from Mecca to Jerusalem and ascended to heaven.

Ahmadinejad has been associated with a radical apocalyptic movement with Iranian Shiism known as the *Hojjatieh Mahdavieh* Society. Mainstream Shiites believe in the eventual return of the Twelfth Imam, who is a direct descendant of Muhammad's son-in-law, Ali, and whose family is viewed by Shiites as the only appropriate successors to Muhammad. The Twelfth Imam went into what Shiites call the "lesser occulation" in the year 874 by which he became invisible and communicated with the outside word through special agents until the year 940, when "the greater occulation"

231

began and his communication with his followers ended; the Twelfth Imam is expected to return in the future as the Mahdi ("the rightly guided one"). This event is expected to usher in a new messianic-like era of global order and justice for Shiites in which Islam will be victorious. The Shiite Mahdi is also supposed to "take vengeance on the enemies of God," although his arrival is an end of time concept for the distant future.[2]

The *Hojjatieh*, which started out in 1953 as a movement against the Bahai faith, believe that the timing of this historical process is not pre-determined; it can be hastened through apocalyptic chaos and violence. And Ahmadinejad has openly stated, "Our revolution's main mission is to pave the way for the reappearance of the Twelfth Imam, the Mahdi."[3] One Western reporter conveyed that Ahmadinejad may have told his cabinet that the Mahdi will arrive within the next two years.[4] From his statements it is clear that the Iranian president sees that it is within man's power to facilitate this process of the end of days. But how exactly is the Mahdi's arrival to be accelerated?

For Ahmadinejad, the destruction of Israel is one of the key global developments that will trigger the appearance of the Mahdi.[5] It was on Iran's annual "Jerusalem Day" on October 26, 2005, that Ahmadinejad made his famous reference to the need to "wipe Israel off the map." What did not receive the same attention was another part of his speech in which he said, "We are now in the process of an historical war between the World of Arrogance [i.e. the West] and the Islamic world." He then added that "a world without America and Zionism" is "attainable."[6] Thus Ahmadinejad was talking about a war against the U.S. and its Western allies.

A month earlier, in his first UN General Assembly address, Ahmadinejad closed with a prayer that the Mahdi's arrival be quickened: "Oh mighty Lord, I pray to you to hasten the emergence of your last repository, the promised one."[7] He was recorded saying that a member of his delegation noticed that he was surrounded by an aura of light during the twenty-seven to twenty-eight minutes that he spoke, which he admit-ted to have felt himself.[8] Ahmadinejad shows all the signs of not only using apocalyptic language, but also believing that he has a personal role in bringing the end of times about.

But what was the connection between Jerusalem and Ahmadinejad's planned final battle? Dr. Bilal Na'im served as an assistant to the head of the Executive Council of Hizballah, the Iranian-controlled Lebanese Shiite terrorist organization. In an essay discussing the details of how the Mahdi is supposed to appear before the world, according to Shiite doctrine, he states that initially the Mahdi reveals himself in Mecca "and he will lean on the Ka'abah and view the arrival of his supporters from around the world."

From Mecca the Mahdi next moves to Karbala in Iraq. But his most important destination, in Na'im's description, is clearly Jerusalem. It is in Jerusalem from where the launching of the Mahdi's world conquest is declared. He explains, "The liberation of Jerusalem is the preface for liberating the world and establishing the state of justice and values on earth."[9] In short, Jerusalem serves as the launching pad for the Mahdi's global jihad at the end of days.

## Sunni Apocalyptic Movements and Jerusalem

This eschatological scenario is not unique to Shiism. In the last five years, there has been a discernable increase in apocalyptic discussions on Sunni jihadist websites, according to which there are now clear signs evident that the Day of Judgment is imminent.[10] There is a common misperception that preoccupation with the coming of the Mahdi occurred only in the world of Shiism; but in fact, Sunni Islam has generated a number of figures who claimed to be the Mahdi, including the famous Mahdi of Sudan who fought General Gordon and the British in the 1880s, and most recently Muhammad al-Qahtani, who with his brother-in-law, Juhaiman al-Utaibi took over the Grand Mosque in Mecca in 1979.[11]

It should be noted that apocalyptic speculation goes back to the beginning of Islam. Indeed, an explanation for the energy and success behind the original Islamic conquests of the seventh century was the belief at the time that the Muslim armies were eradicating evil just before the day of judgment and the end of the world.[12]

There have also been strong counter-currents in Sunni Islam against what might be called Mahdism. The great Islamic philosopher Ibn Khaldun attacked Mahdism as a form of ideological infiltration of Shiism into the Sufi orders of Sunni Islam.[13] He doubted the reliability of the *hadith* literature about the Mahdi, questioning the lines of transmission of these oral traditions.[14] And of course the Ottoman Empire, which was headed by a Sultan who was also caliph of Sunni Islam, fought the Sudanese Mahdi along with the British. Thus there have been powerful voices in Islam against these apocalyptic trends in the world of Sunni Islam, treating Mahdism as almost a deviation from authentic Islam.

In the Koran, there in fact is no reference to the coming of a Mahdi. The end of time is called *al-sa'a* or "the Hour" and it appears in several dozen places in the Koran. There are also many more references in the Koran to "the Day of Resurrection." In the hadith literature, in fact, there is reference to Muhammad saying that he was sent "with a sword" just before the Hour arrives, indicating that at the time of the rise of Islam there was indeed a perception that the end of days was imminent. This was also true of the period of Muhammad's immediate successors. For example, the Muslim historian al-Tabari records a conversation between the second caliph, Umar bin al-Khattab, and a Jew who predicted his conquest of Jerusalem in which Umar asked as well about the coming of the false Messiah, known in Arabic as *al-Dajjal.* The Jew responded, "What are you asking about him, O Commander of the Faithful? You, the Arabs will kill him ten odd cubits in front of the gates of Lydda [near present-day Ben-Gurion international airport of Israel]."[15]

Some of the current apocalyptic speculation began to return to be a part of public discourse back in the 1990s with the publication of a number of popular books that put forward a number of common scenarios. They often began with a region of Central Asia, called in many classical works "Khurasan," which apparently refers to Afghanistan, Turkemenistan, parts of Uzbekistan, and eastern Iran. The Mahdi is supposed to appear here and lead an army that will carry black banners and arrive in Iraq. In a 1993 version of this scenario, the army with its black banners is supposed to advance from "Khurasan" through the area of Iran in the general direction of Syria "with the ultimate goal of establishing the messianic capital in Jerusalem."[16]

The tradition cited about the black banners comes from a hadith attributed to Muhammad that says, "Black flags will go out of Khurasan and nothing shall thwart them until they are firmly hoisted in *Iliya* [based on the old Roman name for Jerusalem, Aelia]."[17] The tradition grew in the eighth century when the Abbasids were seeking to overthrow the Ummayad caliphate, for which Jerusalem was an important symbol of power.[18] This historical context was now forgotten as events in the late 1990s and in the years that followed confirmed many of these apocalyptic scenarios for radical Sunni Muslims. The rise of the Taliban in Afghanistan seemed to resemble the legendary "Khurasan" from where the truly Islamic forces were to begin their advance in the Middle East.[19] For many radical Muslims, the Taliban's special role in the apocalyptic scenario was authenticated when they ordered the destruction of the Buddhist "idols" in the Bamiyan Valley during 1998.[20]

The Taliban were not the only active party in "Khurasan." There were also jihadist forces in the area of Uzbekistan as well, including Hizb ut-Tahrir, whose presence in that area was substantial. A Palestinian radical named Salah al-Din Abu Arafa, writing in 2001, identified Osama bin Laden as an apocalyptic figure who will defeat and ultimately destroy the United States. His book was a bestseller in the territories controlled by the Palestinian Authority.[21] Detailed analyses on websites identifying with al-Qaeda have characterized the confrontation between radical Islam and the West as a sign of the impending Apocalypse, according to which bin Laden's forces are the army of the Mahdi that will eventually conquer Iraq, Syria, Palestine, and *Bayt al-Maqdis*—that is, Jerusalem.[22]

Indeed, it is Jerusalem that plays a particularly critical role in most of these Sunni apocalyptic scenarios. Muhammad Isa Da'ud, an Egyptian who has been living in Saudi Arabia, has written the most detailed and comprehensive accounts about the coming of the Mahdi. He is also one of the most prolific authors in the Arab world on apocalyptic scenarios, having authored at least eight books on the subject in the course of the 1990s that were published in Cairo. But his works have not been endorsed by the clerical establishment.[23] In his book *Armageddon and What Comes After Armageddon*, he writes: "The Mahdi will come to Jerusalem and will enter the building of the caliphate near the al-Aqsa Mosque, the place from which Muhammad ascended to Heaven which is a sign that that the Mahdi will go out from there with conquests and with the honor that he will provide the religion of Allah [for] he will take people out from darkness to light, sending the flag of Islam to all of the world."

What Da'ud describes is not a spiritual conquest of the world but an actual military campaign led by the Mahdi himself. A global war begins, in his narrative, after spies from Rome are caught in Jerusalem trying to assassinate the Mahdi. He then declares his army is moving toward the Vatican after it refuses to turn over the families of the assassins to Mahdi's custody. At that point a series of military campaigns in Europe begins. Sweden accepts Islam voluntarily and Denmark soon falls as well, providing the Mahdi with a northern European base. Britain and France are the last to fall after a ballistic missile attack. Da'ud concludes, "Then what will remain for the Mahdi of Europe is just Italy and the Vatican; at that point the Mahdi declares that it is time to destroy the Cross."[24]

As for Jerusalem, Da'ud portrays a bloodbath. He anticipates that most Jews in Israel will be killed and that 85 percent of the Jews in the world will perish in the Mahdi's campaign.[25] He adds that the Mahdi will also purify Jerusalem of any buildings of Jewish vintage before he establishes the Mahdist capital in the Holy City.[26] This might be interpreted as a need to erase any record of a Jewish presence in Jerusalem or artifacts of a past Jewish civilization

One immediate question that arises from all this literature is its impact. How widespread are these books and are they affecting public opinion in any way? An Egyptian writer, Sayyid Ayyub, who wrote a book called *al-Masih al-Dajjal* (*The Antichrist*), was one of the first of the current wave of authors.[27] His work was described as a "runaway hit" in Egypt and appears to have generated hundreds of other books.[28] Even those who downplay the influence of Islamic apocalyptic literature on the public at large admit that it has a strong following among Islamic radicals.[29] The apocalyptic writings of the slain Saudi militant Juhaiman al-Utaibi, who seized the Grand Mosque in Mecca in 1979 and declared that Muhammad al-Qahtani was the Mahdi, appear on the most important jihadist online library—that of Abu Muhammad al-Maqdisi, the former mentor of the late Abu Musab al-Zarqawi.[30]

Bassam Jarrar, a high-ranking Hamas operative, wrote an apocalyptic work called *The Disappearance of Israel in 2022*, which he claimed sold 30,000 copies in the West Bank alone—given the relatively small size of the Palestinian population, one writer noted that this is like selling two million books in the U.S.[31] He reached this date by making mathematical calculations based on the number of times certain terms are mentioned in the Koran. Jarrar's influence was probably far greater than his book sales even indicate. He was known as one of the most prominent Islamist intellectuals on the West Bank.[32] He was also a representative of the Union of Good, an international umbrella organization of Islamic charities run by Sheikh Yusuf Qaradhawi, the greatest spiritual authority of the Muslim Brotherhood.[33]

Jarrar also taped anti-Semitic lectures on audio cassettes as well, such as "The End of the Israelites." Israeli security forces found dozens of these recordings in the offices of a Hamas-affiliated charity in the West Bank town of Tulkarm, along with cassettes from Saudi Arabia about the Day of Judgement, asserting that the souls of Jews transmigrate after death to the bodies of monkeys and pigs. Israeli authorities detained Jarrar on September 25, 2005, for his involvement in Hamas.[34]

Additionally, Jarrar's predictions about 2022 began to appear in mosque sermons in 2001.[35] And finally, the best testament to his impact is that he seems to have influenced the founder of Hamas and its head, Sheikh Ahmad Yassin, who adopted his analysis about the inevitable disappearance of Israel, only with the slightly modified date of 2027.[36]

Jarrar might claim that his speculations about the future were not part of the apocalyptic trend because he only wrote about Israel in his book, and not the end of days. But, in an internet chat in Arabic on Islamonline, the website of Sheikh Yusuf Qaradhawi, Jarrar extrapolated further on his vision, predicting the rise of Islam as a superpower—what he calls the "Second Global Islamic Kingdom."[37]

Elsewhere he describes how after Muslims recover the al-Aqsa Mosque in Jerusalem, the Mahdi will arrive and lead them to victory over "the Romans and the Christians."[38] Clearly, according to Jarrar's worldview, the elimination of Israel is a prerequisite for the emergence of this global Islamic state. It goes without saying that this includes a radical Islamic takeover of Jerusalem, which paves the way for these ambitions to be realized.

By definition, those advancing an apocalyptic agenda believe that the end of days is near; and as already discussed, these kinds of apocalyptic perceptions probably contributed to the enormous energies that the early armies of Muhammad and his immediate successors exhibited at the dawn of the expansion of Islam. It is not surprising to find that Sheikh Sulayman bin Nasser al-Ulwan, one of Saudi Arabia's leading militant clerics who has supported al-Qaeda and the September 11 attacks, actually encourages the mujahidin to deal with the issue of the coming of the Mahdi and the signs that the Hour have begun.[39] Al-Ulwan was an important force in the jihadist world. He was even mentioned once in an al-Qaeda video clip from December 2001, when a Saudi visitor brings bin Laden a "beautiful fatwa from Sheikh al-Ulwan." His religious rulings appeared on the website of Hamas and other militant Islamist groups across the Middle East.

What emerges from the previous accounts is that according to most Islamic apocalyptic thought, the Muslim conquest of Jerusalem is one of the six signs that are to be counted prior to the arrival of the Hour and the Day of Judgment.[40] There are many different traditions regarding these signs in a literature going back hundreds of years. For example, in one classic fourteenth-century collection by Ibn Kathir, *The Signs Before the Day of Judgment*, there is a report of Muhammad prophesizing the conquest of Constantinople (Istanbul) and Rome as one of the signs of the Hour. But Jerusalem is clearly in Islamic hands before the attacks on Constantinople and Rome are executed. In other words, the conquest of other cities is also part of the apocalyptic sequence in even the more classical works on the subject, but Jerusalem has a unique role in heralding the dawn of this new era.

In most of the currently written apocalyptic scenarios, a new caliphate is established whose capital is Jerusalem that is led by a messianic Mahdi. After facing down the Dajjal, or the Anti-christ, the new caliphate implements a plan of world conquest including, according to one recently posted

Internet book, an outright attack on the United States with "meteors and nuclear missiles."[41] While many of these books sound like a Middle Eastern version of *The Da Vinci Code* combined with the works of Tom Clancy—and they are not approved religious texts—they nonetheless have enormous impact at the popular level, and cannot be dismissed out of hand, particularly in jihadist circles.

## Jerusalem as a Launching Pad for Future Global Jihadism

There is a remaining question of why Jerusalem should have assumed such a significant role in Islamic predictions of this "end of days" battle. Jerusalem, as previously noted, was the third most important holy city in Islam. It might have been expected that the Mahdi would make Mecca into his capital, or perhaps Medina, as in the days of Muhammad. As already noted, the Koran contains considerable details about the Hour and the Day of Judgment. It says nothing about Jerusalem in this regard. Nonetheless, subsequent traditions placed the sounding of the trumpet of the Day of Judgment by the angel Israfil and the beginning of the resurrection in Jerusalem.

As a result, in this apocalyptic literature Jerusalem emerges as the new Islamic capital. It is the focal point of "end of days" activity, according to some Sunni Islamic interpretations. Bassam Jirrar of Hamas has been quoted making this point succinctly: "Islam began in Mecca and Medina and will end in Jerusalem."[42] The relative importance of Jerusalem grows for those engaging in apocalyptic speculation. Significantly, its conquest is also the necessary pre-condition for a full-fledged, worldwide campaign of Islam, led by the messianic Mahdi, to militarily vanquish the rest of the world. Jerusalem, in short, ignites a new and final global jihad. How Jerusalem assumed this additional role as a launching pad for a final battle requires further explanation.

The role of Jerusalem in sparking a renewed jihadist effort can be understood by looking at how current Islamist literature seeks to find a connection between the seventh-century victory of Muhammad over the Jews of the northern Arabian oasis of Khaybar and the future struggle over the fate of Jerusalem.[43] As a matter of background, in the early history of Islam, when Muhammad took his followers from Mecca to live and practice their religion in Medina, it is true that he waged his first military campaign in 624 at the battle of Badr, where he defeated over 1,000 Meccan Arabs with a force of 300 supporters.

But the battle of Badr did not change the overall situation of Muhammad and his followers, who remained based in Medina and under the threat of the Meccans. Further military encounters for the early Muslims in Medina followed, like the attack of the Meccans on Medina that the Muslims managed to blunt in a defensive battle called the "Campaign of the Trench."

But in 628, Muhammad went on the offensive and totally vanquished Khaybar, a large Jewish agricultural settlement a hundred miles north of Medina that had a number of fortresses; at this point in time the Jews were not expelled; they agreed to pay half their harvests as tribute. Three other Arabian Jewish settlements, Fadak, Wadi al-Qura, and Taima, surrendered right after Khaybar's defeat.[44]

In early Islamic history, Khaybar marked a dramatic turning point for the armies of Muhammad. For in early 630, two years after the Khaybar victory, Muhammad returned to Mecca and completed his conquest of the holiest city in Islam. Moreover, shortly thereafter, Muhammad's successor, Abu Bakr, launched one of the greatest military campaigns in history, leading to Islamic expansionism outside of the Arabian peninsula. It eventually brought about the collapse of both the Byzantine and Persian empires and their replacement with an Islamic caliphate ruling vast territories. Thus from a contemporary Islamist perspective posted on the Hamas website:

> The war against the Jews will bring victory afterwards against all enemies . . . the conquest of Mecca and the victories that followed were one of the fruits of the invasion of Khaybar. That is because the victory of the Prophet brought about a collapse of the spirit and morale of the polytheists in Mecca, due to the fall of a strong ally. There is no doubt that the helplessness of the Islamic nation to assist its sons in Bosnia, Chechnya, and other regions emanates from its inability to return the first direction of prayer [Jerusalem].

In other words, according to this analysis the worldwide jihad is not succeeding because Jerusalem has not been taken back from Israel. But if Jerusalem were to be recovered by the Islamic nation, then the spirit and morale of other nations seeking to contain Islamist insurgencies would be broken as a consequence of the Jewish defeat. Furthermore, the fall of Jerusalem would clearly empower and inspire the jihadist campaign that would no longer act with the same sense of "helplessness."

Parenthetically, this was not a completely new idea. A similar sort of analysis was put forward in the early twelfth century by the Syrian Muslim scholar Ali ibn Tahir al-Sulami, who focused on the need to take back Jerusalem during the Crusades in order to set the stage for much greater military victories against the West, including the conquest of Constantinople: "We have heard in what we have heard of a sufficiently documented *hadith*, mentioning in it that the *Rum* [Rome, or more accurately the Byzantines] will conquer Jerusalem for a set period of time, and the Muslims will gather against them, drive them out of it, kill them all except a few of them, [and] then pursue their scattered remnants to Constantinople, descend on it and conquer it."[45]

In this description, it is also noteworthy that the conquest of Jerusalem was supposed to lead to a bloodbath. (In comparison, Saladin managed to get the Crusaders to surrender with light losses for both sides.)

Likewise, the recent Hamas posting about Khaybar recalls a far more violent attack—one that brings about the extermination of its Jewish population—in contrast with the actual historical record: Muhammad in fact subjugated the Jews, took some captives, and forced them to pay tribute; it was the second caliph, Umar, who expelled them entirely from Arabia, with many survivors seeking refuge in Jericho or Tiberias. Using its own reading of history, the Hamas posting reaches rabid anti-Semitic conclusions, asserting that the fate of the Jews must end with their "absolute killing, total destruction and complete extinction."[46] Perhaps with a similar recollection of events, Hizballah named one of its missiles in the 2006 Second Lebanon War "Khaybar-1."

The special role of Khaybar as a rallying cry for jihad is found elsewhere as well. Amrozi bin Nurhasin, facing sentencing for his role in the Bali bombing, shouted in an Indonesian court: "Jews remember Khaybar, the army of Muhammad is coming back to defeat you." There were hardly any Jews left in Indonesia, but reference to Khaybar nonetheless had meaning for a convicted jihadist in Southeast Asia because it meant far more than the destruction of a fortified oasis in seventh-century Arabia.

Finally, the powerful symbolism of Khaybar was also raised by General Hamid Gul, the former pro-Islamist head of Pakistan's Inter-Service Intelligence Directorate who worked closely with bin Laden in the late 1980s and the anti-Soviet Arab mujahidin, who would form the core of al-Qaeda. In a press conference on *al-Jazeera* aired on August 8, 2006, he also reminded his audience that "Mecca was only conquered after the destruction of Khaybar." He also added, "Of course, as long as Khaybar was not destroyed, Islam did not spread."[47]

While Gul did not get into any further level of detail, it was clear that in 2006, there was no Jewish Khaybar to destroy and thereby facilitate the global spread of militant Islam; from the context of his remarks, he was seeking to justify the continuing enmity of a Pakistani militant toward Israel whose defeat, along with the loss of Jerusalem, would have historical repercussions, like the conquest of Khaybar.

Indeed, this link between the past fate of Khaybar and the future fate of Jerusalem has been most explicitly made by an apocalyptic writer named Muhammad Izzat Arif, who refers to seventh-century Khaybar in a 1996 book as "the Jerusalem of the Jews." He interprets the seventh verse of Sura 17 in the Koran not as a recapitulation of the destruction of the first and second Temples but rather as entailing an account of the past attack by the armies of Muhammad on Khaybar and as a future conquest of Jerusalem by Islamic forces.[48]

When will this conquest occur? Is this an idea for the "end of days," in the far distant future? For many of the new apocalyptic writers the final battles of Islam are very close; the Saudi self-declared Mahdi, Muhammad al-Qahtani, emerged in 1979 because that was also the year 1400 according to the Islamic calendar. Another round of speculation focused on the year 2000, even though marking the millennium was related to the Christian calendar.[49] As noted earlier, in many Islamic apocalyptic scenarios, the "signs" of the Hour are the critical determining factor marking the beginning of the end of days. These include the return of Jesus, who kills the *Dajjal,* or Antichrist, and spreads Islam over the whole earth. Before this happens, a group emerges known as *al-Ta'ifa al-Mansura* (the Victorious Community) that will fight for truth and ultimately bring defeat to the Antichrist.

Sheikh Yusuf Qaradhawi, who is probably the leading spiritual authority for most Islamist groups, and as noted previously for the Muslim Brotherhood in particular, appeared on *al-Jazeera* in 2002 and stated that this "Victorious Community" is in fact already here, at present, in Jerusalem: "What I am saying to you is that the 'Community' is [already] in Bayt al-Maqdis—there is Hamas, there is [Palestinian Islamic] Jihad, there are the al-Aqsa Brigades, there are the brigades of the Popular Front [for the Liberation of Palestine]."[50] What this signals is that from Qaradhawi's standpoint, Jerusalem is at present associated with one of the signs of the Hour. His judgment of the precise religious status of the situation would be closely tied to the next developments that transpire on the ground.

This kind of apocalyptic speculation was not unusual for Qaradhawi. In his appearances on *al-Jazeera* in 1999 and 2000, he also spoke about the prophecies of Muhammad concerning the conquest of Constantinople and Rome that in the hadith also herald the coming of the Hour: "Constantinople was conquered, and the second part of the prophecy remains, that is, the conquest of Romiyya. This means that Islam will return to Europe." Qaradhawi is generally careful speaking about moving into Europe by means of preaching and the spread of Islamic ideology, though at one point he openly writes: "Islam will return to Europe as a conqueror and victor, after being expelled from it twice—once from the South, from Andalusia [Spain], and a second time from the East, when it knocked several times on the door of Athens."[51] What is clear from much of the other apocalyptic material is that for these prophecies to be realized, Jerusalem must be taken first.

## Al-Qaeda Begins to Close In

The interest in Jerusalem that has been voiced through various forms of apocalyptic speculation on jihadist websites would have remained completely theoretical had it not been for critical events that transpired, in parallel to this discourse, during 2005 and 2006. As demonstrated earlier, since its formation in the late 1980s, al-Qaeda never made the struggle for Jerusalem its highest priority. The ideological fathers of al-Qaeda like Abdullah Azzam and Ayman al-Zawahiri thought that in order "to liberate" Jerusalem, they needed to tackle the "Near Enemy" first—that is, it was necessary to overthrow the Arab regimes currently governing in Egypt, Jordan, Saudi Arabia, and in the rest of the Middle East.

There were good operational reasons for this strategy, for if Israel succeeded in deterring neighboring states from permitting cross-border terrorist attacks—with the notable exception of the historically weak state of Lebanon—then there was no way for the jihadist groups around the Middle East to wage an effective campaign in the direction of Jerusalem. Undermining the internal stability of these Arab regimes was a prerequisite for any war for Jerusalem.

Moreover, with al-Qaeda's birth in the area of the far-off Hindu Kush mountains of Afghanistan, it was far more natural for the organization to focus on the conflicts in the surrounding areas, like Kashmir, Uzbekistan, Chechnya, and in the Arabian peninsula, where Osama bin Laden and the vast majority of his volunteers were born. Al-Qaeda's growing interest in the Arab-Israeli zone in 2005 did not come about as a result of some dramatic change in this fundamental ideological orientation, but rather because of new strategic opportunities that opened up for the organization in this period that it decided to fully seize upon and exploit.

First, clearly, one of the unintended side effects of the 2003 Iraq War was the emergence of a new global center of Sunni jihadism in the heart of the Arab world, as mujahidin from various Islamic countries joined the Sunni insurgency in western Iraq. (Without delving too deeply into the Iraq War debate, it could be argued that this new center might have emerged without the Iraq War as Saddam Hussein forged ties with al-Qaeda affiliates like *Ansar al-Islam* in Kurdistan, but not on the same order of magnitude; in any case precipitous Coalition withdrawals from Iraq could also greatly enlarge the extent of this problem.) What this effectively meant was that a new potential springboard for al-Qaeda operations was emerging about 300 miles east of Jerusalem that did not exist before.

Al-Qaeda acknowledged this strategic shift in the summer of 2005. Earlier, in October 2004, Abu Musab al-Zarqawi, the Jordanian jihadist who had been one of the leaders of the Sunni insurgents in Iraq, formally made his organization part of the al-Qaeda global network. Zarqawi was not a Palestinian, as former secretary of state Colin Powell once argued before the UN Security Council; in fact, like many jihadists, the struggle for Palestine was not his first priority. Zarqawi came from the al-Khalaylah clan of the Banu Hassan tribe, which was a huge East Bank tribe that had been loyal to King Hussein and the Hashemite throne. His father fought for the Arab Legion in 1948. Zarqawi's tribe was spread across Jordan and even Iraq.[52] With a strong dedication to jihadist ideals to which he became committed, Zarqawi joined the mujahidin in Afghanistan and with the fall of the Taliban he transplanted himself to Iraq.

Ayman al-Zawahiri wrote a letter on July 9, 2005, to Zarqawi, who was now the head of al-Qaeda in Iraq, extolling his fighting "in the heart of the Islamic world, which was formerly the field for major battles in Islam's history, and what will happen, according to what appeared in the Hadiths of the Messenger of God"—Zawahiri was reminding Zarqawi about the final battles at the end of history prophesized, according to Islamic tradition, by Muhammad and recorded as oral traditions. Later in the letter he explained that the Islamic state, which was their common mission to establish, was to be defended by every generation "until the Hour of Resurrection."

Zawahiri added what should be the next stages that al-Qaeda Iraq should follow in order to reach these goals. After defeating the U.S. in Iraq, Zawahiri hoped that Zarqawi would establish an Islamic emirate that could eventually proclaim a caliphate and then "extend the jihad to secular countries neighboring Iraq" (i.e., Egypt, Jordan, and Syria). And in the final stage, Zawahiri recommended al-Qaeda positioning itself for "the clash with Israel." In some respects, the sequence that al-Qaeda had envisioned in the past was still preserved for the takeover of Arab states that was to precede any showdown with Israel.

This jihadist mission as articulated in the letter made additional sense given Zawahiri's stated religious view that "the victory of Islam will never take place until a Muslim state is established in the manner of the

Prophet." He explained that this required any future emirate or caliphate to be centered in "the Levant [replacing Syria, Lebanon, Jordan, and Israel] and Egypt." The Zawahiri letter to Zarqawi was intercepted by the U.S. intelligence establishment and posted on the website of the U.S. director of national intelligence, John D. Negroponte.[53]

What made the Zawahiri letter so significant was that subsequent events showed that it was being operationalized on the ground: al-Qaeda was already moving into Iraq's neighbors even though the war for Iraq had not been decided nor had an Islamic emirate been declared. Al-Qaeda itself was transforming during these years; it was less a centrally controlled international organ and more an ideological movement capable of creating new affiliate groups that undertook devastating operations. For example, a month after the Zawahiri letter was written, on August 19, 2005, al-Qaeda Iraq launched a rocket attack on the Jordanian seaport of Aqaba; one rocket hit the neighboring Israeli resort town of Eilat. In September 2005, there were increasing reports of new jihadist activity in Syria, which ironically had assisted the Iraqi insurgency in the past by serving as a rear base and a conduit for supplies. There were reports of clashes between the Syrian army and an al-Qaeda affiliate called *Jund al-Sham* (Army of the Levant).[54]

Then in early November, al-Qaeda Iraq attacked three Jordanian hotels in Amman with suicide bombers, killing sixty-seven people and wounding more than 200. Finally, on December 27, 2005, al-Qaeda Iraq used an allied organization in southern Lebanon to launch Katyusha rockets on two northern Israeli towns. It was the first time al-Qaeda had struck directly on Israeli territory proper. Observing the growing activity of al-Qaeda within Israel's immediate neighbors, the head of Israeli military intelligence at the time, Major General Aharon Zeevi (Farkash), concluded, "We are not a high priority [for al-Qaeda], but our prioritization is increasing."[55]

A second strategic opportunity for al-Qaeda to enter the heart of the Middle East was created by Israel's own decision to unilaterally disengage from the Gaza Strip in August 2005. With no effective Palestinian security services emerging to replace the Israel Defense Forces, a huge security vacuum was created that al-Qaeda was very willing to fill. Moreover, the Israeli pullout included a withdrawal from what was known as the "Philadelphi Corridor"—a narrow strip of land separating the Gaza Strip from Egyptian Sinai. (The name was randomly given by the Israeli military and had nothing to do with Philadelphia.)

The al-Qaeda presence in Sinai had grown in recent years; its Egyptian affiliate had conducted deadly terrorist attacks against Red Sea resorts like Taba in October 2004 and Sharm al-Sheikh in July 2005. Even before this al-Qaeda activism in Sinai became common, for years Egyptian jihadist groups, seeking to topple the regime of President Husni Mubarak, had targeted the Egyptian tourist industry in order to cripple the Egyptian economy and destabilize the government. Some of these groups that were allied to al-Qaeda continued to have that basic interest. However now they had a new mission as well. With Israel out of the Philadelphi Corridor, the new situation would allow these terrorists based in Sinai to move far more easily into Gaza and smuggle huge amounts of munitions and other arms.

The first evidence of al-Qaeda's entry was disclosed by the Hamas movement, which was already the dominant political force in Gaza. On September 13, 2005, Hamas leader Mahmoud al-Zahar, who would become the Palestinian foreign minister the following year, gave an interview to *Corriere della Sera* in Italy and frankly admitted, "Yes it is true, a pair of men from al-Qaeda has infiltrated into Gaza and other contacts happen by telephone with the centers of the organization in a foreign country." More men and munitions followed. Al-Qaeda sought to systematically expand its presence and recruit new followers.

How extensive was this al-Qaeda presence? Initially, it apparently consisted of efforts "to create ideological and religious cells."[56] For example an organization calling itself "Al-Qaeda Jihad in Palestine" distributed fliers in a Gaza mosque in October 2005 announcing its political program.[57] It specifically called for the revival of the caliphate and the ultimate establishment of an Islamic state across the world. It referred to Muhammad's having already "heralded the fall of Rome and Constantinople" and the return of the caliphate. The leaflet said nothing about Jerusalem, but nonetheless it gave an insight into the worldview of the new organization that appeared to seek to fulfill prophesies about an "end of times" victory against the West, to which it implicitly referred.

But al-Qaeda in Gaza also acquired military capabilities very quickly. In May 2006, even the Egyptian Interior Ministry was taking notice of the growing terrorist infrastructure in Gaza. It divulged that two terrorists involved in an April 24, 2006, terrorist attack on the Red Sea coastal resort of Dahab in Egyptian Sinai had been trained in the use of weapons and explosives in the Gaza Strip.[58] The organization that took credit for the Dahab attack was called *al-Tawhid wal-Jihad*, which was the name of Zarqawi's terrorist network prior to his merger with al-Qaeda. This was not a definite confirmation that the new al-Qaeda presence in Gaza was being used to strike Egypt, but the entire episode had all the hallmarks of an al-Qaeda-connected operation.

An al-Qaeda military effort was initiated in the West Bank as well. In December 2005, Israeli security services arrested two Palestinians from Nablus who had been recruited over the last half-year by Zarqawi's organization, which had been operating out of the northern Jordanian city of Irbid.[59] Their plan had been to use both a suicide bomber and a car bomb sequentially in order to cause mass casualties in the municipal Jerusalem neighborhood of French Hill.

Al-Qaeda wanted them to set up secret cells to attack economic targets as well; training of these newly recruited operatives could be arranged in Iraq or Syria, but it appeared that al-Qaeda preferred to send an instructor of its own from Gaza to the West Bank for military training.[60] The fact that Jerusalem had been one of the first targets of the al-Qaeda cell meant that the organization could be expected to seek to recruit new operatives from the Palestinian population in the eastern part of the city.

Al-Qaeda had multiple incentives to move in this direction. Rumors had been circulating about further Israeli unilateral withdrawals in the West Bank; al-Qaeda was clearly putting the infrastructure in place for that eventuality. As noted in the previous chapter, in early March 2006, even Palestinian Authority president Mahmoud Abbas (Abu Mazen) was taking notice of al-Qaeda's entry into territories that were supposed to be under his control. In an interview with the London-based Arabic daily *al-Hayat*, he admitted, "We have signs about the presence of al-Qaeda in Gaza and the West Bank. This is intelligence information. We're not yet at a situation of control and crackdown. It's security information. The last security report I saw was three days ago. It was the first time that this subject was discussed. It's a very dangerous situation."[61]

What had also changed to make this a far more hospitable environment for militant Islamist groups like al-Qaeda were the results of the January 25, 2006, Palestinian parliamentary elections. The newly elected government of the Palestinian Authority was formed by Hamas, which took credit for having forced Israel's unilateral pullout from Gaza and had enhanced its own public standing as a result. Mahmoud Abbas remained the Palestinian Authority president, but key ministries that also controlled several security forces were in the hands of a militant group that had been designated as an international terrorist organization by both the U.S. and the European Union.

The full meaning of this development became clear in March, when the new Palestinian interior minister, Sa'id Sayyam, specifically stated that he would not order the arrest of terrorist operatives attacking against Israel; the new policy amounted to an open invitation to al-Qaeda or any other group to turn the Palestinian Authority into a base of activity.[62] Experts trained in Lebanon, Iran, and Afghanistan in the use of sophisticated explosive devices reached Gaza in early April.[63]

In the meantime the Syrian-based Hamas leadership abroad, headed by Khaled Mashaal, met openly with known al-Qaeda supporters in Pakistan, Yemen, and in Saudi Arabia.[64] It is important to stress that Hamas was still not al-Qaeda; it wasn't attacking New York, London, or Madrid. But it was acting more like the Taliban regime by turning the territory that it controlled into a sanctuary for global jihadist groups.

In late April 2006, Zarqawi himself made a noticeable comment about the new activity in the Israeli-Palestinian sector: "We are fighting in Iraq and our eyes are in the direction of Beit al-Maqdis [Jerusalem] which will not be returned except by the guiding Koran and by the sword which will be triumphant."[65] He did not speak regularly about Jerusalem but he did adopt apocalyptic references in his speeches just like Zawahiri, such as, "Behold, the spark has been lit in Iraq and its flames will blaze, Allah willing, until they consume the Armies of the Cross in Dabiq."[66]

Zarqawi was referring to one of the events heralding the coming of the Day of Judgment, for the Mahdi, according to Muslim apocalyptic tradition, is supposed to destroy the infidel armies assembling in northern Syria in A'maq and Dabiq.[67] Here Zarqawi assigned to his al-Qaeda forces in Iraq the same task as the Mahdi's army and to himself an apocalyptic role. This might have had nothing to do with Jerusalem, but it was indicative of how versed al-Qaeda's chief in Iraq was about Islam's "end of days" scenarios and the extent to which he sought to apply them to the current situation.

Zarqawi was killed by coalition forces on June 7, 2006. Still, even after his demise, al-Qaeda under his command had positioned itself well to influence the Israeli-Palestinian zone of the Middle East for the first time. Moreover, his successors appeared no less determined to support jihad outside of Iraq as well: "This is also a message to the jihad fighters inside and outside Iraq, assuring them that we are clinging to the principles of truth."[68] They insisted that "jihad continues until the Day of Judgment."[69] They also indicated they planned to strike in Jordan or Lebanon and not confine their militant efforts to Iraq alone.[70] And Hamas continued to speak sympathetically about the jihadist efforts in Iraq; its spokesman, Sami Abu Zuhri, reiterated "its supportive position to all liberation movements and foremost the Iraqi liberation movement, for which Zarqawi was one of the symbols in the face of the American occupation."[71]

In fact, it could be argued that if al-Qaeda in Iraq were ultimately to be weakened after Zarqawi's death, then the organization might have a further incentive to seek the establishment of an alternative sanctuary in one of Iraq's western neighbors. There have been precedents for such a development already. After the U.S. invasion of Afghanistan in 2001, several hundred al-Qaeda operatives took refuge in Lebanon's Ein al-Hilweh refugee camp, where they presumably joined forces with *Asbat al-Ansar*, an al-Qaeda affiliate.[72]

Additionally, on the fifth anniversary of the September 11 attacks, Zawahiri made clear that al-Qaeda sought to retain a strategy of attacking in the core area of the Middle East; he specifically identified the area bordering Israel and the Arab Gulf states. Al-Qaeda's long-term goal was "to liberate all of Palestine and (recapture) land from Spain to Iraq."[73] In the meantime the marked increase of al-Qaeda activity in Lebanon, Syria, Jordan, the Palestinian-controlled areas of the West Bank and Gaza brought the outgoing head of Israeli military intelligence, Major General Farkash, to conclude upon his retirement that "The Middle East is currently standing before a global jihad tsunami."[74]

## Triggering Apocalyptic Conflicts or Averting Them

Jerusalem could easily become the "powder keg" of the Middle East, but not for the reasons usually cited by those coining this expression, who are concerned by any consolidation of Israel's control over a united city.[75] At present, there are two converging trends with respect to Jerusalem that are far more significant. Of these, the first is well advanced, while the second remains in an early stage.

First, it has been clear for more than a decade that Jerusalem has become a focal point for apocalyptic authors whose works have become relatively popular across the Arab world during these years. Their books are not just part of a theoretical discourse, but rather their language is reiterated by some of the most violent terrorist groups presently operating in the Middle East. Apocalyptic leaders see religious scenarios of the end of days fitting into present events and can equally adopt a present course of action to comply with a specific religious scenario. As David Cook of Rice University, one of the leading analysts of this literature, has aptly noted, "apocalyptic materials amount not to mere talk but a necessary prelude to action."[76]

The second trend to watch is the security situation on the ground in the Middle East. The 2003 Iraq War brought the jihadism of Afghanistan to the center of the Arab world. This accelerated the formation of al-Qaeda offshoots in the countries neighboring Iraq: Jordan, Egypt (particularly Sinai), Lebanon, and even Syria have all been affected. The Israeli withdrawal from the Gaza Strip in 2005 created a new sanctuary for this growing al-Qaeda presence and provided rudimentary infrastructure for its expansion into the West Bank.

It also contributed to the 2006 electoral victory of Hamas, which argued that its strategy of armed resistance had been vindicated by the Israeli decision to pull out while under fire from Qassam rockets. Hamas did not fight al-Qaeda's incursion into its domain and even expressed a willingness to harbor its operatives. In the meantime, al-Qaeda in Iraq recruited West Bank Palestinians using cells based in the Jordanian town of Irbid. Jerusalem was one of its first targets. Still, this process is in a very preliminary stage, but could become far more significant in the future, depending on the course of events.

What would happen if the jihadism coming from the East is drawn into Jerusalem so that the more than decade-long trend of apocalyptic speculation about Jerusalem would converge with global jihadist militancy, as represented by al-Qaeda? It should be recalled that Jerusalem may be the third holiest site in classical Islam and is associated primarily with the Night Journey of Muhammad that appears in the Koran. But in the world of apocalyptic speculation, Jerusalem has many other associations—it is the place where the messianic Mahdi is to establish his capital. For that reason, some argue that it also should become the seat of the new caliphate that most Islamist groups—from the Muslim Brotherhood to al-Qaeda— seek to establish. Jerusalem's recapture is seen by some as one of the signs that "the Hour" and the end of times are about to occur. It is also the point where Jesus returns to earth to battle the *Dajjal*. And most importantly, because of these associations, it is the launching pad for a new global jihad powered by the conviction that this time the war will unfold according to a pre-planned religious script, and hence must succeed.

This scenario is not far-fetched. Up until now, the conventional wisdom in Western diplomatic circles has been that one critical way to avert any intensification of the threat of militant jihadist terrorism would be to tackle the most difficult outstanding issues of the Israeli-Palestinian conflict, especially the question of Jerusalem. But given the analysis above, any change in the status quo in Jerusalem could have exactly the opposite effect by confirming, even in part, the narrative suggested in the present-day apocalyptic speculation. Already in the cases of Lebanon and the Gaza Strip, unilateral Israeli pullouts were supposed to stabilize these sensitive border areas, but instead far worse conflicts surprisingly erupted. Given the global scope of the apocalyptic effects of changes in the status of Jerusalem, the results of such diplomatic initiatives would not be confined to the border areas around Israel, but could be felt in the streets of major cities in the West, from New York to London, Paris, or Berlin.

Already back in 1998, Cook's pioneering research into the Muslim apocalyptic materials led him to conclude that any future final status negotiations between Israel and the Palestinian Authority over the future of Jerusalem had very little chance of producing an agreement (a prediction borne out by events at Camp David two years later): "Anything touching the Temple Mount is viewed with acute suspicion—making it particularly unfortunate that negotiations about this site might take place precisely as a heightened suspicion is in the air." The apocalyptic obsessions that were common at the time, he believed, were generating a heightened readiness to accept conspiracy theories about the Antichrist and Jerusalem. He then warned, "Anything said or done by Israelis, Americans, and Europeans that can possibly be twisted to fit this conspiracy will provide fuel for a conflagration."[77] Cook was writing before September 11; his arguments are even stronger given present circumstances.

An optimistic counter-argument might begin by saying that this prognosis is excessively alarmist, since no Israeli government, with the U.S. serving as an honest diplomatic broker, is going to turn over Jerusalem to global jihadist groups. But the concerns outlined here do not require such absurdly extreme scenarios to come to fruition in order for them to be relevant. In the Palestinian Authority, its Fatah president, Mahmoud Abbas, already works with a Hamas prime minister, Ismail Haniyah. In general, Abbas has been extremely reluctant to confront Islamic militants on his own. Hamas, for its part, has welcomed global jihadist groups in the Gaza Strip.

And even the moderate regimes of Egypt and Jordan have shown relative tolerance for the Muslim Brotherhood. They often prefer accommodation to confrontation with these groups, even releasing dangerous jihadist operatives in order to create an environment of reconciliation. (Zarqawi was released from a Jordanian prison in 1999, as a gesture of this sort.) Israel is not going to unilaterally withdraw from the Old City of Jerusalem. But, even after the failure of the Camp David negotiations in 2000, European Union representations to Israel have repeatedly called for a return to those sort of negotiations which, if culminated, would leave much of the Old City and the Temple Mount out of Israel's hands.

Diplomats and intelligence agencies don't normally pore over obscure religious texts about the end of days. But considering their widespread popularity and their particular impact on the issue of Jerusalem, that could be a colossal error. If one day Israel succumbed to the constant barrage of pressures from EU diplomats—backed by certain quarters in the U.S. foreign policy establishment as well—to redivide Jerusalem by relinquishing its holy sites, it might well unleash a new wave of jihadism emboldened by a sense that the traditions of radical Islamists about final battles at the end of history are about to come true. Western diplomats pursuing such a course of action may well believe they are lowering the flames of radical Islamic rage, but in fact they will only be turning up those flames to heights that have not been seen before.

# Chapter 9

# The West and the Freedom of Jerusalem

Just after President George W. Bush won his second term in office in November 2004, British prime minister Tony Blair offered an unusual kind of public congratulations. Rather than give a straightforward statement of best wishes for his ally's reelection, Blair used the opportunity to plunge into a discussion about foreign policy. With the Iraq War under way and allied forces fighting in Afghanistan, he wanted to talk about the necessity of pursuing the war on terrorism by non-military means as well. According to Blair, the diplomatic dimension of this global conflict required the revitalization of the Middle East peace process, which he suddenly characterized as "the single most pressing political challenge in our world today."[1]

It was an astounding assertion. Blair, after all, was putting the urgency of reaching a territorial solution to the Israeli-Palestinian conflict ahead of Iran's drive to obtain nuclear weapons, the continuing efforts of al-Qaeda and the Taliban to regroup along the Afghan-Pakistani border, and the expanding terrorist presence in Iraq. Or perhaps he was suggesting that these broad regional developments stretching thousands of miles across the Middle East could all somehow be redressed by the peace process.

Since September 11, this preoccupation with the Israeli-Palestinian conflict had been a persistent theme in Blair's discussions with Bush on the war on terrorism.[2]

After the July 7, 2005, terrorist bombings in the London underground, he would make the same charge yet again, associating the conflict in the Middle East with the root causes of the London attacks. In reality, it had become clear that those particular bombings against the London subways and transit system emanated from the permissive domestic environment for radical Islamist movements that had grown over the years in so-called "Londonistan," where groups that were illegal in Egypt and Pakistan had thrived for years, publishing jihadist materials that were banned in the Middle East.

Moreover, their goals went far beyond Israel and the Palestinians; for example, the Muslim Brotherhood's London weekly, *Risalat al-Ikhwan* (The Message of the Brotherhood), featured in its 2001 logo: "Our mission: world domination."[3] By 2003, in a post–September 11 environment, the Muslim Brotherhood changed this emblem, but it nonetheless indicated the true scope of jihadi ambitions.

Blair's mindset, which seemed to ignore these developments at home, needs to be placed in a larger context. In the years following the September 11 attacks, there arose two very different intellectual approaches to explain the rage driving radical Islam. Many in Europe, like Blair, stressed that Western policies, including the failure to resolve the issue of Jerusalem, were fueling the flames of that rage. If these grievances could be addressed with something like a resurrection of Clinton's peace proposals, they argued, then some of the underlying causes of terrorism would be removed. This belief made many European officials near-obsessive about the Israeli-Palestinian conflict.

The alternative view was that al-Qaeda and its offshoots were part of an aggressive ideology with global ambitions that did not respond to Western diplomatic initiatives at all. Indeed, the U.S. and its Western allies had defended besieged Muslim populations repeatedly in the 1990s, in Kuwait, Bosnia, and Kosovo, during the very years that al-Qaeda expanded. The same could be said about the Oslo process, with its myriad implementation agreements. As has been pointed out, al-Qaeda did not emerge as a result of any of the Arab-Israeli wars.

In fact, the original al-Qaeda of Osama bin Laden was born in 1989, in the aftermath of the Soviet withdrawal from distant Afghanistan. As it grew, it fed off perceived weakness; its recruiters relied mostly on film clips of its victories and the deaths—especially the beheadings—of its enemy prisoners. Most recruits came from other conflict areas with different concerns like Saudi Arabia, Yemen, Kashmir, and Chechnya. What, for example, did the Israeli-Palestinian conflict have to do with al-Qaeda's vicious attacks against the Shiite population of Iraq and their mosques?

Diplomacy and peacemaking between Israelis and Palestinians have a value in their own right. They are not a pointless exercise if the parties engaged are genuinely committed to reconciliation. And they may offset the resentment of some political groups in the Middle East. But they cannot provide a panacea that could neutralize al-Qaeda's war against the West.[4]

Still, Blair had been a critical ally for Bush who was willing to meet these European concerns halfway, whether they were grounded in a correct analysis of terrorist motivation or not. If Bush wanted Blair and other Europeans on board as full partners in the post–September 11 War on Terror, then he apparently concluded that he had to at least address their foreign policy agenda on Israel and the Palestinians as well.

Meanwhile, in the aftermath of a succession of Palestinian suicide bombing attacks in its cities, Israel decided in 2002 to temporarily send forces into the Palestinian Authority–controlled areas of the West Bank from which the attacks originated. At the end of the initial hostilities, Bush gave a detailed speech on June 24, 2002, outlining his vision of a Palestinian state. Refraining from mentioning Jerusalem, he used carefully crafted language intended to satisfy all parties, asserting that "the Israeli occupation that began in 1967 will be ended through a settlement negotiated between the parties, based on UN Resolutions 242 and 338, with Israeli withdrawal to secure and recognized borders."[5] It appeared, then, that Blair had managed to get Bush more engaged. Blair's hopes that Bush would meet Arafat, however, were dashed when Bush instead called for Arafat's replacement with a new Palestinian leadership.

Blair and the Europeans pressed Bush further, particularly as the Iraq War got under way in 2003. Bush became willing, for the first time, to coordinate U.S. policies on the Arab-Israeli conflict with a diplomatic "Quartet" consisting of the U.S., Russia, the European Union, and the UN secretary-general's office. The Quartet peace plan, known as the Road Map, was issued on April 30, 2003. Like Bush's speech, the plan declined to explicitly mention Jerusalem.

But it did speak about an Israeli withdrawal in the third phase of the plan's implementation based on a shopping list of UN resolutions including 242, 338, and 1397, the last of which referred to the initiative of Saudi Crown Prince Emir (now King) Abdullah—a plan based on a full Israeli withdrawal from all the territories captured in the 1967 Six-Day War, including Jerusalem. With European prodding, the Quartet—including the U.S.—was now inching closer toward an outright call to redivide Jerusalem.

The Bush administration would soon reverse this course, since by the end of 2003 Israeli prime minister Ariel Sharon had preempted any Quartet initiatives; he proposed instead a unilateral Israeli withdrawal from the Gaza Strip and sought written assurances from President Bush about the future of Israel's West Bank territories in return. Rather than obtaining a quid pro quo from the Arab side in exchange for his withdrawal from Gaza, and judging that Arafat was too deeply involved in terrorism and Mahmoud Abbas was too weak, Sharon felt assurances from Washington were far more reliable than any agreement he might sign with the Palestinian side for a Gaza pullout.

As a consequence of this diplomacy, in a letter dated April 14, 2004, Bush told Sharon that the "United States reiterates its steadfast commitment to Israel's security, including secure defensible borders." Bush acknowledged that there were already "major Israeli population centers" in the West Bank, usually described as settlement blocs, and hence ruled out "a complete return to the armistice lines of 1949" which, as noted earlier, had never been final political boundaries. The Bush assurances were not revolutionary; they simply repeated public assurances provided by past secretaries of state from George Shultz to Warren Christopher.

Indeed, Bush's assurances were firmly rooted in the language and history of UN Security Council Resolution 242. His letter did not mention Jerusalem, but the principles he enunciated had implications for territorial modifications around the Holy City as well. After all, Israel had maintained large population centers for nearly thirty years within East Jerusalem and along its outer perimeter, and these certainly would fall under the principles of the Bush letter. Of course, Bush added that the parties themselves would ultimately have to agree on final borders, but at least the letter set forth the U.S. position for future negotiations on the topic. These guarantees rendered a return to the 1967 lines obsolete at best.

European diplomacy, however, was moving in a totally different direction. On October 25, 2004, Javier Solana, the European Union's High Representative for Common Foreign and Security Policy, argued in the German weekly *Der Speigel* that the peace process after the Gaza pullout must "lead to a withdrawal from all occupied territories." Solana's formula essentially called for Jerusalem's division. It was as though he had never read Resolution 242 or was completely unaware of the complex negotiations behind it.

Solana's stance was not unique. Chris Patten, who served as the EU Commissioner for External Relations through 2004, also insisted on the same territorial imperative, declaring, "The ingredients of a peace settlement are well known . . . borders between the two states based on those that existed in 1967 with negotiated territorial swaps." Using softer language than a flat-out call to redivide Jerusalem, he called for "the sharing of Jerusalem as the capital of two states."[6]

In addition to pressing Washington via the Quartet to implement its plans, the European Union sought to exert its own impact on the ground in Jerusalem. Led by the British consulate in East Jerusalem, the European Heads of Mission hammered out a joint document toward the end of 2005 examining ways to avert any further consolidation of East Jerusalem as part of Israel's united capital. The document proclaimed, "The EU Policy on Jerusalem is based on the principles set out in UN Security Council Resolution 242, notably the impossibility of the acquisition of territory by force. In consequence the EU has never recognized the annexation of East

Jerusalem under the Israeli 1980 Basic Law [Basic Law Jerusalem Capital of Israel] which made Jerusalem the 'complete and united' capital of Israel."

The document did not stop with a biased interpretation of Resolution 242 that cited its preamble while ignoring its operative language; it proposed a series of steps meant to undermine Israeli sovereignty in East Jerusalem, claiming that their implementation would help leave Jerusalem open as a future issue for negotiations. The document's operational recommendations included a proposal for the Europeans "to increase project activity in East Jerusalem" including "political projects." It further added a call to "support local and international organizations in their information efforts on East Jerusalem." Solana decided against publishing the document, fearing it would undercut the EU's remaining diplomatic influence with Israel, but it was inevitably leaked to the press.[7] It helped explain a great deal of EU activity over the years.

Through its various programs, the EU was pouring huge funds into both Palestinian and Israeli non-governmental organizations (NGOs) that supported its policies. An Italian organization on the EU payroll, *Centro Italiano per la Pace in Medio Oriente* (Italian Center for Peace in the Middle East), proudly proclaimed, "Jerusalem, according to UN resolution 242, is going to be the capital of the State of Israel and the coming State of Palestine." (Of course, neither Jerusalem nor the Palestinians are even mentioned in 242.) Advancing its agenda through seminars in Milan, Pisa, and Toscana, it claimed to have contributed to the research work for the negotiations at Camp David in 2000, Taba in 2001, and the subsequent, non-official 2003 paper between Israelis and Palestinians known as the Geneva Initiative.[8]

There was also the "Jerusalem Old City Initiative," likewise funded by the EU, whose goal was to "provoke rigorous discussion about future governance options for the Old City." It planned to publicize these "new ways of thinking" through "public education and advocacy."[9] An earlier version of this initiative called for local landscape architects to design an aesthetically appealing plan for redividing Jerusalem. Specifically, they prepared a project for reviving the old "border zone" facing the Damascus Gate of the Old City.[10]

Israelis and Palestinians of all political stripes are of course free to write research papers and propose new ideas. But when this activity is financially underwritten by a foreign power like the European Union, which has its own political agenda connected to the redivision of Jerusalem, then this amounts to interference in the internal affairs of Israel, especially when this effort so completely contradicts the policy of Israel's democratically elected government.

The main problem with the outlook of the European Union is that it is based on a complete misreading of the contemporary Middle East. The Israeli-Palestinian negotiations held in 2000–2001 proved that unbridgeable differences separated even the most liberal Israeli position on Jerusalem from the stance of the mainstream PLO leadership. And none of the non-official negotiations that were held subsequently proved otherwise.[11] While these negotiations were supposed to be predicated on the mutual recognition of the parties, Camp David ended with the PLO leadership denying in toto the historical connections of Israel and the Jewish people to Jerusalem—including the denial of the Temple's very existence.

Moreover, if one looks back at the statements of many PLO leaders even beyond Arafat, it seems doubtful that they were prepared to really compromise in the future; their sole interest in negotiations seemed to be improving their position for future conflict. That was the essence of Faisal al-Husseini's comment that the whole Oslo process was a "Trojan Horse" enabling the PLO to enter Israel's fortifications. As demonstrated earlier, many of Arafat's lieutenants who were well known in the Western media also parroted Arafat's historical rendition of Jerusalem's past, including his creed of Temple Denial. And now, after the January 2006 Palestinian parliamentary elections, the PLO has been replaced by Hamas, the Palestinian branch of the Muslim Brotherhood, which does not hide in any way its intentions to destroy Israel.

Even if the Hamas regime falls or its influence begins to wane, it certainly will remain a dominant factor on the Palestinian scene for the foreseeable future, especially among the Palestinian religious leadership that controls the sermons given in mosques and the management of holy sites. It is important to recall that even in the heyday of PLO hegemony over the Palestinian Authority, Hamas already had enormous influence in the charities and religious associations of the Palestinians. Now the continued diplomatic push for the redivision of Jerusalem, under present circumstances, has become a policy completely divorced from reality.

Furthermore, the call to redivide Jerusalem is also removed from recent events in the Middle East more widely, particularly the increasing power of Iran, which has engaged in a crash program to obtain nuclear weapons. This effort is totally changing the central conflicts of the Middle East; many Arab states now believe the Iranian threat to the entire region completely overshadows the older issues separating Israel and the Palestinians. A new preoccupation with Shiite encirclement—beginning in Iran and extending to the Shiite majority of Iraq, to the Alawis of Syria, and then to Lebanon—is now at the top of the policy agenda of Sunni states, many of which have substantial Shiite minorities. This concern has become the driving force behind the politics of the Middle East.

In parallel, the Sunni extremist threat within Arab states has exerted a profound effect on the religious environment across the Arab world. Indeed, what was called an "evil wind" earlier in this book has been blowing across the Islamic world since the 1990s, making the destruction of holy sites and places of worship far more common than in the past. Looking back on this period, it was the original al-Qaeda which undoubtedly helped spur the Taliban to butcher the Afghan Shiites and blast to pieces the ancient Buddhist statues in the Bamiyan Valley in 2001. The writings of radical Saudi and other Persian Gulf–based clerics who also supported that action have reached millions in the Middle East through the Internet, even appearing on the Hamas website. Anyone suggesting the redivision of Jerusalem must take these region-wide trends into account.

In the meantime, al-Qaeda offshoots have spread to the Arab-Israeli sector of the Middle East, particularly in the area of western Iraq, but also in Egypt, Lebanon, Syria, and Jordan. Their operatives may not have been trained in Afghanistan and they may not receive direct funding from bin Laden's parent organization, but the critical point is that they are ideologically linked to the same network. When Israel pulled out of the Gaza Strip, al-Qaeda cells of this sort reached the Palestinians as well and found refuge in territories dominated by Hamas.

These internal and external developments raise the question of who would look after the holy sites of Jerusalem were Israel to redivide the Holy City—the Palestinian version of the Taliban?

Indeed, the whole story of the Gaza pullout demonstrates how in the Middle East well-intentioned plans for dealing with terrorism can totally backfire. Many in the international community thought that Israel's unilateral disengagement from the Gaza Strip and the addressing of the Palestinians' territorial grievances against Israel would reduce the flames of radical Islamic rage. That perception certainly underpins in part Solana's enthusiasm for a complete Israeli withdrawal, including in Jerusalem.

But instead, in the security vacuum that disengagement created, a new sanctuary for global jihad emerged. Even Egypt admitted that terrorists striking their Red Sea Sinai resorts had been trained in Gaza. The West got the very opposite of what it bargained for. Moreover, the fact that Israel faced a two-front war in August 2006 that was launched from the very territories from which it had unilaterally withdrawn—from southern Lebanon six years earlier and from the Gaza Strip the year before—indicated that the underlying motivation for the conflict on the part of the Islamist movements around Israel was not territorial but part of a larger antipathy against anyone associated with the West, including Israel.

Under such circumstances, withdrawals don't ameliorate hostile intentions but they can aggravate them. For what historically fed the growth of Islamic terrorism since 1989 had been its growing sense of victory and not its political grievances over any specific territorial dispute. When the Soviets finally ended their long war in Afghanistan and withdrew, that did not put an end to the mujahidin armies that multiplied there over the previous decade. Indeed, the Arab mujahidin regrouped to form al-Qaeda and were imbued with the conviction that they had just defeated one superpower and could even consider launching a jihad on the other superpower as well.

For the same reason, Hamas was not weakened by the Israeli withdrawal from Gaza which, according to the prevalent international view, should have diminished its influence among the Palestinians and caused them to see that new diplomatic options were possible. Instead, Hamas won the Palestinian elections in the wake of the Israeli pullout. It argued before the Palestinian public that its rocket attacks had succeeded in forcing Israel out and that armed resistance worked. Few in the West understood the empirical evidence in Afghanistan, Lebanon, and now in the Gaza Strip proving that withdrawal in the face of a radical Islamic threat simply fuels jihad. It is like trying to put out a fire with gasoline.

In the case of Jerusalem, no one is proposing a unilateral Israeli withdrawal from the Old City. But even if negotiations were to occur and Israel lost its nerve by deciding, under enormous international pressure, to concede the ancient parts of its national capital, it is extremely doubtful that the flames of radical Islamic rage would be lowered. Jerusalem is not just another contested area like the Gaza Strip; it is a city loaded with layers of deep religious meaning of which most diplomats and policy makers who call for its redivision are hardly aware. All the evidence presented throughout this book in fact indicates that an Israeli withdrawal from the Old City could spur jihadist motivation to an all-time high.

In other words, the proposed redivision of Jerusalem risks reigniting the very rage that the Europeans are seeking to extinguish by diplomatic means. Understanding the impact of religious trends on political violence is not an exact science, but there are strong undercurrents in the Middle East that cannot be ignored. For radical Islam, Jerusalem was never a high priority, but if the West offers the Holy City on a silver platter, many radical groups would not be apathetic or indifferent. As things stand today, such a move will be perceived as confirming the apocalyptic scenarios that have captured the imagination of many in the radical Islamic camp (both Shiites and Sunnis) who believe that their future control of Jerusalem is the first step for spectacular jihadist victories against the West.

Among the Shiites, the driving force popularizing this mode of thinking has been no less than the president of Iran, Mahmoud Ahmadinejad, whose public appearances have been largely absorbed with the return of the lost Imam as the Mahdi, "the rightly guided one." In November 2005, he declared explicitly that his mission was to prepare the groundwork for the lost Imam's reappearance.[12] This Shiite eschatology has been directly tied to the issue of Jerusalem, given the timing and content of the Iranian president's comments.

For example, one Hizballah theoretician succinctly stated, "The liberation of Jerusalem is the *preface* for liberating the world and establishing the [Mahdi's] state of justice and values on earth [emphasis added]."[13] In other words, the assault on Jerusalem is the first stage in a much larger campaign of global warfare.

This theme surfaces elsewhere. A Hizballah book published in Beirut in late 2006 titled *Ahmadinejad and the Next Global Revolution* expands on the upcoming return of the Mahdi and his worldwide campaign. In the earliest stages of the future conflict, the radical Shiite text, which goes out of its way to compliment the Iranian president, envisions Ahmadinejad taking command over the Mahdi's army in the battle to take Jerusalem, thus setting the stage for the worldwide campaign that would follow. The book is excerpted on a Sunni website expressing concern about the ideologies that it contains.[14] Rather than diminish such wild apocalyptic speculations with their clear jihadist overtones, ill-conceived Western policies on Jerusalem could just feed them and enhance their importance.

It would be one thing if this apocalyptic speculation were confined merely to peripheral individuals on the religious fringe. Yet not only is this literature extremely popular in Middle Eastern bookstores, but, as was shown, it also surfaces in the thinking of some of the most important clerics in radical Sunni Islam, including Sheikh Yusuf Qaradhawi, the highest religious authority for the worldwide Muslim Brotherhood. As noted earlier, he appeared on *al-Jazeera* in 2002 announcing that an end of days group called *al-ta'ifa al-mansura*, or the "victorious community," had already positioned itself in Jerusalem and is ready to fight the *Dajjal*, or Antichrist, in a great battle.

The same Qaradhawi invoked on other occasions what he called the prophecies of Muhammad by talking about Islam returning to Europe "as a conqueror." He foresaw the future fall of Rome, and he also dropped passing references to Andalus, once Islamic Spain (though he often conditioned this commentary by expressing his desire to recover these territories through preaching alone). The ideological energies of Qaradhawi and his followers are not confined to political change in the Middle East alone, but rather are directed to the West as a whole.

Thus a line of policy that has been adopted to enhance the security of London, Paris, and Rome, or of any European city where militant elements reside could unleash a new jihadist drive, energizing those who feel empowered by the fact that their worldview will have been vindicated. Jerusalem, which had been a lower priority for al-Qaeda throughout the 1990s, if suddenly thrust onto center stage by misplaced Western diplomacy, could trigger ideological responses that would only complicate the efforts of the U.S. and its allies to contain the outburst of radical Islamic movements.

And what if Jerusalem were internationalized? Would that solve something? It was the European Union that in 1999 resurrected the internationalization concept contained in UN General Assembly Resolution 181. When the UN was still seriously considering internationalization back in 1949, it was Jordan's King Abdullah who vociferously opposed the idea on the grounds that this would put the "infidel" in control of the city. Abdullah was a moderate leader under strong British influence at the time, but he knew what chords to strike in the Islamic world to wage his struggle against internationalization among Arab audiences in states that opposed Hashemite authority in Jerusalem.

It doesn't take much imagination to consider how the idea of internationalization would be greeted by radical Islamist elements across the Middle East. Indeed, al-Qaeda had just waged a ten-year war to remove the "infidels" from the Arabian peninsula, which hosts the primary holy sites of Islam, Mecca and Medina. It should have come as no surprise that in the aftermath of Camp David, Arafat rejected proposals for the internationalization of the Temple Mount, even if they incorporated representation from the Organization of Islamic States and the Arab League.[15] He obviously cared far more how an idea would go over on *al-Jazeera* or in the Egyptian press than on the editorial pages of the *New York Times*. In short, internationalization would not provide a solution to the needs of the increasingly dominant radical elements of the Islamic world.

And even if the Arab world accepted internationalization, who would be in charge of protecting Jerusalem—the UN? The record of UN forces has been extremely negative over the last decade starting in the Balkans and Rwanda and more recently in southern Lebanon. Israel's own historical experience with the UN in Jerusalem has been nothing short of disastrous. The UN did not lift a finger when its Jewish population of 100,000 was put under siege, even though it had previously adopted the recommendation of the General Assembly to put Jerusalem under UN authority.

It was only the nascent Israeli army that broke through to resupply Jerusalem's civilians with food and water. The UN also failed to respond to repeated pleas to get the Arab Legion to halt its devastating bombardment of the synagogues of the Old City's Jewish Quarter. It is for these reasons that Israel's first prime minister, David Ben-Gurion, concluded that the UN resolution recommending internationalization had lost all moral force and was "null and void."

True, the UN helped broker the postwar armistice agreements between Jordan and Israel in 1949. And a UN officer on the ground chaired the Mixed Armistice Commissions that the agreements created to oversee their implementation. But when the Jordanians violated Article VIII of the agreement by refusing to permit freedom of access of Israeli worshipers to the Old City in general and to the Western Wall in particular, the UN did nothing.

Nor did the Security Council seek the repeal of Jordanian laws restricting the rights of Christian institutions in Jerusalem. As already noted, possibly the UN's most significant religious intervention during the years of Jordanian rule was a letter by the UN Truce Supervision Organization on November 30, 1964, demanding that Israel switch off Chanukkah lights that were lit in the Israeli enclave on Mt. Scopus because they might offend the Jordanians.[16]

## The Peace of Jerusalem

If there is no realistic negotiated solution for Jerusalem and internationalization is not an option either, then what is the likely fate of the Holy City? Frankly, we can expect continuing Israeli sovereignty over a united city which, given the history of Jerusalem, is the best possible outcome. The historical record has shown that only a free and democratic Israel can truly protect the freedom of Jerusalem for all faiths.

What about Palestinian and broader Arab opinion? It needs to be made clear that no one is asking the Palestinian Authority to formally sign on to such an arrangement at another Camp David summit. Not all conflicts are resolved by formal agreements negotiated at great summit meetings; sometimes the parties reach a modus vivendi that is not imposed from above, but rather built up from the ground. While not ideal, it nonetheless addresses many—though not all—of each side's principal concerns.

In the history of the Israeli-Palestinian conflict, sometimes reaching an imperfect arrangement has been easier than the completion of formal negotiations. In the late 1920s, British high commissioner Sir John Chancellor presented Jerusalem mufti Hajj Amin al-Husseini two alternatives—a political settlement with the Jews over the Western Wall or a much worse international solution. Husseini preferred the latter, as long as he did not have to sign a document relinquishing a single one of his perceived political rights. By refusing to compromise at Camp David and at all the negotiations that followed, Arafat and the Palestinian leadership around him appeared to be driven by the same set of considerations.

A number of measures need to be taken in the period ahead. First, there is already an Islamic authority representing the interests of the Muslim world with whom it is possible to work. For example, there is a Jordanian administrative role on the Temple Mount that was reinstated after the 1967 Six-Day War, leaving Israel clearly responsible for security. Thus despite the harsh memories on the Israeli side of Jordan's invasion of Jerusalem in 1948, the two sides have come a long way in building up mutual confidence, even with respect to religious administration in Jerusalem. This cooperation was formalized in a 1994 Israeli-Jordanian agreement known as the Washington Declaration that was incorporated into the treaty of peace between both countries. It stated, "Israel respects the present special role of the Hashemite Kingdom of Jordan in the Muslim holy shrines in Jerusalem. When negotiations on the permanent status will take place, Israel will give high priority to the Jordanian historic role in these shrines."

In 1988, King Hussein declared that he was cutting his kingdom's administrative ties with the West Bank, although he retained his religious ties to Jerusalem. Indeed, the Jordanian Ministry of *Awqaf* (Religious Endowments) Affairs has paid the salaries of Waqf officials to this very day.

During the years of Oslo, Jordan lost much of its influence over the administration of Islamic affairs on the Temple Mount to the Palestinian Authority, but it has been seeking to recover it as of late. Today, there is no Palestinian Authority Minister of Awqaf sitting in Jerusalem, as in the times of Arafat.

The latest evidence of this increased Jordanian interest was disclosed in mid-October 2006, when it was revealed that King Abdullah II had expressed interest in building a fifth minaret on the Temple Mount's eastern wall, near the Golden Gate.[17] The Jordanians also signaled their continuing religious role in the area, when they undertook renovations in the Dome of the Rock, especially the replacement of its carpets in October 2006. Before any further construction projects of significance on the Temple Mount are implemented, however, a broader change in the overall situation there should take place.

Right now, what goes on in the Temple Mount area is highly secretive; Israel opened up the Temple Mount to limited visits by members of all faiths. The entire area now needs to be fully accessible, including for purposes of archaeological oversight, in order to prevent the further destruction of ancient antiquities by irresponsible Islamic groups. This would be facilitated by giving the international media full access to the area at times that do not conflict with Muslim prayer.

Second, Arab states like Saudi Arabia should quietly support the moderate role of Jordan in these administrative issues. No state should have an interest in radical Islamic sermons in the al-Aqsa Mosque calling for the overthrow of current Arab regimes. It is not at all clear if the Saudi establishment is fully aware of what different groups associated with the Muslim Brotherhood have been planning. For example, the proposal of the Northern Branch of the Islamic Movement in Israel to bring Zamzam water from Mecca to the Temple Mount is intended to elevate Jerusalem's Islamic credentials by adopting ceremonies normally reserved for Mecca.

Saudi Arabia may be opposed to Israel, but do the Saudis actually support such initiatives? Do they want to fund them? Centuries ago Ibn Taymiyya opposed religious innovations like the performance of rituals in Jerusalem that are reserved for Mecca. Moreover, these ideas today are advanced in many cases by those supportive of jihadist tendencies, especially those seeking an immediate reestablishment of the caliphate to replace Arab governments. Since 2003, with the escalation of al-Qaeda attacks inside Saudi Arabia, there is a growing awareness in the Saudi leadership that these radicalizing trends can come back to haunt the kingdom and undermine its stability.

Third, it must be remembered that Jerusalem is not just a diplomatic question. It involves the relationships of the three great monotheistic faiths. For Jerusalem sits on an inter-civilizational seam and what happens in the Holy City can have implications—both negative and positive—for how these religions will relate to one another in the future. The visit of Pope John Paul II to the Western Wall closed a historical circle in the relations between Christianity and Judaism, breaking with older theological patterns of thought in the Church that needed the ruins of a defeated Jerusalem as proof of Christianity's emergence as a replacement for the earlier Israelite faith.

When Islam came out of the Arabian peninsula in the seventh century, it came into contact with other civilizations and religious groups. Part of that first contact involved direct military confrontation and outright conquest. But part of it was also surprisingly tolerant given the era in which it occurred. Radical Islamists who look back to the first four "rightly guided caliphs" perhaps forget that it was the second caliph, Umar bin al-Khattab, who allowed the Jews to return to Jerusalem after five centuries of Roman and then Byzantine rule. Saladin would do the same several hundred years later.

Since there were no existing synagogues under Umar's administration, the returning Jews had to erect new prayer houses, one of which was under the Temple Mount itself. And it was the very same Umar bin al-Khattab who would not pray at the Church of the Holy Sepulchre, according to Islamic tradition, because he was concerned that future generations of Muslims might then turn it into a mosque.

The Islamic world will have to decide its own future course by itself, and outsiders can only hope that its future struggle for ideas will invoke those historical periods in which there was genuine curiosity about the ideas and history of the earlier monotheistic faiths and not an effort to erase them or eradicate what is left of their historical archaeological legacy.

Keeping Jerusalem open for all faiths is a historical responsibility of the State of Israel. Yet, Jerusalem has been at the heart of a great internal debate in Israel and the Jewish world more broadly. Many with a more particularistic orientation understand its reunification in 1967 as part of the national renewal of a people who had faced centuries of exile and even extermination just a few decades earlier. It was where the Jews first restored a clear-cut majority back in 1863 at a time when the world began to recall and recognize their historical rights and title. Jerusalem was the meeting point between the nation's ancient history and its modern revival.

Others with a more universalistic view make a priority of integrating the modern State of Israel with the world community by using Jerusalem as a bargaining chip in a peace process presently under the auspices of the EU, Russia, the UN, and the U.S. In fact, the elaborate international ceremonies of world leaders orchestrated around the signing of each peace accord in the 1990s were intended to remind Israelis that their international acceptance as well as the normalization of their relations with their Arab neighbors was tied to this very diplomatic process.

The clash between the particularistic instincts inside Israel and its universalistic hopes has lain at the heart of the country's political debate for forty years. Jerusalem is where these two national instincts converge, for by protecting Jerusalem under Israeli sovereignty, the State of Israel also serves a universal mission of keeping the holy city truly free and accessible for peoples of all faiths. Particularists will have to understand that there are other religious groups with a stake in the future of the Holy City, while universalists will have to internalize that they have a great national legacy worth protecting for the world and that conceding it would condemn it to total uncertainty at best.

This duality was once understood in ancient times, when protecting the freedom of Jerusalem meant keeping it open as a place of pilgrimage to Jews and Gentiles alike. As described earlier, the Temple service included offerings for the peace of all the nations of the world. These religious principles, reflected in the prophetic traditions of Isaiah and Micah

as well, should be a source of current inspiration, even if the ancient services on which they were based are no longer practiced.

Modern Israel has faced a constant security challenge in recent years,
forcing it to address tough dilemmas as Jerusalem's custodian. During
times of elevated threat levels, for example, it has had to limit the age
groups of Palestinians from the West Bank entering Jerusalem in order to
reduce the risk of suicide bombing attacks. Clearly, in a more peaceful
environment, such regulations would be completely unnecessary, as was
the case before the current wave of militant Palestinian violence began. But
circumstances presently require that a delicate balance be maintained
between the needs of vigilance and a policy of wide-open entry to
Jerusalem's most sensitive sites. Israel has also had to take action against a
tiny internal faction who do not care about the holy sites of others, by
employing its security establishment and its criminal justice system.

Israel's security challenge has required it to extend its security fence
around Jerusalem as well, in order to prevent Hamas suicide bombers
strolling unobstructed into the heart of the city to attack crowded public
areas. Christian institutions near Jerusalem's municipal borders were concerned about being cut off from the Holy City, despite the many crossing
points the fence will have. In response to the request by the main Christian churches, the Israeli defense establishment managed to include nineteen out of twenty-two Christian sites inside the new fence.[18] Of course,
had the Palestinian Authority dismantled the terrorist groups in the areas
under its jurisdiction, the fence would have been totally unnecessary. But
after more than a thousand Israelis died from these attacks since the Oslo
Agreement was signed, it has become essential for Israel's defense. Outside
Jerusalem, the fence could make the movement of pilgrims on special holidays more difficult in certain areas, but it will save the lives of all
Jerusalem's civilians, which is both Israel's paramount responsibility and
ultimately the supreme religious value for all faiths.

Keeping Jerusalem united and free under the sovereignty of Israel is
not a break from international norms or practice. Historically, there have
been international claims that other holy cities be internationalized as well.
This was the case with Istanbul, the seat of Eastern Orthodox Christian-

ity after the fall of the Ottoman Empire. Furthermore, some called for Mecca's internationalization after the Saudis captured the city in the 1920s, when Indian Muslims became concerned by the implications of Wahhabi rules for the practice of other Islamic traditions. But these challenges eventually abated. Ultimately, there is no reason why Israel's role in Jerusalem cannot come to be accepted as well.

It has now been close to forty years since Israel reunited Jerusalem after the 1967 Six-Day War. Access to the Holy City has grown, new religious seminaries have been built, holy shrines have been restored, and Jerusalem's ancient heritage has been unveiled as never before. Jerusalem's multitude of visitors has included peace-loving pilgrims from every continent, including from countries with which Israel has no diplomatic relations. What should now be clear is that no other state or international body can truly protect the peace, freedom, and religious pluralism of the Holy City for all mankind. Rather than fight against the unity of Jerusalem, the world community should come forward to embrace it.

# Obama, Bush, and Jerusalem

On June 4, 2008, then-senator Barack Obama thrust Jerusalem into the 2008 presidential campaign when he addressed the American Israel Public Affairs Committee (AIPAC). He declared that "Jerusalem will remain the capital of Israel, and it must remain undivided." It was the strongest statement made on Jerusalem by a U.S. presidential candidate in years and was greeted by the thousands who heard him at the annual AIPAC event with a standing ovation. But Obama immediately came under criticism by the Palestinians who did not like his reference to an "undivided" Jerusalem. A day later, Obama appeared on CNN with correspondent Candy Crowley, and issued a clarification, saying that Jerusalem would be one of the issues the parties themselves would have to negotiate in the future. The *Washington Post*'s Glenn Kessler charged that Obama had backtracked on his earlier public declaration.[1]

Obama defended himself against the charge of backtracking on Jerusalem to Katie Couric on CBS, as follows:

> Well, if you look at what happened, there was no shift in policy or backtracking in policy. We just had phrased it poorly in the speech.

That has happened and will happen to every politician. You're not always gonna hit your mark in terms of how you phrase your policies. But my policy hasn't changed, and it's been very consistent. It's the same policy that Bill Clinton has put forward, and that says that Jerusalem will be the capital of Israel, that we shouldn't divide it by barbed wire, but that, ultimately that is a final status issue that has to be resolved between the Palestinians and the Israelis.[2]

In other words, his insistence that Jerusalem remain undivided, as he was now explaining, did not necessarily mean keeping it united under the single sovereignty of Israel, but only meant that Jerusalem should not be divided *physically*—by barbed wire, for example. He carefully did not rule out dividing Jerusalem *politically* between parts that would be under the sovereignty of Israel and parts under the sovereignty of the Palestinians, with no barrier between them. That was not exactly what his audience at the AIPAC conference had understood from his words in June 2008. Jerusalem remained a potent political topic not only in the Middle East, but in the United States, especially among religious voters.

Obama's passing reference to Clinton's 2001 proposals—which are examined in chapter 6—was significant, for it showed how much his predecessor's ideas still gripped the imagination of policymakers in Washington. It was common to hear in foreign policy research institutes in the United States the refrain "We all know what the shape of the final settlement will look like." In June 2003, for example, Clinton's National Security Advisor, Sandy Berger, made this very point at the Council on Foreign Relations: "I believe that the contours that we were talking about at Camp David and that later were put out in the Clinton plan in December and then later even further developed in Taba are ultimately the contours that we will embrace."[3]

The Clinton Plan envisioned a re-division of Jerusalem along ethnic lines: areas where Jews live would remain with Israel while areas where Palestinian Arabs live would be transferred to a future Palestinian state. Given the layout of Jerusalem neighborhoods, that might produce a checkerboard of sovereignties, which would be unmanageable. While

Israel and the Palestinians never signed a binding treaty accepting it, the idea of an ethnic re-dividing of Jerusalem remains popular among foreign policymakers in the Obama administration as it was in the Clinton administration.

President George W. Bush was largely silent on the issue of Jerusalem. His April 14, 2004 letter to Ariel Sharon dealt with the ultimate fate of settlement blocs in the West Bank, some of which surrounded Jerusalem. But while Bush affirmed that Israel should not have to return to the 1949 Armistice Lines (also known as the pre-1967 borders), he did not specifically address the issue of Jerusalem. President Bush did, however, provide an important emotional reference to Jerusalem in his Knesset address on May 15, 2008, honoring Israel's 60th anniversary, when he said:

> Sixty years ago, on the eve of Israel's independence, the last British soldiers departing Jerusalem stopped at a building in the Jewish quarter of the Old City. An officer knocked on the door and met a senior rabbi. The officer presented him with a short iron bar—the key to the Zion Gate—and said it was the first time in 18 centuries that a key to the gates of Jerusalem had belonged to a Jew. His hands trembling, the rabbi offered a prayer of thanksgiving to God, "Who had granted us life and permitted us to reach this day." Then he turned to the officer, and uttered the words Jews had awaited for so long: "I accept this key in the name of my people."[4]

Bush's words acknowledged the historical link of the Jewish people to their ancient capital and implied his own recognition of the Israeli claim to Jerusalem's Old City. But beyond the eloquence of his remarks for the Israelis who heard them, they had no practical significance for the development of U.S. policy, though American public opinion still overwhelmingly supports the idea of Jerusalem remaining united, especially when the future of the holy sites is taken into account.[5]

While the Obama administration appears to be clinging to former president Bill Clinton's proposals of re-dividing Jerusalem, Israeli opinion is moving in a very different direction. For example, in October 2007,

Israel's Dahaf Institute, which ran polls for Israel's largest newspaper, *Yediot Ahronot*, found that 63 percent of all Israelis rejected any compromise on Jerusalem.[6] At the same time, another important Israeli pollster, the Midgam Institute, found that 67 percent opposed dividing Jerusalem—even in exchange for a permanent status agreement (an official recognition of Israel's right to exist) and a declaration of an "end of conflict" with the Arab world.[7] A year later, in October 2008, the Herzliya Interdisciplinary Center's Lauder School released a poll indicating that 85 percent of Israelis opposed dividing Jerusalem.[8] For young people between the ages of 18 and 24, the percentage of those opposed to re-dividing Jerusalem actually went up to 90 percent. Israelis in repeated polls wanted to keep their capital united.

Israelis voiced strong support for an undivided Jerusalem because they had seen several territorial withdrawals in recent years backfire; every pullout weakened Israeli security. For example, after the 1993 Oslo Accords, in which Israel pledged to redeploy forces from parts of Gaza and the West Bank, Palestinian terrorists began a campaign of suicide bombing attacks in the heart of Israeli cities, especially in Jerusalem, causing more than 1,000 fatalities. When Israel withdrew from the Gaza Strip in 2005, Hamas massively escalated its rocket attacks on Israeli civilians.

As a result of these experiences, public opinion understandably hardened. In the debate over Jerusalem's future, the argument was made that even if Israel pulled out of the outer Arab neighborhoods of Jerusalem alone, those areas would be taken over by Hamas, which would deploy in them the very same Qassam rockets and long-range mortars that were being used in Gaza against Israeli towns and cities.[9]

Moreover, in addition to these concerns with security, long-standing historical and religious ties of Israelis still bound them to their capital. In fact, the entire Israeli political spectrum shifted to the right between the parliamentary elections of 2006 and 2009. The conservative bloc in the Knesset held 50 seats in 2006; it held 65 (out of 120) in 2009.[10]

There was one exception to this trend in Israeli opinion: Prime Minister Ehud Olmert. Elected in 2006, he began a series of private negotiations with the Palestinian Authority Chairman, Mahmoud Abbas, which included discussions of the status of Jerusalem. After leaving office, Olmert confessed to having met with Abbas in September 2008 and having offered the Palestinian leader nearly 94 percent of the West Bank and even some pre-1967 Israeli territory.[11] In the past, Olmert had openly discussed his willingness to withdraw from Jerusalem neighborhoods that were populated by Palestinian Arabs. Presumably, he made that offer as well.

The bombshell Olmert dropped about his secret talks was that he also proposed withdrawing Israeli sovereignty over what negotiators call "the Holy Basin"—the territory in the heart of Jerusalem that covers the Old City, the Mount of Olives, and possibly other contiguous areas—where the main holy sites of Christianity, Judaism, and Islam are concentrated. Olmert envisioned the area being administered by a consortium of Saudis, Jordanians, Israelis, Palestinians, and Americans.

In these negotiation sessions, Olmert had worked alone. He did not come to Abbas with a negotiating team. He did not seek the authorization of his cabinet for these positions. His public standing was badly damaged as he came under a criminal investigation on charges of bribery and corruption.

The senior ministers from Olmert's own political party, Kadima, gave no indication that they were prepared to re-divide Jerusalem the way the prime minister was suggesting. Deputy Prime Minister Shaul Mofaz, who as chief of staff of the Israel Defense Forces (IDF) presented the IDF General Staff's opposition to the Clinton proposals in 2000, stood firm in insisting Jerusalem remain united. Vice Prime Minister and Foreign Minister Tzipi Livni, who was responsible for the official negotiating track between Israel and the Palestinian Authority (which she conducted with Abu Ala'), was conspicuously silent on the issue, and did not come to Olmert's defense. Aaron Abramovich, her director-general who ran the Israeli Foreign Ministry, subsequently disclosed that her diplomatic team did not negotiate with the Palestinians about Jerusalem.[12] There was a clear gap between Olmert and his key ministers.

The plain fact was Olmert would not have secured a parliamentary majority in the Knesset for any concessions on Jerusalem. As rumors about Olmert's conciliatory positions spread, 70 members of the Knesset, a clear parliamentary majority, signed a letter to President Bush opposing any change in the current municipal boundaries of Jerusalem. The signatories included seventeen members of Olmert's own party or its coalition partners.

Despite the unprecedented territorial concessions that Olmert offered the Palestinians—including in the very heart of Jerusalem—he was not able to clinch an agreement with Abbas, who demanded that Israel go even further. In September 2008, he told the Israeli Hebrew daily, *Haaretz*: "There are various proposals regarding borders and the refugee issue, but they have remained proposals only, and all six central issues of the final status agreement have remained open. I cannot say there has been agreement on a single issue. The gap between the sides is very large."[13]

This was a significant and even historical admission. Abbas was repeating in 2008 what Arafat had done at Camp David in 2000. After Israel offered unprecedented concessions to the Palestinian leadership—even in the heart of Jerusalem—to reach a peace settlement, Abbas was saying that it was not enough and that the gap between the parties was too wide. His argument raised fundamental questions about whether further diplomatic efforts on the same basis made sense.

But the Obama administration came into office with a strong sense that the United States needed to invest far greater diplomatic energy to reach an Israeli-Palestinian agreement of the sort that had eluded the administrations of George W. Bush and Bill Clinton. Jerusalem would inevitably be a central issue in any such effort.

In the Israeli elections of 2009, Prime Minister Olmert decided not to run again. The new prime minister, Benjamin Netanyahu, reverted to the position that had been held by Prime Ministers Yitzhak Rabin and Ariel Sharon that Jerusalem must remain united under the sovereignty of Israel. This had been Netanyahu's position during his first term in office between 1996 and 1999, and he enunciated it before a joint session of the U.S. Congress at that time. Now, speaking on Ammunition Hill on May 21, 2009, where one of the most difficult battles in Jerusalem was fought during the 1967 Six Day War, he declared:

United Jerusalem is the capital of Israel. Jerusalem has always been— and will always be—ours. It will never be divided or cut in half.

Jerusalem will remain only under Israel's sovereignty. In united Jerusalem, the freedom of access for all three religions to the holy sites will be guaranteed, and it is the only way to guarantee that members of all faiths, minorities and denominations can continue living here safely.[14]

# New Areas of U.S.-Israeli Friction in Jerusalem

Tensions between Israel and the Obama administration soon became apparent. For example, during her first visit to Israel in March 2009, Secretary of State Hillary Clinton openly criticized plans by the Jerusalem municipality to demolish illegal Palestinian houses. The houses had been built without a license in an area that had been zoned as Jerusalem park land for many years, since the time of the British Mandate. The area where the illegal construction had taken place was known as the King's Garden, which the Palestinians called the *al-Bustan* (literally, "the Garden") Neighborhood.

Clinton said: "Clearly this kind of activity is unhelpful and not in keeping with the obligations entered into under the 'road map.'"[15] This interpretation of the April 30, 2003, "Performance-Based Roadmap" that had been issued by a diplomatic quartet consisting of the United States, Russia, the European Union, and the United Nations Secretariat, was surprising. Previous Israeli governments had never understood that roadmap to prohibit Israel from enforcing its building codes in Jerusalem. They drew a distinction between the West Bank and East Jerusalem, which Israel annexed in 1967 and where Israeli law fully applied.

Indeed, this distinction was made formally by the Israeli government on May 25, 2003, when it accepted the Roadmap with certain reservations. It stipulated that Jerusalem was an issue for future permanent status talks and not covered by the confidence-building measures that the Roadmap envisioned for the interim period. During that time, even the 1993 Oslo Agreements acknowledged Jerusalem as under Israeli jurisdiction, meaning Israel would be responsible for zoning and planning in the Holy City. But in 2009, Hillary Clinton was not just making a one-time comment about Israeli demolition orders for illegal construction. As she explained: "It is an issue we intend to raise with the government of Israel and the government at the municipal level in Jerusalem."

Geographically, the King's Garden is adjacent to the City of David, which was the center of the original biblical Jerusalem at the time of the First Temple. In 1967, there were only four structures on the periphery of the King's Garden; by 2009, there were eighty-eight.[16] Any major city, like New York or London, would take measures against illegal structures, especially if they were built on public land that was supposed to be a city park. Clinton's involvement in an internal Israeli legal issue seemed unusual, unless the Obama administration meant to give a nod to Palestinian political aspirations by trying to restrict Israel's exercise of its sovereignty in the eastern parts of Jerusalem.

Israeli settlements on the West Bank were another area, with direct implications for Jerusalem, where friction grew between the Obama administration and Israel. The Obama team declared its determination to get Israel to halt any construction in its West Bank settlements, even if it was only for the "natural growth" of the population.[17] The Israeli government argued that it did not intend to build new settlements, but needed to provide the Israeli population of the West Bank with schools, clinics, and housing that would accommodate natural growth. In any case, the territory was disputed. Just as Israelis were building new homes in the area, so were Palestinians.

In the past, American officials had regarded the Israeli settlements differently. Eugene Rostow, a former dean of Yale Law School who was also Undersecretary of State in the Johnson years, wrote years later that Israel has an "unassailable" legal right to establish settlements in the West Bank.[18] In contrast, the Carter administration saw the settlements as illegal. The Reagan administration and its successors did not challenge the legality of settlements, but questioned their advisability, describing them as "obstacles to peace." The Obama administration has tried to keep its position somewhat ambiguous. In June 2009, the *Washington Post* reported that a State Department spokesman repeatedly refused to answer whether the Obama administration viewed Israeli settlements on the West Bank as illegal.[19]

The heart of the legal debate over the West Bank settlements concerned Article 49 in the 1949 Fourth Geneva Convention. It outlawed the forcible transfer of populations out of occupied territories. The law was based explicitly on the experience of Europe under the Nazis. The question was whether this law applied to the voluntary movement of Israelis into areas captured by the Israel Defense Forces in the Six Day War. For the most part, American jurists utterly rejected applying Article 49 to Israeli settlements on the West Bank.

During the administration of George H. W. Bush, the U.S. ambassador to the United Nations in Geneva, Morris Abram, explained that he had been on the U.S. staff at the Nuremberg trials and hence was familiar with the "legislative intent" behind the Fourth Geneva Convention. He confirmed that it applied to forcible evictions of people such as occurred in the Second World War and not to the case of Israeli settlements. Of course, many Israeli jurists found the application of anti-Nazi laws against Israel to be not just legally wrong but morally offensive.

Though administration policies differed over the course of the more than forty years since the 1967 Six Day War, the State Department generally treated East Jerusalem differently than the rest of the West Bank, and did not count Israeli residents of East Jerusalem in its statistics of Israeli settlements.[20] More recently at the end of the Bush administration, Secretary of State Condoleezza Rice admonished Israel for building new housing units in the neighborhood of Har Homa, which was on the eastern side of Jerusalem.[21] In contrast, while not publicly backing the original construction of Har Homa in 1997, the Clinton administration twice vetoed efforts by the Arab bloc to have Israel condemned in the UN Security Council for the neighborhood's development.

In June 2009, U.S. State Department Spokesman Ian Kelly was asked whether the Obama administration's demand that Israel halt construction projects on the West Bank also applied to Jewish neighborhoods in East Jerusalem. He answered in the affirmative: "We're talking about all settlement activity, yes, the area across the line (the 1967 border)."[22] There were also reports that the Obama administration was disturbed by Israeli plans to build a new 200-room hotel in East Jerusalem which was located a little more than 100 yards from the walls of the Old City.[23]

In recent years, Israel had made the argument that it was important to draw a distinction between Israeli construction in areas that Israel will ultimately retain anyway in any peace settlement and other types of construction. It tried to reach quiet agreements with the Bush administration on these issues. If the Obama administration tries to prevent Israeli construction in Israeli neighborhoods in Jerusalem—neighborhoods that all Israeli governments envision remaining part of Israel—the city will remain a potential diplomatic flashpoint.

There were other developments in the Obama administration's policy on Jerusalem that gave observers concern. In the 1990s, the U.S. Congress passed the Jerusalem Embassy Act requiring the U.S. Government to transfer the U.S. Embassy from Tel Aviv to Jerusalem. The law provided that the president could issue a waiver of the law if he felt it was necessary. George W. Bush's presidential waiver contained a clause that said: "My administration remains committed to beginning the process of moving our embassy to Jerusalem."[24] While Bush had made a commitment to move the U.S. Embassy, he ultimately did not follow through, signing waiver after waiver. At the very minimum, he kept his political commitment to moving the embassy alive, by preserving this formal language in the waiver. But the Obama administration has dropped the formal sentence about being committed to moving the embassy. All in all, while U.S.-Israel relations remain strong, there is considerable worry on the Israeli side about the direction of U.S. policy under the new administration, and about its commitment to Israel and a unified Jerusalem.

## What Narrative for Jerusalem?

President Obama raised the issue of Jerusalem himself, in his June 4, 2009 address at Cairo University. The declared purpose of his speech in the Egyptian capital was to reduce the tensions that had grown in recent years between the West and the Islamic world. Admittedly, this was not going to be a balanced presentation between the interests of Israel and the Arab world, but rather would be tailored to reach out to Islamic concerns. As a result, Obama adopted in his address a point of view that appeared to veer away from how Israel saw its conflict with the Palestinians and the Arab world, as well as how Israel defined the issue of sovereignty over Jerusalem.

Obama said, "All of us have a responsibility to work for the day when the mothers of Israelis and Palestinians can see their children grow up without fear; when the Holy Land of the three great faiths is the place of peace that God intended it to be; when Jerusalem is a secure and lasting home for Jews and Christians and Muslims, and a place for all the children of Abraham to mingle peacefully together as in the story of Isra— (applause)—as in the story of Isra, when Moses, Jesus, and Muhammad, peace be upon him, joined in prayer."[25]

Obama was making reference to the Islamic tradition that after his Night Journey from Mecca to Jerusalem, Muhammad ascended to heaven and on the way prayed with the earlier prophets. That Obama chose this Islamic reference and not a universalistic vision from Judaism or Christianity about Jerusalem is not surprising, given that he was engaged in an outreach effort to Muslims. But there was one problematic element in his remarks. He described a day in the future when "Jerusalem is a secure and lasting home" for all three great faiths. On that day, according to Obama, Jerusalem will be a place "for all the children of Abraham to mingle peacefully together...."[26]

Ironically, that day when members of all three great faiths could finally pray in Jerusalem actually came to pass forty-two years before Obama's speech, when the Israel Defense Forces re-united the Holy City. As described in earlier chapters, the holy sites of Jerusalem prior to the 1967 Six Day War were not equally accessible to all faiths: under Jordanian administration, Christians found their institutions under restrictions, while the Jewish people were denied access to their holy sites, such as the Western Wall. Under Israel, the freedom of Jerusalem was restored.

But Obama implied that today, under Israeli rule, Christians, Jews, and Muslims cannot enjoy freedom in Jerusalem, that Jerusalem under Israel is not a "secure and lasting home" for all three faiths.[27] Obama did not say, specifically, what sort of settlement he wanted in Jerusalem, but he did make clear that a united Jerusalem under Israeli jurisdiction was inadequate.

In other parts of his Cairo speech, Obama correctly confronted extremist elements in the Muslim world that engage in "Holocaust

Denial." In the Jerusalem section of his speech, he had the opportunity—which he let pass, unfortunately—to refute another sort of denial: the disturbing trend of "Temple denial," according to which the most basic elements of the biblical history of Jerusalem, common to Jews and Christians, are rejected out of hand. By denying the basics of Jewish history that have been well-established by ample archaeological evidence, the Palestinian leadership, in particular, has been undermining the principle of mutual recognition that must be the foundation of any meaningful peace process in the future.

It has been nearly a decade since Yasser Arafat denied at Camp David in front of President Clinton that the Temple was ever in Jerusalem. "Temple Denial" is still very much a part of the Palestinian narrative. For example, the Palestinian Authority's Minister of Agriculture, Mahmoud al-Habash, explained on Palestinian Authority television on April 16, 2009, that "truly religious Jews truly believe—and they have stated this on more than one occasion—that the Temple was never in the Holy City."[28]

The official newspaper of the Palestinian Authority, *al-Hayat al-Jadida*, used terms like "an imaginary Hebrew history."[29] Another term, "the alleged Temple," was used on Palestinian Authority television on May 1, 2009.[30] Dr. Marwan Abu Khalaf, the director of the Archaeological Institute at al-Quds University, appeared on Palestinian Authority television earlier in the year on February 27, 2009, saying that the archaeological treasures in Jerusalem "refute the Israeli claims...."[31] He added that the relics in the Holy City say, "We are Arab, we are Muslim, we are Christian." He refused to recognize the rich archaeological evidence authenticating Jerusalem's biblical past.

But that past will not go away, for striking artifacts keep being discovered that link Jerusalem to its ancient past and even to the Temple itself. In October 2008, the Israeli Antiquities Authority revealed that in excavations conducted just north of Jerusalem, a fragment of a sarcophagus cover was found. Engraved on the fragment was a remarkable Hebrew inscription that read: "Ben HaCohen Hagadol"—which translates to "the Son of the High Priest."[32] It was the High Priest who officiated at the Temple service in ancient Jerusalem. The professional estimate of when the son of the high priest lived was between the years 30 and 70 CE, or around the time of the destruction of the Temple by the Roman Empire. Thus, while the Palestinian Authority media used every opportunity to deny Jerusalem's past, archaeologists are discovering precisely the opposite as new revelations come out linking the Holy City and its ancient heritage.

The denial of the Jewish connection to Jerusalem continues, however, at the highest level of Palestinian officialdom. The Palestinian Authority Prime Minister Salam Fayyad, known for his pragmatic, pro-American orientation, spoke in the UN General Assembly on November 12, 2008, at a special meeting on "The Dialogue of Religions and Cultures."[33] He devoted a large portion of his address to the issue of Jerusalem. It was an opportunity for Fayyad to reach out to his Israeli neighbors with a positive vision for the future.

Instead Fayyad ignored them and their history: "As we speak about religious tolerance, we must speak about the City of Jerusalem, the City of Peace, the land of prophets, the first of their two Qiblas, the third holiest shrine of Islam, the place of ascension of the Prophet Muhammad (Peace be upon him) and the place of resurrection of Jesus Christ (Peace be upon him)."[34] In Fayyad's definition of Jerusalem, there was no King David or King Solomon—in fact, no Jewish connection whatsoever. It is telling that he gave this speech at a United Nations event dedicated to inter-religious dialogue. The one-sidedness of the Palestinian prime minister only confirmed yet again why it is only democratic Israel that can truly safeguard all of Jerusalem's holy sites and be the best guardian of them in the future.

When Israeli prime ministers speak about Jerusalem they always envision Israel as the protector of the Holy City for all three great monotheistic faiths: Judaism, Christianity, and Islam. The continuing influence of Temple Denial—and historical denial, more generally—among Palestinian Arab elites illustrates how far the Arab-Israeli peace process must still go before any real and permanent breakthroughs will become possible. For at the root of any meaningful peace process must be the idea of mutual recognition. Understanding the deep historical connections of the Jewish people to Jerusalem (which is detailed in the Hebrew Bible), is an important first step that the Arab peoples must take. The Obama administration could play an important role if it reaffirmed the historical rights of Israel in Jerusalem and thereby reinforced the kind of realism that will be necessary for a stable peace to emerge.

# ❈❈❈ Appendix

## Excerpts from an 1864 British Consular report on Jerusalem demographics in 1863

> Report on the Commerce of Jerusalem during the year 1863

> Population and Industries
>
> The population of the Sandjak may be estimated at 200,000, divided into the three sects of Mahometans, Christians, and Jews,

The population of the
city of Jerusalem is computed,
at 15,000, of whom about
4,500 Moslems, 8,000 Jews
and

the rest Christians of
various denominations.

Foreign Office Records (FO), 195/808, British National Archives

## The Palestine Mandate

July 24, 1922
The Council of the League of Nations:

Whereas the Principal Allied Powers have agreed, for the purpose of giving effect to the provisions of Article 22 of the Covenant of the League of Nations, to entrust to a Mandatory selected by the said Powers the administration of the territory of Palestine, which formerly belonged to the Turkish Empire, within such boundaries as may be fixed by them; and

Whereas the Principal Allied Powers have also agreed that the Mandatory should be responsible for putting into effect the declaration originally made on November 2nd, 1917, by the Government of His Britannic Majesty, and adopted by the said Powers, in favor of the establishment in Palestine of a national home for the Jewish people, it being clearly understood that nothing should be done which might prejudice the civil and religious rights of existing non-Jewish communities in Palestine, or the rights and political status enjoyed by Jews in any other country; and

**Whereas recognition has thereby been given to the historical connection of the Jewish people with Palestine and to the grounds for reconstituting their national home in that country;** and

Whereas the Principal Allied Powers have selected His Britannic Majesty as the Mandatory for Palestine; and

Whereas the mandate in respect of Palestine has been formulated in the following terms and submitted to the Council of the League for approval; and

Whereas His Britannic Majesty has accepted the mandate in respect of Palestine and undertaken to exercise it on behalf of the League of Nations in conformity with the following provisions; and

Whereas by the afore-mentioned Article 22 (paragraph 8), it is provided that the degree of authority, control or administration to be exercised by the Mandatory, not having been previously agreed upon by the Members of the League, shall be explicitly defined by the Council of the

League of Nations; confirming the said Mandate, defines its terms as follows:

ARTICLE 1. The Mandatory shall have full powers of legislation and of administration, save as they may be limited by the terms of this mandate.

ART. 2. **The Mandatory shall be responsible for placing the country under such political, administrative and economic conditions as will secure the establishment of the Jewish national home, as laid down in the preamble, and the development of self-governing institutions, and also for safeguarding the civil and religious rights of all the inhabitants of Palestine, irrespective of race and religion.**

ART. 3. The Mandatory shall, so far as circumstances permit, encourage local autonomy.

ART. 4. An appropriate Jewish agency shall be recognized as a public body for the purpose of advising and co-operating with the Administration of Palestine in such economic, social and other matters as may affect the establishment of the Jewish national home and the interests of the Jewish population in Palestine, and, subject always to the control of the Administration to assist and take part in the development of the country.

The Zionist organization, so long as its organization and constitution are in the opinion of the Mandatory appropriate, shall be recognized as such agency. It shall take steps in consultation with His Britannic Majesty's Government to secure the co-operation of all Jews who are willing to assist in the establishment of the Jewish national home.

ART. 5. The Mandatory shall be responsible for seeing that no Palestine territory shall be ceded or leased to, or in any way placed under the control of the Government of any foreign Power.

ART. 6. The Administration of Palestine, while ensuring that the rights and position of other sections of the population are not prejudiced, shall facilitate Jewish immigration under suitable conditions and shall encourage, in co-operation with the Jewish agency referred to in Article 4, close settlement by Jews on the land, including State lands and waste lands not required for public purposes.

ART. 7. The Administration of Palestine shall be responsible for enacting a nationality law. There shall be included in this law provisions framed so as to facilitate the acquisition of Palestinian citizenship by Jews who take up their permanent residence in Palestine.

ART. 8. The privileges and immunities of foreigners, including the benefits of consular jurisdiction and protection as formerly enjoyed by Capitulation or usage in the Ottoman Empire, shall not be applicable in Palestine.

Unless the Powers whose nationals enjoyed the afore-mentioned privileges and immunities on August 1st, 1914, shall have previously renounced the right to their re-establishment, or shall have agreed to their non-application for a specified period, these privileges and immunities shall, at the expiration of the mandate, be immediately reestablished in their entirety or with such modifications as may have been agreed upon between the Powers concerned.

ART. 9. The Mandatory shall be responsible for seeing that the judicial system established in Palestine shall assure to foreigners, as well as to natives, a complete guarantee of their rights. Respect for the personal status of the various peoples and communities and for their religious interests shall be fully guaranteed. In particular, the control and administration of Waqfs shall be exercised in accordance with religious law and the dispositions of the founders.

ART. 10. Pending the making of special extradition agreements relating to Palestine, the extradition treaties in force between the Mandatory and other foreign Powers shall apply to Palestine.

ART. 11. The Administration of Palestine shall take all necessary measures to safeguard the interests of the community in connection with the development of the country, and, subject to any international obligations accepted by the Mandatory, shall have full power to provide for public ownership or control of any of the natural resources of the country or of the public works, services and utilities established or to be established therein. It shall introduce a land system appropriate to the needs of the country, having regard, among other things, to the desirability of promoting the close settlement and intensive cultivation of the land.

The Administration may arrange with the Jewish agency mentioned in Article 4 to construct or operate, upon fair and equitable terms, any public works, services and utilities, and to develop any of the natural resources of the country, in so far as these matters are not directly undertaken by the Administration. Any such arrangements shall provide that no profits distributed by such agency, directly or indirectly, shall exceed a reasonable rate of interest on the capital, and any further profits shall be utilized by it for the benefit of the country in a manner approved by the Administration.

ART. 12. The Mandatory shall be entrusted with the control of the foreign relations of Palestine and the right to issue exequaturs to consuls appointed by foreign Powers. He shall also be entitled to afford diplomatic and consular protection to citizens of Palestine when outside its territorial limits.

ART. 13. **All responsibility in connection with the Holy Places and religious buildings or sites in Palestine, including that of preserving existing rights and of securing free access to the Holy Places, religious buildings and sites and the free exercise of worship, while ensuring the requirements of public order and decorum, is assumed by the Mandatory, who shall be responsible solely to the League of Nations in all matters connected herewith, provided that nothing in this article shall prevent the Mandatory from entering into such arrangements as he may deem reasonable with the Administration for the purpose of carrying the provisions of this article into effect; and provided also that nothing in this mandate shall be construed as conferring upon the Mandatory authority to interfere with the fabric or the management of purely Moslem sacred shrines, the immunities of which are guaranteed.**

ART. 14. A special commission shall be appointed by the Mandatory to study, define and determine the rights and claims in connection with the Holy Places and the rights and claims relating to the different religious communities in Palestine. The method of nomination, the composition and the functions of this Commission shall be submitted to the Council of the League for its approval, and the Commission shall not be appointed or enter upon its functions without the approval of the Council.

ART. 15. The Mandatory shall see that complete freedom of conscience and the free exercise of all forms of worship, subject only to the maintenance of public order and morals, are ensured to all. No discrimination of any kind shall be made between the inhabitants of Palestine on the ground of race, religion or language. No person shall be excluded from Palestine on the sole ground of his religious belief.

The right of each community to maintain its own schools for the education of its own members in its own language, while conforming to such educational requirements of a general nature as the Administration may impose, shall not be denied or impaired.

ART. 16. The Mandatory shall be responsible for exercising such supervision over religious or eleemosynary bodies of all faiths in Palestine as may be required for the maintenance of public order and good government. Subject to such supervision, no measures shall be taken in Palestine to obstruct or interfere with the enterprise of such bodies or to discriminate against any representative or member of them on the ground of his religion or nationality.

ART. 17. The Administration of Palestine may organize on a voluntary basis the forces necessary for the preservation of peace and order, and also for the defense of the country, subject, however, to the supervision of the Mandatory, but shall not use them for purposes other than those above specified save with the consent of the Mandatory. Except for such purposes, no military, naval or air forces shall be raised or maintained by the Administration of Palestine.

Nothing in this article shall preclude the Administration of Palestine from contributing to the cost of the maintenance of the forces of the Mandatory in Palestine.

The Mandatory shall be entitled at all times to use the roads, railways and ports of Palestine for the movement of armed forces and the carriage of fuel and supplies.

ART. 18. The Mandatory shall see that there is no discrimination in Palestine against the nationals of any State Member of the League of Nations (including companies incorporated under its laws) as compared with those of the Mandatory or of any foreign State in matters concerning taxation, commerce or navigation, the exercise of industries or professions, or in the treatment of merchant vessels or civil aircraft. Similarly, there shall be no discrimination in Palestine against goods originating in or destined for any of the said States, and there shall be freedom of transit under equitable conditions across the mandated area.

Subject as aforesaid and to the other provisions of this mandate, the Administration of Palestine may, on the advice of the Mandatory, impose such taxes and customs duties as it may consider necessary, and take such steps as it may think best to promote the development of the natural resources of the country and to safeguard the interests of the population. It may also, on the advice of the Mandatory, conclude a special customs agreement with any State the territory of which in 1914 was wholly included in Asiatic Turkey or Arabia.

ART. 19. The Mandatory shall adhere on behalf of the Administration of Palestine to any general international conventions already existing, or which may be concluded hereafter with the approval of the League of Nations, respecting the slave traffic, the traffic in arms and ammunition, or the traffic in drugs, or relating to commercial equality, freedom of transit and navigation, aerial navigation and postal, telegraphic and wireless communication or literary, artistic or industrial property.

ART. 20. The Mandatory shall co-operate on behalf of the Administration of Palestine, so far as religious, social and other conditions may permit, in the execution of any common policy adopted by the League of Nations for preventing and combating disease, including diseases of plants and animals.

ART. 21. The Mandatory shall secure the enactment within twelve months from this date, and shall ensure the execution of a Law of Antiquities based on the following rules. This law shall ensure equality of treatment in the matter of excavations and archaeological research to the nationals of all States Members of the League of Nations.

(1) "Antiquity" means any construction or any product of human activity earlier than the year 1700 A. D.

(2) The law for the protection of antiquities shall proceed by encouragement rather than by threat.

Any person who, having discovered an antiquity without being furnished with the authorization referred to in paragraph 5, reports the same to an official of the competent Department, shall be rewarded according to the value of the discovery.

(3) No antiquity may be disposed of except to the competent Department, unless this Department renounces the acquisition of any such antiquity.

No antiquity may leave the country without an export license from the said Department.

(4) Any person who maliciously or negligently destroys or damages an antiquity shall be liable to a penalty to be fixed.

(5) No clearing of ground or digging with the object of finding antiquities shall be permitted, under penalty of fine, except to persons authorized by the competent Department.

(6) Equitable terms shall be fixed for expropriation, temporary or permanent, of lands which might be of historical or archaeological interest.

(7) Authorization to excavate shall only be granted to persons who show sufficient guarantees of archaeological experience. The Administration of Palestine shall not, in granting these authorizations, act in such a way as to exclude scholars of any nation without good grounds.

(8) The proceeds of excavations may be divided between the excavator and the competent Department in a proportion fixed by that Department. If division seems impossible for scientific reasons, the excavator shall receive a fair indemnity in lieu of a part of the find.

ART. 22. English, Arabic and Hebrew shall be the official languages of Palestine. Any statement or inscription in Arabic on stamps or money in Palestine shall be repeated in Hebrew and any statement or inscription in Hebrew shall be repeated in Arabic.

ART. 23. The Administration of Palestine shall recognize the holy days of the respective communities in Palestine as legal days of rest for the members of such communities.

ART. 24. The Mandatory shall make to the Council of the League of Nations an annual report to the satisfaction of the Council as to the measures taken during the year to carry out the provisions of the mandate.

Copies of all laws and regulations promulgated or issued during the year shall be communicated with the report.

ART. 25. In the territories lying between the Jordan and the eastern boundary of Palestine as ultimately determined, the Mandatory shall be entitled, with the consent of the Council of the League of Nations, to postpone or withhold application of such provisions of this mandate as he may consider inapplicable to the existing local conditions, and to make such provision for the administration of the territories as he may consider suitable to those conditions, provided that no action shall be taken which is inconsistent with the provisions of Articles 15, 16 and 18.

ART. 26. The Mandatory agrees that, if any dispute whatever should arise between the Mandatory and another member of the League of Nations relating to the interpretation or the application of the provisions of the mandate, such dispute, if it cannot be settled by negotiation, shall be submitted to the Permanent Court of International Justice provided for by Article 14 of the Covenant of the League of Nations.

ART. 27. The consent of the Council of the League of Nations is required for any modification of the terms of this mandate.

ART. 28. In the event of the termination of the mandate hereby conferred upon the Mandatory, the Council of the League of Nations shall make such arrangements as may be deemed necessary for safeguarding in perpetuity, under guarantee of the League, the rights secured by Articles 13 and 14, and shall use its influence for securing, under the guarantee of the League, that the Government of Palestine will fully honor the financial obligations legitimately incurred by the Administration of Palestine during the period of the mandate, including the rights of public servants to pensions or gratuities.

The present instrument shall be deposited in original in the archives of the League of Nations and certified copies shall be forwarded by the Secretary-General of the League of Nations to all members of the League.

Done at London the twenty-fourth day of July, one thousand nine hundred and twenty-two.

(emphasis added)

— 4 —

## THE HARAM.

### HISTORICAL SKETCH

The words al-Haram al-Sharif, which can perhaps best be rendered by "The August Sanctuary", denote the whole of the sacred enclosure which it is the object of this Guide to describe. Its plan is roughly that of a rectangle whose major axis runs from north to south; its area is approximately 145,000 square metres. If you wish to have some idea of its extent and to see it whole before proceeding to examine it in detail, you would be well-advised to begin your visit by walking to the north-west corner, and there, ascending the flight of steps which lead up to the disused building on the right, you will see the whole area spread before you. The view shown on the frontispiece (Fig. 1) was taken, although at a considerable altitude, from the very spot where you are standing.

The two principal edifices are the Dome of the Rock, on a raised platform in the middle, and the mosque of al-Aqsa against the south wall. Other buildings which we shall consider later lie dotted about here and there. On the left, along the east wall, the double portals of the Golden Gate appear. On every side, trees break the prospect, which lend a peculiar charm to the scene. The site is one of the oldest in the world. Its sanctity dates from the earliest (perhaps from pre-historic) times. Its identity with the site of Solomon's Temple is beyond dispute. This, too, is the spot, according to the universal belief, on which "David built there an altar unto the Lord, and offered burnt offerings and peace offerings". (1)

But, for the purposes of this Guide, which confines itself to the Moslem period, the starting-point is the year 637 A.D. In that year, the Caliph Omar occupied Jerusalem and one of his first acts was to repair to this site, which had already become sacred in the eyes of Moslems as the place to which the Prophet was one night miraculously translated. The site had long since been neglected. The Caliph and his four thousand followers found little more than desolation and rubbish. There were the ruined walls of the Herodian and Roman periods, the remains of an early basilica (probably on the present site of al-Aqsa), and the bare Rock. Yet from this rock had the Prophet, according to the tradition, ascended to heaven on his steed. So the Caliph ordered a mosque to be erected by its side. His orders were executed, and the building was seen and described by Bishop Arculf who visited Jerusalem about 670 A.D. But no vestige of it remains to-day, save for the name "Mosque of Omar" which is still, but quite wrongly, sometimes used for the Dome of the Rock.

With the reign of 'Abdul-Malek ibn Marwan, the Umayyad, (685-705 A.D.), the history of the present buildings begins. Jeru-

---

(1) 2 Samuel XXIV, 25.

# Selections from United Nations
# General Assembly Resolution 181
# November 29, 1947

Part III-City of Jerusalem

A. SPECIAL REGIME

The City of Jerusalem shall be established as a corpus separatum under a special international regime and shall be administered by the United Nations. The Trusteeship Council shall be designated to discharge the responsibilities of the Administering Authority on behalf of the United Nations.

B. BOUNDARIES OF THE CITY

The City of Jerusalem shall include the present municipality of Jerusalem plus the surrounding villages and towns, the most eastern of which shall be Abu Dis; the most southern, Bethlehem; the most western, 'Ein Karim (including also the built-up area of Motsa); and the most northern Shu'fat, as indicated on the attached sketch-map (annex B).

C. STATUTE OF THE CITY

The Trusteeship Council shall, within five months of the approval of the present plan, elaborate and approve a detailed statute of the City which shall contain, inter alia, the substance of the following provisions:

Government machinery; special objectives. The Administering Authority in discharging its administrative obligations shall pursue the following special objectives:

To protect and to preserve the unique spiritual and religious interests located in the city of the three great monotheistic faiths throughout the world, Christian, Jewish and Moslem; to this end to ensure that order and peace, and especially religious peace, reign in Jerusalem;

To foster cooperation among all the inhabitants of the city in their own interests as well as in order to encourage and support the peaceful development of the mutual relations between the two Palestinian peoples throughout the Holy Land; to promote the security, well-being and any constructive measures of development of the residents having regard to the special circumstances and customs of the various peoples and communities.

Governor and Administrative staff. A Governor of the City of Jerusalem shall be appointed by the Trusteeship Council and shall be responsible to it. He shall be selected on the basis of special qualifications and without regard to nationality. He shall not, however, be a citizen of either State in Palestine.

The Governor shall represent the United Nations in the City and shall exercise on their behalf all powers of administration, including the conduct of external affairs. He shall be assisted by an administrative staff classed as international officers in the meaning of Article 100 of the Charter and chosen whenever practicable from the residents of the city and of the rest of Palestine on a non-discriminatory basis. A detailed plan for the organization of the administration of the city shall be submitted by the Governor to the Trusteeship Council and duly approved by it.

Local autonomy

The existing local autonomous units in the territory of the city (villages, townships and municipalities) shall enjoy wide powers of local government and administration.

The Governor shall study and submit for the consideration and decision of the Trusteeship Council a plan for the establishment of special town units consisting, respectively, of the Jewish and Arab sections of new Jerusalem. The new town units shall continue to form part the present municipality of Jerusalem.

Security measures

The City of Jerusalem shall be demilitarized; neutrality shall be declared and preserved, and no para-military formations, exercises or activities shall be permitted within its borders.

Should the administration of the City of Jerusalem be seriously obstructed or prevented by the non-cooperation or interference of one or more sections of the population the Governor shall have authority to take such measures as may be necessary to restore the effective functioning of administration.

To assist in the maintenance of internal law and order, especially for the protection of the Holy Places and religious buildings and sites in the city, the Governor shall organize a special police force of adequate strength, the members of which shall be recruited outside of Palestine. The Governor shall be empowered to direct such budgetary provision as may be necessary for the maintenance of this force.

Legislative organization

A Legislative Council, elected by adult residents of the city irrespective of nationality on the basis of universal and secret suffrage and proportional representation, shall have powers of legislation and taxation. No legislative measures shall, however, conflict or interfere with the provisions which will be set forth in the Statute of the City, nor shall any law, regulation, or official action prevail over them. The Statute shall grant to the Governor a right of vetoing bills inconsistent with the provisions referred to in the preceding sentence. It shall also empower him to promulgate temporary ordinances in case the Council fails to adopt in time a bill deemed essential to the normal functioning of the administration.

Administration of justice

The Statute shall provide for the establishment of an independent judiciary system, including a court of appeal. All the inhabitants of the city shall be subject to it.

Economic union and economic regime

The City of Jerusalem shall be included in the Economic Union of Palestine and be bound by all stipulations of the undertaking and of any treaties issued therefrom, as well as by the decisions of the Joint Economic Board. The headquarters of the Economic Board shall be established in the territory City. The Statute shall provide for the regulation of economic matters not falling within the regime of the Economic Union, on the basis of equal treatment and non-discrimination for all members of the United Nations and their nationals.

Freedom of transit and visit: control of residents

Subject to considerations of security, and of economic welfare as determined by the Governor under the directions of the Trusteeship Council, freedom of entry into, and residence within the borders of the City shall be guaranteed for the residents or citizens of the Arab and Jewish States. Immigration into, and residence within, the borders of the city for nationals of other States shall be controlled by the Governor under the directions of the Trusteeship Council.

Relations with Arab and Jewish States. Representatives of the Arab and Jewish States shall be accredited to the Governor of the City and charged with the protection of the interests of their States and nationals in connection with the international administration of the City.

### Official languages

Arabic and Hebrew shall be the official languages of the city. This will not preclude the adoption of one or more additional working languages, as may be required.

### Citizenship

All the residents shall become ipso facto citizens of the City of Jerusalem unless they opt for citizenship of the State of which they have been citizens or, if Arabs or Jews, have filed notice of intention to become citizens of the Arab or Jewish State respectively, according to Part 1, section B, paragraph 9, of this Plan.

The Trusteeship Council shall make arrangements for consular protection of the citizens of the City outside its territory.

### Freedoms of citizens

Subject only to the requirements of public order and morals, the inhabitants of the City shall be ensured the enjoyment of human rights and fundamental freedoms, including freedom of conscience, religion and worship, language, education, speech and press, assembly and association, and petition.

No discrimination of any kind shall be made between the inhabitants on the grounds of race, religion, language or sex.

All persons within the City shall be entitled to equal protection of the laws.

The family law and personal status of the various persons and communities and their religious interests, including endowments, shall be respected.

Except as may be required for the maintenance of public order and good government, no measure shall be taken to obstruct or interfere with the enterprise of religious or charitable bodies of all faiths or to discriminate against any representative or member of these bodies on the ground of his religion or nationality.

The City shall ensure adequate primary and secondary education for the Arab and Jewish communities respectively, in their own languages and in accordance with their cultural traditions.

The right of each community to maintain its own schools for the education of its own members in its own language, while conforming to such educational requirements of a general nature as the City may impose, shall not be denied or impaired. Foreign educational establishments shall continue their activity on the basis of their existing rights.

No restriction shall be imposed on the free use by any inhabitant of the City of any language in private intercourse, in commerce, in religion, in the Press or in publications of any kind, or at public meetings.

Holy Places Existing rights in respect of Holy Places and religious buildings or sites shall not be denied or impaired.

Free access to the Holy Places and religious buildings or sites and the free exercise of worship shall be secured in conformity with existing rights and subject to the requirements of public order and decorum.

Holy Places and religious buildings or sites shall be preserved. No act shall be permitted which may in any way impair their sacred character. If at any time it appears to the Governor that any particular Holy Place, religious building or site is in need of urgent repair, the Governor may call upon the community or communities concerned to carry out such repair. The Governor may carry it out himself at the expense of the community or communities concerned if no action is taken within a reasonable time.

No taxation shall be levied in respect of any Holy Place, religious building or site which was exempt from taxation on the date of the creation of the City. No change in the incidence of such taxation shall be made which would either discriminate between the owners or occupiers of Holy Places, religious buildings or sites or would place such owners or occupiers in a position less favourable in relation to the general incidence of taxation than existed at the time of the adoption of the Assembly's recommendations.

Special powers of the Governor in respect of the Holy Places, religious buildings and sites in the City and in any part of Palestine.

The protection of the Holy Places, religious buildings and sites located in the City of Jerusalem shall be a special concern of the Governor. With relation to such places, buildings and sites in Palestine outside the city, the Governor shall determine, on the ground of powers granted to him by the Constitution of both States, whether the provisions of the Constitution of the Arab and Jewish States in Palestine dealing therewith and the religious rights appertaining thereto are being properly applied and respected.

The Governor shall also be empowered to make decisions on the basis of existing rights in cases of disputes which may arise between the different religious communities or the rites of a religious community in respect of the Holy Places, religious buildings and sites in any part of Palestine.

In this task he may be assisted by a consultative council of representatives of different denominations acting in an advisory capacity.

## D. DURATION OF THE SPECIAL REGIME

The Statute elaborated by the Trusteeship Council the aforementioned principles shall come into force not later than 1 October 1948. It shall remain in force in the first instance for a period of ten years, unless the Trusteeship Council finds it necessary to undertake a re-examination of these provisions at an earlier date. After the expiration of this period the whole scheme shall be subject to examination by the Trusteeship Council in the light of experience acquired with its functioning. The residents the City shall be then free to express by means of a referendum their wishes as to possible modifications of regime

# Israel-Jordan Armistice Agreement
## April 3, 1949

### Preamble

The Parties to the present Agreement, Responding to the Security Council resolution of 16 November 1948, calling upon them, as a further provisional measure under Article 40 of the Charter of the United Nations and in order to facilitate the transition from the present truce to permanent peace in Palestine, to negotiate an armistice;

Having decided to enter into negotiations under United Nations chairmanship concerning the implementation of the Security Council resolution of 16 November 1948; and having appointed representatives empowered to negotiate and conclude an Armistice Agreement;

The undersigned representatives of their respective Governments, having exchanged their full powers found to be in good and proper form, have agreed upon the following provisions:

### Article I

With a view to promoting the return of permanent peace in Palestine and in recognition of the importance in this regard of mutual assurances concerning the future military operations of the Parties, the following principles, which shall be fully observed by both Parties during the armistice, are hereby affirmed:

1. The injunction of the Security Council against resort to military force in the settlement of the Palestine question shall henceforth be scrupulously respected by both Parties;

2. No aggressive action by the armed forces-land, sea, or air-of either Party shall be undertaken, planned, or threatened against the people or the armed forces of the other; it being understood that the use of the term planned in this context has no bearing on normal staff planning as generally practised in military organisations;

3. The right of each Party to its security and freedom from fear of attack by the armed forces of the other shall be fully respected;

4. The establishment of an armistice between the armed forces of the two Parties is accepted as an indispensable step toward the liquidation of armed conflict and the restoration of peace in Palestine.

### Article II

With a specific view to the implementation of the resolution of the Security Council of 16 November 1948, the following principles and purposes are affirmed:

1. The principle that no military or political advantage should be gained under the truce ordered by the Security Council is recognised;

2. **It is also recognised that no provision of this Agreement shall in any way prejudice the rights, claims and positions of either Party hereto in the ultimate peaceful settlement of the Palestine question, the provisions of this Agreement being dictated exclusively by military considerations.**

### Article III

1. In pursuance of the foregoing principles and of the resolution of the Security Council of 16 November 1948, a general armistice between the armed forces of the two Parties-land, sea and air-is hereby established.

2. No element of the land, sea or air military or para-military forces of either Party, including non-regular forces, shall commit any warlike or hostile act against the military or para-military forces of the other Party, or against civilians in territory under the control of that Party; or shall advance beyond or pass over for any purpose whatsoever the Armistice Demarcation Lines set forth in articles V and VI of this Agreement; or enter into or pass through the air space of the other Party.

3. No warlike act or act of hostility shall be conducted from territory controlled by one of the Parties to this Agreement against the other Party.

### Article IV

1. The lines described in articles V and VI of this Agreement shall be designated as the Armistice Demarcation Lines and are delineated in

pursuance of the purpose and intent of the resolution of the Security Council of 16 November 1948.

2. The basic purpose of the Armistice Demarcation Lines is to delineate the lines beyond which the armed forces of the respective Parties shall not move.

3. Rules and regulations of the armed forces of the Parties, which prohibit civilians from crossing the fighting lines or entering the area between the lines, shall remain in effect after the signing of this Agreement with application to the Armistice Demarcation Lines defined in articles V and VI.

### Article V

1. The Armistice Demarcation Lines for all sectors other than the sector now held by Iraqi forces shall be as delineated on the maps in annex I to this Agreement, and shall be defined as follows:

(a) In the sector Kh Deir Arab (MR 1510-1574) to the northern terminus of the lines defined in the 30 November 1948 Cease-Fire Agreement for the Jerusalem area, the Armistice Demarcation Lines shall follow the truce lines as certified by the United Nations Truce Supervision Organisation;

(b) In the Jerusalem sector, the Armistice Demarcation Lines shall correspond to the lines defined in the 30 November 1948 Cease-Fire Agreement for the Jerusalem area;

(c) In the Hebron-Dead Sea sector, the Armistice Demarcation Line shall be as delineated on map 1 and marked B in annex I to this Agreement;

(d) In the sector from a point on the Dead Sea (MR 1925-0958) to the southernmost tip of Palestine, the Armistice Demarcation Line shall be determined by existing military positions as surveyed in March 1949 by United Nations observers, and shall run from north to south as delineated on map 1 in annex I to this Agreement.

### Article VI

1. It is agreed that the forces of the Hashemite Jordan Kingdom shall replace the forces of Iraq in the sector now held by the latter forces, the

intention of the Government of Iraq in this regard having been communicated to the Acting Mediator in the message of 20 March from the Foreign Minister of Iraq authorising the delegation of the Hashemite Jordan Kingdom to negotiate for the Iraqi forces and stating that those forces would be withdrawn.

2. The Armistice Demarcation Line for the sector now held by Iraqi forces shall be as delineated on map 1 in annex I to this Agreement and marked A.

3. The Armistice Demarcation Line provided for in paragraph 2 of this article shall be established in stages as follows, pending which the existing military lines may be maintained:

(a) In the area west of the road from Baqa to Jaljulia, and thence to the east of Kafr Qasim: within five weeks of the date on which this Armistice Agreement is signed;

(b) In the area of Wadi Ara north of the line from Baqa to Zubeiba: within seven weeks of the date on which this Armistice Agreement is signed;

(c) In all other areas of the Iraqi sector: within fifteen weeks of the date on which this Armistice Agreement is signed.

4. The Armistice Demarcation Line in the Hebron-Dead Sea sector, referred to in paragraph (c) of article V of this Agreement and marked B on map 1 in annex I, which involves substantial deviation from the existing military lines in favour of the forces of the Hashemite Jordan Kingdom, is designated to offset the modifications of the existing military lilies in the Iraqi sector set forth in paragraph 3 of this article.

5. In compensation for the road acquired between Tulkarem and Qalqiliya, the Government of Israel agrees to pay to the Government of the Hashemite Jordan Kingdom the cost of constructing twenty kilometres of first-class new road.

6. Wherever villages may be affected by the establishment of the Armistice Demarcation Line provided for in paragraph 2 of this article, the inhabitants of such villages shall be entitled to maintain, and shall be protected in, their full rights -of residence, property and freedom. In the event any of the inhabitants should decide to leave their villages, they shall be

entitled to take with them their livestock and other movable property, and to receive without delay full compensation for the land which they have left. It shall be prohibited for Israeli forces to enter or to be stationed in such villages, in which locally recruited Arab police shall be organised and stationed for internal security purposes.

7. The Hashemite Jordan Kingdom accepts responsibility for all Iraqi forces in Palestine.

8. The provisions of this article shall not be interpreted as prejudicing, in any sense, an ultimate political settlement between the Parties to this Agreement.

9. The Armistice Demarcation Lines defined in articles V and VI of this Agreement are agreed upon by the Parties without prejudice to future territorial settlements or boundary lines or to claims of either Party relating thereto.

10. Except where otherwise provided, the Armistice Demarcation Lines shall be established, including such withdrawal of forces as may be necessary for this purpose, within ten days from the date on which this Agreement is signed.

11. The Armistice Demarcation Lines defined in this article and in article V shall be subject to such rectification as may be agreed upon by the Parties to this Agreement, and all such rectifications shall have the same force and effect as if they had been incorporated in full in this General Armistice Agreement.

### Article VII

1. The military forces of the Parties to this Agreement shall be limited to defensive forces only in the areas extending ten kilometres from each side of the Armistice Demarcation Lines, except where geographical considerations make this impractical, as at the southernmost tip of Palestine and the coastal strip. Defensive forces permissible in each sector shall be as defined in annex II to this Agreement. In the sector now held by Iraqi forces, calculations on the reduction of forces shall include the number of Iraqi forces in this sector.

2. Reduction of forces to defensive strength in accordance with the preceding paragraph shall be completed within ten days of the establishment of the Armistice Demarcation Lines defined in this Agreement. In the same way the removal of mines from mined roads and areas evacuated by either Party, and the transmission of plans showing the location of such minefields to the other Party, shall be completed within the same period.

3. The strength of the forces which may be maintained by the Parties on each side of the Armistice Demarcation Lines shall be subject to periodical review with a view toward further reduction of such forces by mutual agreement of the Parties.

### Article VIII

1. A Special Committee, composed of two representatives of each Party designated by the respective Governments, shall be established for the purpose of formulating agreed plans and arrangements designed to enlarge the scope of this Agreement and to effect improvements in its application.

2. **The Special Committee shall be organised immediately following the coming into effect of this Agreement and shall direct its attention to the formulation of agreed plans and arrangements for such matters as either Party may submit to it, which, in any case, shall include the following, on which agreement in principle already exists: free movement of traffic on vital roads, including the Bethlehem and Latrun-Jerusalem roads; resumption of the normal functioning of the cultural and humanitarian institutions on Mount Scopus and free access thereto; free access to the Holy Places and cultural institutions and use of the cemetery on the Mount of Olives; resumption of operation of the Latrun pumping station; provision of electricity for the Old City; and resumption of operation of the railroad to Jerusalem.**

3. The Special Committee shall have exclusive competence over such matters as may be referred to it. Agreed plans and arrangements formulated by it may provide for the exercise of supervisory functions by the Mixed Armistice Commission established in article XI.

## Article IX

Agreements reached between the Parties subsequent to the signing of this Armistice Agreement relating to such matters as further reduction of forces as contemplated in paragraph 3 of article VII, future adjustments of the Armistice Demarcation Lines, and plans and arrangements formulated by the Special Committee established in article VIII, shall have the same force and effect as the provisions of this Agreement and shall be equally binding upon the Parties.

## Article X

An exchange of prisoners of war having been effected by special arrangement between the Parties prior to the signing of this Agreement, no further arrangements on this matter are required except that the Mixed Armistice Commission shall undertake to re-examine whether there may be any prisoners of war belonging to either Party which were not included in the previous exchange. In the event that prisoners of war shall be found to exist, the Mixed Armistice Commission shall arrange for all early exchange of such prisoners. The Parties to this Agreement undertake to afford full co-operation to the Mixed Armistice Commission in its discharge of this responsibility.

## Article XI

1. The execution of the provisions of this Agreement, with the exception of such matters as fall within the exclusive competence of the Special Committee established in article VIII, shall be supervised by a Mixed Armistice Commission composed of five members, of whom each Party to this Agreement shall designate two, and whose Chairman shall be the United Nations Chief of Staff of the Truce Supervision Organisation or a senior officer from the observer personnel of that organisation designated by him following consultation with both Parties to this Agreement.

2. The Mixed Armistice Commission shall maintain its headquarters at Jerusalem and shall hold its meetings at such places and at such times as it may deem necessary for the effective conduct of its work.

3. The Mixed Armistice Commission shall be convened in its first meeting by the United Nations Chief of Staff of the Truce Supervision Organisation not later than one week following the signing of this Agreement.

4. Decisions of the Mixed Armistice Commission, to the extent possible, shall be based on the principle of unanimity. In the absence of unanimity, decisions shall be taken by a majority vote of the members of the Commission present and voting.

5. The Mixed Armistice Commission shall formulate its own rules of procedure. Meetings shall be held only after due notice to the members by the Chairman. The quorum for its meetings shall be a majority of its members.

6. The Commission shall be empowered to employ observers, who may be from among the military organisations of the Parties or from the military personnel of the United Nations Truce Supervision Organisation, or from both, in such numbers as may be considered essential to the performance of its functions. In the event United Nations observers should be so employed, they shall remain under the command of the United Nations Chief of Staff of the Truce Supervision Organisation. Assignments of a general or special nature given to United Nations observers attached to the Mixed Armistice Commission shall be subject to approval by the United Nations Chief of Staff or his designated representative on the Commission, whichever is serving as Chairman.

7. Claims or complaints presented by either Party relating to the application of this Agreement shall be referred immediately to the Mixed Armistice Commission through its Chairman. The Commission shall take such action on all such claims or complaints by means of its observation and investigation machinery as it may deem appropriate, with a view to equitable and mutually satisfactory settlement.

8. Where interpretation of the meaning of a particular provision of this Agreement, other than the preamble and articles I and II, is at issue, the Commission's interpretation shall prevail. The Commission, in its discretion and as the need arises, may from time to time recommend to the Parties modifications in the provisions of this Agreement.

9. The Mixed Armistice Commission shall submit to both Parties reports on its activities as frequently as it may consider necessary. A copy of each such report shall be presented to the Secretary-General of the United Nations for transmission to the appropriate organ or agency of the United Nations.

10. Members of the Commission and its observers shall be accorded such freedom of movement and access in the area covered by this Agreement as the Commission may determine to be necessary, provided that when such decisions of the Commission are reached by a majority vote United Nations observers only shall be employed.

11. The expenses of the Commission, other than those relating to United Nations observers, shall be apportioned in equal shares between the two Parties to this Agreement.

### Article XII

1. The present Agreement is not subject to ratification and shall come into force immediately upon being signed.

2. This Agreement, having been negotiated and concluded in pursuance of the resolution of the Security Council of 16 November 1948 calling for the establishment of an armistice in order to eliminate the threat to the peace in Palestine and to facilitate the transition from the present truce to permanent peace in Palestine, shall remain in force until a peaceful settlement between the Parties is achieved, except as provided in paragraph 3 of this article.

3. The Parties to this Agreement may, by mutual consent, revise this Agreement or any of its provisions, or may suspend its application, other than articles I and III, at any time. In the absence of mutual agreement and after this Agreement has been in effect for one year from the date of its signing, either of the Parties may call upon the Secretary-General of the United Nations to convoke a conference of representatives of the two Parties for the purpose of reviewing, revising, or suspending any of the provisions of this Agreement other than articles I and III. Participation in such conference shall be obligatory upon the Parties.

4. If the conference provided for in paragraph 3 of this article does not result in an agreed solution of a point in dispute, either Party may bring the matter before the Security Council of the United Nations for the relief sought on the grounds that this Agreement has been concluded in pursuance of Security Council action toward the end of achieving peace in Palestine.

5. This Agreement is signed in quintuplicate, of which one copy shall be retained by each Party, two copies communicated to the Secretary-General of the United Nations for transmission to the Security Council and to the United Nations Conciliation Commission on Palestine, and one copy to the United Nations Acting Mediator on Palestine.

Done at Rhodes, Island of Rhodes, Greece, on the third of April one thousand nine hundred and forty-nine in the presence of the United Nations Acting Mediator on Palestine and the United Nations Chief of Staff of the Truce Supervision Organisation.

For and on behalf of the Government of the Hashemite
Jordan Kingdom
Signed:        Colonel Ahmed Sudki El-Jundi
               Lieutenant-Colonel Mohamed Maayte

For and on behalf of the Government of Israel
Signed:        Reuven Shiloah
               Lieutenant-Colonel Moshe Dayan

(Geographic and weapons annex have been removed, see especially bolded sections above)

# UN Security Council Resolution 242
## November 22, 1967

*The Security Council,*

*Expressing* its continuing concern with the grave situation in the Middle East,

*Emphasizing* the inadmissibility of the acquisition of territory by war and the need to work for a just and lasting peace in which every State in the area can live in security,

*Emphasizing further* that all Member States in their acceptance of the Charter of the United Nations have undertaken a commitment to act in accordance with Article 2 of the Charter,

1. *Affirms* that the fulfillment of Charter principles requires the establishment of a just and lasting peace in the Middle East which should include the application of both the following principles:

(i) Withdrawal of Israeli armed forces from territories occupied in the recent conflict;

(ii) Termination of all claims or states of belligerency and respect for and acknowledgement of the sovereignty, territorial integrity and political independence of every State in the area and their right to live in peace within secure and recognized boundaries free from threats or acts of force;

2. *Affirms further* the necessity

(a) For guaranteeing freedom of navigation through international waterways in the area;

(b) For achieving a just settlement of the refugee problem;

(c) For guaranteeing the territorial inviolability and political independence of every State in the area, through measures including the establishment of demilitarized zones;

3. *Requests* the Secretary General to designate a Special Representative to proceed to the Middle East to establish and maintain contacts with the

States concerned in order to promote agreement and assist efforts to achieve a peaceful and accepted settlement in accordance with the provisions and principles in this resolution;

4. *Requests* the Secretary-General to report to the Security Council on the progress of the efforts of the Special Representative as soon as possible.

*Adopted unanimously at the 1382nd meeting*

# UN Security Council Resolution 338
## October 22, 1973

The Security Council,

1.  Calls upon all parties to the present fighting to cease all firing and terminate all military activity immediately, no later than 12 hours after the moment of the adoption of this decision, in the positions they now occupy;

2.  Calls upon the parties concerned to start immediately after the cease-fire the implementation of Security Council resolution 242 (1967) in all its parts;

3.  Decides that, immediately and concurrently with the cease-fire, negotiations start between the parties concerned under appropriate auspices aimed at establishing a just and durable peace in the Middle East.

## International Interpretations of the Negotiations over UN Security Council Resolution 242 and Subsequent National Positions: Selected Quotations

### Great Britain

George Brown, British foreign secretary in 1967, on January 19, 1970:

"I have been asked over and over again to clarify, modify or improve the wording, but I do not intend to do that. The phrasing of the Resolution was very carefully worked out, and it was a difficult and complicated exercise to get it accepted by the UN Security Council.

"I formulated the Security Council Resolution. Before we submitted it to the Council, we showed it to Arab leaders. The proposal said 'Israel will withdraw from territories that were occupied,' and not from 'the' territories, which means that Israel will not withdraw from all the territories." (*Jerusalem Post*, January 23, 1970)

Michael Stewart, secretary of state for foreign and commonwealth affairs, in reply to a question in Parliament, November 17, 1969:

Question: "What is the British interpretation of the wording of the 1967 Resolution? Does the Right Honourable Gentleman understand it to mean that the Israelis should withdraw from all territories taken in the late war?"

Mr. Stewart: "No, Sir. That is not the phrase used in the Resolution. The Resolution speaks of secure and recognized boundaries. These words must be read concurrently with the statement on withdrawal."

Michael Stewart in a reply to a question in Parliament, December 9, 1969:

"As I have explained before, there is reference, in the vital United Nations Security Council Resolution, both to withdrawal from territories and to secure and recognized boundaries. As I have told the House previously, we believe that these two things should be read concurrently and that the omission of the word 'all' before the word 'territories' is deliberate."

### United States

President Lyndon Johnson, September 10, 1968:

"We are not the ones to say where other nations should draw lines between them that will assure each the greatest security. It is clear, however, that a return to the situation of 4 June 1967 will not bring peace. There must be secure and there must be recognized borders. Some such lines must be agreed to by the neighbors involved."

Joseph Sisco, assistant secretary of state, July 12, 1970, on NBC's *Meet the Press*:

"That Resolution did not say 'withdrawal to the pre-June 5 lines.' The Resolution said that the parties must negotiate to achieve agreement on the so-called final secure and recognized borders. In other words, the question of the final borders is a matter of negotiations between the parties."

Eugene V. Rostow, professor of law and public affairs, Yale University, who in 1967 was under-secretary of state for political affairs:

" ... paragraph I (i) of the Resolution calls for the withdrawal of Israeli armed forces 'from territories occupied in the recent conflict,' and not 'from the territories occupied in the recent conflict.' Repeated attempts to amend this sentence by inserting the word 'the' failed in the Security Council. It is, therefore, not legally possible to assert that the provision requires Israeli withdrawal from all the territories now occupied under the cease-fire resolutions to the Armistice Demarcation lines." (*American Journal of International Law*, Volume 64, September 1970, 69.)

### USSR

Deputy Foreign Minister Vasily Kuznetsov, November 11, 1967:

" ... phrases such as 'secure and recognized boundaries.' What does that mean? What boundaries are these? Secure, recognized-by whom, for what? Who is going to judge how secure they are? Who must recognize them?...There is certainly much leeway for different interpretations which retain for Israel the right to establish new boundaries and to withdraw its troops only as far as the lines which it judges convenient."

### France

Armand Berard, permanent representative to the UN, November 22, 1967:

"We must admit, however, that on the point which the French delegation has always stressed as being essential-the question of withdrawal of the occupation forces-the resolution which has been adopted, if we refer to the French text which is equally authentic with the English, leaves no room for any ambiguity, since it speaks of withdrawal *'des territoires occupés,'* which indisputably corresponds to the expression "occupied territories."

### Canada

George Ignatieff, permanent representative to the UN, November 9, 1967:

"If our aim is to bring about a settlement or a political solution, there must be withdrawal to secure and recognized borders."

### Brazil

Geraldo de Carvalho Silos, permanent representative to the UN, November 22, 1967:

"We keep constantly in mind that a just and lasting peace in the Middle East has necessarily to be based on secure, permanent boundaries freely agreed upon and negotiated by the neighboring States."

# Selections from the Israel-Palestine Liberation Organization Declaration of Principles (Oslo Accord) September 13, 1993

The Government of the State of Israel and the Palestinian team representing the Palestinian people agree that it is time to put an end to decades of confrontation and conflict, recognize their mutual legitimate and political rights, and strive to live in peaceful coexistence and mutual dignity and security to achieve a just, lasting and comprehensive peace settlement and historic reconciliation through the agreed political process. Accordingly, the two sides agree to the following principles.

### Article 1 AIM OF THE NEGOTIATIONS

The aim of the Israeli Palestinian negotiations within the current Middle East peace process is, among other things, to establish a Palestinian Interim Self-Government Authority, the elected Council, (the "Council") for the Palestinian people in the West Bank and the Gaza Strip, for a transitional period not exceeding five years, leading to a permanent settlement **based on Security Council Resolutions 242 and 338**.

It is understood that the interim arrangements are an integral part of the whole peace process and that the negotiations on the permanent status will lead to implementation of **Security Council Resolution 242 and 338**.

### Article V TRANSITIONAL PERIOD AND PERMANENT STATUS NEGOTIATIONS

1. The five-year transitional period will begin upon the withdrawal from the Gaza strip and Jericho area.

2. Permanent status negotiations will commence as soon as possible, but not later than the beginning of the third year of the interim period between the Government of Israel and the Palestinian people representatives.

3. **It is understood that these negotiations shall cover remaining issues, including: Jerusalem**, refugees, settlements, security arrangements, border, relations and cooperation with their neighbors, and other issues of common interest.

4. The two parties agreed that the outcome of the permanent status negotiations should not be prejudiced or preempted by agreements reached for the interim period

(emphasis added)

# The Washington Declaration:
## Israel-Jordan-The United States
## July 25, 1994

A. After generations of hostility, blood and tears and in the wake of years of pain and wars, His Majesty King Hussein and Prime Minister Yitzhak Rabin are determined to bring an end to bloodshed and sorrow. It is in this spirit that His Majesty King Hussein of the Hashemite Kingdom of Jordan and Prime Minister and Minister of Defense, Mr. Yitzhak Rabin of Israel, met in Washington today at the invitation of President William J. Clinton of the United States of America. This initiative of President William J. Clinton constitutes an historic landmark in the United States' untiring efforts in promoting peace and stability in the Middle East. The personal involvement of the President has made it possible to realise agreement on the content of this historic declaration.

The signing of this declaration bears testimony to the President's vision and devotion to the cause of peace.

B. In their meeting, His Majesty King Hussein and Prime Minister Yitzhak Rabin have jointly reaffirmed the five underlying principles of their understanding on an Agreed Common Agenda designed to reach the goal of a just, lasting and comprehensive peace between the Arab States and the Palestinians, with Israel.

1. Jordan and Israel aim at the achievement of just, lasting and comprehensive peace between Israel and its neighbours and at the conclusion of a Treaty of Peace between both countries.

2. The two countries will vigorously continue their negotiations to arrive at a state of peace, based on Security Council Resolutions 242 and 338 in all their aspects, and founded on freedom, equality and justice.

3. **Israel respects the present special role of the Hashemite Kingdom of Jordan in Muslim Holy shrines in Jerusalem. When negotiations on the permanent status will take place, Israel will give high priority to the Jordanian historic role in these shrines. In addition**

**the two sides have agreed to act together to promote interfaith relations among the three monotheistic religions.**

4. The two countries recognise their right and obligation to live in peace with each other as well as with all states within secure and recognised boundaries. The two states affirmed their respect for and acknowledgment of the sovereignty, territorial integrity and political independence of every state in the area.

5. The two countries desire to develop good neighbourly relations of cooperation between them to ensure lasting security and to avoid threats and the use of force between them.

C. The long conflict between the two states is now coming to an end. In this spirit the state of belligerency between Jordan and Israel has been terminated.

D. Following this declaration and in keeping with the Agreed Common Agenda, both countries will refrain from actions or activities by either side that may adversely affect the security of the other or may prejudice the final outcome of negotiations. Neither side will threaten the other by use of force, weapons, or any other means, against each other and both sides will thwart threats to security resulting from all kinds of terrorism.

E. His Majesty King Hussein and Prime Minister Yitzhak Rabin took note of the progress made in the bilateral negotiations within the Jordan-Israel track last week on the steps decided to implement the sub- agendas on borders, territorial matters, security, water, energy, environment and the Jordan Rift Valley.

In this framework, mindful of items of the Agreed Common Agenda (borders and territorial matters) they noted that the boundary sub-commission has reached agreement in July 1994 in fulfillment of part of the role entrusted to it in the sub-agenda. They also noted that the sub-commission for water, environment and energy agreed to mutually recognise, as the role of their negotiations, the rightful allocations of the two sides in Jordan River and Yarmouk River waters and to fully respect and comply with the negotiated rightful allocations, in accordance with agreed acceptable principles with mutually acceptable quality. Similarly, His Majesty King Hussein and Prime Minister Yitzhak Rabin expressed their deep satisfaction and pride in the work of the trilateral commission in its meeting held in Jordan on Wednesday, July 20th 1994, hosted by the Jordanian Prime Minister, Dr. Abdessalam al-Majali, and attended by Secretary of State Warren Christopher and Foreign Minister Shimon Peres. They voiced their pleasure at the association and commitment of the United States in this endeavour.

F. His Majesty King Hussein and Prime Minister Yitzhak Rabin believe that steps must be taken both to overcome psychological barriers and to break with the legacy of war. By working with optimism towards the dividends of peace for all the people in the region, Jordan and Israel are determined to shoulder their responsibilities towards the human dimension of peace making. They recognise imbalances and disparities are a root cause of extremism which thrives on poverty and unemployment and the degradation of human dignity. In this spirit His Majesty King Hussein and Prime Minister Yitzhak Rabin have today approved a series of steps to symbolise the new era which is now at hand:

1. Direct telephone links will be opened between Jordan and Israel.

2. The electricity grids of Jordan and Israel will be linked as part of a regional concept.

3. Two new border crossings will be opened between Jordan and Israel-one at the southern tip of Aqaba-Eilat and the other at a mutually agreed point in the north.

4. In principle free access will be given to third country tourists traveling between Jordan and Israel.

5. Negotiations will be accelerated on opening an international air corridor between both countries.

6. The police forces of Jordan and Israel will cooperate in combating crime with emphasis on smuggling and particularly drug smuggling. The United States will be invited to participate in this joint endeavour.

7. Negotiations on economic matters will continue in order to prepare for future bilateral cooperation including the abolition of all economic boycotts.

All these steps are being implemented within the framework of regional infrastructural development plans and in conjunction with the Jordan-Israel bilaterals on boundaries, security, water and related issues and without prejudice to the final outcome of the negotiations on the items included in the Agreed Common Agenda between Jordan and Israel.

G. His Majesty King Hussein and Prime Minister Yitzhak Rabin have agreed to meet periodically or whenever they feel necessary to review the progress of the negotiations and express their firm intention to shepherd and direct the process in its entirety.

H. In conclusion, His Majesty King Hussein and Prime Minister Yitzhak Rabin wish to express once again their profound thanks and appreciation to President William J. Clinton and his Administration for their untiring efforts in furthering the cause of peace, justice and prosperity for all the peoples of the region. They wish to thank the President personally for his warm welcome and hospitality. In recognition of their appreciation to the President, His Majesty King Hussein and Prime Minister Yitzhak Rabin have asked President William J. Clinton to sign this document as a witness and as a host to their meeting.

His Majesty King Hussein—Prime Minister Yitzhak Rabin—President William J. Clinton

(emphasis added)

# Letter from President George W. Bush
## to Prime Minister Ariel Sharon
## April 14, 2004

His Excellency Ariel Sharon Prime Minister of Israel
Dear Mr. Prime Minister,

Thank you for your letter setting out your disengagement plan.

The United States remains hopeful and determined to find a way forward toward a resolution of the Israeli-Palestinian dispute. I remain committed to my June 24, 2002, vision of two states living side by side in peace and security as the key to peace, and to the roadmap as the route to get there.

We welcome the disengagement plan you have prepared, under which Israel would withdraw certain military installations and all settlements from Gaza, and withdraw certain military installations and settlements in the West Bank. These steps described in the plan will mark real progress toward realizing my June 24, 2002, vision, and make a real contribution towards peace. We also understand that, in this context, Israel believes it is important to bring new opportunities to the Negev and the Galilee. We are hopeful that steps pursuant to this plan, consistent with my vision, will remind all states and parties of their own obligations under the roadmap.

The United States appreciates the risks such an undertaking represents. I therefore want to reassure you on several points.

First, the United States remains committed to my vision and to its implementation as described in the roadmap. The United States will do its utmost to prevent any attempt by anyone to impose any other plan. Under the roadmap, Palestinians must undertake an immediate cessation of armed activity and all acts of violence against Israelis anywhere, and all official Palestinian institutions must end incitement against Israel. The Palestinian leadership must act decisively against terror, including sustained, targeted, and effective operations to stop terrorism and dismantle terrorist capabilities and infrastructure. Palestinians must undertake a comprehensive and fundamental political reform that includes a strong parliamentary democracy and an empowered prime minister.

Second, there will be no security for Israelis or Palestinians until they and all states, in the region and beyond, join together to fight terrorism and dismantle terrorist organizations. **The United States reiterates its steadfast commitment to Israel's security, including secure, defensible borders,** and to preserve and strengthen Israel's capability to deter and defend itself, by itself, against any threat or possible combination of threats.

Third, Israel will retain its right to defend itself against terrorism, including to take actions against terrorist organizations. The United States will lead efforts, working together with Jordan, Egypt, and others in the international community, to build the capacity and will of Palestinian institutions to fight terrorism, dismantle terrorist organizations, and prevent the areas from which Israel has withdrawn from posing a threat that would have to be addressed by any other means. The United States understands that after Israel withdraws from Gaza and/or parts of the West Bank, and pending agreements on other arrangements, existing arrangements regarding control of airspace, territorial waters, and land passages of the West Bank and Gaza will continue.

The United States is strongly committed to Israel's security and well-being as a Jewish state. It seems clear that an agreed, just, fair and realistic framework for a solution to the Palestinian refugee issue as part of any final status agreement will need to be found through the establishment of a Palestinian state, and the settling of Palestinian refugees there, rather than in Israel.

**As part of a final peace settlement, Israel must have secure and recognized borders, which should emerge from negotiations between the parties in accordance with UNSC Resolutions 242 and 338. In light of new realities on the ground, including already existing major Israeli populations centers, it is unrealistic to expect that the outcome of final status negotiations will be a full and complete return to the armistice lines of 1949,** and all previous efforts to negotiate a two-state solution have reached the same conclusion. It is realistic to expect that any final status agreement will only be achieved on the basis of mutually agreed changes that reflect these realities.

I know that, as you state in your letter, you are aware that certain responsibilities face the State of Israel. Among these, your government has stated that the barrier being erected by Israel should be a security rather than political barrier, should be temporary rather than permanent, and therefore not prejudice any final status issues including final borders, and its route should take into account, consistent with security needs, its impact on Palestinians not engaged in terrorist activities.

As you know, the United States supports the establishment of a Palestinian state that is viable, contiguous, sovereign, and independent, so that the Palestinian people can build their own future in accordance with my vision set forth in June 2002 and with the path set forth in the roadmap. The United States will join with others in the international community to foster the development of democratic political institutions and new leadership committed to those institutions, the reconstruction of civic institutions, the growth of a free and prosperous economy, and the building of capable security institutions dedicated to maintaining law and order and dismantling terrorist organizations.

A peace settlement negotiated between Israelis and Palestinians would be a great boon not only to those peoples but to the peoples of the entire region. Accordingly, the United States believes that all states in the region have special responsibilities: to support the building of the institutions of a Palestinian state; to fight terrorism, and cut off all forms of assistance to individuals and groups engaged in terrorism; and to begin now to move toward more normal relations with the State of Israel. These actions would be true contributions to building peace in the region.

Mr. Prime Minister, you have described a bold and historic initiative that can make an important contribution to peace. I commend your efforts and your courageous decision which I support. As a close friend and ally, the United States intends to work closely with you to help make it a success.

Sincerely,

George W. Bush

(emphasis added)

# UN Charter

## CHAPTER VI: PACIFIC SETTLEMENT OF DISPUTES

Article 33

1. The parties to any dispute, the continuance of which is likely to endanger the maintenance of international peace and security, shall, first of all, seek a solution by negotiation, enquiry, mediation, conciliation, arbitration, judicial settlement, resort to regional agencies or arrangements, or other peaceful means of their own choice.

2. The Security Council shall, when it deems necessary, call upon the parties to settle their dispute by such means.

Article 34

The Security Council may investigate any dispute, or any situation which might lead to international friction or give rise to a dispute, in order to determine whether the continuance of the dispute or situation is likely to endanger the maintenance of international peace and security.

Article 35

1. Any Member of the United Nations may bring any dispute, or any situation of the nature referred to in Article 34, to the attention of the Security Council or of the General Assembly.

2. A state which is not a Member of the United Nations may bring to the attention of the Security Council or of the General Assembly any dispute to which it is a party if it accepts in advance, for the purposes of the dispute, the obligations of pacific settlement provided in the present Charter.

3. The proceedings of the General Assembly in respect of matters brought to its attention under this Article will be subject to the provisions of Articles 11 and 12.

Article 36

1. The Security Council may, at any stage of a dispute of the nature referred to in Article 33 or of a situation of like nature, recommend appropriate procedures or methods of adjustment.

2. The Security Council should take into consideration any procedures for the settlement of the dispute which have already been adopted by the parties.

3. In making recommendations under this Article the Security Council should also take into consideration that legal disputes should as a general rule be referred by the parties to the International Court of Justice in accordance with the provisions of the Statute of the Court.

Article 37

1. Should the parties to a dispute of the nature referred to in Article 33 fail to settle it by the means indicated in that Article, they shall refer it to the Security Council.

2. If the Security Council deems that the continuance of the dispute is in fact likely to endanger the maintenance of international peace and security, it shall decide whether to take action under Article 36 or to recommend such terms of settlement as it may consider appropriate.

Article 38

Without prejudice to the provisions of Articles 33 to 37, the Security Council may, if all the parties to any dispute so request, make recommendations to the parties with a view to a pacific settlement of the dispute.

## CHAPTER VII: ACTION WITH RESPECT TO THREATS TO THE PEACE, BREACHES OF THE PEACE, AND ACTS OF AGGRESSION

Article 39

The Security Council shall determine the existence of any threat to the peace, breach of the peace, or act of aggression and shall make recommendations, or decide what measures shall be taken in accordance with Articles 41 and 42, to maintain or restore international peace and security.

Article 40

In order to prevent an aggravation of the situation, the Security Council may, before making the recommendations or deciding upon the measures provided for in Article 39, call upon the parties concerned to comply with such provisional measures as it deems necessary or desirable. Such provisional measures shall be without prejudice to the rights, claims, or position of the parties concerned. The Security Council shall duly take account of failure to comply with such provisional measures.

Article 41

The Security Council may decide what measures not involving the use of armed force are to be employed to give effect to its decisions, and it may call upon the Members of the United Nations to apply such measures. These may include complete or partial interruption of economic relations and of rail, sea, air, postal, telegraphic, radio, and other means of communication, and the severance of diplomatic relations.

Article 42

Should the Security Council consider that measures provided for in Article 41 would be inadequate or have proved to be inadequate, it may take such action by air, sea, or land forces as may be necessary to maintain or restore international peace and security. Such action may include demonstrations, blockade, and other operations by air, sea, or land forces of Members of the United Nations.

Article 43

1. All Members of the United Nations, in order to contribute to the maintenance of international peace and security, undertake to make available to the Security Council, on its call and in accordance with a special agreement or agreements, armed forces, assistance, and facilities, including rights of passage, necessary for the purpose of maintaining international peace and security.

2. Such agreement or agreements shall govern the numbers and types of forces, their degree of readiness and general location, and the nature of the facilities and assistance to be provided.

3. The agreement or agreements shall be negotiated as soon as possible on the initiative of the Security Council. They shall be concluded between the Security Council and Members or between the Security Council and groups of Members and shall be subject to ratification by the signatory states in accordance with their respective constitutional processes.

## Article 44

When the Security Council has decided to use force it shall, before calling upon a Member not represented on it to provide armed forces in fulfillment of the obligations assumed under Article 43, invite that Member, if the Member so desires, to participate in the decisions of the Security Council concerning the employment of contingents of that Member's armed forces.

## Article 45

In order to enable the United Nations to take urgent military measures, Members shall hold immediately available national air-force contingents for combined international enforcement action. The strength and degree of readiness of these contingents and plans for their combined action shall be determined within the limits laid down in the special agreement or agreements referred to in Article 43, by the Security Council with the assistance of the Military Staff Committee.

## Article 46

Plans for the application of armed force shall be made by the Security Council with the assistance of the Military Staff Committee.

## Article 47

1. There shall be established a Military Staff Committee to advise and assist the Security Council on all questions relating to the Security Coun-

cil's military requirements for the maintenance of international peace and security, the employment and command of forces placed at its disposal, the regulation of armaments, and possible disarmament.

2. The Military Staff Committee shall consist of the Chiefs of Staff of the permanent members of the Security Council or their representatives. Any Member of the United Nations not permanently represented on the Committee shall be invited by the Committee to be associated with it when the efficient discharge of the Committee's responsibilities requires the participation of that Member in its work.

3. The Military Staff Committee shall be responsible under the Security Council for the strategic direction of any armed forces placed at the disposal of the Security Council. Questions relating to the command of such forces shall be worked out subsequently.

4. The Military Staff Committee, with the authorization of the Security Council and after consultation with appropriate regional agencies, may establish regional sub-committees.

Article 48

1. The action required to carry out the decisions of the Security Council for the maintenance of international peace and security shall be taken by all the Members of the United Nations or by some of them, as the Security Council may determine.

2. Such decisions shall be carried out by the Members of the United Nations directly and through their action in the appropriate international agencies of which they are members.

Article 49

The Members of the United Nations shall join in affording mutual assistance in carrying out the measures decided upon by the Security Council.

Article 50

If preventive or enforcement measures against any state are taken by the Security Council, any other state, whether a Member of the United

Nations or not, which finds itself confronted with special economic problems arising from the carrying out of those measures shall have the right to consult the Security Council with regard to a solution of those problems.

### Article 51

Nothing in the present Charter shall impair the inherent right of individual or collective self-defence if an armed attack occurs against a Member of the United Nations, until the Security Council has taken measures necessary to maintain international peace and security. Measures taken by Members in the exercise of this right of self-defence shall be immediately reported to the Security Council and shall not in any way affect the authority and responsibility of the Security Council under the present Charter to take at any time such action as it deems necessary in order to maintain or restore international peace and security.

### CHAPTER XII: INTERNATIONAL TRUSTEESHIP SYSTEM

### Article 80

1. Except as may be agreed upon in individual trusteeship agreements, made under Articles 77, 79, and 81, placing each territory under the trusteeship system, and until such agreements have been concluded, nothing in this Chapter shall be construed in or of itself to alter in any manner the rights whatsoever of any states or any peoples or the terms of existing international instruments to which Members of the United Nations may respectively be parties.

2. Paragraph 1 of this Article shall not be interpreted as giving grounds for delay or postponement of the negotiation and conclusion of agreements for placing mandated and other territories under the trusteeship system as provided for in Article 77.

## ◈◈◈ Acknowledgments

Anyone who has taken upon themselves to write books knows that they cannot be finished without the support provided by friends and colleagues. In this case, this book would not have been completed without the constant encouragement of my own family, and above all my wife, Ofra, who stood behind my undertaking this project along with Yael and Ariel from day one.

During the years that I have been involved in researching and writing on the issues of the contemporary Middle East, I have been indebted to Ronald S. Lauder, who has been both a constant friend and mentor.

There are also a number of individuals with whom I shared the ideas behind this book. There is a scholar in England who follows the affairs of the Middle East and shall remain unnamed, with whom I discussed the urgency of this project. As in the past, Allen Roth provided ideas that helped me with the design and shape of this project at an early stage. I would also like to acknowledge the advice of Dr. Eilat Mazar, who was willing to share her extensive knowledge of the archaeology of Jerusalem and the Temple Mount, as well as her most recent work in the City of David. Rabbi Joseph Telushkin provided indispensable advice on Jewish history and theology. Dr. Martin Kramer took time out of his busy schedule to provide feedback on one particularly difficult chapter on Islamic apocalyptic thought. Dr. Rivka Fishman was extremely generous with her time commenting on both the Roman and early Christian (Byzantine) periods in Jerusalem, as well as her knowledge of ancient Greek texts. Dr. Joel Fishman read some of the early manuscript and shared with me his broad historical perspective. David Parsons, of the International Christian

Embassy, read through my text on Christianity and made extremely useful recommendations.

As in my previous books, I have had several important intellectual allies, who have been indispensable. First, Lt. Col. (res.) Jonathan Dahoah Halevi again demonstrated his first-class research skills in the world of radical Islam, as he combed obscure websites and studied Arabic texts from all over the Arab world. Second, Jeffrey Helmreich read, re-read, and made detailed comments on every chapter of this book, sharing his first-class knowledge of legal theory, which he is studying at UCLA, and diplomatic history. Dr. Reuven Erlich, who heads the Intelligence and Terrorism Information Center at the Center for Special Studies, was always willing to share documentation and provide research tips in a timely fashion. He also introduced me to Dr. Yoram Kahati, who shared his extensive knowledge on radical Islamic groups. Reuven Berko shared his insights in the complexities of Jerusalem, as well. And finally, as in my last books, both Gene and Nadia Kleinhendler also read earlier chapters and provided both encouragement as well as useful criticism.

I owe a tremendous special debt to Yehuda Mali and David Beeri, who are opening the eyes of many visitors to Jerusalem and inspiring thousands with the latest discoveries about its ancient heritage.

James S. Snyder, director of the Israel Museum, and his team were extremely helpful in locating and explaining archaeological artifacts used for this book.

A virtual army of research assistants stood behind this book. Again, Zachary K. Goldman provided me with critical documents at a very early stage of this project. Amir Tsemach was highly motivated in providing materials as well. David Keyes resumed my past collaboration with him on studying the lessons of the Camp David/Taba period from 2000–2001 and produced first-class analytical work in this area. My daughter Yael Gold took time off from the Technion and went through historical materials in Hebrew from the same period and provided meticulous summaries and analysis as well. Benny Silberman volunteered to help in the final weeks of research and contributed his useful findings to this work.

Four individuals came in at the very end of this project and provided critical advice. Shammai Fishman shared his knowledge of the Muslim Brotherhood and Yechiel Leiter opened up before me his tremendous knowledge of Hebrew Bible. Aron U. Raskas came up with extremely important suggestions for the final text as did David Goder, who was intimately involved in my past writing projects.

I must express my appreciation for the entire team at the Jerusalem Center for Public Affairs, who put in extra hours while I was busy with this book, especially our director general, Chaya Herskovic. I am especially grateful to Rachel Elrom, who put in long hours helping me put this manuscript in shape and whose watchful eye corrected errors before they were even typed.

I owe a special debt of gratitude to the whole team at Regnery, starting with Jeffrey J. Carneal, president of Eagle Publishing, and Marjory G. Ross, president and publisher of Regnery Publishing, as well as Harry Crocker, who understood at the outset the importance of this project. My daily contacts at Regnery were with Miriam Moore, who took the leading role as project director of the book, providing critical comments and constructive feedback as we progressed through the project. I would like to acknowledge as well the hard work of Jack Langer, who edited the text, and Amanda Larsen, who handled much of the graphic work. All of them demonstrated extraordinary patience and professionalism as we worked on this text together.

Finally, my agent Richard Pine read carefully my proposal for this book at the outset and provided important input into its refinement. His faith in this project and his encouraging messages while it was being written all contributed to its successful completion.

## Introduction

1.  The State Department's Aaron Miller later recalled, "On the event of the Camp David summit, I would argue to you, no atmosphere or environment was worse for a high-level meeting between Israelis and Palestinians. There was more suspicion on the part of Barak and Arafat in July 2000, as a consequence of broken promises, unfulfilled agreements, the power of the weak versus the power of the strong on the ground. It was not, in my judgement, an auspicious occasion for a high-level summit." "Lessons of Arab-Israeli Negotiating: From Negotiations Look Back and Ahead," April 25, 2005, Middle East Institute, Washington, D.C.

2.  Dennis Ross, *The Missing Peace: The Inside Story of the Fight for Middle East Peace* (New York: Farrar, Straus and Giroux, 2004), 690.

3.  Ruth Lapidoth and Moshe Hirsch, eds., Document 37, "Israel's Protection of the Holy Places Law, 5727-1967, 27 June 1967," *The Jerusalem Question and Its Resolution: Selected Documents* (Dordrecht: Martinus Nijhoff Publishers, 1994), 169.

4.  "Palestinian Summer Camp Offers the Games of War," *New York Times*, August 3, 2000. The armed conquest of Jerusalem was clearly at the forefront of the camp's indoctrination efforts. According to the article, "many [camp attendees] predicted that their generation would someday take up arms against Israel over Jerusalem." A fifteen-year-old boy told the *Times*, "If we can get Jerusalem without weapons, it is better. But if there is a need to liberate Jerusalem with weapons, we will be ready for that."

5.  Madeleine Albright, *Madam Secretary: A Memoir* (New York: Miramax Books, 2003), 496.

6.  State of Israel, Ministry of Foreign Affairs, Sharm El-Sheikh Fact-Finding Committee, "First Statement of the Government of Israel," December 28, 2000), 61–63.

7.  *Al-Safir*, March 3, 2001, trans. *MEMRI*.

8.  "Bus Shooting Caps Turbulent Day in Middle East," CNN.com, October 7, 2000.

9.  Ibid.

10. Richard A. Clarke, *Against All Enemies: Inside America's War on Terror* (New York: Free Press, 2004), 224.
11. Ibid.
12. Bernard Lewis, "License to Kill: Usama bin Laden's Declaration of Jihad," *Foreign Affairs*, November/December 1998.
13. David Cook, *Contemporary Muslim Apocalyptic Literature* (Syracuse: Syracuse University Press, 2005), 174.
14. Montasser al-Zayyat, *The Road to al-Qaeda: The Story of Bin Laden's Right-Hand Man* (London: Pluto Press, 2004), 62.
15. Ari Shavit, "End of a Journey," *Ha'aretz*, September 13, 2001.
16. Shlomo Ben-Ami, *Scars of War, Wounds of Peace: The Israeli-Arab Tragedy* (Oxford: Oxford University Press, 2006), 270.
17. Ross, 756.
18. "High Marks: Ariel Sharon Gets Warm Greetings from the White House, Congress and American Jews," *Baltimore Jewish Times*, March 23, 2001.
19. Ross, 694.
20. Benny Morris, "Camp David and After: An Interview with Ehud Barak," *New York Review of Books*, August 9, 2001.
21. "Interview with Yasser Arafat," MEMRI, Special Dispatch Series No. 428, October 11, 2002.
22. Al-Ayyam, July 27, 2000, trans. MEMRI.
23. Charles Enderlin, *Shattered Dreams: The Failure of the Peace Process in the Middle East 1995–2002* (New York: Other Press, 2002), 272.
24. *Le Monde*, September 25, 2000.
25. Yael Yehoshua, "Abu Mazen: A Political Profile," MEMRI, April 29, 2003, quoting Kul Al-Arab, August 25, 2000; http://www.memri.org/bin/articles.cgi?Area=sr&ID=SR01503.
26. Romesh Ratnesar, "The Peacemaker: An Israeli Colonel Tries to Keep Jerusalem's Temple, Sacred to Muslim and Jew, From Exploding," *Time*, October 5, 2003. See PaleoJudaica.com: http://paleojudaica.blogspot.com/2003_10_05paleojudaica_arhive.html.
27. Yitzchak Reiter, *From Jerusalem to Mecca and Back: The Islamic Consolidation of Jerusalem* (Jerusalem: The Jerusalem Institute for Israel Studies, 2005), 40.
28. "Jordanian Professor/Terrorist on Saudi Al-Majd TV Says Kings David & Solomon Were Muslims Who Today Would Have Fought Israel, Supports Leading Holocaust Denier," MEMRI, Special Dispatch Series No. 1030, November 22, 2005.
29. Reiter, 48.
30. Israel Finkelstein and Neil Silberman, *The Bible Unearthed: Archaeology's New Vision of Ancient Israel and the Origin of Its Sacred Texts* (New York: Touchstone, 2001), 128.
31. David Van Biema, "Judaism's Stake: The Mysteries of Solomon's Temple," *Time*, April 16, 2001.

32.  Nadia Abu El-Haj, *Facts on the Ground: Archaeological Practice and Territorial Self-Fashioning in Israeli Society* (Chicago: University of Chicago Press, 2001), 147.

33.  Ibid., 250.

34.  Daniel Lazare, "False Testament: Archaeology Refutes the Bible's Claim to History," (Criticism), *Harper's*, March 2002.

35.  Eliat Mazar, "Did I Find King David's Palace?" *Biblical Archaeological Review*, January/February 2006.

36.  Shahar Ilan, "Gems in the Dirt," *Haaretz Magazine*, October 14, 2005.

37.  Baydawi writes that the masjid al-Aqsa was bayt al-maqdis, "because there was no mosque at that time behind it."

38.  Yohanan Friedmann, trans., *The History of al-Tabari: Volume XII, The Battle of al-Qadisiyyah and the Conquest of Syria and Palestine* (Albany: State University of New York Press, 1992).

39.  "Israelis and Palestinians Contest Holy Shrine," Associated Press, October 11, 2000.

40.  CNN.com, "Bus Shooting Caps Turbulent Day in Middle East."

41.  "First Statement of the Government of Israel," 86–87.

42.  Associated Press, "Fire Breaks Out at the Church of the Nativity," May 2, 2002. http://www.foxnews.com/story/0,2933,51678,00.html.

43.  "Greedy Monsters Ruled Church," *Washington Times*, May 15, 2002.

44.  Ahmed Rashid, *Taliban: Militant Islam, Oil and Fundamentalism in Central Asia* (New Haven: Yale University Press, 2000), 201.

45.  "Arab Intellectual on the Worsening Situation of Christians in the Muslim World," MEMRI Special Dispatch, Reform Project No. 1150, April 28, 2006.

46.  Ibid.

47.  Richard Z. Chesnoff and Robin Knight, "A Helping Hand from Saudi Arabia: Who Funds Hamas?" *U.S. News & World Report*, July 8, 1996.

48.  http://www.palestine-info.net/arabic/fatawa/index.htm.

49.  "Al-Zarqawi's Message to the Fighters of Jihad in Iraq on September 11, 2004," MEMRI Special Dispatch Series No. 785, September 15, 2004.

50.  "Leading Sunni Sheikh Yousef Al-Qaradhawi and Other Sheikhs Herald the Coming Conquest of Rome," MEMRI, Special Dispatch Series No. 447, December 6, 2002.

51.  Philip Webster and Richard Ford, "Extremist Clerics Face Prosecution for Backing Terror," *Times*, July 14, 2005.

52.  "Saudi Cleric Nasser bin Suleiman al-'Omar," MEMRI, Special Dispatch Series No. 1154, May 4, 2006.

53.  David Cook, "Muslim Fears of the Year 2000," *Middle East Quarterly*, June 1998.

54.  Timothy R. Furnish, *Holiest Wars: Islamic Mahdis, Their Jihads, and Osama bin Laden* (Westport: Praeger Books, 2005), 18.

55.   Ehud Ya'ari, "'Harmagadun' Now," *Jerusalem Report*, May 12, 2003.
56.   Shlomo Ben-Ami, *Scars of War, Wounds of Peace: The Israeli-Arab Tragedy* (Oxford: Oxford University Press, 2006), 265.

## Chapter 1: Jerusalem: The Legacy of Ancient Israel

1.    Book of Deuteronomy, 3:25: see Commentary of Rashi, who defines "that goodly mountain" as Jerusalem.
2.    The tribe of Judah briefly captured Jerusalem just after the death of Joshua ben Nun, according to Judges (1:8), but subsequently lost control of the city. Meir Ben-Dov, *Historical Atlas of Jerusalem* (New York: Continuum, 2002), 40–41.
3.    The commentary of the great biblical commentator Rashi on this verse identifies Mt. Moriah as the location of Jacob's dream.
4.    U. Cassuto, "Jerusalem in the Pentateuch," *Biblical & Oriental Studies*, Volume 1: Bible (Jerusalem: The Magnes Press, 1973), 78.
5.    Adapted from William G. Dever, *What Did the Biblical Writers Know & When Did They Know It? What Archaeology Can Tell Us about the Reality of Ancient Israel* (Grand Rapids: William B. Eerdmands Publishing Company, 2001), 218. YHWH refers to the Hebrew name for God.
6.    Meir Ben-Dov, Mordechai Naor, and Zeev Aner, The Western Wall (Hakotel), (Bat-Yam: Ministry of Defense Publishing House, 1987), 81–89.
7.    It is notable that the Hebrew word for these pilgrimage festivals in Jerusalem, hag, closely resembles the Arabic word for the pilgrimage to Mecca, hajj, that became one of the pillars of Islam centuries later.
8.    Midrash Rabah, Chapters 45 and 49.
9.    Zev Vilnay, *Legends of Jerusalem* (Jerusalem: Sefer Ve Sefel Publishing, 2004), 7–8. See also "Even Shtiah," Encyclopedia Talmudit (Jerusalem: Talmudic Encylcopedia, 1990), 85. The foundation stone is mentioned in Mishnah Yoma, Chapter 53, Mishnah 2. In Tractate Yoma of the Talmud (54:b), reference is made to the Mishnah and is explained as follows: "A stone was there in the Holy of Holies from the days of the early prophets, and it was called Shetiyah (foundation)." See Talmud Bavli, Tractate Yoma, Volume II, Schottestein Edition (Brooklyn: Mesorah Publications, 2005), 54b1.
10.   David Van Biema, "Judaism's Stake: The Mysteries of Solomon's Temple," *Time*, April 16, 2001.
11.   Daniel Lazare, "False Testament: Archaeology Refutes the Bible's Claim to History" (Criticism), *Harper's*, March 2002.
12.   Eilat Mazar, "Did I Find King David's Palace?" *Biblical Archaeological Review*, January/ February 2006. André Lemarie, "The United Monarchy: Saul, David and Solomon," in Hershel Shanks, ed., *Ancient Israel: From Abraham to the Roman Destruction of the Temple* (Washington: Bibli-

cal Archaeological Society/Prentine Hall, 1999), 117. Kathleen Kenyon and Yigal Shiloh dated the stepped-stone structure to the time of David and Solomon; Amihai Mazar has also written that the "stepped structure…may tentatively be attributed to the tenth century B.C.E." See Amihai Mazar, *Archaeology of the Land of the Bible 10,000–586 B.C.E.* (New York: Doubleday, 1990), 374. Israel Finkelstein has disagreed with these views. See Israel Finkelstein and Neil Asher Silberman, *David and Solomon: In Search of the Bible's Sacred Kings and the Roots of Western Tradition* (New York: Free Press, 2006), 270.

13. K. A. Kitchen, *On the Reliability of the Old Testament* (Grand Rapids: William B. Eerdmans Publishing Company, 2003), 93.

14. James B. Pritchard, ed., *The Ancient Near East: Volume 1, An Anthology of Texts and Pictures* (Princeton: Princeton University Press, 1958), 209–210. The French scholar André Lemaire has examined the Moabite Stone in the Louvre. Upon finding the phrase "the House of [D]avid;" he inserted the missing "D," which is the only reading that makes sense. See Kitchen, 92–93. The "Mesha Stone" today is kept at the Oriental Institute of the University of Chicago.

15. Kitchen, 92.

16. Israel Finkelstein and Neil Asher Silberman, *The Bible Unearthed: Archaeology's New Vision of Ancient Israel and the Origin of Its Sacred Texts* (New York: Touchstone, 2001), 129.

17. Gabriel Barkay, "The Iron Age II-III"; Amnon Ben-Tor, ed., *The Archaeology of Ancient Israel* (New Haven: Yale University Press, with the Open University of Israel, 1992), 307.

18. Dever, 131–32. For a different view of the Solomonic gates, see Finkelstein and Silberman, *The Bible Unearthed*, 138–40. They argue that the prototypes in northern Syria for what Yadin concluded were Solomon's cities were built a half century after Solomon. But what if the north Syrian structures did not serve as the prototypes for construction by King Solomon?

19. Yigael Yadin, *The Art of Warfare in Biblical Lands*, Volume Two (New York: McGraw-Hill Book Company, 1963), 288.

20. Simon Goldhill, *The Temple of Jerusalem* (Cambridge: Harvard University Press, 2005), 43. Goldhill writes, "Ezekiel was a priest who was exiled to Babylon, where he was inspired to deliver judgments and prophecies which make up the Book of Ezekiel. Central to this book too is an image of the Temple." Amihai Mazar also notes that "Detailed descriptions of the Solomonic temple appear in 1 Kings 5:16–6:38 and 2 Chronicles 4. To those may be added the firsthand evidence of Ezekiel (Chapters 40–44), (emphasis added). See A. Mazar, 376.

21. Eilat Mazar, *The Complete Guide to the Temple Mount Excavations* (Shoham Academic Research and Publication, 2002), 9. See also analysis of Ernest-Marie Lapperrousaz, in Lemaire, 117.

22. Daniel J. Elazar, *Covenant and Polity in Biblical Israel* (New Brunswick: Transaction Publishers, 1995), 163. Michael Walzer, Exodus and Revolution (New York: Basic Books, 1985).

23. Norman Podhoretz, *The Prophets: Who They Were, What They Are* (New York: The Free Press, 2002), 191.

24. Pritchard, 198–201.

25. John Bright, *A History of Israel* (London: SCM Press Ltd., 1974), 288.

26. Ibid., 315–17.

27. Ibid., 318–19.

28. Rabbi Joseph Telushkin, *Biblical Literacy* (New York: William Morrow and Company, 1997), 270–73.

29. Bright, 321–22.

30. Midrash Rabbah, Chapters 45 and 49.

31. Ibid.

32. "For when Alexander while still far off saw the multitude in white garments the priests at their head clothed in linen, and the high priest in a robe of hyacinth-blue and gold, wearing on his head the mitre with the golden plate on it on which was inscribed the name of God, he approached alone and prostrated himself before the Name and first greeted the high priest.... Then he went up to the temple, where he sacrificed to God under the direction of the high priest, and showed due honour to the priests and to the high priest himself." See Josephus, *Jewish Antiquities Books IX–XI* (Cambridge: Harvard University Press, 1956), 475–77.

33. David Golan, "Josephus, Alexander's Visit to Jerusalem, and Modern Historiography" in Uriel Rappaport, ed., Josephus Flavius: *Historian of Eretz-Israel in the Hellenistic-Roman Period* [in Hebrew] (Jerusalem: Yad Izhak Ben Zvi, 1982), 29–55.

34. Talmud Bavli, *Tracdate Yoma*, Volume II, Schottenstein Edition (Brooklyn: Mesorah Publications, 2005), 69a4.

35. Herod was from an Idumean family that converted to Judaism. Though despised for murdering Hasmoneans and members of the Sanhedrin, his Jewishness was not challenged by Jewish sources. Eusebius, one of the Church fathers, nonetheless called Herod "a foreigner": "Herod was the first foreigner to hold the sovereignty of the Jewish nation...." Eusebius, the Ecclesiatical History (Cambridge: Cambridge University Press, 1965), 49.

36. The Romans captured Josephus and subsequently gave him Roman citizenship and a stipend, which allowed him to chronicle the revolt.

37. Josephus, *The Jewish War* (London: Penguin Books, 1981), 156–58.

38. Ibid., 164.

39. Ibid., 27.

40. Neil Faulkner, *Apocalypse: The Great Jewish Revolt Against Rome AD 66–73* (Gloucestershire: Tempus Publishing, Ltd., 2004), 288.

41. Ibid., 189.

42. Menachem Stern, *Greek and Latin Authors on Jews and Judaism, Volume 2: From Tacitus to Simplicius* (Jerusalem: The Israel Academy of Sciences and Humanities, 1980), 64.

43. Karen Armstrong, *Jerusalem: One City, Three Faiths* (New York: Ballantine Books, 1997), 153.

44. Gedaliah Alon, *The Jews in Their Land in the Talmudic Age* (Jerusalem: The Magnes Press, The Hebrew University, 1984), 629.

45. Eric H. Cline, *Jerusalem Besieged: From Ancient Canaan to Modern Israel* (Ann Arbor: University of Michigan Press, 2004), 128–29.

46. Hadrian's name was Aelia Hadrianus, while the name Capitolina refers to the cult of Capitoline in Rome. See Cline, 131.

47. "Since the days the wicked empire has taken over, laying upon us its evil decrees, keeping us from the [study] of Torah and the life of mitzvot] ... " Tractate Baba Batra 60b, cited in Alon, 584.

48. Maimonides, Mishna Torah, "The Laws of Judges," Chapter 11, Law 3 (Jerusalem: Wagsal, 1990), 207.

49. Yigael Yadin, *Bar-Kochba: The Rediscovery of the Legendary Hero of the Last Jewish Revolt Against Imperial Rome* ( London: Weidenfeld and Nicolson, 1971), 81–85.

50. Lawrence H. Schiffman, *From Text to Tradition: A History of Second Temple and Rabbinic Judaism* (Hoboken: Ktav Publishing, 1991), 245.

51. Cited in Alon, 593.

52. Josephus, 189.

53. Faulkner, 383–86.

54. Alon, 613–15. Historians do not have a unanimous view as to whether Bar Kochba captured Jerusalem. The Christian historian Eusebius writes of Hadrian as the last conqueror of Jerusalem after Vespasian. This implies that Hadrian captured the city from Jewish authorities during the Bar Kochba revolt. Jewish sources in the Midrash support this view. The fact that the Roman historian Dio Cassius is silent on the issue of Jerusalem constitutes a source of doubt about when Bar Kochba reached the Holy City.

55. Alon, 607.

56. Some of the Greek-named rebels may have been Hellenized Jews, but this does not negate the fact that Gentiles also participated in the revolt.

57. Alon, 628.

58. Lawrence H. Schiffman, *Who Was a Jew?: Rabbinic and Halakhic Perspectives on the Jewish-Chrisitian Schism* (Hoboken: Ktav Publishing House, 1985), 76. There are widely differing interpretations of Jewish-Christian relations in the first and second centuries. Lee Levine writes of the trend of "the Jerusalem authorities to persecute the church time and again." He also reports that the high priest Ananus ordered the execution of the Apostle James. See Lee I. Levine, *Jerusalem: Portrait of the City in the Second Temple Period* (New York: Jewish Publication Society, 2002), 206. Karen

Armstrong, in contrast, conveys a different version of James's death: the high priest condemned James to death in 62 C.E. for "breaking the law," but eighty Pharisees protest the sentence to Rome, on James's behalf, and die with him. See Armstrong, 151.

David Flusser explains that "Annas" was a Sadducean high priest who convened the Sanhedrin to judge James, but that the Pharisees charged that the session was illegal. David Flusser, *Jesus* (Jerusalem: The Magnes Press, 1997), 146. In another account, Ananus was deposed after only three months in office for ordering the execution by the Jewish king Agrippas II and the Roman procurator Festus. See John Dominic Crossan and Jonathan L. Reed, *Excavating Jesus: Beneath the Stones, Behind the Texts* (New York: HarperCollins, 2001), 35, 47.

59.  Alon, 593.
60.  Aharon Oppenheimer, "The Bar Kochba Revolt", in Z. Baras, S. Safrai, M. Stern, and Y. Tsafrir, eds., *Eretz Israel: From the Destruction of the Second Temple to the Muslim Conquest Volume I* (Jerusalem: Yad Ben Tzvi, 1982), 73.
61.  Midrash Shmot Rabbah, 2:5.
62.  Michael Avi-Yonah, *In the Days of Rome and Byzantium* [in Hebrew] (Jerusalem: The Bialik Institute, 1970), 64–67.
63.  Leonard Victor Rutgers, "Diaspora Synagogues: Synagogue Archaeology in the Greco-Roman World" in Steven Fine, ed., *Sacred Realm: The Emergence of the Synagogue in the Ancient World* (Oxford: Oxford University Press, 1996), 84–88.
64.  Steven Fine, "From Meeting House to Sacred Realm: Holiness and the Ancient Synagogue" in ibid., 26. See also Mishnah Rosh Ha-Shanah, 4:1–3.
65.  Mordecai Naor, *City of Hope: Jerusalem from Biblical to Modern Times* (Jerusalem: Yad Izhak Ben-Zvi, 1997), 81.
66.  Moshe Gil, *A History of Palestine: 634–1099* (Cambridge: Cambridge University Press, 1992), 3.
67.  Ibid., 2.
68.  Ibid., 3.
69.  Ibid.
70.  Naor, 96. H. H. Ben-Sasson, ed., *A History of the Jewish People* (Cambridge: Harvard University Press, 1976), 312.
71.  Dan Bahat, "Jerusalem Down Under: Tunneling Along Herod's Temple Mount Wall," *Biblical Archaeological Review*, November/December 1995.
72.  Gil, 72.
73.  Ibid., 171.
74.  Salo Wittmayer Baron, *A Social and Religious History of the Jews: Late Middle Ages and Era of European Expansion, 1200–1650*, Volume 4 (New York: Columbia University Press, 1965), 95.
75.  Arie Morgenstern, "Dispersion and the Longing for Zion, 1240–1840," *Azure*, No. 12, Winter 2002, 86–87.

76. Ibid., 87.
77. Hans Lewy, Alexander Altmann, and Isaac Heinemann, eds., *Three Jewish Philosophers* (New Milford: The Toby Press, 2006), 109.
78. Ibid., 108.
79. *The Twelve Prophets* [in Hebrew] (Jerusalem: Mosad Harav Kook, 1990), 33.

## Chapter 2: Christianity and Jerusalem

1. Hershel Shanks, "Where Jesus Cured the Blind Man," *Biblical Archaeology Review*, September/October 2005, 16–23.
2. John Dominic Crossan and Jonathan L. Reed, *Excavating Jesus: Beneath the Stones, Behind the Texts* (New York: HarperCollins, 2001), 321.
3. Karen Armstrong, *Jerusalem: One City, Three Faiths* (New York: Ballantine Books, 1996), 159.
4. Ibid., 161.
5. David Chidester, *Christianity: A Global History* (London, Penguin Books, 2000), 29–31.
6. Gedaliah Alon, *The Jews in Their Land in the Talmudic Age* (Cambridge: Harvard University Press, 1996), 295.
7. Lawrence H. Schiffman, *From Text to Tradition: A History of Second Temple & Rabbinic Judaism* (Hoboken: Ktav Publishing House, 1991), 152–54.
8. Peter Walker, "Jerusalem in the Early Christian Centuries," in W. L. Walker, ed., *Jerusalem Past and Present in the Purposes of God* (Cambridge: Tyndale House, 1992), 83.
9. W. L. Walker, *Jesus and the Holy City: New Testament Perspectives on Jerusalem* (Grand Rapids: William B. Eerdmans Publishing Co., 1996), 321.
10. Chidester, 46–64.
11. W. L. Walker, *Jesus and the Holy City*, 322.
12. Armstrong, 171.
13. Bernard Wasserstein, *Divided Jerusalem: The Struggle for the Holy City* (New Haven: Yale University Press, 2002), 5.
14. Ibid.
15. James Carroll, *Constantine's Sword: The Church and the Jews: A History* (Boston: Houghton Mifflin, 2001), 166–71.
16. Kirsopp Lake, trans., *Eusebius: The Ecclesiastical History* (Cambridge: Harvard University Press, 1965), See introductory essay, xi.
17. Chidester, 46–64.
18. W. L. Walker, *Jesus and the Holy City*, ix.
19. Eusebius, *The Proof of the Gospel*, W. J. Ferrar, ed. and trans., Book VIII.
20. James Carroll has traced this shift back to the time of the Gospels, whom he charged "deflected blame away from the Romans and onto the Jews...." See Carroll, 85.

21. Beginning in the 1880s, many Protestants identified the site of Jesus' burial and resurrection at an alternative location in Jerusalem called the Garden Tomb.

22. Colin Chapman, *Whose Holy City?: Jerusalem and the Future of Peace in the Middle East* (Grand Rapids: Baker Books, 2005), 59.

23. Ibid., 180.

24. Carroll, 195.

25. Bat-Sheva Albert, "The Impact of Jerusalem on Liturgy and Architecture in the Carolingian Empire" [in Hebrew], *Cathedra*, July 2003.

26. Peter Walker, "Jerusalem in the Early Christian Centuries," 84–87.

27. Cited by Alon, 594.

28. Andrew S. Jacobs, *The Holy Land and Christian Empire in Late Antiquity* (Stanford: Stanford University Press, 2004), 162.

29. Rivka Gonen, *Contested Holiness: Jewish, Muslim and Christian Perspectives on the Temple Mount in Jerusalem* (Jersey City: Ktav Publishing House, Inc, 2003), 82.

30. Cited in Eric Cline, *Jerusalem Besieged: From Ancient Canaan to Modern Israel* (Ann Arbor: University of Michigan Press, 2004), 138.

31. Gonen, 123.

32. Ibid., 84.

33. Jacobs, 150–51.

34. Meir Ben-Dov, *Historical Atlas of Jerusalem* (New York: Continuum Publishing Group, 2002), 161–62.

35. Gonen.

36. Armstrong, 252. Abdul Aziz Duri, "Jerusalem in the Early Islamic Period: 7th–11th Centuries AD," in Kamil J. Asali, ed., *Jerusalem in History: 3000 BC to the Present Day* (London: Kegan Paul International, 1989), 113.

37. Armstrong, 272.

38. Ibid., 259.

39. Cline, 160. See also Moshe Gil, "Political History of Jerusalem in the Early Islamic Period"; Joshua Prawer, *The History of Jerusalem: The Early Islamic Period* [in Hebrew] (Jerusalem: Yad Izhak Ben-Zvi, 1987), 29.

40. Piers Paul Read, *The Templars* (London: Phoenix Press, 1999), 70.

41. Jonathan Riley-Smith, *The Crusades: A History* (New Haven: Yale University Press, 2005), 12.

42. These texts are taken from Fordham University's "Medieval Sourcebook"—"Urban II (1088–1099): Speech at Council of Clermont, 1095, Five Versions of the Speech" http://www.fordham.edu/ halsall/source/urban2-5vers.html.

43. Ibid.

44. Norman Cohn, *The Pursuit of the Millennium* (Oxford: Oxford University Press, 1970), 75.

45. Thomas Asbridge, *The First Crusade: A New History* (New York: The Free Press, 2004), 35.

46. Armstrong, 266.

47. Ibid., 272. See also Carroll, 255, where he concludes: "Crusading fever meshed with millennial fever, and soon enough the present moment was widely experienced as nothing less that the dawn of the apocalyptic age." See commentary by Professor Bernard McGinn of the University of Chicago on the Crusades on PBS Frontline's "Apocalypse: The Evolution of Apocalyptic Belief and How It Shaped the Western World," http://www.pbs.org/wgbh/pages/frontline/shows/apocalyse/explanation-/crusades.html and Richard Landes, *Encyclopedia of Millenialism and Millenial Movements* (New York: Routledge, 2000), 330.

48. Riley-Smith, 24.

49. Carroll, 257.

50. Riley-Smith, 24.

51. Ibid., 10–11: "The increased traffic had probably reflected that as the year 1000 approached the Last Days were near, for it was to be in Jerusalem that the final acts in this dimension—the appearance of the Anti-Christ, the return of the Savior, the earliest splitting of tombs and reassembling of bones and dust in the General Resurrection—would take place."

52. Armstrong, 266.

53. Asbridge, 48.

54. Ibid., 57–63.

55. Joshua Prawer, "The Political History of Crusader and Ayyubid Jerusalem" in Joshua Prawer, ed., *The History of Jerusalem: Crusaders and Ayyubids* (1099–1250), (Jerusalem: Yad Izhak Ben-Zvi Publications, 1991), [in Hebrew], 2–3.

56. Asbridge, 300.

57. Joshua Prawer, "The Jewish Community in Jerusalem During the Crusader Period" in Prawer, 195.

58. F. E. Peters, Jerusalem: *The Holy City in the Eyes of Chroniclers, Visitors, Pilgrims and Prophets from the Days of Abraham to the Beginnings of Modern Times* (Princeton; Princeton University Press, 1985), 285.

59. Riley-Smith, 43.

60. Prawer, "The Jewish Community in Jerusalem During the Crusader Period," 196.

61. Peters, 290.

62. Prawer, "The Jewish Community in Jerusalem During the Crusader Period," 197–98.

63. Riley-Smith, 48.

64. Armstrong, 275.

65. Prawer, "The Jewish Community in Jerusalem During the Crusader Period," 201.

66. Joseph Brennan, "Jerusalem—A Christian Perspective;" John M. Oesterreicher, *Jerusalem* (New York: The John Day Company, 1974), 227–28.

67. Graham Tomlin, "Protestants and Pilgrimage," in Craig Bartholomew and Fred Hughs, eds., *Exploration in a Christian Theology of Pilgrimage* (New York: Ashgate Publishing Company, 2004), 110.

68.   Arthur Eyffinger, "How Wondrously Moses Goes Along with the House of Orange! 'Hugo Grotuis' 'De Repulica Emendana' in the Context of the Dutch Revolt," *Hebraic Political Studies*, Fall 2005, Volume 1, Number 1, 85–97.

69.   Peter W. L. Walker, "Jerusalem and the Church's Challenge," in W. L. Walker, ed., *Jerusalem Past and Present in the Purposes of God* (Cambridge: Tyndale House, 1992), 175–204.

70.   Chidester, 544.

71.   David Brog, *Standing with Israel: Why Christians Support the Jewish State* (Lake Mary: FrontLine, 2006), 100.

72.   Ibid., 82–83.

73.   Address by President Weizmann in Jerusalem, December 1, 1948. Meron Medzini, ed., *Israel Foreign Relations: Selected Documents 1947–1974* (Jerusalem: Ministry for Foreign Affairs, 1976), 221.

74.   See Statement to the Trusteeship Council by Ambassador Abba Eban, February 20, 1950. Medzini, 234.

75.   Ibid.

76.   *Middle East Insight*, Vol. XIV, No. 1, January/February 1999, 32.

77.   Carroll, 600.

78.   Sergio I. Minerbi, "Pope John Paul II and the Jews: An Evaluation" *Jewish Political Studies Review*, Spring 2000.

## Chapter 3: Jerusalem as the Third Holiest Place in Classical Islam

1.   Hava Lazarus-Yafeh, "Jerusalem and Mecca," *Judaism*, Spring 1997.

2.   Phillip Hitti, *History of the Arabs* (New York: St. Martin's Press, 1970), 115–16.

3.   Moshe Gil, *A History of Palestine*, 634–1099 (Cambridge: Cambridge University Press, 1992), 96.

4.   Mohammed Abdul Hameed Al-Khateeb, *Al-Quds: The Place of Jerusalem in Classical Judaic and Islamic Traditions* (London: Ta-Ha Publishers, 1998), 120.

5.   Ibid.

6.   Kanan Makiya, *The Rock: A Tale of Seventh-Century Jerusalem* (London: Constable, 2002), 291.

7.   Martin Kramer, "The Temples of Jerusalem" PeaceWatch #277, September 18, 2000, Washington Institute for Near East Policy.

8.   Yitzhak Hasson, "Jerusalem in the Muslim Perspective: The Qur'an and Tradition Literature," in Joshua Prawer, ed., *The History of Jerusalem: The Early Islamic Period (638–1099)* (Jerusalem: Yad Izhak Ben-Zvi, 1987), 287–88.

9.   C. E. Bosworth, E. Van Donzel, W. Heinrichs, and Ch. Pellat, eds., "Mi'radj," *The Encyclopedia of Islam Volume VII*, (Leiden: E. J. Brill, 1993), 98.

10. Bernard Lewis, "I'm Right, You're Wrong and Go to Hell" *Atlantic Monthly*, May 2003.

11. S. D. Goitein, *Jews and Arabs: Their Contacts Through the Ages* (New York: Schocken Books, 1967), 86–87.

12. Gil, 11.

13. Bernard Lewis, "Politics and War"; Joseph Schacht, *The Legacy of Islam* (London: Oxford University Press, 1974), 182.

14. Bernard Lewis, *The Political Language of Islam* (Chicago: University of Chicago Press, 1991), 75–76.

15. Bernard Lewis, "License to Kill: Usama bin Ladin's Declaration of Jihad," *Foreign Affairs*, November/ December 1998, 16.

16. Gil, 111.

17. Hitti, 169.

18. W. Montgomery Watt, *Islamic Political Thought* (Edinburgh: Edinburgh University Press, 1968), 17.

19. C. E. Bosworth, E. Van Donzel, W. Heinrichs, and Ch. Pellat, eds., "Al-Kuds," *The Encyclopedia of Islam*, Volume V (Leiden: E. J. Brill, 1986), 323.

20. Gil, 43.

21. Philip Hitti, *Makers of Arab History* (New York: Harper Torchbooks, 1968), 28.

22. F. E. Peters, *Jerusalem: The Holy City in the Eyes of Chroniclers, Visitors, Pilgrims, and Prophets from the Days of Abraham to the Beginnings of Modern Times* (Princeton: Princeton University Press, 1985), 176.

23. Philip Hitti, *History of the Arabs*, 145.

24. Bosworth, et al., "Al-Kuds."

25. Peters, 190.

26. Yohanan Friedman, trans., *The History of al-Tabari: The Battle of al-Qadisiyyah and the Conquest of Syria and Palestine* (Albany: State University of New York Press, 1992), 194–95.

27. Peters, 195–96.

28. Ibid, 184.

29. Gil, 73.

30. Ibid., 70–71.

31. Ibid., 70.

32. Ibid., 71.

33. Shmuel Berkovits, *"How Dreadful Is This Place!"*: *Holiness, Politics and Justice in Jerusalem and the Holy Places in Israel* (Jerusalem: Carta, 2006), 102. Berkovits notes that the great Israeli historian Bentzion Dinur first raised the possibility back in 1929 of there being a synagogue on the Temple Mount for 400 years until the First Crusade.

34. Karen Armstrong, *Jerusalem: One City, Three Faiths* (New York: Ballantine Books, 1997), 233. Moshe Gil, "The Jewish Community" in Joshua Prawer, ed., *The History of Jerusalem: The Early Islamic Period* (638–1099), (Jerusalem: Yad Izhak Ben-Zvi, 1987), 142.

35. Mark. R. Cohen, *Under Crescent and Cross: The Jews in the Middle Ages* (Princeton: Princeton University Press, 1994), 54–60.

36. Eilat Mazar, *The Complete Guide to the Temple Mount Excavations* (Jerusalem: Shoham Academic Research and Publication, 2002), 94.

37. Abdul Aziz Duri, "Jerusalem in the Early Islamic Period: 7th–11th Centuries AD," Kamil J. Asali, ed., *Jerusalem in History: 3000BC to the Present Day* (London: Kegan Paul International, 1997), 112.

38. Bosworth, et al., "Mi'radj," 97.

39. Ignaz Goldziher, *Muslim Studies* (London: George Allen & Unwin, 1971), 44, footnote 3.

40. Abdul Aziz Duri,109.

41. Ghada Hashem Talhami, "The Modern History of Jerusalem: Academic Myths and Propaganda," *The Middle East Journal*, February 2000.

42. Bosworth, et al., "Al-Kuds," 325.

43. Armstrong, 237.

44. Bernard Lewis, "The Revolt of Islam: When Did the Conflict with the West Begin and How Could It End?" *Atlantic*, November 19, 2001.

45. Oleg Grabar, *The Dome of the Rock* (Cambridge: Belknap/Harvard Unviersity Press, 2006), 90–92.

46. Moshe Sharon, "Islam on the Temple Mount," *Biblical Archaeological Review*, July/August 2006, 42.

47. Rivka Gonen, *Contested Holiness: Jewish, Muslim and Christian Perspectives on the Temple Mount in Jerusalem* (Jersey City: Ktav Publishing House, 2003), 87.

48. Hitti, *The Arabs in History*, 221.

49. Ibid.

50. Cohen, 58.

51. Peters, 235–238.

52. Abdul Azuz Duri, 113.

53. Armstrong, 246.

54. Bosworth, et al., "Al-Kuds," 326.

55. Amin Maalouf, *The Crusades Through Arab Eyes* (New York: Schocken Books, 1984), xvi.

56. Emmanuel Sivan, "The Sanctity of Jerusalem in Islam During the Period of the Crusades," in Joshua Prawer and Hagi Ben Shamai, eds., *The Book of Jerusalem: The Crusader and Ayyubid Period* (Jerusalem: Yad Izak Ben Zvi, 1991) [in Hebrew], 288.

57. Sharon, 45.

58. Ibid., 46.

59. Talhami.

60. Peters, 244. The Andalusian legal expert Abu Bakr al-Tartushi, who visited Jerusalem in 1091, reported the popular belief of its residents that if they performed some of the rites in Jerusalem that were normally reserved for the pilgrimage to Mecca every four years, then that would be counted as a real pilgrimage to Mecca. He criticized these practices as bid'a—innovation. See Abdul Aziz Duri,116.

61. Sivan, 290.
62. Bosworth, et al., "Al-Kuds," 332.
63. Hitti, *History of the Arabs,* 645–46.
64. Eric H. Cline, *Jerusalem Besieged: From Ancient Canaan to Modern Israel* (Ann Arbor: University of Michigan Press, 2004), 184.
65. Niall Christie, "A Translation of Extracts from Kitab al-Jihad of 'Ali ibn Tahir al-Sulami (d. 1106)": http://www.arts.cornell.edu/prh3/447/texts/Sulami.html. The Arabic text appears in an article by Emmanuel Sivan, in *Journal Asiatique* 254 (1966), 206–22.
66. Jonathan Riley-Smith, *The Crusades: A History* (New Haven: Yale University Press, 2005), 110.
67. Stanley Lane-Poole, *Saladin: All-Powerful Sultan and the Uniter of Islam* (New York: Cooper Square Press, 2002), 199.
68. Lewis, "License to Kill."
69. Meir Ben-Dov, *Historical Atlas of Jerusalem* (New York: Continuum Publishing Group, 2002), 214.
70. Peters, 353.
71. Donald Little, "Jerusalem under the Ayyubids and the Mamluks: 1187–1516 AD," *Asali,* 180.
72. Armstrong, 298.
73. Ibid.
74. Little, 183.
75. Ibid.
76. Ibid.
77. Ben-Dov, 219.
78. Bosworth, et al., "Al-Kuds," 331.
79. Sivan, 295.
80. Peters, 373.
81. Ibid., 377.
82. Ibid., 376.
83. Armstrong, 313.
84. Ibid., 310.
85. Sivan, 301.
86. Peters, 417–21.
87. Mordechai Naor, *City of Hope: Jerusalem from Biblical to Modern Times* (Jerusalem: Yad Izhak Ben-Zvi, 1997), 161.
88. Peters, 406.
89. Oleg Graber, "The Haram al-Sharif: An Essay in Interpretation," BRIIFS, Vol. 2, No. 2, Autumn 2000, Royal Institute for Inter-Faith Studies.
90. K. J. Asali, "Jerusalem Under the Ottomans: 1516-1831 AD," in Asali, ed., 201–02.
91. Ibid., 204.
92. Armstrong, 323–27.
93. Naor, 186.
94. Asali, 209.

## Chapter 4: Jerusalem and the Birth of Modern Israel

1. Yehoshua Ben-Arieh, *Jerusalem in the 19th Century* (New York: St. Martin's Press, 1984), 268.
2. Amnon Cohen found that the Ottoman census in the sixteenth century underestimated the Jewish population of Jerusalem by approximately 20 percent. See Amnon Cohen, *The Jewish Community in Jerusalem in the 16th Century* (Jerusalem: Yad Izhak ben Zvi, 1982), [in Hebrew], 38.
3. "Report on the Commerce of Jerusalem in the Year 1863," British consulate in Jerusalem, May 1864, Foreign Office Records (FO), 195/808, British National Archives.
4. Martin Gilbert, "Jerusalem: A Tale of One City," *New Republic*, November 14, 1994.
5. Barbara Tuchman, *Bible and Sword: England and Palestine from the Bronze Age to Balfour* (Ballantine Books, 1984), 337.
6. Eric. H. Cline, *Jerusalem Besieged: From Ancient Canaan to Modern Israel* (Ann Arbor: The University of Michigan Press, 2004), 227.
7. David Brog, *Standing with Israel: Why Christians Support the Jewish State* (Lake Mary: Front Line, 2006), 99–101.
8. Ruth Lapidoth and Moshe Hirsch, eds., *The Jerusalem Question and Its Resolution: Selected Documents* (Dordecht: Martinus Nijhoff Publishers, 1994).
9. These treaties eventually resulted in the emergence of the modern Middle Eastern states of Saudi Arabia, Qatar, Kuwait, Jordan, and Iraq.
10. Document 75: "(Lausanne), Treaty of Peace with Turkey and Accompanying Straits Convention and Declaration on the Administration of Justice, 24 July 1923," in J. C. Hurewitz, ed., *The Middle East and North Africa in World Politics: A Documentary Record—Volume 2: British-French Supremacy, 1914–1945* (New Haven: Yale University Press, 1979).
11. Ibid., Document 70: "The Mandate for Palestine," July 24, 1922, 305–06.
12. Ibid., Document 34: "Tentative Recommendations for President Wilson by the Intelligence Section of the American Delegation to the Peace Conference," January 21, 1919, 132–36.
13. Douglas Feith, William V. O'Brien, Eugene V. Rostow, *Israel's Legitimacy in Law and History* (New York: Center for Near East Policy Research, 1993). See chapter by Paul S. Riebenfeld, 51.
14. Elihu Lauterpacht, *Jerusalem and the Holy Places* (London: The Anglo-Israel Association, 1968), 7.
15. Hurewitz, ed., Document 69: "Statement of British Policy (Churchill Memorandum), on Palestine" July 1, 1922, 301–05.
16. Ibid., Document 13, "The Husayn-McMahon Correspondence," 46–56.
17. Palestine: A Study of Jewish, Arab, and British Policies, Published for the Esco Foundation for Palestine, Inc. (New Haven: Yale University Press, 1947), 187.
18. Joshua Teitelbaum, *The Rise and Fall of the Hashemite Kingdom of Arabia* (New York: New York University Press, 2001), 195.
19. Esco Report, 143.

20. Hurewitz, ed., Document 33: "Amir Faisal's Memorandum to the Supreme Council at the Paris Peace Conference" January 1, 1919, 132.
21. Esco Report, 143.
22. According to oral and written sources about the largest Bedouin tribe in the Negev area of what is today the State of Israel, arrived to the area about 600 years ago. Like most Negev Bedouin, they trace their origins to the Arabian peninsula, particularly the Hijaz and the Nejd. In contrast, the Bedouin tribes of the Galilee are connected to tribes in western Iraq and the northern Syrian desert. See Joseph-Ben David, *The Bedouins in Israel— Land Conflicts and Social Issues* (Jerusalem: The Jerusalem Institute for Israel Studies, 2004), [in Hebrew], 30, 68.

    In general, Palestine had absorbed considerable Arab immigration in recent centuries, including Sudanese who arrived with the Egyptians in the 1830s. Many Gazans had Egyptian origins. See Esco Report, 462. During the 1930s the Jewish Agency protested to the British authorities about the scale of Arab immigration into Palestine that mostly came from Syria and Transjordan, as well as from Egypt. The Royal Institute for International Affairs cited an interview with the Syrian newspaper, *La Syrie*, with the governor of the Hauran district in southern Syria, who stated that 30,000 to 36,000 Hauranese entered Palestine in a period of a few months. The Jewish Agency charged that these Hauranese workers were behind the outbreak of the disturbances that began in Jaffa in 1936. See Esco Report, 682–83, 805.
23. Memorandum to the Secretary of State, May 17, 1939, *Foreign Relations of the United States*, 1939, Volume 4 (Washington: U.S. Government Printing Office, 1955), 757.
24. Esco Report, 467.
25. Philip Mattar, *The Mufti of Jerusalem: Al-Hajj Amin Al-Husayni and the Palestinian National Movement* (New York: Columbia University Press, 1988), 6.
26. C. E. Bosworth, E. Van Donzel, B. Lewis, and C. H. Pellat, eds., "Al-Kuds," *The Encyclopedia of Islam* (Leiden: E.J. Brill, 1986), 333.
27. Ibid.
28. Palestine Royal Report, July 1937, Chapter II, 40, cited in Eli E. Herz, Reply to the Advisory Opinion of 9 July 2004 in the Matter of the Legal Consequences of the Construction of a Wall in the Occupied Palestinian Territory as Submitted by the International Court of Justice, (Forest Hill: Myths and Facts, 2005), 29.
29. Ibid., 31.
30. Bernard Wasserstein, *Divided Jerusalem: The Struggle for the Holy City* (New Haven: Yale University Press, 2002), 4–5.
31. Esco Report, 1155.
32. J. C. Hurewitz, *The Struggle for Palestine* (New York: Schocken Books, 1976), 77–78.

33. Riebenfeld, 41. Paul Riebenfeld was a Zionist delegate to the Permanent Mandates Commission of the League of Nations from 1937 to 1939.
34. Martin Gilbert, *Jerusalem in the Twentieth Century* (New York: John Wiley & Sons, 1996), 174–77.
35. Lauterpact, 16.
36. Lapidoth and Hirsch, eds., Document 4B, "Statement to the Ad Hoc Committee on the Palestine Question by the Representative of the Jewish Agency for Palestine, 2 October 1947," 12.
37. Gilbert, *Jerusalem in the Twentieth Century*, 179.
38. Trygve Lie, *In the Cause of Peace* (New York: Macmillan, 1954), 174.
39. Gilbert, *Jerusalem in the Twentieth Century*, 218.
40. Ibid., 214–24.
41. Ibid., 219.
42. Quoted in Shlomo Slonim, *Jerusalem in America's Foreign Policy, 1947–1997* (The Hague: Kluwer Law International, 1998), 79.
43. "Jerusalem Facing Danger of Destruction, April 1, 1948," in Meron Medzini, ed., *Israel's Foreign Relations* (Jerusalem: Ministry for Foreign Affairs, 1976), 217–19.
44. Cited in Gilbert, *Jerusalem in the Twentieth Century*, 220.
45. Lapidoth and Hirsch, eds., Document 8, "Progress Report on the U.N. Mediator on Palestine, 16 September 1948 (extracts)," 22.
46. Gilbert, *Jerusalem in the Twentieth Century*, 223.
47. "Statement to the Knesset by Prime Minister Ben-Gurion, 5 December 1949," in Medzini, ed., 224.
48. Ibid.
49. Ibid., 226.
50. Gilbert, 19.
51. Lauterpacht, 22. See also Yehuda Z. Blum, "The Juridicial Status of Jerusalem," in Msgr. John M. Oesterreicher and Anne Sinai, *Jerusalem* (New York: John Day, 1974), 110.
52. Chaim Herzog, *The Arab-Israeli Wars: War and Peace in the Middle East* (New York: Vintage Books, 1984), 106.
53. Lapidoth and Hirsch, eds., Document 16: "Statement by the Foreign Minister of Israel, Moshe Sharett in the U.N. General Assembly on the Position of the Government of Israel Concerning the Proposed Internationalization of Jerusalem, 25 November 1949," 75. The exact number of fallen Israelis in Jerusalem was 1,490.
54. Netanel Lorch, ed., *Major Knesset Debates, 1948–1981: The Constituent Assembly—First Knesset 1949–1951* (Jerusalem: Jerusalem Center for Public Affairs, 1993), 574.
55. Ibid., 589.
56. "The Consul in Jerusalem (Burdett), to the Secretary of State" May 20, 1949, *Foreign Relations of the United States 1949*, Volume VI (Washington: U.S. Government Printing Office, 1977), 1039–41.

## Chapter 5: Jerusalem, the Palestinian Arabs, and the Hashemite Kingdom of Jordan

1. For an excellent summary of the Palestinian Arab point of view see Henry Cattan, *Jerusalem* (London: Saqi Books, 2000). See also Document 22, "The Arab Case for Palestine: Evidence Submitted by the Arab Office, *Jerusalem*, to the Anglo-American Committee of Inquiry, March 1946," Walter Laqueur and Barry Rubin, eds., *The Israeli-Arab Reader: A Documentary History of the Middle East Conflict* (New York: Penguin Books, 1991), 94.

2. Ibid.

3. J. C. Hurewitz, *The Struggle for Palestine* (New York: Schocken Books, 1976), 18–19.

4. Said K. Aburish, *Arafat: From Defender to Dictator* (New York: Bloomsbury Publishing, 1998), 15.

5. Phillip Mattar, *The Mufti of Jerusalem: Al-Hajj Amin al-Husayni and the Palestinian National Movement* (New York: Columbia University Press, 1988), 16–17. The Nebi Musa festival was a local tradition that grew over the centuries after local Muslims decided that Moses was buried just southwest of Jericho and not east of the Jordan. The shrine marking the tomb of Moses was built in the thirteenth century and became a palce of pilgrimage for local Muslims who would gather in Jerusalem before heading to the site. See Bernard Wasserstein, *Divided Jerusalem: The Struggle for the Holy City* (New Haven: Yale University Press, 2002), 102.

6. Wasserstein, 104.

7. Martin Gilbert, *Jerusalem in the Twentieth Century* (New York: John Wiley & Sons, 1996), 90.

8. Mattar, 23.

9. Gilbert, 119.

10. Esco Foundation for Palestine, *Palestine: A Study of Jewish, Arab, and British Policies*, Volume Two (New Haven: Yale University Press, 1947), 600.

11. See letter of Harry Sacher in the *Times*, August 29, 1929, quoted in Gilbert, 124.

12. Amikam Elad believes that "towards the end of the seventeenth century the place where al-Buraq was fastened was still identified as that on the outside south-west corner of the wall of the Haram, just as it was described by Ibn al-Faqih and by Ibn Abd Rabbihi in the tenth century." Cited by Wasserstein, 324–25.

13. Shmuel Berkovits, *The Battle for the Holy Places: The Struggle over Jerusalem and the Holy Sites in Israel, Judea, Samaria, and the Gaza District* (Or Yehuda: Hed Arzi, 2000), [in Hebrew], 109–10.

14. "Waqf" in Cyrile Glasse, ed., *The Concise History of Islam* (London: Stacey International, 1991), 417.

15. Mattar, 54.

16. Ibid.
17. *Report of the Commission Appointed by His Majesty's Government in the United Kingdom of Great Britain and Northern Ireland, and with the Approval of the Council of the League of Nations, to Determine the Rights and Claims of Moslems and Jews in Connection with the Western or Wailing Wall at Jerusalem* (London: His Majesty's Stationery Office, 1931).
18. Ibid.
19. Esco Report, 614.
20. Y. Porath, *The Palestinian Arab National Movement: 1929–1939 From Riots to Rebellion* (London: Frank Cass, 1977), 10.
21. Martin Kramer, *Islam Assembled: The Advent of the Muslim Conferences* (New York: Columbia University Press, 1986), 129.
22. Porath, 11.
23. Gilbert, 132.
24. Porath, 12.
25. Meron Benvenisti, *City of Stone: The Hidden History of Jerusalem* (Berkley: University of California Press, 1996), 79.
26. Michael C. Hudson, "The Transformation of Jerusalem: 1917–1987 AD," in Kamil J. Asali, ed., *Jerusalem in History: 3000 BC to the Present Day* (Kegan Paul International, 1997), 256.
27. Document 4: "UN General Assembly Resolution 181 on the Future Government of Palestine," Ruth Lapidoth and Moshe Hirsch, eds., *The Jerusalem Question and Its Resolution: Selected Documents.* (Dordrecht: Martinus Nijhoff Publishers, 1994), 13–14.
28. Thomas A. Indinopulos, *Jerusalem: A History of the Holiest City as Seen Through the Struggles of Jews, Christians, and Muslims* (Chicago: Ivan R. Dee, 1994), 300. and Karen Armstrong, *Jerusalem: One City, Three Faiths* (New York: Ballantine Books, 1997), 389.
29. Tawfik al-Khalil, *Jerusalem from 1947 to 1967* (Amman: Economic Press, no date given), 90–92.
30. Raphael Israeli, *Jerusalem Divided: The Armistice Regime 1947–1967* (London: Frank Cass, 2002), 58.
31. Martin Gilbert, "Jerusalem: A Tale of One City," *New Republic*, November 14, 1994.
32. Israeli, 58.
33. Document 24, "Resolutions Concerning the Annexation of the West Bank (including East Jerusalem), to the Kingdom of Transjordan," Lapidoth and Hirsch, eds., 47.
34. HRH Crown Prince Hassan bin Talal, *A Study on Jerusalem* (London: Longman Group, 1979), 27.
35. Gilbert, *Jerusalem in the Twentieth Century*, 247.
36. Wasserstein, 186.
37. Quoted in Gilbert, *Jerusalem in the Twentieth Century*, 249. See also Wasserstein, 189.

38. Daniel Pipes, "The Muslim Claim to Jerusalem" *Middle East Quarterly*, September 2001.

39. Kimberly Katz, *Jordanian Jerusalem: Holy Places and National Spaces* (Gainsville: University Press of Florida, 2005), 85.

40. Gilbert, *Jerusalem in the Twentieth Century*, 248.

41. Mattar, 132.

42. Ibid., 136.

43. Quoted by Yosef Tekoah, Israel's permanent representative to the United Nations in a letter to the UN secretary-general, March 5, 1968. See Msgr. John M. Oesterreciher and Anne Sinai, eds., *Jerusalem* (New York: John Day, 1974), 281.

44. Gilbert, *Jerusalem in the Twentieth Century*, 226.

45. Ibid., 223.

46. According to Amos Elon, after the Jewish Quarter surrendered, twenty-two of the twenty-seven synagogues in the Old City were burned down by a mob, while the remaining five synagogues were sacked by the Jordanian Army. Elon does not count study halls or Yeshivot, but his data on synagogues is illuminating. See Amos Elon, *Jerusalem: City of Mirrors* (New York: HarperCollins/Flamingo, 1996), 81.

47. Marie Syrkin, "The Siege of Jerusalem" in Oesterreciher and Sinai, 79.

48. Gabriel Padon, "The Divided City: 1948–1967" in ibid., 101.

49. United Nations, General Assembly, Thirty-Second Session, Official Records, 47th Plenary Meeting, October 26, 1977. A/32/PV.47 See statement of Ambassador Chaim Herzog before the UN General Assembly.

50. Israeli, 74.

51. Padon, 102.

52. Wasserstein, 193.

53. Address of Foreign Minister Abba Eban to the Knesset, June 30, 1971. See John M. Oesterreicher, "Jerusalem the Free," in Oesterreciher and Sinai, 258.

54. Wm. Roger Louis, *The British Empire in the Middle East 1948–1951: Arab Nationalism, the United States and Postwar Imperialism* (Oxford: Oxford University Press, 1985), 579.

55. Document 31, "Aide Memoire Delivered by the United States Department of State to the Prime Minister of Jordan Concerning the Intention of Jordan to Treat the City of Jerusalem as Its Second Capital, 5 April 1960," in Lapidoth and Hirsch, 160.

56. Katz, 88.

57. Wasserstein, 250. Wasserstein noted that there was no mention of Jerusalem either in its ten-point political statement issued in Cairo on June 8, 1974.

58. Guy Bechor, *Lexicon of the PLO* (Tel Aviv: Ministry of Defense Publishers, 1991), [in Hebrew], 158.

59. Moshe Shemesh, *The Palestinian Entity 1959–1974: Arab Politics and the PLO* (London: Frank Cass, 1996), 45.
60. Ibid., 52.
61. Aburish, 7–11.
62. Ibid., 17.

## Chapter 6: Jerusalem and the Arab-Israeli Peace Process

1. Document 39, "Nasser's Speech to Arab Trade Unionists," May 26, 1967, Walter Laqueur and Barry Rubin, eds., *The Israeli-Arab Reader: A Documentary History of the Middle East Conflict* (New York: Penguin Books, 1984), 176.
2. Yehuda Z. Blum, "The Juridicial Status of Jerusalem," Msgr. John M. Oesterreicher and Anne Sinai, eds., *Jerusalem* (New York: John Day, 1974), 116.
3. These details of the Jordanian artillery barrage appear in Michael Oren, *Six Days of War: June 1967 and the Making of the Modern Middle East* (New York: Ballantine Books, 2003), 187.
4. Cited in Shlomo Slonim, *Jerusalem in America's Foreign Policy, 1947–1997* (The Hague: Kluwer Law International, 1998), 191.
5. Oren, 186.
6. Slonim, 192.
7. Document 32, "Israel's Protection of the Holy Places Law," June 27, 1967, Ruth Lapidoth and Moshe Hirsch, eds., *The Jerusalem Question and Its Resolution: Selected Documents* (Dordecht: Martinus Nijihoff Publishers, 1994), 169.
8. Document 45, "Statement made by the Government of Israel on Payment for Damages Caused to Churches and to Church Property in Wars Since 1948, September 11, 1968," in Lapidoth and Hirsch, 231.
9. See Document 100, "The Report of the Commission of Investigation in the Events on the Temple Mount, October 8, 1990," in Lapidoth and Hirsh, 466.
10. See Letter of Foreign Minister Abba Eban to the Secretary-General, July 10, 1967. Cited in Elihu Lauterpacht, *Jerusalem and the Holy Places* (London: The Anglo-Israel Association, 1968), 50.
11. Document 167, Julius Stone, "Israel, the United Nations and International Law," John Norton Moore, *The Arab-Israeli Conflict, Volume IV: The Difficult Search for Peace* (1975–1988), Part One (Princeton: Princeton University Press, 1991), 815.
12. Stephen M. Schwebel, "What Weight to Conquest?" *American Journal of International Law*, Volume 64 (1970).
13. Dore Gold, *Tower of Babble: How the United Nations Has Fueled Global Chaos* (New York: Crown Forum, 2005), 45.
14. Slonim, 195.
15. Arthur Lall, *The UN and the Middle East Crisis, 1967* (New York: Columbia University Press, 1968), 242.

16. "Foreign Relations of the United States, 1967–1968, volume XIX, Arab-Israeli Crisis and War 1967," http://www.state.gov/r/pa/ho/frus/johnsonlb/xix/28070.htm.

17. Ovadia Soffer, *The UN as Peacemaker* (Irchester: Mark Saunders Books, 1971), 92.

18. Alan Dershowitz, *The Case for Israel* (Hoboken: John Wiley & Sons, 2003), 96.

19. Slonim, 201.

20. Bernard Wasserstein, *Divided Jerusalem: The Struggle for the Holy City* (New Haven: Yale University Press, 2002), 231.

21. Ibid.

22. "American Answers to Jordanian Questions," October 1978, Appendix H, William B. Quandt, *Camp David: Peacemaking and Politics* (Washington: The Brookings Institution, 1986), 388–96.

23. Wasserstein, 248.

24. Howell Raines, "Reagan Urges Link to Jordan and Self-Rule by Palestinians," Transcript of Speeches, *New York Times*, September 2, 1982. Privately, the Reagan administration did not oppose the participation of East Jerusalem Palestinians in Palestinian elections, but it still insisted on Jerusalem remaining united.

25. Secretary of State George Shultz's address, September 16, 1988: http://www.findarticles.com/p/articles/mi_m1079/is_n2140_v88/ai_6876262.

26. Nabil Shath, "The Oslo Agreement" (an interview), *Journal of Palestine Studies*, Volume XXIII, Autumn 1993, Issue 89, 7.

27. Ibid.

28. Maariv, October 14, 2006.

29. Reported by Agence France Presse, June 27, 1995.

30. Israel Ministry of Foreign Affairs, *The Peace Process—Key Speeches by Israeli Leaders*, "PM Rabin in Knesset—Ratification of Interim Agreement," October 5, 1995.

31. CNN, "Text of Ambassador Albright's Speech to the UN on Mideast," March 18, 1994.

32. Bill Clinton, *My Life* (New York: Random House, 2004), 679.

33. Transcript, HBO History Makers Series: Samuel Berger, former national security advisor [Rush Transcript: Federal News Service, Inc.] Council on Foreign Relations, New York, New York, September 11, 2006.

34. Benny Morris, "Camp David and After: An Exchange-1. An Interview with Ehud Barak," *New York Review of Books*, June 13, 2002. http://www.nybooks.com/articles/15501.

35. Menachem Klein, *Shattering a Taboo: The Contacts Toward a Permanent Status Agreement in Jerusalem 1994–2001* [in Hebrew] (Jerusalem: The Jerusalem Institute for Israel Studies, 2001), 21.

36. Thomas L. Friedman, "Foreign Affairs; Bibi's Playbook," *New York Times*, December 4, 1997.

37. Dennis Ross, *The Missing Peace: The Inside Story of the Fight for Middle East Peace* (New York: Farrar, Straus and Giroux, 2004), 208.

38. David Makovsky, "Taba Mythchief," *National Interest*, Spring 2003, 124, see especially footnote 8.

39. Yael Yehoshua, "Abu Mazen: A Political Profile" MEMRI, Special Report Number 15, April 29, 2003.

40. Ibid.

41. Gilead Sher, *Just Beyond Reach: The Israeli-Palestinian Peace Negotiations 1999–2001* (Tel Aviv: Yedioth Ahronot Books, 2001) [in Hebrew]. Sher explains that Barak's backchannel team in the Stockholm channel put off the issue of Jerusalem for a later stage. Shlomo Ben-Ami, *Scars of War, Wounds of Peace* (Oxford: Oxford University Press, 2006), 252. Ben-Ami reports his optimistic impressions from the Stockholm channel.

42. Haaretz, July 28, 2000.

43. Ibid.

44. Ross, 690; Morris.

45. Charles Enderlin, *Shattered Dreams: The Failure of the Peace Process in the Middle East 1995–2002* (New York: Other Press, 2002), 230.

46. Haaretz, July 28, 2000; Yotam Feldner, "The Formulae for a Settlement in Jerusalem," MEMRI, September 13, 2000.

47. Al-Hayat (London-Beirut), November 23–24, 2000, translated by MEMRI, November 28, 2000.

48. Ross, 701.

49. Ibid., 707–08.

50. "East Jerusalem and the Holy Places at the Camp David Summit," MEMRI, August 28, 2000, quoting al-Hayat al-Jadida, August 10, 2000.

51. Interview with Charlie Rose on the Middle East Peace Talks, July 27, 2000.

52. See letter of Giddi Grinstein, in "Camp David: An Exchange," *New York Review of Books*, September 20, 2001.

53. Wasserstein, 315.

54. *Jerusalem Post*, August 25, 2000.

55. Interview with Charlie Rose, September 12, 2000.

56. Klein, 53.

57. *New York Times*, January 6, 2001.

58. "Arafat's Letter of Reservations to President Clinton," January 3, 2001, MEMRI.

59. Ibid.

60. Yehoshua.

61. Ross, 721.

62. Ben-Ami, 327.

63. Shlomo Ben-Ami, *A Front Without a Rearguard: A Voyage to the Boundaries of the Peace Process* (Tel Aviv: Yedioth Books, 2004) [in Hebrew], 308–09.

64. Al-Ayyam, January 28, 2001, MEMRI.

65. Makovsky, 123.

66. Al-Ayyam, January 29, 2001, MEMRI.

67. Quoted by Makovsky, 124.

68. Al-Quds, January 28, 2001, MEMRI.
69. For references on the German Note Verbale episode, including activities at the UN, see Dore Gold, *Jerusalem in International Diplomacy* (Jerusalem: Jerusalem Center for Public Affairs, 2001), 35.
70. MEMRI Special Dispatch No. 155, "Three Palestinian Viewpoints on the Intifada and the Future of the Palestinian State," November 22, 2000.
71. "Faysal al-Husseini in His Last Interview" MEMRI Special Dispatch No. 236, July 2, 2001.
72. "Have the Palestinians Abandoned a Negotiated Settlement?" Jerusalem Issue Brief, *Jerusalem Center for Public Affairs*, September 6, 2001.
73. Palestinian Authority and PLO Non-Compliance with Signed Agreements and Commitments: A Record of Bad Faith and Misconduct (Jerusalem: Government Press Office, 2000), 10.

## Chapter 7: The Evil Wind: Radical Islam, the Destruction of Holy Sites, and Jerusalem

1. Bernard Lewis, "License to Kill: Usama bin Laden's Declaration of Jihad" *Foreign Affairs*, November/December 1998, 14–19.
2. This was the analysis of Abu Musab al Suri, who first met bin Laden in 1988, and wrote a book on him titled *The International Islamic Resistance Call* that was published on jihadist websites. See Peter L. Bergen, *The Osama bin Laden I Know: An Oral History of al Qaeda's Leader* (New York: Free Press, 2006), 114.
3. Hamid Algar, *Wahhabism: A Critical Essay* (Oneonta: Islamic Publications International, 2002), 9.
4. Mamoun Fandy, *Saudi Arabia and the Politics of Dissent* (New York: Palgrave, 1999), 191.
5. Stephen Schwartz, "From Mecca to Jerusalem," TechCentralStation.com, April 15, 2005.
6. Ibid. See also http://www.workforislam.com/html/News/rajab.htm. Sheikh al-Manajid argues that there is no proof the the isra and the mir'aj indeed occurred in the month of Rajab. And if they did occur in Rajab, no ceremony should be practiced since its source is not from the Prophet, his companions, or from the people of his era.
7. Richard Mitchell, *The Society of Muslim Brothers* (Oxford: Oxford University Press, 1993), 57–58.
8. Reuven Paz, "From Riyadh 1995 to Sinai 2004: The Return of Al-Qaeda to the Arab Homeland," PRISM Series of Global Jihad, No. 3/2— October 2004, The Global Research in International Affairs Center (GLORIA).
9. Montasser al-Zayyat, *The Road to al-Qaeda: The Story of Bin Laden's Right-Hand Man* (London: Pluto Press, 2004), 62.
10. Ibid.
11. Fawaz A. Gerges, *The Far Enemy: Why Jihad Went Global* (Cambridge: Cambridge University Press, 2005), 11.

12. David Cook, *Contemporary Muslim Apocalyptic Literature* (Syracuse: Syracuse University Press, 2005), 174.
13. Paz.
14. Michael Griffin, Rea*ping the Whirlwind: Afghanistan, Al Qa'ida and the Holy War* (London: Pluto Press, 2003), 237.
15. Ahmed Rashid, "After 1,700 Years, Buddhas Fall to Taliban Dynamite," *Daily Telegraph*, March 12, 2001.
16. Ahmed Rashid, *Taliban: Militant Islam, Oil and Fundamentalism in Central Asia* (New Haven; Yale University Press, 2000), 85.
17. Robert Fisk, "The Taliban, the Buddhas and the Saudi Connection," *Independent*, March 13, 2001.
18. Rashid, 201.
19. Ibid., 139.
20. Fandy, 206.
21. Ibid.
22. Algar, 43.
23. Irfan Ahmed, "The Destruction of Holy Sites in Mecca and Medina," http://www.islamicmagazine.com/issue-15/preserving-heritage/the destruction-of-holy-sites-in-mecca-and-m.html.
24. http://www.oqlaa.com/?section=fatawa_view&id=39.
25. http://saaid.net/Warthah/Al-Alwan/4htm.
26. http://www.palestine-info.net/arabic/fatawa/index.htm.
27. http://www.themodernreligion.com/jihad/afghan/qaradawi-latest.html. See also a February 15, 2006, interview with Qaradhawi at http://www.qaradhawi.net/site/topics/articel.asp?cuno=2&itemno=4166&version=1&template id=105&parentid=16.
28. Ursula Lindsey, "Egypt's Grand Mufti Issues Fatwa: No Sculpture," *Christian Science Monitor*, April 18, 2006.
29. Dore Gold, *Hatred's Kingdom: How Saudi Arabia Supports the New Global Terrorism* (Washington: Regnery, 2004), [Updated paperback edition], 217.
30. Alex Rodriguez, "Iraqi Shrine Blast Suspect Caught," *Chicago Tribune*, June 28, 2006.
31. Moonjan Momen, *An Introduction to Shi'i Islam: The History and Doctrines of Twelver Shi'ism* (New Haven: Yale University Press, 1985), 144.
32. "Freedom House Calls for Action after Pakistan Massacre" October 29, 2001, Center for Religious Freedom, Freedom House: http://freedomhouse.org/religion/news/bn2001/bn-2001-10-29.htm.
33. Justus Reid Weiner, *Human Rights of Christians in Palestinian Society* (Jerusalem: Jerusalem Center for Public Affairs, 2005), 4–5.
34. Mitchell, 222.
35. Ibid., 229.
36. Weiner, 10.
37. Harry de Quetteville, "'Islamic Mafia' Accused of Persecuting Holy Land Christians," *Daily Telegraph*, September 9, 2005.
38. Weiner, 9.
39. Ibid., 26.

40. Official Vatican spokesmen gave contradictory versions of what transpired; Michel Sabah, Latin patriarch of Jerusalem (the first Palestinian ever appointed to this position), said that the Palestinians were not armed and were willingly given asylum in the church. In contrast, the Franciscans, who represented the Catholic Church as the custodians of the Holy Land (Custodia Francisca Terra Sancta), put out a statement saying that what had occurred was "a violent invasion effected by armed men who thereafter barricaded themselves there." See Sergio Minerbi, "The Vatican and the Standoff at the Church of the Nativity" *Jerusalem Viewpoints*, Number 515, March 15, 2004, Jerusalem Center for Public Affairs. Associated Press, "Fire Breaks Out at the Church of the Nativity," May 2, 2002, http://www.foxnews.com/story/0,2933,51678,00.html. "Greedy Monsters Ruled Church," *Washington Times*, May 15, 2002.

41. "Arab Intellectual on the Worsening Situation of Christians in the Muslim World," MEMRI Special Dispatch Series No. 1150, April 28, 2006.

42. Israeli-Palestinian Interim Agreement on the West Bank and the Gaza Strip (Jerusalem: Ministry of Foreign Affairs, 1995), See Article 9, Paragraph 2, 14.

43. Shmuel Berkovits, *The Battle for the Holy Places* (Jerusalem: Jerusalem Institute for Israel Studies/ Hed Arzi Publishing House, 2000) [in Hebrew], 165.

44. Nachman Tal, "The Islamic Movement in Israel," Strategic Assessment, Volume 2, Number 4, February 2000, Jaffee Center for Strategic Studies, Tel Aviv University.

45. Ibid.

46. Tal. Since 1996, there have been two different factions in the Islamic movement in Israel: the "Southern Faction," headed by Sheikh Abdullah Darwish, which is willing to run in Israeli parliamentary elections, and the "Northern Faction," headed by Sheikh Ra'id Salah, which rejects any integration with the State of Israel and is also far more radical in its outlook.

    In 2005, a Haifa court sentenced Sheikh Salah to three and a half years in prison—which included a suspended sentence because of a plea bargain—for funneling cash to Hamas.

47. Raphael Israeli, *Fundamentalist Islam and Israel: Essays in Interpretation* (Lanham: University Press of America, 1993), 103.

48. Raphael Israeli, "The Islamic Movement in Israel," *Jerusalem Letter*, Number 416, October 15, 1999.

49. Berkovits.

50. Ibid., 167.

51. Ibid., 74–77. Berkovits has fully examined the understandings between the Waqf and the Israeli Police in Jerusalem. What made this issue more complicated was the unauthorized decision of the Israeli police commander in Jerusalem, Arieh Amit, to put the earlier oral understandings in writing in a letter to the Waqf, which forced them to deny their existence. The Netanyahu government would argue that it was not made aware of the Waqf's written response to Amit.

52. Ibid., 105.

53. "Letter Dated 26 September 1996 from the Permanent Representative of Saudi Arabia to the United Nations Addressed to the President of the Security Council," S/1996/790.

54. Mark Ami-El "The Destruction of the Temple Mount Antiquities" Jerusalem Viewpoints, Number 483, August 1, 2002. Ami-El's analysis is based on discussions with Israeli archeologist Eilat Mazar. See also "The Al-Aqsa Institute for Developing Islamic Sites," http://www.islamonline. net/arabic/famous/2004/07/article03.shtml.

55. Ibid.

56. Adnan Husseini, "Work at the Temple Mount," Letters to the Editor, *Washington Post*, July 27, 2000.

57. "PA Minister: The Intifada Was Planned from the Day Arafat Returned from Camp David" MEMRI Special Dispatch No. 194, March 9, 2001.

58. Shmuel Berkovits, *"How Dreadful is this Place!": Holiness, Politics and Justice in Jerusalem and the Holy Places in Israel* (Jerusalem: Carta, 2006) [in Hebrew], 402–03.

59. "Moving Zamzam Waters to the Temple Mount" May 24, 2001. http://islamonline.net/Arabic/news/2001-05/25/article3.shtml.

60. Dan Diker, "The Expulsion of the Palestinian Authority from Jerusalem and the Temple Mount," *Jerusalem Issue Brief*, Jerusalem Center for Public Affairs, August 5, 2004.

61. "Temple Mount Mosques Continue to Serve as Breeding Grounds for Anti-Israeli and Anti-American Incitement in the Post-Arafat Era," Intelligence and Terrorism Information Center and the Center for Special Studies, Special Information Bulletin, December 2004.

62. "The Temple Mount Mosques as a Focus for Incitement and Inflammation against the United States and its Allies," Intelligence and Terrorism Information Center at the Center for Special Studies, Special Information Bulletin, June 2003.

63. http://www.islamonline.net/SiteDirectory/English/subcategories.asp?id =387 http:www.alokab.com/forums/lofiversion/index.php/tl5253.html.

64. Asaf Maliach, "The Islamic Liberation Party: From Pragmatism to Radicalism?" Institute for Counter-Terrorism, December 6, 2005, http:// www.ict.org.il/articles/articledet.cfm?articleid=551.

65. Zeyno Baran, "Fighting the War of Ideas," *Foreign Affairs*, November/ December 2005, 68.

66. Zeyno Baran, *Hizb ut-Tahrir: Islam's Political Insurgency* (Washington: The Nixon Center, 2004), 19–20.

67. Baran, "Fighting the War of Ideas," 69.

68. Olivier Roy, *Globalized Islam: The Search for a New Ummah* (New York: Columbia University Press, 2004).

69. Baran, "Fighting the War of Ideas," 77–78.

70. Lt. Col. (res.), Jonathan D. Halevi, "Understanding the Direction of the New Hamas Government: Between Tactical Pragmatism and Al-Qaeda

Jihadistsm," *Jerusalem Viewpoints*, Jerusalem Center for Public Affairs, May 1, 2006.

71. Ibid.


# Chapter 8: Jerusalem as an Apocalyptic Trigger for Radical Islam

1. Bernard Lewis, "August 22: Does Iran Have Something in Store," *Wall Street Journal*, August 8, 2006.
2. "Hidden Imam" in Cyril Glasse, *The Concise Encyclopedia of Islam* (London: Stacey International, 1991), 155.
3. Patrick Poole, "Ahmadinejad's Apocalyptic Faith," FrontPageMagazine.com, August 17, 2006. Scott Peterson, "Waiting for the Rapture in Iran," *Christian Science Monitor*, December 21, 2005. Jackson Diehl, "In Iran, Apocalypse vs. Reform," Washington Post, May 11, 2006. John Daniszzewski, "Messianic Fervor Grows Among Iran's Shiites," *Los Angeles Times*, April 15, 2006.
4. Diehl.
5. See also "Ayatollah Nouri-Hamedani: 'Fight the Jews and Vanquish Them So as to Hasten the Coming of the Hidden Imam," MEMRI Special Dispatch No. 897, April 22, 2005. Ayatollah Nouri-Hamedani met with members of the Mahdaviyat Studies Institute, which studies the doctrine of the Hidden Imam.
6. "Iranian President at Tehran Conference: 'Very Soon, This Stain of Disgrace [i.e. Israel] Will Be Purged From the Center of the Islamic World—and This Is Attainable,'" MEMRI, Special Dispatch No. 1013, October 28, 2005.
7. Address by H.E. Dr. Mahmoud Ahmadinejad, president of the Islamic Republic of Iran, before the sixtieth session of the UN General Assembly, September 7, 2005, www.un.org.
8. Anton La Guardia, "'Divine Mission Driving Iran's New Leader," Daily Telegraph, January 14, 2001. See also Charles Moore, "There's A Method in the Mahdi Madness of Iran's President," *Daily Telegraph*, January 14, 2006.
9. http://albehari.tripod.com/quds4.htm.
10. Reuven Paz, "Hotwiring the Apocalypse: Jihadi Salafi Attitude towards Hizballah and Iran," The Project for the Research of Islamist Movements (PRISM), *Global Research in International Affairs* (GLORIA), Volume 4 (2006), Number 4 (August 2006).
11. Tomothy R. Furnish, *Holiest Wars: Islamic Mahdis, Their Jihadis, and Osama bin Laden* (Westport: Praeger Publishers, 2005), 30–71.
12. David Cook, *Understanding Jihad* (Berkley: University of California Press, 2005), see all of chapter 1.
13. Furnish, 74.

14.   Aziz al-Azmeh, Ibn Khaldun: An Essay in Reinterpretation (London: Frank Cass, 1982), 80. Mohammed Abdul Hameed al-Khateeb, Al-Quds: *The Place of Jerusalem in Classical Judaic and Islamic Traditions* (London: Ta-Ha Publishers, 1998), 166.

15.   *The History of al-Tabari: The Battle of al-Qadasiyyah and the Conquest of Syria and Palestine*, Yohanan Freidman, trans. (Albany; State University of New York Press, 1992), 189.

16.   David Cook, *Contemporary Muslim Apocalyptic Literature* (Syracuse: Syracuse University Press, 2005), 173. See also references to the article of Osama Azzam, from March 9, 2003, cited in Reuven Paz, "Global Jihad and the Sense of Crisis: Al-Qai'idah's Other Front," Intelligence and Terrorism Information Center, Center for Special Studies.

17.   Moshe Gil, *A History of Palestine: 634–1099* (Cambridge: Cambridge University Press, 1992), 297.

18.   Ibid.

19.   Thus an Egyptian apocalyptic writer named Amin Jamal al-Din identifies the Taliban with the black flags supporting the Mahdi. The Western war on Afghanistan serves as "the precursor of the battle of Armageddon." Cook, *Contemporary Muslim Apocalyptic Literature*, 180.

20.   Ibid., 175–76.

21.   Ibid., 181.

22.   Paz, 5.

23.   Barbara Freyer Stowasser, "The End Is Near: Minor and Major Signs of the Hour in Islamic Texts and Contexts," http://research.yale.edu/ycias/database/files/MESV6-3.pdf#search=%22%22Muhammad%20Daud%22%22.

24.   Muhammad Isa Da'ud, Armageddon and What Is After Armageddon (Cairo: Madbuli al-Saghir, undated), [in Arabic], 165–205.

25.   Cook, *Contemporary Muslim Apocalyptic Literature*, 140.

26.   Ibid.

27.   Gershom Gorenberg, *The End of Days: Fundamentalism and the Struggle for the Temple Mount* (Oxford: Oxford University Press, 2000), 185.

28.   Ibid., 189.

29.   Ehud Ya'ari, "Mahdi Now," *Jerusalem Report*, March 24, 2003.

30.   Paz, "Hotwiring the Apocalypse," 4.

31.   Gorenberg, 193.

32.   Ziad Abu-Amr, *Islamic Fundamentalism in the West Bank and Gaza: Muslim Brotherhood and Islamic Jihad* (Bloomington: Indiana University Press, 1994), 32.

33.   "The Distribution of Virulent Anti-Israeli and Anti-Semitic Hate Propaganda Continues in the West Bank and Gaza Strip, Although Incitement in the Official Media Has Abated under Abu Mazen," Intelligence and Terrorism Information Center for Special Studies at the Center for Special Studies, December 5, 2005.

34.   Ibid.

35. Itamar Marcus, "Islam Is at War Against the Jews and Israel in Palestinian Authority Religious Teaching" Special Report No. 37, March 2002, Palestinian Media Watch. See also Itamar Marcus, Palestinian Media Watch, "Palestinian TV. Radio, Newspapers—in Teaching the Islamic Attitude Toward Jews—Have Fueled an Intense Hatred for Israel and Promoted Violent Jihad," July 22, 2001.

36. Al-Bayan (UAE), July 10, 2003.

37. http://www.islamonline.net/net/livedialogue/arabic/ Browse.asp?hGuestID=t2gH5q.

38. http://islamicweb.com/goldenbook/israel.htm.

39. Paz, "Hotwiring the Apocalypse," 5.

40. For a conventional view of Islamic eschatology, see al-Khateeb, 176. According to a hadith collected by al-Bukhari, "it is related that 'Awf ibn Malik said, "I went to the Prophet, may Allah bless him and grant him peace, during the Tabuk expedition while he was in a hide tent. He said, 'Count six signs before the Hour: my death, then the conquest of Jerusalem, then a plague which will carry you off like the sheep disease, the the increase of wealth so that a man will be given a hundred dinars and remain displeased, the a civil war (fitna), which will not fail to enter every house of the Arabs, and then a truce between you and the Greeks who will act treacherously and come at you under eighty flags with twelve thousand men under every flag.'" From the website SunniPath, see the Sahih Collection of al-Bukhari at http://www.sunnipath.com/Resources/Printmedia/ Hadith/H0002P0000.aspx.

41. A radical Islamic perspective summarizing the current eschatological thinking about Jerusalem may be found in Khaled Abul Wahhab, The End of Israel and the United States of America, www.go.ac.kalwid/index.htm, 2004.

42. Gorenberg, 191.

43. Mukhlis Barzak, Al-Wa'ad Min Khaibar illa al-Quds, http:// www.palestine-info.info/arabic/books/alwad/2.htm (this book appears on the website of Hamas).

44. Carl Brockelmann, *History of the Islamic Peoples* (New York: Capricorn Books, 1960), 28.

45. Niall Christie, "A Translation of Extracts from Kitab al-Jihad of 'Ali ibn Tahir al-Sulami (d. 1106)," http://www.arts.cornell.edu/prh3/447/ texts/Sulami.html. The Arabic text appears in an article by Emmanuel Sivan, in *Journal Asiatique* 254 (1966), 206–22.

46. Barzak.

47. "Former Pakistan Intelligence Chief on Al-Jazeera: 'Israel Is Our Main Enemy'; as Mel Gibson Said, 'The Jews Caused All the Wars,'" MEMRI Special Dispatch No. 1254, August 17, 2006.

48. David Cook, *Contemporary Muslim Apocalyptic Literature*, 113.

49. David Cook, "Muslim Fears of the Year 2000," *Middle East Quarterly*, June 1998.

50. http://www.qaradawi.net/site/topics/article.asp?cuno=2&item no=2509&version=1&template id=105&parent id=16.

51. "Leading Sunni Sheikh Yousef Al-Qaradhawi and Other Sheikhs Herald the Coming Conquest of Rome," MEMRI Special Dispatch Series No. 447, December 6, 2002.

52. Loretta Napoleoni, *Insurgent Iraq: Al Zarqawi and the New Generation* (London: Constable, 2005), 30.

53. http://www.dini.gov/release_letter_101105.html. See also Rita Katz, "The Coming New Wave of Jihad," *Boston Globe*, March 13, 2006.

54. "Syrian Security Forces Kill Five Militants in Clash," Al-Sharq al-Awsat, September 4, 2005.

55. "IDF Intelligence: Al-Qaeda Already Operating in Gaza," *Maariv* [Hebrew], October 17, 2005.

56. This was the interpretation of Major General Yair Naveh, who commanded the Israeli Central Command. See Yaakov Katz, "Naveh: Zarqawi Trying to Get Better Grip," *Jerusalem Post*, February 22, 2006.

57. "Communique from "Al-Qaida's Jihad in Palestine," Evan Kohlmann, ed., Global Terroralert, October 6, 2005, http://www.globalterroralert.com/pdf/1005/qaidapalestine1005.pdf.

58. "The Egyptian Interior Ministry Exposed Operative Collaboration between Terrorist Elements in Sinai (Connected to the Global Jihad and Suspected of Involvement in the Arracks at Dahab), and Palestinian Terrorist Elements in the Gaza Strip (Whose Identity is Unclear)," Intelligence and Terrorism Information Center at the Center for Special Studies, May 26, 2006.

59. "A Terrorist Cell Was Exposed in Nablus Which Was Handled by Global Jihad Operatives in Jordan. Palestinian Terrorists Suggested a Mass-Murdeer Attack in Jerusalem and the Global Jihad Financed Its Preparations," Intelligence and Terrorism Information Center at the Center for Special Studies, March 22, 2006.

60. Ibid.

61. Ghasan Charbel, "Abu Mazen: 'There Are Signs of Al-Qaeda in Gaza and the West Bank, and the Consequences Will Destroy the Entire Region.'" Al-Hayat, March 3, 2006, http://english.daralhayat.com/Spec/03-2006/Article-20060303-c098ab0b-c0a8-10ed-00c1-5565d99ff30d/story.html.

62. Lt. Col. (res.) and Jonathan D. Halevi, "Understanding the Direction of the New Hamas Government: Between Tactical Pragmatism and Al-Qaeda Jihadism," *Jerusalem Viewpoints*, Number 542, May 1, 2006.

63. Amos Harel, "IDF: Gaza Is Wide Open to Weapons Smuggling and Entry of Terrorists," *Haaretz*, April 6, 2006.

64. Halevi.

65. Al-Jazeera, April 26, 2006, http://www.al-jazeera.net/news/archives?ArchiveId=324854.

66. "Al-Zarqawi's Message to the Fighters of Jihad in Iraq on September 11, 2004," MEMRI Special Dispatch Series No. 785, September 15, 2004.

67. Ibid.
68. "Commander of Shura Council of Jihad Fighters in Iraq: Al-Zarqawi's Death Will Be Incentive for Jihad and Martyrdom" MEMRI Special Dispatch No. 1192, June 28, 2006.
69. Ibid. See also Youssef Ibrahim, "Zarqawi May Be Dead, but His Terrorist Creed Lives on in the Mosques," *New York Sun*, June 12, 2006.
70. Evan Kohlmann, "Al-Zarqawi Group Aims to Strike Beyond Iraq," MSNBC, July 25, 2006.
71. Khaled Abu Toameh, "Hamas Denies Statement Mourning Zarqawi," *Jerusalem Post*, June 11, 2006.
72. Jonathan Schanzer, *Al-Qaeda's Armies: Middle East Affiliate Groups & the Next Generation of Terror* (Washington: The Washington Institute for Near East Policy, 2005), 49.
73. Miral Fahmy, "Al-Qaeda Threatens Attacks in Gulf, Israel," Reuters, September 11, 2006.
74. Yaakov Katz, "General Predicts 'Global Jihad Tsunami,'" *Jerusalem Post*, May 15, 2006.
75. International Crisis Group, "The Jerusalem Powder Keg," August 2, 2005, http://www.crisigroup. org/home/index.cfm?id=3588.
76. Cook, "Muslim Fears of the Year 2000."
77. Ibid.

## Chapter 9: The West and the Freedom of Jerusalem

1. "Blair Calls for World to Unite After Bush Win," Associated Press, November 4, 2004, http://www.foxnews.com/story/0,2933,137541,00.html.
2. Con Coughlin, *American Ally: Tony Blair and the War on Terror* (New York: HarperCollins, 2006), 155–56, 164–65, 177, 184–85, 193–94, 227–28.
3. "London: A Center-Stage for Radical Islamic Incitement to Anti-American and Anti-Israeli Violence and Hatred," Intelligence and Terrorism Information Center at the Center for Special Studies.
4. Dennis Ross, *The Missing Peace: The Inside Story of the Fight for Middle East Peace* (New York: Farrar, Straus and Giroux, 2004), 783.
5. "President Bush Calls for New Palestinian Leadership," The White House, June 24, 2002. http://www.whitehouse.gov/news/releases/ 2002/06/20020624-3.html.
6. Chris Patten, *Not Quite the Diplomat: Home Truths About World Affairs* (London: Allen Lane, 2005), 197.
7. Nicholas Watt, "EU Shelves East Jerusalem Report over Fear of Alienating Israel," *Guardian*, December 13, 2005.
8. http://www.cipmo.org/attivita/eu-projects_en.html. Whether the EU also financed the well-known Geneva Initiative that proposed dividing Jerusalem is unclear. Its leaders, former Israeli justice minister Yossi Beilin and former Palestinian information minister Yasser Abd Rabbo, met with Solana and Patten, along with European Commission president Ramano Prodi, on February 2, 2004. According to the Europeans' account, the

Geneva team sought EU political and financial support for their initiative. See Euromed Synopsis, weekly newsletter of the Euro-Mediterranean Partnership and the MEDA Programme, Issue No. 258, February 5, 2004.

9.   Search for Common Ground in the Middle East, Program Update 2006. To its credit, Search for Common Ground, which is a U.S.-based as well as a European-based organization, is transparent about its funding sources. It explains that its activities "are funded by the European Union and the Canadian, Dutch, German, Norwegian, Spanish, UK, and US governments." The U.S. involvement, while troubling, has to be weighed against the involvement of multiple European countries.

10.  Michael Bell, Michael J. Molloy, John Bell, and Maraketa Evans, *The Jerusalem Old City Initiative: Discussion Document* (Toronto: University of Toronto, no date given). The University of Toronto summary of the initiative states that it was subsidized by Canada's Department of Foreign Affairs. There is no mention of the EU at this stage.

11.  The acclaimed Geneva Agreement, reached between Israeli and Palestinian on official teams in late 2003, showed signs of falling apart even before it was formally announced. For example, in the document's pre-amble, it clearly states that it was "[a]ffirming that this agreement marks the recognition of the right of the Jewish people to statehood..." Yet in the London-based Arabic daily *al-Hayat* on October 14, 2003, Qaddoura Fares, one of the leaders of the Palestinian delegation denied that Geneva Agreement stated that Israel will be a Jewish state. See Y. Yehoshua, "Palestinian Reactions to the 'Geneva Understanding," MEMRI, Inquiry and Analysis Series—No. 154, November 11, 2003. What Camp David had shown was that backchannel understandings reached between Israel and the Palestinians in the past melted down when the moment of truth arrived and they were tested in official negotiations.

12.  Al-Sharq al-Awsat, November 19, 2005.

13.  http://albehari.tripod.com/quds4.htm.

14.  http://www.alrased.net.

15.  Moshe Amirav, *The Palestinian Struggle for Jerusalem* (Jerusalem: The Jerusalem Institute for Israel Studies, 2002) [in Hebrew], 63.

16.  Raphael Israeli, *The Armistice Regime: 1947–1967* (London: Frank Cass, 2002), 74.

17.  Edgar Lefkovits, "Jordan Plans New Temple Mt. Minaret," *Jerusalem Post*, October 11, 2006.

18.  Amnon Ramon, "The Christian Institutions and the Separation Fence in the Jerusalem Area" in Israel Kimhi, (ed.) *The Security Fence in Jerusalem: Its Impact on the City's Residents* [in Hebrew] (Jerusalem: The Jerusalem Institute for Israel Studies, 2006), 111–118.

## Afterword

1.   Glen Kessler, "Obama Clarifies Remarks on Jerusalem," *The Washington Post*, The Trail: A Daily Diary of Campaign 2008, June 5, 2008; available

online at: http://blog.washingtonpost.com/44/2008/06/05/obama_back-tracks_on_jerusalem.html.

2.  "Obama: Surge Doesn't Meet Long-Term Goals," CBS News, July 22, 2008.

3.  U.S. Grand Strategy in the Middle East," Meeting Held at the Council on Foreign Relations, June 5, 2003. Transcript available at: http://www.cfr.org/publication/6046/us_grand_strategy_in_the_middle_east.html.

4.  George W. Bush, "Sixty Years of Israel's Independence: Address to Members of the Knesset," May 15, 2008; available online at: http://www.presidentialrhetoric.com/speeches/05.15.08.html.

5.  The American pollster Frank Luntz conducted a public opinion survey in the United States on January 31, 2009, in which he asked: "And if you had to choose between Israel and the Palestinian Authority, who would you trust most to protect the holy sites in Jerusalem?"
    The answers of the general public were 71.1 percent said they trusted Israel while only 24 percent said they trusted the Palestinians Authority. Looking at how American voters came down on the question, Luntz found that 61.1 percent of Obama voters preferred Israel, while 89.2 percent of McCain voters trusted Israel more to protect the holy sites of Jerusalem.

6.  YNET, October 9, 2007.

7.  Midgam Survey supplied by the Midgam Institute to the author.

8.  Ephraim Yaar and Yonatan Lipsky, *The IDB Survey on Patriotism in Israel* (Herzliya: The Lauder School of Government, Diplomacy, and Strategy, The Interdisciplinary Center, 2008), 21.

9.  Nadav Shragai, *Jerusalem: The Dangers of Division: And Alternative to Separation from the Arab Neighborhoods* (Jerusalem: Institute for Contemporary Affairs\Jerusalem Center for Public Affairs, 2008).

10. Yehuda Ben Meir, "The Elections in Israel: Initial Observations and Coalition Prospects," The Institute for National Security Studies, Tel Aviv University, February 12, 2009.

11. Kevin Peraino, "Olmert's Lament," *Newsweek*, June 22, 2009.

12. Aluf Ben and Barak Ravid, "Men, a Security Fence, and a Camera," *Haaretz*, May 15, 2009.

13. Akiva Eldar, "Abbas to *Haaretz*: We Will Compromise on Refugees," *Haaretz*, September 14, 2008.

14. Address by PM Netanyahu on the occasion of Jerusalem Day State Ceremony, Ammunition Hill, Jerusalem, May 21, 20009. www.pmo.gov

15. Barak Ravid, "Clinton: Israel's Demolition of East Jerusalem Homes Harms Peace Efforts," *Haaretz*, April 13, 2009.

16. Pini Waichselbaum, Building Inspections Department, Jerusalem Municipality Power Point, 2009.

17. "Obama Rejects 'Natural Growth' Exceptions to Settlement Halt, Clinton Says", AFP, May 27, 2009.

18. Eugene Rostow, "Resolved: Are the Settlements Legal? Israeli West Bank Policy," *New Republic*, October 21, 1991.

19. Glenn Kessler, "Old Legal Opinion Raises New Questions," *Washington Post*, June 17, 2009.
20. Steven J. Rosen, "Obama and a Settlements Freeze," *Middle East Forum*, January 28, 2009.
21. Susan Page and Richard Wolf, "Rice Rebukes Israel for Divisive Building Plans," *USA Today*, December 12, 2007.
22. Tova Lazaroff and Hillary Leila Krieger, "US: Settlement Freeze Must Include J'lem," *Jerusalem Post*, June 23, 2009.
23. Akiva Eldar, "U.S. Demands Israel Halt Construction in East Jerusalem Market," *Haaretz*, June 6, 2009.
24. Kerry Picket, "Obama Drops Key Clause in Jerusalem Embassy Memo," *Washington Times* (weblog), June 5, 2009.
25. The White House, "Remarks by the President on a New Beginning," Cairo University, Cairo, Egypt, June 4, 2009.
26. Ibid.
27. Ibid.
28. Itamar Marcus and Noaz Cohen, "Jerusalem under Palestinian Assault: Palestinian Authority's Unprecedented Campaign of Historical Revision and Libels about Jerusalem," Palestinian Media Watch, May 26, 2009.
29. *Al-Hayat al-Jadida*, March 4, 2009; Ibid.
30. Ibid.
31. Ibid.
32. Israeli Ministry of Foreign Affairs, "Excavations North of Jerusalem Reveal Sarcophagus Fragment Inscribed 'Son of the High Priest.'" October 6, 2008.
33. Permanent Observer Mission of Palestine to the United Nations, Statement by H.E. Dr. Salam Fayyad, Prime Minister of the Palestinian Authority before the High-level Meeting of the United Nations General Assembly on the Dialogue of Religions and Cultures, Under Agenda Item 45: "Culture of Peace." New York, November 12, 2008.
34. Ibid.

# Index